# PROSPECT FOR AMERICA

# PROSPECT FOR AMERICA

The Rockefeller Panel Reports

DOUBLEDAY & COMPANY, INC.
GARDEN CITY, NEW YORK
1961

# Contents

Report II

## INTERNATIONAL SECURITY: THE
## MILITARY ASPECT

Report III

## FOREIGN ECONOMIC POLICY
## FOR THE TWENTIETH CENTURY

Report IV

## THE CHALLENGE TO AMERICA:
## ITS ECONOMIC AND SOCIAL
## ASPECTS

Report V

THE PURSUIT OF EXCELLENCE:
EDUCATION AND THE FUTURE
OF AMERICA

Report VI

## THE POWER OF THE
## DEMOCRATIC IDEA

# Special Studies Project
# Planning Committee

Laurance S. Rockefeller, (Chairman since May 26, 1958).
Nelson A. Rockefeller, (Chairman, resigned May 26, 1958).

Dana S. Creel
Nancy Hanks
Emmet John Hughes
Francis A. Jamieson*
Henry A. Kissinger
John E. Lockwood
Oscar M. Ruebhausen

## STAFF

Nancy Hanks, Executive Secretary
John R. Kennedy
Sylvia Drucker
Julie North
James N. Drayton

* Deceased.

# Preface

I

The reports here published are the result of more than one hundred American citizens thinking and working together over a period of four years. They are citizens of experience and capacity. They have felt—and, in these reports, they express—concern for the state of their nation and its future.

The Special Studies Project of the Rockefeller Brothers Fund, organized in 1956, sought to do three things:

1. To define the major problems and opportunities that will challenge the United States over the next ten to fifteen years;

2. To clarify the national purposes and objectives that must inspire and direct the meeting of such great challenges; and

3. To develop a framework of concepts and principles on which national policies and decisions can be soundly based.

This project grew out of a belief that the United States, in the middle of the twentieth century, found itself in a critical situation requiring the urgent attention of thoughtful citizens.

As a nation we had progressed in our domestic development to an extent hardly imaginable a few short decades ago. Internationally, we had emerged as the strongest nation and the best hope of freedom in an explosive world.

Yet, our achievements and our strengths, because of their very magnitude, appeared in some ways to have outrun our goals. There was more than paradox, there was peril in such a situation. A nation which does not shape events through its own sense of purpose eventually will be engulfed in events shaped by others.

The age in which we live is one of deep and widespread ferment. We have been witnessing a revolution in politics, social order, science, economics, diplomacy, and weapons. We are being challenged to responsible and inspired action not alone by a technical revolution, but even more by people new to political freedom on every continent, by people alive to the possibility of achieving personal dignity in their own lifetime, by people exhilarated with the prospect of shaping their own destiny.

Throughout this world alive with hope and change stalks the Communist challenge. It is a challenge organized to exploit every human hope and disappointment for its own ends. The challenge is ruthless and total. It is a challenge not merely to the power or structure of free nations but to the very values and principles from which free civilization draws its meaning and vitality. Since America finds itself both guardian and protagonist of this free civilization, it is America, above all, that is challenged.

Spurred by this sense of paradox and of peril, the Special Studies Project enlisted some of our ablest and most respected citizens to think in long-range terms about the prospect for America. The intent has been to discover how our values, our goals, and our material strength could be united in powerful mutual support to advance the cause of justice and dignity among men and nations.

This, then, has been an effort to look upon America as it is, at this critical time, to try to discern what is expected of America— and what America must expect of itself.


II


This has necessarily been a long labor.

The Special Studies Project began with an invitation in 1956 to leaders from many walks of life and of many shades of opinion. They were invited to meet and examine the most critical problems facing the nation over the next ten to fifteen years. Before this group held its first meeting, some one hundred thoughtful individuals were asked to write papers defining (each in his respective sphere of competence) the problems and opportunities to be weighed. These papers helped channel the subsequent discussion.

More precise organization of the project quickly followed. One group could hardly review all issues. Accordingly, the original panel was set up as an Overall Panel of some thirty members to guide the entire project. In addition to holding formal meetings, many of them continuing for several days, the members of this Overall Panel gave the equivalent of months of their time to the review and revision of documents, to meetings and consultation.

The Overall Panel, individually and as a group, was distinguished by its active and continuous personal participation in the whole enterprise.

At the same time, subpanels were created to explore specific areas of national life. The membership of these subpanels totaled one hundred and eight. They held sixty-eight formal meetings, and uncounted discussions in smaller groups, in the course of preparing their reports. Each of these subpanels followed a basic formula of organization: (a) a chairman and three or four members from the Overall Panel, (b) four or five individuals with specialized experience in the particular field under review, and (c) three or four of the authors who had prepared papers for the panels to consider.

Over a three year period, beginning in mid-1957, drafts of the several reports came before the subpanels and the Overall Panel for the weighing and testing of ideas, and for the language which could best express them. It was a demanding and dedicated group effort.

From January of 1958 to September of 1960, the reports of the panels have been published as each has been concluded. Although not every member of the Overall Panel necessarily endorsed every detail, all approved the substance of the reports and urged action on the recommendations.

Inevitably—despite the long-term perspective of each study—the reports published over this period contain occasional references to strictly contemporaneous situations, such as the recession in 1958. The reports in this volume are not edited to remove such references. These reports, in the form in which they were originally released, state the views of a concerned and responsible group of citizens as they appraised the state of their nation in the sixth decade of the twentieth century.

We cannot assess the ultimate value of what these men and women have done. We do know, however, that their reports have significantly challenged wide public interest and discussion. We can, also, express one conviction: the participants themselves have given a demonstration of democracy at work.

We have had the privilege of witnessing, in the Special Studies Project, a rare spirit of responsibility. Each time these men and women met, people of quite different persuasions and views tested their good will, their tolerance of dissent, their capacity to work toward common conclusions. All this, in itself, was an exercise in democracy. We are indeed proud and grateful to have been associated with the men and women who, intelligently and devotedly, made it this.

Such an undertaking itself marks one of the great distinctions between a free society and one that is enslaved. There is *dialogue* in a democracy—a dialogue not only between great political parties but between the people and their government. In this dialogue, the conversation is mutual and continuing. Both not only speak but also listen. Each deeply affects the other's capacity for thinking and for acting. By contrast, the political conversation in a tyranny is basically a *monologue*: the state talks, the people listen.

This project, then, has been a sustained effort to contribute to the dialogue by which we Americans live—the dialogue in which the voices of alert and concerned citizens may be heard by the leadership of a nation, both within and without the government.

By more and many such efforts, we may hope that the dialogue of American democracy, over the years, will continue to prove itself a thing of vigor and truth.

LAURANCE S. ROCKEFELLER
*President*

on behalf of
The Rockefeller Brothers Fund Trustees

DETLEV W. BRONK
WALLACE K. HARRISON
ABBY ROCKEFELLER MAUZE
ABBY M. O'NEILL
DAVID ROCKEFELLER
JOHN D. ROCKEFELLER 3RD
MARTHA B. ROCKEFELLER
NELSON A. ROCKEFELLER
WINTHROP ROCKEFELLER

*November 1960*

# Introduction

BY THE OVERALL PANEL

I

We who have taken part in this project have done so in the conviction that the United States has come to a crucial point in its history.

The signs are all around us. Probably never have these signs—of growth and change, of danger and dilemma—so abounded in all spheres of our national life. From the security of our nation to the renewal of our cities, from the education of our young to the well-being of our old, from the facts of military might to the subtle substance of spiritual strength—everything seems touched by challenge.

The number and the depth of the problems we face suggest that the very life of our free society may be at stake.

We are concerned that there has not been enough general understanding of the issues confronting us, not enough sense of urgency throughout our nation about the mortal struggle in which we are engaged. Without this awareness, the challenge to our values and to our society cannot be—and has not yet been—fully met.

II

What is the essence of this society whose defense and enrichment is our great task? A democracy such as ours—neither monolithic in structure nor dogmatic in creed, but capable of reaching a consensus and acting as a nation—gives no simple or symmetrical answer. Its very diversity is part of the answer. Diversity means a society of individuals free to be themselves so long as they respect this right in others. It means multiplicity of views and attitudes; it means a pluralism of institutions.

Yet there *is* an American consensus and what lies at the heart of it is clear. It is our belief in the individual as the supreme fact of life, his spiritual and material well-being as the supreme test of the way a society is working. This is not, of course, a peculiarly American notion, but it has given a special accent to all American history. It comes close to stating the central purpose of American life. And it is based upon age-old religious, moral, and cultural traditions—above all, on the concept of the worth and sanctity of the individual as set forth in the teachings of Judaism and Christianity.

The conflict dividing the world and challenging America is much more than a struggle against communism. It is a struggle *for* something. It requires us, ultimately, not merely to repel the ambitions, or reject the assertions, of totalitarians. It summons us to proclaim and to apply our own convictions of the worth of the individual, to be true to our own beliefs of justice and law, to attack ignorance, poverty, and misery, and, by so doing, to be of help to all free men.

### III

In this spirit, we have weighed the great matters before the nation. Although the six studies we have made divide evenly between subjects traditionally called "foreign" and "domestic," we doubt that this distinction any longer has much meaning, for nothing that America is or does can fail to affect the world. Whatever America seeks to *do* in the world, it must first *be* at home. What the world suffers or feels, America eventually must bear or share.

We look at the state of this world in the first of these reports: *The Mid-Century Challenge to U. S. Foreign Policy.* We find a world seething with change, astir with something more profound than the surface clash of Soviet and American national policies. It is astir, in fact, with the sense of freedom that the American example has done so much to foster. It is equally astir with the demand of underprivileged people for more of the necessary things of life. These people are challenging America to inspire and help lead the way toward a new world order based on our own concepts of freedom and human dignity.

Something much more than conventional national security or containment of hostile aggression is demanded of us. We must seek—for nothing less will suffice—a world in which nations live at peace, in ways that foster justice, so that all men are free to realize their own development and pursue their own aspirations. We are required, then, to strengthen the conditions of freedom at home and to help build them everywhere in the world. We are required to strive to prevent not only World War III but also conflict between the Western and Eastern worlds, now in closer contact than ever in history. We are required as Americans, in short, to think and act like pioneers in the vast enterprise of building a new political order.

While such a world is in the building, however, we cannot neglect a more immediate order of the day: securing the defenses of our own nation. The revolution in technology that makes this task so urgent also makes it more complex than ever. The speed of invention quickens the rate of obsolescence not only of weapons but of policy and strategies. The new weaponry threatens to give ominous advantage to an aggressor. Security becomes precarious and must constantly be redefined. Hence the dilemmas weighed in the second report: *International Security: The Military Aspect.*

The issues involved here test the democratic process in new ways —in the speed of decision required, in the complexity of the matters for decision, in the exigencies of secrecy and security.

We have yet to solve most of these issues. Nor do we believe that the defenses we have built are wholly sufficient.

While strength alone will not guard or secure our future, strength is essential to assure that there will be a future to defend. This strength—both for America and for all free nations—must be, at base, more than military. Among other things, it must be economic. And it must be a growing strength to match and meet new needs and demands. Economic growth is of vital importance to the realization of the aspirations of people everywhere in the world.

The forces of aspiration, of revolution, and of growth in the economic sphere are surveyed in the third and fourth of our reports: *Foreign Economic Policy for the Twentieth Century* and

*The Challenge to America: Its Economic and Social Aspects.*
Across the globe, peoples newly free from colonialism are committed to struggle against an even more ancient enemy—poverty.
To aid them in this struggle—and to combat the deceptions in
Communist promises—new demands are being made on the resources of all free nations. The need will tax these resources in
more than a material sense: it will test the capacity of these nations
to plan and work together in a crucial common cause.

The vigor and growth required of the American economy are
not—let it be stressed—ends in themselves. They are the means of
contributing to the human betterment which is the central purpose
of our society.

Economic growth depends essentially on healthy and expanding private enterprise. Social institutions, private philanthropy,
and government action, however, are required to complement
individual initiative in channeling economic growth toward human well-being.

There are many problems yet to be solved in encouraging
and achieving the growth of which we are capable. Agriculture,
transportation, and urban congestion are illustrations of these. We
examine these problem areas as well as what must still be done
to strengthen some of the basic elements of individual and family
welfare—good education, equality of opportunity, job security,
good health, adequate housing, and expanding cultural horizons.

The abiding concern of our society for the individual, for the
fullest and wisest development of his resources, is closely examined
in the fifth of our reports: *The Pursuit of Excellence: Education
and the Future of America.* If we cannot be content with what we
have built to date in the structure of our national defenses, we
have even less reason for self-congratulation on the structure of our
school system. Nor is the matter simply one of formal education.
The challenge is to our whole society. As our society becomes more
complex and intricate, it demands ever more urgently not only
the development of talent which is skilled and dedicated, but the
nurture of free, reasoning, and responsible individuals.

This latter aspect of the challenge is explored further in our
final report: *The Power of the Democratic Idea.* The power of the
idea rests in the belief that only free men can ever really understand this complex world. Only free men can manage its complex-

ity, and only free men can have the opportunity for the spiritual, moral, and intellectual growth that our times require. Only free men can really develop that deep consensus of mind and spirit that gives strength and continuity to the democratic society they create and which in turn serves their purposes.

In our democratic society, the role of the state, and of all our institutions, is to serve the individual. The citizen is not their servant: they are his. But the individual, in his turn, recognizes that he himself, in concert with others, is the servant of the greater ideals and values of human worth.

Our institutions—political, social, economic, cultural—must continuously be examined to determine how well they are serving the individual's real needs, his pressing demands, and his supreme purposes.

IV

Over the last four years, while these studies have been in progress, the details of life around us have been shifting constantly. But the basic problems to be met and the basic decisions to be made have remained with us. Indeed, the urgency has become greater than ever as time has passed.

The surface signs of change in our lives are as plain as the deeper upheavals. One by one, the great leaders of the World War II era are departing from the scene. More than half the population living today is too young to have been aware of the great events and currents of that time. For them, it is an era past and gone. Now, pressing in upon them, comes a future in which great danger is linked with great opportunity.

The foreground of the world scene seems filled with violence and conflict: new nations catapulting onto the stage, the compelling desire of millions for fuller and better daily lives, the search for a social order within which human hopes can be realized, the surge of nationalist passions, the widening chasm between nations rich and poor—and, in addition to all of this, there is the ever-present menace of imperialist communism.

Within America, prosperous and technically at peace, the problems multiply: the slow progress in solving racial tension, the continuing question of economic growth with stability, the complex agricultural problem, the deterioration of our cities, the financial difficulties of transportation, the need for more schools, more teachers, and improved quality in education.

At the same time the capacity for human betterment has never been greater. The decades ahead offer an opportunity unparalleled in history for man to realize his aspirations for freedom and dignity.

Peril and possibility, then, make ours a time of momentous decision.

At issue is nothing less than the future of America and the freedom of the world.

LAURANCE S. ROCKEFELLER, president, Rockefeller Brothers Fund, Inc.; chairman of the panel.

ADOLF A. BERLE, JR., senior partner, Berle, Berle and Brunner; professor of law, Columbia University; former Ambassador to Brazil; former Assistant Secretary of State.

CHESTER BOWLES, member of Congress; former Ambassador to India; former Governor of Connecticut.

ARTHUR F. BURNS, president, National Bureau of Economic Research; professor of economics, Columbia University.

LUCIUS D. CLAY, general, U. S. Army (ret.); chairman, Continental Can Company, Inc.; former commander-in-chief, U. S. Forces in Europe, and Military Governor, U. S. Zone, Germany.

JOHN COWLES, president, *Minneapolis Star and Tribune*; chairman, *The Des Moines Register and Tribune*.

JUSTIN W. DART, president, Rexall Drug and Chemical Company.

JOHN S. DICKEY, president, Dartmouth College.

JOHN W. GARDNER, president, Carnegie Corporation of New York; president, Carnegie Foundation for the Advancement of Teaching.

LESTER B. GRANGER, executive director, National Urban League, Inc.

CARYL P. HASKINS, president, Carnegie Institution of Washington.

THEODORE M. HESBURGH, president, University of Notre Dame; commissioner, Civil Rights Commission; member,

National Science Board; permanent delegate of Vatican City to the International Atomic Energy Agency; member, Advisory Committee, United States Committee for the United Nations.

MARGARET HICKEY, public affairs editor, *Ladies' Home Journal*.

OVETA CULP HOBBY, president and editor, *The Houston Post*; former Secretary of Health, Education and Welfare; former director of the WACS.

DEVEREUX C. JOSEPHS, former chairman, New York Life Insurance Company; former chairman, President's Committee on Education beyond High School.

MILTON KATZ, director, International Legal Studies, Harvard University Law School; former Ambassador and chief in Europe of the Marshall Plan.

JAMES R. KILLIAN, JR., chairman of the corporation, Massachusetts Institute of Technology; former special assistant to the President for science and technology.

HENRY R. LUCE, editor-in-chief, *Time, Life, Fortune*.

THOMAS B. McCABE, president, Scott Paper Company; former special assistant to the Secretary of State and Foreign Liquidation Commissioner.

JAMES McCORMACK, major general, U. S. Air Force (ret.); vice-president, Massachusetts Institute of Technology; former director of research and development, U. S. Air Force; former director of military applications, Atomic Energy Commission.

RICHARD P. McKEON, Department of Philosophy, University of Chicago; former member, United States delegation to the General Conferences of UNESCO; former member, United States National Commission for UNESCO.

LEE W. MINTON, president, Glass Bottle Blowers' Association of the United States and Canada.

CHARLES H. PERCY, president, Bell and Howell Company; trustee, University of Chicago; chairman of the board, Fund for Adult Education, Ford Foundation.

JACOB S. POTOFSKY, general president, Amalgamated Clothing Workers of America.

ANNA M. ROSENBERG, public and industrial relations consultant; former Assistant Secretary of Defense for Manpower and Personnel; former regional director, War Manpower Commission.

DEAN RUSK, president, The Rockefeller Foundation; former Assistant Secretary of State.

DAVID SARNOFF, chairman of the board, Radio Corporation of America.

CHARLES M. SPOFFORD, partner, Davis Polk Wardwell Sunderland and Kiendl; former permanent representative to NATO.

EDWARD TELLER, professor at large of physics, University of California, Berkeley; associate director, University of California Radiation Laboratories.

FRAZAR B. WILDE, chairman of the board and president, Connecticut General Life Insurance Company; chairman, Commission on Money and Credit.

———————

ROBERT B. ANDERSON, resigned from the panel in June 1957 on his appointment as Secretary of the Treasury.

GORDON DEAN, senior vice-president—nuclear energy, General Dynamics Corporation, was a member of the panel until his death, August 16, 1958.

NELSON A. ROCKEFELLER, chairman of the panel until May 26, 1958.

———————

HENRY A. KISSINGER, Center for International Affairs, Harvard University, served as director of the project until his resignation, June 30, 1958, and thereafter as a consultant.

NANCY HANKS, executive secretary.

# PROSPECT FOR AMERICA

Report I

# THE MID-CENTURY CHALLENGE TO U.S. FOREIGN POLICY

(First published December 8, 1959)

# Introduction by Panel I

The world is going through a period of profound and rapid change, placing upon men and nations unusual strains which will endure as far as we can see into the future. After the burst of energies now loosed in all realms of life—in basic discoveries, in technology, in population growth, in human expectations—the tide may abate and future generations may be able to settle down to consolidate and enjoy their gains. Or it may be that the wave of change is cumulative and will demand of men hereafter an adaptability and resourcefulness such as we can now only dimly imagine. For the living generation and its children, the question is not relevant. We shall spend our lives in the midst of change. We shall do well—indeed, we shall survive—in proportion as we can understand what is going on in our civilization, can in some measure adjust ourselves to it, and can in some measure shape it.

In the order of things with which foreign policy is concerned, change manifests itself in many ways. The old system of empire through which much of the world was governed for at least a century—its commerce sustained, its differences adjusted, its peace in the main preserved—has broken down irreparably. The balance of power in its older forms no longer exists. Many new nations have arisen on waves of nationalist feelings, just when older nations have begun to sense from their own experience that nationalism is rapidly changing in nature. World powers have come freshly on the stage; but the nature of power under modern conditions has been so suddenly and basically transformed that the newcomers alternate between feeling themselves capable of unprecedented achievements and feeling themselves confined and lacking in essential means to satisfy their needs.

As in other fields of modern life, changes in foreign policy go far deeper than working out novel arrangements or combinations. Statesmen discover that they are not merely making different moves upon an old chessboard. The rules of the game have changed. The chessboard itself may be said to have disappeared. Nations and alliances, spheres of interest and balances of power, appear in new forms. The present competition between the Soviet dictatorship and the United States is essentially different from the traditional concept of balance of power. NATO has features that set it apart from military alliances as they have formerly existed. Even the distinction between a state of peace and war has been blurred by new forms of national conflicts that do not seem to have the aspects or consequences of either. In result, words which form the vocabulary of historic diplomacy—sovereignty, independence, neutrality, nonintervention, internationalism—describe only imperfectly the actualities to which they refer.

To get changes recognized, to inject new facts into the political process, are recognized tasks of statesmanship. At present these tasks are formidable. Policies lag behind awareness; awareness lags behind the constantly evolving reality. Even responsible leaders find it hard to adjust their minds to the existing, but rapidly passing, state of things. The public at large, disturbed by recurrent crises, often indifferent or poorly informed, thinks in terms of the past decade or even century—when any one year brings changes enough to require a review of policy. As a result, the image of the world existing in the public mind is often strangely unreal. Lacking a secure footing in reality, men tend to project themselves into a nonexistent future or else into an irretrievable past.

The need to shape valid policies, fitted to present realities and sensitive to coming changes, falls at a time when questions other than those in the realm of foreign policy are gaining ascendancy in the minds of men. Beneath the threat of total destruction there is growing everywhere hope of unprecedented gains in standards of living, providing not merely material advantage but the basis for a more worthy existence. Peoples long without a decent share of the good things of life begin to make their wants felt. The "rising expectations" which supply so considerable a part of the revolutionary ferment of the modern age exist as strongly in rich as in poor nations. New vistas of opportunity unfold, and amid the preoccupations thus engendered, foreign policy is bound to take on a new tone and character.

That such bright prospects should exist side by side with the grim portents of the new weapons of destruction gives to this age a special poignancy. It could be said that modern life thus acquires a quality quite its own—except that a like quality is known to all ages that, through religious faith, have deeply apprehended as reality both heaven and hell. In terms of foreign policy, as we shall point out in this report, the rising hopes for domestic prosperity put certain definite challenges to the United States. For the moment, it is enough to suggest that the forces of change running through the world have a different dimension than that immediately evident to statesmen and diplomats. Not only are forms of international life in the crucible, but even the texture of men's individual existences, the pattern of their hopes, and the scheme of things they live by. Out of new plenty they are resolved to make a new civilization, using production as a means to a better life for all.

In these circumstances, we believe the United States can well make a fresh appraisal of its foreign policy. This report, the result of a group effort by Panel I of the Special Studies Project, reflects our substantial agreement, though not every member of the panel subscribes to every detail. The report looks to the future, sometimes trying to see forward for the next ten years, sometimes beyond. Given the pace of events, only by trying to look ahead can one hope to hit the target of the present. It is not the purpose of this report to grapple with a large number of specific situations that are now the concern of officials responsible for day-to-day decisions.

The report attempts, therefore, to indicate directions and priorities. It may suggest considerations that the policy maker in office may be too constrained or too harried to weigh; it may open minds to the possibilities of the future. No one who tries to look even ten years ahead can expect not to be very often wrong. But it is certain that one would be fatally wrong if one failed to look ahead, assuming that the present foreign policies of the United States are fixed and permanent. What do remain fixed are American ideals and values. Foreign policy seeks to give these reality. In so doing, it will in the years ahead surely call for the most sustained and concerted efforts by the American people.

*DEAN RUSK, president, The Rockefeller Foundation; former Assistant Secretary of State; chairman of Panel I.

*ADOLF A. BERLE, JR., senior partner, Berle, Berle and Brunner; former Assistant Secretary of State and Ambassador to Brazil.

HADLEY CANTRIL, chairman, The Institute for International Social Research.

SAVILLE R. DAVIS, managing editor, *The Christian Science Monitor.*

JOSEPH E. JOHNSON, president, Carnegie Endowment for International Peace.

MAX F. MILLIKAN, director, The Center for International Studies, Massachusetts Institute of Technology.

PHILIP E. MOSELY, director of studies, Council on Foreign Relations.

JOHN W. NASON, president, Foreign Policy Association.

*JACOB S. POTOFSKY, general president, Amalgamated Clothing Workers of America.

JOHN D. ROCKEFELLER 3rd, trustee, Rockefeller Brothers Fund, Inc.; president, The Asia Society.

*DAVID SARNOFF, chairman of the board, Radio Corporation of America.

*CHARLES M. SPOFFORD, partner, Davis Polk Wardwell Sunderland and Kiendl; former permanent representative to NATO.

EDWIN F. STANTON, former Ambassador to Thailand; trustee, The Asia Society.

JOHN ANDREWS KING, JR., secretary, International Legal Studies, Harvard Law School; secretary of Panel I.


This report was written principally by Mr. August Heckscher, director of The Twentieth Century Fund, under the direction of the panel. The panel appreciates the generous help of distinguished experts throughout the preparation of this report.

* Also Overall Panel members.

# I. The Nature of Foreign Policy

The United States as it moves down the second half of the twentieth century finds itself in a world of great dangers and great opportunities. Through actions and choices in the field of foreign policy, the United States must come to terms with this world. It must show how it means to use the power that has been bestowed upon it and how it can best live up to responsibilities that, sometimes in spite of itself, have been thrust upon it.

The panel is convinced that the foreign policy of the United States must be a positive force, helping in measurable ways to shape a world in which freedom is expanding and peace becomes the normal condition of men's lives. There have been times in the experience of the United States when its foreign policy seemed comparatively unimportant and other times when it naïvely supposed itself capable at a stroke of making over the world in a utopian image. The present generation must establish a sane but imaginative concept of what foreign policy can accomplish and then go on and do the work that it will require.

## DEVELOPMENT OF AMERICAN FOREIGN POLICY

Alone among modern nations, the United States passed through a large part of its national existence without feeling itself actively and intimately involved with countries outside its borders. It lived and grew not recognizing itself to be part of any concert of nations. While the United States was expanding across the continent, its statesmen believed themselves immune from the kind of problems that plagued the countries of the Old World.

Their predecessors, the men who had established the Republic and guided it through the first, dangerous epoch, were not so innocent. They knew well enough that the sea was not an un-breachable barrier to conquest. *The Federalist* papers gave frequent warnings of involvement if the states should persist in going their separate ways. They saw the states being drawn into conflicts with each other and in turn drawing European countries into alliances with the separate groupings. The American statesmen of this classic period did not assume that adoption of the Constitution would by itself end danger of intrusions of foreign interest. The New World had been the object of imperial ambitions since its discovery; it would continue to be so except as a wise foreign policy made it secure.

The key to this security was, in their minds, a close affinity with the power that controlled the Atlantic approaches. To them, England might be an old enemy and a present source of annoyance. But it was also, regardless of its intentions or motives, an essential element in the nation's capacity to develop itself and reach its natural westward limits. Jefferson, while engaged in a war with England, could still express his concern lest Bonaparte should conquer Russia and then overcome Britain. This connection with Britain becomes clear in considering the Monroe Doctrine. Without the British fleet, Monroe's declaration to protect the hemisphere against European imperialisms would have been merely rhetorical, a promise incapable of being made good.

What was evident to Monroe and to his Secretary of State, John Quincy Adams, was unfortunately forgotten during much of the remaining century. The American statesmen of those years liked to think that they were favored by providence, not by human arrangements. Behind the largely unrecognized relationship to Britain, the Americans felt able to make the broad declarations that satisfied national vanity or to engage in marginal interventions on the world scene.

The result was that Americans forgot the nature of foreign policy; they lost the habit and the techniques of practicing one. Thus, they failed to recognize that their safety existed only so long as Britain was not challenged by a new hegemony on the continent. They watched the rise of German power before World War I with little sense of what it meant to their interests, only to repeat the same error in the years leading up to World War II.

In this same period, Americans developed an exaggerated faith in the efficacy of words and in the formulation of abstract principles. They had seen prior to 1914 a long period of peace among the great powers, with their own interests being protected and many liberal advances being achieved in different parts of the world. These developments had been occurring without any particular efforts on the part of the United States and seemingly in accord with its grandly phrased declarations. It was not surprising that words, rather than deeds, came to appear the principal ingredient of foreign policy.

## LIMITS OF FOREIGN POLICY

The experience resulting from two world wars shows how hard it is to come to terms with reality: to create a foreign policy that can be adequately supported, to find a right relationship between national aims and the power the state can ultimately muster. In a difficult period of chastening and education, not the least important lesson that the United States has had to learn is that it cannot do everything, and certainly cannot do it cheaply, easily, without sacrifice and effort.

In many quarters of American opinion the emphasis after World War II came to be not on the possibilities and scope of foreign policy but on its limitations. The country was told persuasively that not everything that happened in the world, for good or for bad, was attributable to its policies. Changes might occur that it did not foster and that it could not have prevented, at least without a disproportionate expenditure of effort and lives. Parties changed, revolutions were fought, hopes for freedom rose and fell. In much of this, it was pointed out, the United States could not be expected to have a dominant voice.

To be patient, limited in one's hopes, prepared for one's share of disappointments and harassments: this was the spirit of foreign policy as it appeared to many when the American people awoke from their long dream of isolation.

## NEED FOR A POSITIVE OUTLOOK

The time has now come when we once more must establish the positive nature of foreign policy. In doing so, we cannot go back to an earlier mood, when in our neglect of the underlying situation we gave an exaggerated weight to declarations of moral principles and universal truths.

We cannot do everything through declarations of principle, as we certainly cannot do everything through force. The constant weight of American power, moral as well as military, needs to be channeled in purposeful and useful ways. Amidst the deep currents, the United States is not merely a nation, but a polarizing and dynamic force exerting intended influence and unintended gravitational pull or repulsion beyond its borders, moving (by historical standards) with great speed and huge mass. The American whole is more, in the international equation, than the sum of its various parts, economic, military, technical, and spiritual. This force cannot be described merely as an aggregate of American economic productivity, or of fire power, or of organizational and social inventiveness; it is also animated by a high degree of consensus based on moral and political beliefs.

The United States, consequently, for better or worse, must be viewed as a political and ideological influence backed by tremendous power.

Recognition of this quality of the United States as a symbol—often plainer to others than to ourselves—is at the beginning of an adequate view of foreign policy. What we are is in itself an element, conceivably a decisive element, in the total balance; what we do or refrain from doing affects other peoples in ways beyond our knowing. Our leadership would be felt even were we to seek to avoid exercising it. Precise balancing of commitment to available force, however necessary in our day-to-day decisions, is not the end of the matter for the United States. There remains, over and above this kind of calculus, the imponderable impact of the country as a whole—the impact that its example and beliefs are, at their best, capable of exerting.

The time has now come when the great possibilities of foreign policy need to be stressed. The emphasis on limits has been useful, but the other side of the medal needs to be examined.

As modern life develops in its complexity, it offers a wide variety of means and methods. The lives of people touch at innumerable points; the range of their interest increases. The greater part of this report is concerned with governmental policies and official action. But at every juncture where the American image impinges on the world, private citizens make their influence felt and contribute to the attraction or repulsion that is a vital element in the country's total power. The traveler, the exchange student, the businessman, the labor leader become spokesmen of the nation's purposes. In particular, three areas outside the official sphere need to be stressed:

## Voluntary Associations

The American people are intimately involved with a vast and growing complex of international relationships that, in reflecting the common concerns of men, cut across national and cultural frontiers. The immensely successful International Geophysical Year was sponsored and developed by private groups, with the government lending its support. Universities, scientific and scholarly associations, private foundations, and religious organizations are active elements in a variety of international communities, which flourish underneath and sometimes despite the issues that preoccupy governments. American policy is committed to encouraging such groups, affording them freedom to speak and act with the greatest diversity.

## Economic Contacts

Economics provides a channel of influence far deeper than it has been accorded in traditional diplomatic concepts. This has been fully discussed in another report of this series, *Foreign Economic Policy for the Twentieth Century*. As an exporter of capital and technical skills, America has played an increasingly important role. It is important also to think of the power that is exerted by reciprocal or absorptive means. America is one of the world's major buyers of goods and raw materials; the internal life of many countries is vitally affected by these purchases. Too often the significance of this role has not been adequately appraised.

American private enterprises conduct operations in all parts of the world. Foreign private enterprises are found throughout the United States. Labor leaders in America are in contact with their fellows elsewhere. The marketing of goods between our country and others goes on continuously. The sum of all these contacts constitutes a basic reality of international economic relations.

### Cultural Relationships

The United States' influence in the world is, of course, strongly affected by the impact of American ideas and fashions, by American books, plays, paintings, movies, science, and music. Yet reciprocal relationships, which have been emphasized in regard to economic policy, need to be equally stressed where intellectual and cultural matters are involved. The capacity of the United States to appreciate and enjoy intellectual achievements of other peoples not only enriches our own life but generates an important element of power. The United States as an absorber and mediator of diverse cultural strains is a force in the world that it could not be if it sought merely to promote the adoption of its own ideas by others.

The manifold and intricate quality of modern free society—its richness in the fields of nongovernmental group activity, of economic and cultural interests—thus gives to foreign policy a scope that goes far beyond the activities of small groups of officials or well-publicized negotiations. This is not to underestimate the need for vision and courage at the highest levels of diplomacy as an essential factor in a positive foreign policy. But we must never forget that the opportunities for effective action and influence are wide—far wider than the official channels through which a government's influence is exerted.

## IMPORTANCE OF IDEALS

To stress opportunities is inevitably to come up against the problem of the relation between realism and idealism in foreign policy. The United States has been criticized both at home and abroad for its reliance upon what seems a purely idealistic formulation of the world's thorny issues. Nevertheless, whenever it has wielded effective power in the world, its ideals and its moral convictions have played a vital part in its decisions.

Whenever, on the contrary, the United States has tried to act without moral conviction, or in ways that went counter to its basic beliefs, it has found itself inhibited and has ultimately had to rechart its course. Proposals for an imperial venture in the

Philippines withered before the tendency to independence, which we instinctively favored. The attempt to be "realistic" in French Indochina—supporting a colonial power so as to contain communism—was a faltering effort partly because of the realization that we were going against our natural respect for national independence. A "settlement" with the Soviet Union that would legitimize Soviet rule over Poles, Czechs, Hungarians, and others would run counter to these same deeply rooted instincts. Examples could be multiplied. While it is true that every nation seeks to justify its actions in ways that conform to its image of morality, America is committed to the basic idea of the consent of the governed. It is bound, therefore, to a peculiar degree to act in accordance with what it believes to be its own character.

Those who mistrust idealism in foreign affairs maintain that a nation's self-interest is not to be confused with its preferences and desires. The world is what it is; regimes come and go, and we must deal with nations according to their relationship to the national security and well-being. There is for Americans a certain valuable corrective in this view. In extending and withholding diplomatic recognition, the United States has too often acted as if it were trying to insist that the world must conform to its liking or else be beyond notice and contact. In the granting of aid it has had recurrently to combat a temptation to make its gifts dependent on its recipients' conforming to our economic experience and preferences.

There is indeed an order of things fixed by geographical and other facts that endures beyond the surface changes of regime. Even so radical a transformation as Russia underwent at the time of the Revolution did not wholly alter the relationships that had existed between it and the United States through the nineteenth century. It had been, despite ideological differences, a potential ally in the rear of potential enemies. It remained so, as shown in World War II, after the ideological difference had been rendered even more profound by the switch from czarism to communism.

Yet when all that has been said, Americans continue to believe deep-down that force by itself is not power; that ideals and values are among the essential components of strength in a democracy. Our own actions are made what they are—effective or frustrated —in large part by the degree to which they are in conformance with what we basically believe to be right. Similarly, our relationships to other countries are inevitably affected by the values they uphold as well as by their estimate of ours.

Ideas and ideals are thus to the United States an essential element of reality. How to translate those ideas and ideals into policy is a continuing problem of statesmanship. To press specific forms of democracy upon countries whose ideas run in other directions can obviously be self-defeating. At the same time, the loss of democratic values in any country now free would be a severe setback for civilization as we understand it. In an area where so much depends upon the sensitivity, firmness, and imagination of men dealing with specific situations, perhaps the most that can be said is that the promotion of our ideological interests must be on a different plane and on a different time schedule from the promotion of those interests more directly related to our security. We cannot safely accept, even briefly, the development of a power vacuum at any crucial point in our line of defense. We cannot, on the other hand, hope to effect an immediate transformation in a regime that has developed along lines hostile to freedom. In such a case, our task must be conceived as a long-range one of persuasion, assisted by the force of example and by the whole weight of America's record and achievements.

Because the United States' desire for a world of expanding freedom cannot be realized at one step does not make it any less important. It is, indeed, the grand objective of foreign policy that the world order shall be of a kind in which the United States can be at home—spiritually, economically, and politically.

To sum up, this report takes the position that foreign policy must be conceived as a positive, active force. Since World War II there have been patient and often highly successful efforts to make our influence felt and to give our ideals a reality in the eyes of other peoples. In contrast to earlier periods, we have accepted deep commitments and continuing responsibilities. But the period ahead will see still greater opportunities and greater demands upon the United States. Unless in these years we go beyond the protection of our more obvious and immediate interests—unless we take a real part in shaping an environment congenial to freedom—we shall find that we have failed to make even our immediate interests secure.

# II. The American Objective

What are the objectives of American policy? At this stage in the report, we shall try to state these objectives in their simplest form —both what as a nation we seek and what we do not. Any definition of aims begins with the fact that the United States has no territorial ambitions. That is a negative fact but one of profound significance to the country's basic purposes and hopes. The report proceeds to speak of survival and of peace as objectives, but it maintains that these are not in themselves sufficient for a viable foreign policy in the second half of the century. Nothing less than an image of what this world might be—a world organized so as to assure peace and freedom for all—can provide a goal large enough to harness our energies and give direction to our efforts.

## NO TERRITORIAL AIMS

That it is not the objective of the United States to extend its territorial dominion may seem obvious to Americans. But in fact the opposite has been the rule through much of our own history and for most nations. The United States has provided an example of territorial expansion—by settlement, by purchase, by war. By the beginning of the twentieth century the present boundaries of the United States had been filled out and the transient dream of further empire once and for all renounced. That no territorial ambitions or desires now stir America, that there is not even debate on this point, needs to be stressed.

If this country were not profoundly agreed on this point, it could not pursue without confusions or misunderstandings its ideological interests in world affairs. This report takes a strong position on what it conceives to be the need for affirmative measures in building new supranational organizations and new regional associations. Such a role could not be played in good conscience if there were doubts as to America's disinterestedness.

It is not a small thing that a nation of such power as the United States has been so free for so long of territorial ambitions. This can be said, we hope, without immodesty. It needs to be said, for it is a major fact of today's world.

## THE ISSUE OF SURVIVAL

It needs next to be said that the American objective includes the basic, fundamental one of national survival.

A nation, like an individual, need perhaps give no reason for wanting to survive. A deep instinct and an unreasoning will are, in the last analysis, what count. But the age in which we live justifies making this objective explicit and affirming it solemnly. The threat to the survival of the United States is today greater than this country has ever experienced, even in its first uncertain years as a nation. It is confronted by a hostile power system equipped with weapons of destruction that pose for the rest of the world the issue of survival in its starkest form.

In the moral crises that these new weapons present, moreover, there is particular need to be clear on the issue of the continued existence of our nation. The price of survival will not be cheap in terms of the effort and the will that must go into maintaining strong arms, dependable allies, and confident friends. Moreover, it is imperative, in our present situation, that the United States have the kind of military establishment that allows it to respond to limited attacks with limited means, keeping for itself a wide option in the face of intermediate threats or aggressions. But if worst comes to worst, if despite all efforts the choice is posed as that between an all-out war and submission to nuclear blackmail, such a war must be faced. The destruction it could wreak on us and on others is fearful to consider. But failure to face up to the threat of such a war undermines the hope of achieving any sort of tolerable world order. It would have the inevitable result of encouraging demands that we had announced in advance we would not resist.

To put such a price upon national survival, when nationalism can no longer have the absolute meaning it once did, may seem a paradox. The time may come—and we hope it may come before too many decades are out—when survival will not be posed in its present terms. For the time being there is no other course for Americans than to act for the preservation of our nation-state, and to act on such a scale and with such means as the threat to its existence may make necessary.

Putting the issue in terms of survival confronts foreign policy with its grimmest decision: the resort to force and the possible use of weapons dangerous to civilization itself. It confronts the citizens and their leaders with the ultimate question: Upon what grounds do they deem their survival as a nation a good for the sake of which such grave perils must be faced? For Americans, the answer must be that, despite shortcomings and defects, they conceive the United States as standing for enduring values deeply rooted in the aspirations of man. Nothing less than that conviction can sustain them against the final test.

## THE SEARCH FOR PEACE

Peace is obviously one of the grand objectives of American foreign policy. The American people do not like war, have never liked it, and find their attitude powerfully reinforced by the form that future wars must take. The only question is whether peace shall be the whole aim of foreign policy; whether everything shall be yielded to that end. Clearly the answer must be *no*. The risks that arise from the possibility of war are great. But by resolutely accepting the risk—and by that alone—we gain a decent chance of avoiding it.

Apart from this grim logic there is another reason why peace cannot be made our sole objective. It is the same reason why giving one man a responsibility for peace—or one department or one party—is bound to prove illusory. Peace is not a single or simple thing. It can only be the result of a nation's total policies, within the total policies of all the other nations. It is the end product of a wide series of arrangements, institutions, habits, and organizations, all in working order. A foreign policy that devoted itself exclusively to avoiding war would neglect the constructive aspects out of which a true peace must develop. A free nation that sought nothing but peace would gain peace only at the price of its freedom.

In this area, as in that of national survival, we meet a paradox. The nation, regardless of risks, must preserve itself, just at a point where the significance of the nation-state is declining. So the possibility of war must be faced even though it is difficult to conceive of war as a suitable instrument of policy. In simpler ages it may have been possible to live without this tension and ambiguity; the nature of the present situation offers no escape. However unthinkable war may be in one sense, our safety and hope lie in thinking about it coolly and realistically.

## A NOTE ON THE NATIONAL INTEREST

The pursuit of "national interest" has traditionally been the framework within which the aims of foreign policy have been defined. In this report we use the phrase as little as possible, for it seems to us to express too narrowly what foreign policy in our age must aim to do. Today, the national interest cannot be fulfilled within the limits of the nation itself. Nor can it be achieved apart from the interests of the citizens who compose the nation. If survival were the sole end of foreign policy, if preservation of existing boundaries were the end, then one could justify the use of this abstraction. But as we see the world today, the interest of the United States, like the national interests of all other nations, can only be fulfilled within an order far wider than its own geographical limits.

The idea of the "national interest" had value when the international order was more or less fixed and comprehensible. Within this order, nations could hope to maneuver so as to protect their interests and gain legitimate advantages. But when the international order is in flux, or when a new order waits to be created, responsibilities are thrust on some nations that call them to undertakings far beyond anything suggested by their own immediate interests.

The England whose example spread independent parliamentary democracies—or the America that bound Europe's wounds after World War II—was acting upon a concept of the common good which went beyond older and narrower notions of national interest. Both these nations saw their task as creating a structure within which the separate interests of many diverse peoples could be pursued. Britain, it is true, prospered within the situation it had shaped by its sustained efforts. The United States believed, and rightly, that its long-range security and well-being would be enhanced under the Marshall Plan.

This panel believes that the United States has an objective that needs to be defined in new terms, broader than the old concept of "national interest." This objective is to foster the development of a world order in which all peoples can live in security and realize their fullest potentialities. We shall sketch in broad strokes some of the elements of such an order so far as it now appears to the American people and as their consensus has defined it.

## THE IDEAL AMERICA

To attain an understanding of an ideal world order we must begin by sketching an ideal America. Foreign policy inevitably reflects a nation's values and experience as they have developed in its domestic life. Policy otherwise would lack roots and substance. Conversely, American development toward the ideal is dependent upon an essentially congenial world environment. The underlying unity of the world today, the degree to which it is made one by instancy of communication and the rapid spread of ideas, means that the environment must eventually be as broad as the globe itself.

The United States at its best has always seen its national life as an experiment in human liberty. It established its independence and made its Constitution in an age of large and liberal hopes, when reason seemed capable of taming the essential violence of man's nature. The fact that the new nation was set apart on a continent, which almost seemed to have been preserved hidden from mankind until the time was ripe, gave it a special character from the beginning.

A sense of being watched—in an almost Biblical sense of being judged—has remained with the United States. Others have contributed to this sense by their high expectations of American performance. In its naïve form, this sense has been the basis of the American's concern with what travelers thought of this country; it remains today in the anxiety to be "liked" abroad, to be popular, and to have tangible evidences of gratitude for his good deeds.

On a deeper level, Americans have cared what history thought of them, what the ultimate judgment would be upon their work. They have known that the hopes of the world were, in some measure, bound up with their success.

The deep contradictions within the American system that derive from slavery—and that carry forward in today's problems of adjusting relations between races—appear to unsympathetic outsiders as a denial of the American claim. Certainly they open the United States to charges of self-righteousness and hypocrisy. In fairness, it should be noted that the treatment of caste or color forms in many modern societies a discordant note. There are difficult situations in other countries where racially diverse groups are in daily contact, but it is fair to say that no other nation combines, in quite the same degree, a passion for equality with the residue of a social order that involved inequality of race.

Seen from within, these deviations from our own ideal have a kind of fearful justification: they testify to the struggle for mastery of its soul, which every human entity must endure before it can validate its claim to leadership in wider realms. The burden of slavery lies deep in the history of America. It was not an evil lightly to be extirpated, a condition to be cured by effortless progress or easy reform. The violence and passion of the Civil War bear witness to that. Today's struggles are transferred to the social and judicial spheres, but let no one suppose that the old passions do not still burn. It is as if America were compelled in every generation to prove its fidelity to the ideal—not by words, not by gestures in the foreign field, but by harsh, unremitting, often bitter contests within its depths, among its own people.

For the ideal exists. It is the core of a consensus that unites all parties and all sections of the country, and it is alive not least among those who resist its immediate fulfillment. The total substance of what Americans desire and intend for their nation is not summed up in any document; it certainly is not put in the form of dogmas that can be exported or imposed on other peoples.

Perhaps the heart of the matter is, nevertheless, in the Declaration of Independence.

As a nation we really do believe that the state exists for man, not the other way around. The "consent of the governed" is therefore a basic test of good institutions. It is not always a simple concept to live up to in a day when mass pressures tend to induce conformity or routine acquiescence rather than the live consent of a democratic government at its best. Nor is it always easy to apply the criterion to governments abroad. But anyone who seeks to predict how the United States will react to a particular regime would do worse than ask to what degree the people of the land in question genuinely consent to the acts of their government.

The American people believe, also, that "all men are created equal"—not just men of one nation or race—and that they are endowed by their Creator with certain unalienable rights. Life, liberty, and the pursuit of happiness are fundamental among these rights.

It would be comforting to say that in this advanced age the words have new meanings: that the right to life means fullness of life, self-realization, enhancement of the human personality; that liberty and happiness mean the attainment of these things in a refined and subtle degree. The words do indeed have these new shades and colors. But they retain their primary, blunt significances as well. This is an age when millions of people have been deliberately murdered; when in wide areas oppression to the point of slavery remains a fact; when the simplest elements of happiness —enough to eat, adequate shelter, the most common enjoyments —are lacking in great portions of the globe. In such an age, it is important to reiterate in their plainest form the rights we deem to be unalienable and God-given. If these rights are not fully established in fact, they are enduring aspirations and motivate our society at its best.

In the United States "the pursuit of happiness" has indeed attained dimensions that statesmen of the classic age could not have foreseen. The possibilities of material abundance on this continent outreach what all but utopians have previously imagined. We are resolved to go forward to exploit for human well-being everything that science and technology can offer. At the same time, we realize that this very abundance brings new psychological and moral problems. Can happiness be attained under a flood of material goods? Can boredom be escaped when the compulsion to work is drastically lessened? The answers to these questions may take a long while to work out effectively, especially because of a widespread reluctance in these times to think about problems directly and frankly in moral terms. But this is a passing phase, and we are confident that Americans will increasingly seek answers to these questions in their own way, with a deep continuing concern that spiritual qualities assert themselves over the tide of material things.

The American creed as thus briefly summed up can be fulfilled only under conditions of peace and in a world so organized as to make possible free exchange, free communication, and free movement of people and goods. No one nation and no one geographic area alone is capable of preserving the basic rights of man. It is impossible to conceive enduring prosperity for America when large parts of the world struggle in want or oppression. The American ideal—in both its philosophical and its practical form—connotes a sense of growing freedom and well-being. It is not an ideal that can live a shrinking existence, fenced in and defensive. Freedom is part of the world, or it does not have a valid existence anywhere.

## AMERICAN CONCEPTION OF THE IDEAL WORLD

We now come back to the kind of world which forms, as we see it, the ultimate objective of foreign policy.

The American objective is a world at peace, based on separate political entities acting as a community.

Within this community there need not and should not be uniformity: diversity of religion, culture, philosophy, social organization, expression, and ideals is to be expected. It is for each people, in its own way, to discover and work out the form of social organization most satisfactory to it. The international community thus conceived ought to include any state that does not insist on imposing its way of life on others. Any Communist state that is prepared to assume the responsibilities and self-restraints of international life can be an acceptable and constructive member of that group.

Such a community of states must build up institutions and arrangements permitting all its members to function and progress, assisting those that may need help. This is required for many reasons. Among them are increasing population, rising standards of living, heightened expectations, need of greater economic interchange, immediacy of communication, and vastly increased contact between communities and peoples. No substantial area of the earth's surface can now exist without such contacts, friendly or hostile. Present reality offers a single alternative: struggle or co-operation. In another generation, with population doubled in many areas, co-operation may well be the condition of survival.

Institutions binding on all the diverse nations of the world can arise only as the result of acknowledged needs and be chosen only by free consent. The common denominator between the ninety-odd countries now existing is comparatively low. Effective universal arrangements exist largely in technical fields where nations agree to act together to achieve practical results. This area of common action must be constantly enlarged as new developments and as increasing awareness of the world's underlying unity make it possible. Meanwhile, the United States can well encourage "open end agreements"—agreements on specific points concluded among those nations prepared to adopt them but with the door kept open for other nations to join as they conceive it their interest to do so.

Alongside institutions aimed at action on a world scale, there exist already great regions whose necessities and values require a high content of common action—Western Europe, the Western Hemisphere, and the Middle East are obvious examples. In each of these (as also in some other regions) needs are accompanied by a large factor of common regional experience and knowledge and of clear advantage in joint action. As we see it, any world community will include strong regional organizations. The development of these is already on foot; but the need outruns present measures, which often fail to keep pace with obvious necessity and also with what the peoples concerned are ready to accept.

As technical arrangements, often originated on the regional level, develop to a point where there is world-wide recognition of their need and agreement on their substance, they should be institutionalized at the international level. Changing attitudes and conditions will hasten, perhaps to a far greater degree than can now be thought likely, developments in this direction. Certain activities already affect the health and safety of mankind. Defense against disease epidemics and the attacks of pathogens and pests on basic food crops are examples of the growing range of action by a world community. Wherever possible, universalist attitudes deserve encouragement so that the world may pass from feeling the "interdependence of doom" to interdependence in many other, more hopeful forms, including the conservation of vital resources, improvement of standards of health and economic well-being.

The hoped-for result is peace in a world divided into smaller units, but organized and acting in common effort to permit and assist progress in economic, political, cultural, and spiritual life. Such a community must facilitate the freest and fullest access by everyone to the thinking of everyone. It must allow for the widest diversity of ideas, social structure, and forms of expression compatible with the functioning of the community. It would presumably consist of regional institutions under an international body of growing authority—combined so as to be able to deal with those problems that increasingly the separate nations will not be able to solve alone.

Such, in broadest outline, is the image of the world whose building the United States sees as the grand objective of its foreign policy. It is not only by desire that the United States seeks such a world but by necessity. It is not only by the old standards of "national interest" but because the United States cannot hope to become its fullest self except within an environment where new needs are met by new institutions.

# III. The Growth of Community

The image of an ideal world, sketched in the foregoing pages, is not drawn out of thin air. It has already begun to take shape. The British Commonwealth of Nations forms one of the earliest and most significant of modern groupings; the French Community forms one of the most recent. In two areas in particular we see regional associations vitally related to American policy: these are the Western Hemisphere and the Atlantic community. At the same time, the United Nations provides a vigorous example of a growing institution at the world level. The effectiveness of American policy will be judged in large part by the degree to which it succeeds in helping to keep these existing associations —regional and universal—in sound health and on the path of progress.

There are other areas, such as Africa and Asia, where regional life is taking on new forms. But in these the United States does not have the same degree of responsibility as it does in the American and Atlantic communities. Here the United States is able to exert direct influence; its leadership and active help form important ingredients in the developing situations. Results in these areas will demonstrate to the world what as a people we value and are really seeking.

## THE ATLANTIC COMMUNITY

The United States has always been part of the Atlantic world. It was its child and spiritual heir. It survived and grew up within the shadow of Europe's rivalries. Even during the long period of westward expansion and territorial consolidation, when the United States seemed to dwell apart, links of common interest and common ideals were strong. There was an Atlantic community even when Americans were least aware of it. There is an Atlantic community today, with its life consciously drawn together and organized. In terms of culture, political values, economics, and defense, the United States is bound up with the solidarity and progress of the European peoples, as they are with us.

A military alliance attests the common defense needs of the community. We shall speak specifically of the North Atlantic Treaty Organization and its military problems in connection with the Russian threat and the cold war. Here it must be pointed out that NATO is in many ways different in nature from the alliances that have appeared and vanished through modern history. Although NATO came into being for defense against Soviet threats of expansion, it has deeper roots, and in one form or another it must survive whatever transformations in the world situation the next decades may bring.

At times the community underpinning the alliance has not been sharply in evidence. Temporary slackening of Soviet pressure brings out fissures and division among the nations until it has sometimes appeared as if only external threats held the Atlantic world together. Conversely, an intensification of Soviet maneuvers has created strain. Rather than gear the alliance to Soviet actions, it is the task of statesmanship to make clear the reality of the underlying ties.

Historical contingency has made NATO the most striking of the institutions of the Atlantic community. In a way this is unfortunate, for many diverse activities depend on NATO and are closely related to it, thus running the risk of being colored by military considerations. Yet in the life of the world, historical need rather than order and logic is likely to be controlling; wisdom calls for a flexible approach to organizational structure. Such developing political institutions as the NATO parliamentarians, frank face-to-face exchanges among leaders of the member states, and occasional NATO conferences like that held in London in June of 1959, are part of the process by which the common interests of the community are given form.

Common policies of governments of the Atlantic community toward problems outside the framework of the alliance need to be extended as far as feasible. The Atlantic community is involved with more than the welfare and defense of the Atlantic region; it can prosper only insofar as it is part of a functioning world order. Admittedly, there are obstacles. Ill will aroused against any one European nation, as a result of colonial issues, tends to be expressed against all of them. Similar difficulties arise in connection with different attitudes of NATO countries toward problems of the Far East. Insofar as the Atlantic governments can formulate policies of a broad political and strategic nature, the strength of the whole free world is increased. It can be increased also through the embryonic and necessarily cautious steps for establishing Atlantic community co-operation in aid to underdeveloped countries.

Development of a unified Europe is in line with the interests of the Atlantic community as a whole as well as of the United States. The United States has encouraged the economic and political unity of Western Europe; it must continue to do so in every way possible. It must be prepared for the sake of this larger goal to accept such incidental disadvantages as may come from increasing economic integration of Europe. Our long-standing dislike of doing anything that may sectionalize the world economy must give way here, as perhaps in other areas, to a recognition of the value of regional arrangements. It is strongly to be hoped that the division between countries composing the common market and those in the free-trade area will represent only a stage in the development of Europe's economic integration. By the same token it is to be hoped that these economic developments will be reinforced by European political institutions of equal scope and significance.

This developing Europe must keep the door open to those nations and peoples that historically have been associated with it and are now drawn into the Soviet orbit. The peoples of the satellite countries share the great European tradition; they must be welcomed into its intellectual and cultural life at every opportunity. This European civilization, restored and healed, will again be part of a broader Atlantic community. Such a development will enlarge the Atlantic world, though it should not be conceived as extending the NATO military arrangements. It is of the utmost importance that over the next decade the goal of a reunited Europe be kept vividly alive and that political and economic institutions be kept flexible so as not to risk making present divisions seem permanent.

Political and economic unity must, finally, be matched in the field of a European defense system. When the establishment of the European Defense Community was being debated, the United States was well aware of this need. The fact that those efforts proved abortive then should not blind us now to the necessity of exploring new possibilities in existing circumstances.

The NATO states can make their military contribution by providing a powerful and versatile defense organization, combined with a strong will to resist aggression in whatever form it occurs. In this posture lies the best assurance of peace and continued freedom. As and when continental Western Europe secures for itself atomic weapons, its statesmen will be faced with heavy responsibility to organize these weapons within the overall defenses of the Atlantic community—not succumbing to the temptation to duplicate the categories in which the United States is concentrating its major effort. Rather, in the common interest it must be hoped it will use its new weapons to increase its capacity to resist aggression against its own territory.

Assuming Europe will possess atomic arms, it would seem desirable that it create an atomic pool that will complement other forms of European co-operation.

Increasing European unity and strength might be criticized as a step toward greater divergence between United States and European policy. Adjustments will undoubtedly be needed as such a partnership takes shape. However, true Atlantic unity can best be fostered by the growing cohesion and integration of Europe. The Atlantic community must be one that has in it nothing of subordination or inequality. It must be a regional grouping with shared responsibilities, continuous consultation, and joint decision making.

## THE INTER-AMERICAN COMMUNITY

Equally important is the other great region of which the United States is a part—that of the Western Hemisphere, with Canada and Latin America forming with ourselves the major components.

Canada is actually a kind of hinge between the two regional systems. Its position in the North Atlantic and its Common-

wealth ties link it with Great Britain and thence with the continent. The sharing of interests and ideals with the United States
makes for a relationship far more intimate than one based on
mere physical proximity. A long history of amicable dealings and
the famous example of the unguarded border speak for bonds of
a unique kind. These are reinforced by strategic considerations
in a day when the most likely route of attack upon this continent
is over the top of the world, across the pole. The fact that there
have been economic difficulties between the United States and
Canada in recent years emphasizes the need for close consultation
on all common matters. There must be a genuine concern for
the interests of a neighbor that has its own aspirations and has
already shouldered at least its full share of responsibility in world
tasks.

More complex is the problem in community building presented
by twenty countries to the south of the United States. Their
importance cannot be overestimated. Here is a population already
larger than the population of the United States and expanding
at a faster rate. Here is a trade roughly equal to our trade with
Europe. Here are natural resources that offer enormous fields for
development.

The countries of Central and South America provide a field of
constructive action by which the claims of the United States to
world leadership may well be judged. If Soviet strategy sets the
breakup of the Atlantic community at the top of its political
agenda, there is no question but that it is working hard to divide
the United States from its Latin American neighbors.

Unlike Europe and even Asia, our opportunities in regard to
the Western Hemisphere have failed to evoke the continuous
interest of the American people. Too often Latin American relations have been handled absent-mindedly until some incident
or crisis compelled attention.

This has not always been so. The Monroe Doctrine was an act
of far-reaching creative statesmanship that should have set the
stage for a continuous and enlarging preoccupation of the United
States with this area. In raising a bulwark against colonial ventures
in the southern continent, American statesmen established the
enduring pattern of our interests and involvement. In the nineteenth century they sealed off the vast inter-American area against
the kind of intrusion which in that period made an imperial patch-

work of Africa, and they kept the way free for development in the Americas of independent self-governing nations. At the same time, perhaps building better than they knew, they developed a triple Latin American-United States-European relationship. Great Britain's support of Monroe's declaration found an echo in 1941–45, when all the Central and South American countries declared war against Hitler's Germany.

The Organization of American States is the longest established regional group of the modern world. It provides a valuable example of how regional peace-keeping systems stand as a substructure basic to the court of last resort represented by the United Nations. The place of the United States within the OAS puts our policy and our diplomacy to the test in acting vigorously, with intimate knowledge of complex trends and changing personalities, while maintaining the respect for independence that a system of self-governing units requires.

The United States must join in creating a viable economic and political order for the southern continent adequate to meet the sweeping social changes that are clearly needed, and for a continuously expanding economic system. The United States must be prepared to make a contribution that is large, sustained, and well-planned. Such a contribution, needless to say, can be made only on the basis of organized and effective efforts within Latin America itself. If we on our side have the need for more constructive action, it needs to be said that the leaders of the South American countries have tasks of their own to face up to.

In another report in this series, *Foreign Economic Policy for the Twentieth Century*, the panel urges steps toward a common market in Latin America; workable procedures for moderating extreme price fluctuations in basic commodities; ways for the co-operative promotion of general economic growth and development; establishment of an Inter-American Payments Union; and steps toward greater co-operation in social objectives, in education, low-cost housing, health, and technical assistance.

These objectives, spelled out in detail in the other report, the panel considers basic prerequisites to the development of a full community of interests and to general well-being within the hemisphere. The organization of the Inter-American Development Bank is an important step forward, but we urge once more thoughtful consideration of the whole range of recommendations.

In addition, the United States should take a sympathetic interest in regional discussions among the Central American states for common action in economic, education, health, and other matters. Yet even if these objectives were all achieved, the task in this hemisphere would not be completed.

Beyond everything that statesmanship and economics can accomplish there must be an effort of the intellect and of the spirit to comprehend what is going on in the depths of this complex area, to sort out the elements that create a common denominator between so many disparate national strivings, and to build on these for the long future. Latin America is passing through a period of intense cultural activity. In the exchange of scholars, scientists, and literary figures, one sees evidence of a groping for the things that shall bring the whole Latin American civilization to a new level of self-conscious unity.

The United States cannot hope to play in the life of the continent the role that its position should justify, and that incidentally its own position and well-being require, unless it can put itself in tune with the political and cultural movements. Latin America, despite some setbacks and diversions, appears to be building toward new forms of regional international organization, and its leaders want North Americans to think with them. Genuine understanding is needed. This kind of understanding is not achieved without effort or sustained without attention, but in the final analysis it may be no less important than economic support.

## THE UNITED NATIONS

In addition to participating directly in the development of two regional groups, the United States has participated fully and from the start in the United Nations, the international organization that today holds out the reasonable hope of being able to take over more and more functions and to assume increasingly large responsibilities. In supporting the spirit and letter of the Charter, the United States has shown that it gives more than lip service to the indispensable world order that, as we have seen, is basic to the American consensus. The UN is proof of our conviction that problems which are of world-wide impact must be dealt with through institutions global in their scope. It should stand as one of the principal vehicles through which our foreign policy is expressed.

The United Nations plays a vitally important role in the development of a functioning international system. Through its role in the emergence of new nations, it has helped to keep a world order which is dynamic, yet peaceful, and hospitable to forces of change and growth. In many aspects of life, nationalistic rivalries must give way before a common world need, and these are now being dealt with by the specialized agencies of the UN. They include, among others, health, children's welfare, cultural activities, and agricultural research. This part of the UN's work, too often unnoticed because it is non-controversial, needs to be fully developed. New areas of common interest need to be constantly defined and to be implemented at the international level.

The United States should be anxious, in particular, to make additional use of the UN in its approach to economic aid. International agencies for economic and technical assistance and training can bring dividends far more significant than the gratitude that a single contributor of economic aid may expect—but rarely gets—from the recipient country. Drawing the United Nations into economic development helps to mobilize the capacities of other countries in fields where the United States does not have the experience or skill to do the job alone. Participation by the Soviet Union in these activities may make a real contribution toward bridging over the chasm that separates the two ideological systems.

The UN, besides, gives to international diplomacy a field of operations that at certain junctures can be of crucial importance. The expanding role of the Secretary General puts at the disposition of the nations an international civil servant of high prestige whose disinterestedness and skill are highly beneficial to all. In the complex and continuing negotiations that must go on for years in such an area as disarmament, many approaches, many occasions and personalities must be available. The scene must shift; bilateral and multilateral talks can be expected to succeed one another. One of the great objectives must be to keep hope alive and the possibilities of discussion open. In this involved process the UN with its international staff can make a major contribution. Its watchfulness, its experience, its increasing authority as the embodiment of expert knowledge and skills make its services in this field hard to overestimate.

The UN stands, finally, as a symbol of the world order that will one day be built. The United States has need of symbols as well as power in its foreign policy. To measure the UN's contribution, one need only ask how much meaner and poorer, how much less touched by hope or reason would be the world scene if it suddenly ceased to exist.

## THE NATURE OF ORDER IN THE WORLD

This experience of the United States in regional groupings and in the world organization gives substance to its image of an ideal world. As Americans, we are not talking of things that we have not known at first hand. Imperfect as we recognize these beginnings to be, we see in them the possibility of a development that can immensely benefit men and nations over wide areas of the globe. On the basis of this still fragmentary knowledge, we can generalize; perhaps we can even predict.

Let us try, then, to state briefly what this panel has in mind when it speaks of the opportunity before America of helping to shape a new world order. The phrase could easily be misunderstood. It could be taken as meaning a *Pax Americana:* an imperial ambition to call nations into being, to set them against one another in a balance of power, to divide and break up any too massive concert. We do not have that in mind. Nor do we have in mind, as could conceivably be supposed, spreading American ways of doing things across the globe, hoping to duplicate elsewhere the particular kind of life that now exists within the boundaries of the United States.

This panel thinks, rather, of an order in the world that makes it possible for all nations to develop, to create conditions in which their citizens can have the fullest opportunity for self-realization and self-fulfillment, where every kind of humane aspiration can reach the light. The steady rise in living standards, with the gradual abolition of poverty in all countries, is one element of this order. So is the growth of a wide complex of institutions, which makes it possible for citizens of all countries to deal freely with one another, to move about without hindrance, to conduct their affairs with a minimum of frustration and heat.

The highest expression of such an order is a sense that all men are brothers, deeply concerned in each other's fate. Next to that is a kind of neighborliness, which makes it possible for men and women from anywhere in the world to talk with each other civilly, not unduly impressed by differences between them nor overly anxious that all should speak in the same accents.

The instrument through which this order is to be achieved can perhaps best be described as Law. International law has its part to play, and its rapid development would be one unmistakably hopeful sign. If governments can agree to submit more and more of their difficulties to adjudication before the World Court, this would be a mark of significant progress.

We also think of law in a much broader sense, as recognized custom, as accepted ways of dealing with one another, as the slow accretion of consent and accord. Law in this sense can arise where men come to know one another well and manage their joint affairs with instinctive confidence. It can arise in agencies of the international body or wherever officials of various nations gather to accomplish some agreed-on purpose. It will sometimes be codified and made explicit. More often it will exist in shared understandings and tacit approvals. It will usually not be enforceable in any strict legal sense, but it will live and grow because nations recognize increasingly that the things that need to be done in the world can only be accomplished where men bear and forbear within broad limits set by their common experience.

This kind of order, we submit, is compatible with the basic American character. Tentative and experimental as its development must be, such an order offers the best hope of a world in which the potentialities of the twentieth century can be realized for the benefit of all.

# IV. The Communist Threat

The American objective of a global community at peace confronts the world as it actually exists, with its ideological conflicts, its propagandas, its economic inequalities, and its menacing arms race. The goal as we have described it in preceding sections can be sought only by taking these into account. Coming thus from a statement of the ideal to a consideration of actual circumstances, we cannot but be conscious of a descent from uncluttered space into an atmosphere full of troubles and ambiguities.

Yet that is no reason either to despair of the ultimate goal or to lack resolution for facing immediate necessities. Foreign policy, especially in such an age as ours, must be carried on with a two-fold sense of time. There are things that must be done in the present—and nothing should cause the prudent statesman to defer them; there are other things that must wait. Time gained can, if we use it well, provide an opportunity for the working out of slowly maturing forces that can transform the world scene and perhaps bring mankind back from the abyss into which it now peers.

The great and immediate threat is posed, obviously, by the Communist rulers of Russia and China. There are other problems in the world, to be sure. In certain areas where Soviet influence has been felt only indirectly and at the fringes, the problems have been complex and are often still unsolved. In the Middle East for a full decade after World War II, the United States and Britain, despite similar fundamental interests, were unable to effectuate any broad settlement. Nationalistic fervors, technological developments, racial and religious animosities, and economic revolutions —these, quite apart from communism, put Western policy makers to the test. So it is and has been elsewhere in the world.

Nevertheless, it is the two Communist states—their strategy backed by tenacious dogma—that pose the immediate danger. Even where the direct threat of aggression is played down, they exacerbate and exploit every issue in their relentless search for advantage. It is necessary now to look somewhat closely at the precise nature of this threat and at the means of its implementation.

## THE BASIC SOVIET THREAT

The geographic size, the wealth, the comparative self-sufficiency of the United States should not be allowed to conceal this country's true situation. In respect to the rest of the world, the United States is a comparatively small part of a continent set off the shores of Europe and Asia. Its security depends upon its relations to the major powers in that great land mass. In the past, the United States has instinctively felt threatened when a European conqueror seemed capable of gaining hegemony in Europe —whether it was Bonaparte in the nineteenth century or Hitler in the twentieth.

Today, the basic objective of the Soviets falls within the historic pattern of European conquerors. There is no doubt but that their aim has been and remains that of bringing Europe under their control. At earlier crises in our history the fear has been that such a conqueror would turn the sea forces of Great Britain against the United States. With the coming of the missile age the nature of the menace alters; yet the isolation that would be imposed upon the United States if Soviet aims in Europe were to succeed is still something that Americans would rather not contemplate.

The approaches to the Pacific coast of the United States have also been a preoccupation of United States diplomacy, reinforced by commercial and ideological considerations. The essential interest was that neither Russia nor Japan should achieve hegemony in this area. For half a century the integrity and strength of China was a constant United States objective.

It was not until the twentieth century that the possibility arose of a single hostile force dominating the whole Eurasian continent, stretching from the Atlantic to the Pacific shores. This possibility was brought to the point of serious issue under the Axis powers—

the German-Japanese alliance. It has emerged once more with the alliance of the Soviets with Communist China.

Thus Soviet power stands today—an aggressive military force backed by tenaciously held dogma—active on both the European and Asian scenes. Its position in regard to the United States has been radically changed from what it was before 1945. Prior to that date it was not in the forefront; it was contained and remote. Indeed, being behind potentially aggressive powers—behind France in the nineteenth century and Germany and Japan in the early twentieth—Russia was on the whole a stabilizing factor. This situation always made it conceivable that at key points its interests and those of the United States would conform. In World War II that situation was realized. The result was an alliance—but an alliance subject to the strains that different historical experiences and profoundly opposed ideologies made inevitable.

In the wake of World War II the position of Russia vis-à-vis the United States was drastically transformed. The European countries were then economically and politically weakened; the United States had disarmed precipitately. China was torn by civil war. The Soviet government found what appeared congenial conditions for advancing its strategic aims. It prepared to absorb into its empire those countries that its armies occupied at the close of hostilities. It planned by revolutionary subversion and propaganda to extend westward the Communist ideology and power. In Asia its strategy was to base its advances upon a communized China. The net effect was to be the enforced isolation of the United States, reducing it to an island without allies and without access to vital resources.

This underlying, basic Soviet danger has not been as well understood in the United States as it should be. It has been necessary to drum up support for United States policy by stressing imminent threats and crises and by harping on the less attractive features of communism, including the brutalities of the regime and the persistent exploitation of its own and other peoples. The panel does not underestimate the dangers inherent in communism per se nor the degree to which its practices and ideology are abhorrent to our citizens. But even without these, the United States would still find itself hazardously situated in regard to an aggressive, imperialist Russia. Certainly the situation will not be changed by a lull in the crises that have served to keep the United States awake.

The position of the United States is in need of constant, unremitting defense; it cannot be otherwise until the threats against it have been reduced or removed. Declarations of peaceful intent are not in themselves enough. But opportunities for promising negotiation should be followed up vigorously in order to make such modest advances as are possible or to clarify the real issues.

It may be that conditions will alter and that the Soviet leadership will give proof of a new approach toward the settlement of disputes. The panel has noted with interest the statement made by Premier Khrushchev in Peiping (September 30, 1959) following his first visit to America:

"Therefore we, on our part, must do everything possible to preclude war as a means for settling outstanding questions. These questions must be solved through negotiations . . . we must reason realistically and correctly understand the present situation, and this certainly does not mean that since we are so strong we should test the stability of the capitalist system by force. This would be wrong. The peoples would never understand and would never support those who took into their heads to act in this way . . . Even such a noble and progressive system as socialism cannot be imposed by force of arms against the will of the people."

If events indicate that such a statement is a basic Soviet policy, there is hope for settling some of the more troublesome questions. If, however, negotiations disclose that the Soviet Union is determined to remain an aggressive and expansive force, the free world is confronted with the same somber issues with which it has been plagued since World War II.

In any case, the free world, as a basic tenet of policy, must not permit the Communist states to extend their rule. The Berlin situation is a cardinal example. The manner in which the crisis was precipitated by the Soviet government and the kind of arrangements that it has proposed indicate that they are more interested in pursuing their political and strategic aims than in settling an international issue. The United States cannot accept, under the guise of compromise or the easing of tensions, measures that would abandon West Berlin to Communist rule, dissolve NATO, allow West Germany to fall within the Soviet orbit, or otherwise undermine the free states of Europe.

The stakes in this area go to the heart of free world security. It is not beyond the realm of possibility that the Soviets should prove ready to negotiate seriously on safeguards for the freedom of West Berlin or to accept a united Germany, which is not a Soviet pawn and is so integrated in a true European order as to remove earlier fears of German domination of the continent. Possibilities must be kept open, but the West cannot afford to accept illusory agreements that in fact jeopardize the security of Europe. The undermining of NATO and the communization of Germany cannot be permitted. Any weakening of resolve where these matters are concerned, any confusion of purpose could cause a rapid and fatal deterioration of the world situation.

## PRESENT SOVIET TACTICS

Russia today is in a period of rapid growth in its economy, of large scientific and technological gains, and perhaps of social developments that will give a greater place within its system to the individual and to the wants of the consuming public. It is a great power in the world scales. It is not great, as some Americans for too long liked to suppose, because it got an atom bomb through espionage or the fruits of conquest and built an aggressive military machine on foundations of ignorance, squalor, and oppression. Under the rigors of war and the Soviet system, there has survived much that gave pre-Soviet Russia distinction in the intellectual and cultural life of Europe; and communism, though at enormous human costs, has performed prodigious feats in creating its present productive system. The tendency to misjudge Russia—both to overestimate and to underestimate it—has been so persistent that a clear realization of its character seems the beginning of political wisdom.

This progress in the internal life of Russia, combined with the kind of resistance it has met in the world outside, shapes the Soviet tactic as we face it today. It is a new tactic, more subtle and complex but no less menacing than the old. The underlying objective of domination remains, now often disguised in a doctrine of historical inevitability. But active probing and overtly aggressive moves have been supplemented by rivalry with the West in the technological and economic field. The present Russian leadership has declared it will equal, and by 1970 surpass, the

United States in total output and also per capita production. It relies on the possibility of exporting on a large scale capital goods and technological skills, combined with a capacity to manipulate and absorb the surpluses of the underdeveloped areas. It sees its example appealing to peoples who must accomplish much in a short time and its techniques more readily applicable to their needs than those of the more advanced capitalist economies. If Soviet aims were merely greater economic welfare for itself and for its neighbors, it might be cause for rejoicing. In fact, however, supported by propaganda, infiltration, and subversion, aided by the implied threat of its military power, the Soviet regime gives every evidence that it hopes to expand until it has gained a clear preponderance of power in the world.

This basic strategy conforms to what the Soviet leaders must recognize to be rebuffs to their attempts at overt seizures and aggressions. Western Europe has stood solid, with no Soviet advance beyond those areas occupied at the war's end by Soviet troops—indeed with withdrawals from such areas as Yugoslavia and eastern Austria. The people of the satellite countries of Eastern Europe have not yielded their basic character, and various degrees of freedom have even here reasserted themselves. The communization of the vast population of China, achieved in the first postwar phase and with the support of considerable Soviet power, cannot be overlooked. Yet of the new nations created since the war, none, with the exception of North Vietnam and North Korea, has fallen to communism. Examples of brutal repression, as in Hungary and Tibet, have meanwhile unmasked Communist pretensions.

In brief, communism as an exportable commodity has apparently failed; it has not advanced by persuasion but sustains and expands its power primarily through force. Within the Soviet empire itself, ideological fanaticism has been yielding perceptibly to emphasis on material standards and incentives not different from those that exist in other countries and in any bureaucracy. In foreign policy the U.S.S.R. acts increasingly as a nationalistic entity—a powerful and aggressive nationalistic entity—but stripped of much of the revolutionary appeal with which it formerly expected to conquer men's minds. Communist parties in other countries may still provide allies of varying dependability. Russia's massive weight may attract allies. Its practice of infiltration, sub-

version, and para-military activities may still be effective in overturning enfeebled or demoralized social systems. But all this is
quite different from the quasi-religious ardor with which communism once expected to sweep the world.

The possibility cannot be ruled out that the Soviet leadership,
if it secures a clear superiority in the arms race, will use this
advantage to blackmail or to attack its major opponent without
warning. That possibility must at all costs be forestalled. Under
present conditions, and for as long as necessary, the strength of
the Western deterrent must be maintained, with clear realization
that this cannot be done easily or once and for all. To be in a
position to strike the second retaliatory blow requires a far higher
level of preparedness than is required for striking a first blow under
conditions of surprise. Given this position, the rivalry between the
two systems can be kept in a field where the people of the free
world—provided they are ready to expend the vast effort required
—should feel themselves capable of meeting it on its own terms.

The Soviet leaders understand calculations of power. Their
record and the guiding dogma of Lenin show them notoriously
lacking in scruples when it is to their advantage to disregard their
signed agreements. Nevertheless, even in dealing with such adversaries, agreements can be shaped that are real because they conform to their power interests, and compliance can be further
assured by vigilance and effective safeguards. The Soviet leaders
will not readily give up positions that a preponderance of force
permits them to hold, nor will they easily refrain from taking
what the weakness of others exposes to their grasp. When they
talk of settlements, they mean almost invariably settlements on
their own terms. Yet they are subject to their own necessities
and to pressures both internal and external. It is the continuing
task of Western leaders to maintain the kind of strength that
constrains Soviet ambition and then to feel out the points at
which specific accords may be ratified.


## DEFENSE IN EUROPE

The primary defense effort of the free world has been concentrated in Europe. Here, as we have seen, a community of
peoples and nations already existed, capable of organizing themselves for defense of their common values. The proposal to re-

build Europe under the Marshall Plan had been made before the nature of the cold war was clear. It was a natural sequence— though a decisive and dramatic one—to bring the countries of Western Europe together in a defensive military alliance. That alliance was in answer to Soviet threats. It was also the expression of a deep unity within the Atlantic community.

The danger to NATO is that, as the direct military threat changes its form, the degree of coalescence will also diminish. Disturbing differences of opinion and clashes of interest have indeed occurred. The answer, in part, lies in keeping vivid the underlying sense of community through discussions in NATO and at all levels of regional association. It lies also with the strategic role and importance of NATO, discussed by the Special Studies defense panel in its report, *International Security: The Military Aspect.*

The NATO concept of defense has gone through various phases, from thinking of it merely as a tripwire which would serve to engage the nuclear power of the United States, to thinking of it as being in itself capable of withstanding the onslaught of Russian power. Today, in a period when both sides are armed with nuclear power, NATO has a well-defined and indispensable role. That role is to provide a shield that will assure its ability to meet aggression from the East with forces graduated to the scale and nature of the attack. The maintenance of adequate ground troops in Europe can alone give assurance that the West will not find itself caught in the dilemma of being unable to respond to military incidents except by unloosing total nuclear war.

There is a moral problem also. It must be the constant aim of the West to do everything possible to avoid a nuclear holocaust. This is a duty owed not only to the living generation but to generations still unborn. The West cannot be said to have met this responsibility even halfway so long as it does not maintain the NATO defense forces at a level where they can meet and contain aggressions undertaken by conventional as well as by atomic arms. The obligation to keep up the shield of NATO lies heavily on the European countries as well as on the United States. It is regrettable that the agreed minimum NATO goals have never been met. Where so much is at stake it seems inconceivable that any lack of concerted effort or common sacrifice should be permitted.

In relation to missile warfare and the deterrent power of the

West, NATO is going through a transitional stage. The establishment of European bases for intermediate-range missiles was, we believe, a necessary answer to the Soviet announcement that it possessed operational intercontinental missiles. The importance of these bases may diminish in the future. However that may be, a joint defense effort to prevent less than all-out attacks will remain a vital concern of the Atlantic nations. The full development of intercontinental missiles will not provide a substitute for this joint effort; on the contrary, it will reinforce the need for it.

In short, the defense of Western Europe must remain a cooperative undertaking with NATO as its backbone. The allied military establishment in Europe represents a reciprocal dependence. It exists not in the interest of the United States merely, but of a genuine common cause. With the coming of long-range missiles, it will become increasingly necessary for the West to be able to meet the threat of aggression locally and by means adapted to the nature of the attack.

## COMMUNIST CHINA

The integrity and progress of China were major objectives of American foreign policy from the time of the establishment of The Open Door policy in 1899. Involvement in World War II was foreshadowed for the United States—quite apart from what was happening in Europe—when Japan's path of conquest was laid out across China. A consistent war aim of the United States was an independent China restored in its territorial integrity. The frustration of this long-standing aim by China's communization and resulting attitude caused quite literally a revolution in United States policy for Asia. The fact that the "China problem" has been so difficult to debate rationally is a measure of the shock to United States thinking. There is no use trying to minimize the blow. The United States has been left to pick up pieces represented by Formosa and the Chinese Nationalists, saving what it can for the cause of freedom and as reminders of its once-great hopes for the Chinese people.

Toward mainland China the alternatives of policy are, for the short run, lacking in creative possibilities. The value of diplomatic recognition and admission to the United Nations can be variously debated. In any case these somewhat technical questions do not go to the heart of the problem. For at the heart is the fanatical dedication of the Communist Chinese leaders to the Communist faith and methods, their apparent determination to be an enemy of the United States, and their aggressive tendencies as shown in Korea, Tibet, India, and elsewhere. These facts would remain whether China was in the United Nations or not, whether officially recognized by the United States or not.

What self-interest and enlightened policy do require of the United States at this juncture is a candid recognition of what Communist China is and where it is going. For too many Americans, the assumption has seemed to be that China's absence from the United Nations could mean its absence from their minds. It has been supposed that its real power was decisively affected by whether or not it was represented in Washington or in the debates in the United Nations. The need for complete knowledge of what is going on in China is so paramount that lesser interests or concerns should give way to insure full reporting by Americans on the spot.

China today is being moved by obscure and perhaps contradictory forces. It is difficult to determine at a particular moment whether it is giving priority to its avowedly expansionist external aims or to its fierce pressure for internal growth and industrialization. It is difficult to account for all its moods and methods, varying from relative quiescence to the extreme bellicosity of its course since 1958. The country is in the throes of a vast and brutal revolution; shifting policies and changing emphases seem to be part of its violent inner dynamism.

What is clear is that Communist China is in a posture that, in past historical experience, has almost invariably led to aggression. It has a rapidly growing population, a shortage of vital resources, and a fanatical ideology. Around a large part of its perimeter exist "soft" situations, making infiltration, subversion, and outright conquest seem easy or inviting prospects. Moreover, it looks upon the United States as its supreme enemy, the one major obstacle to its domination of the Asian continent. China's overriding political and strategic aim is, undoubtedly, to undermine American influence, to separate the United States from its friends and supporters in Asia, and to force the withdrawal of United States defensive forces.

The present relations between Soviet Russia and Red China do not lend themselves to simple analysis. It is perhaps enough to assert here that these two Communist countries may not always be drawn together by common interests. In regard to China, the Soviets may find themselves being committed to greater risks than they had counted on. The problems of dealing with countries around the border of the Communist world, the difficulties of keeping China supplied with needed capital goods, the new appearance China will present if armed with atomic weapons—these and other factors provide substance enough for strains in an alliance that now seems structurally and ideologically strong. But it is not reasonable to expect such developments to reveal themselves within a short-time span or in a form that will necessarily ease the situation of the free world. Nor can effective results be anticipated from policies specifically designed to drive a wedge between Moscow and Peiping. What we can know for certain is that we shall be much preoccupied over the coming decade with the relations between the two great Communist powers.

For the present we must avoid, wherever possible, courses of action that seem to drive China closer to the Soviets; and we must be prepared for new situations as relations between these two massive powers undergo change. We must, above all, give sympathetic and imaginative consideration to the problems and the hopes of the countries around the rim of Asia. In the next section of this report, we shall look specifically at those countries of Asia (as well as of the Middle East and Africa) where it is a vital interest of the United States and of the free world that communism be forestalled from extending its domination. The secure independence of the countries around the rim of Asia, their progress in terms of human welfare and political maturity, their growing capacity to defend themselves—these the United States desires to see and, insofar as it can, to help. But such objectives cannot be thought of as related exclusively or even principally to the problems of power and military security. They must be ends pursued for their own sake.

In the long run, it is only as the free countries of Asia realize their own potentialities and fulfill their own destiny that there can be established on the continent of Asia the kind of order and balance that restrains the aggressive tendencies of Communist China.

## ONE CO-ORDINATED CONFLICT

This brief and necessarily limited review of the nature and dimensions of the Communist threat should not obscure what is one of the most important facts about the cold war; namely, that it is being waged by Communists as *one* conflict. There are many scenes and many methods; but there are central aims and more or less co-ordinated methods. Military, political, economic, and psychological means are employed alternately or in combination as the situation indicates. If one is played down for a season or in a particular part of the globe, that does not mean that in the total scheme it has assumed any less importance. The answering strategy of the West, and of the United States in particular, must be similarly composed of diverse elements, seen in the context of the whole and effectively harmonized.

In other reports in the series, the panels make their recommendations in the fields of military and economic policy. Here we only reiterate that a strong atomic capability, combined with defense measures adequate to meet the whole spectrum of possible threats, is essential as a means to restrict the conflict to channels where it can be decided otherwise than by mutual suicide and universal destruction. Broad policies looking to sustained economic and technical co-operation and unimpeded exchange of goods and services are likewise indispensable elements in the protracted struggle. Combined with these are such political factors as have been discussed here, along with the whole range of actions that make it their aim to influence the outlook and psychology of the opposing side.

As a people who tend to take up one problem at a time, Americans are disposed to see a general shift for the better when a particular form of tension is relaxed. This is not a safe attitude in the present circumstances. Tenacity of purpose as well as capacity for sacrifice, sustained over a long period, will be needed to meet the present challenge. It will test all the qualities of purpose and leadership that a democracy can muster.

# V. The Asian Rim, the Middle East, and Africa

The three geographical areas dealt with in this section of the report—immense in scope and in significance for the future—have in the more distant past been outside the direct range of United States commitments. The United States was from the beginning involved in Europe; its concern with Latin America was early established. But until the turn of the century, the countries of the Asian rim from Suez to Singapore, the Middle East, and Africa were considered responsibilities of the European powers or as engaged in rivalries in which the United States had no part. American cultural and humanitarian influences were felt in significant but limited ways. Outside of these, nothing much in the way of action seemed either feasible or desirable.

This situation was drastically changed by a number of simultaneous developments. The imperial order began to dissolve rapidly after World War II. The establishment of new nations brought into play the United States' traditional and deeply felt interest in the growth of freedom across the globe. On top of all these was added the cold war. The United States saw rightly that if these areas were not to become subject to communism, the influence and help of the free nations would have to be effectively concerted.

The United States must be continually conscious of the complexity of the problems in these new areas of its concern and of the weight that must be given to developments that it cannot and should not seek to control. New nations have their own interests and their pride. Older nations, many of them going back in history ages before the United States was born, maintain traditions and values that adjust themselves slowly to the twentieth-century world. Matters that seem simple and self-evident to the United States may well appear in a different light to these diverse peoples and nations. Throughout all this area, on two continents and amid situations characterized by the greatest variety and complexity, the United States must find ways of acting with clearness of view and competence of means but without seeking to impose its own will or its ready-made solutions. The United Nations and its specialized agencies provide an important channel for such action.

In all these areas, the threat of Communist imperialism is making itself felt with varying degrees of intensity and immediacy. This fact cannot be ignored by United States policy makers. Yet the struggle against communism will surely be lost if nothing else but the threat is seen. Fortunately, the United States can keep the clear conviction that in acting according to its own best instincts and traditions it is meeting the deep necessities of the cold war. The development of free institutions, economic progress, and advancing well-being will, if consistently and imaginatively furthered, prove not only desirable in itself but the best over-all strategy for warding off the expansion of the Communist empires.

## THE RIM OF ASIA

The problems in the wide arc that runs from Japan in the north to India in the south were bound to be difficult in the post-colonial age. The newly won independence of many nations within this area could not be expected to bring with it the trained groups necessary to effective political and economic organization. The growth of regionalism met inevitable barriers. The lines of transport, trade, and communication still ran back to the metropolitan countries, and there was little enough—apart from anti-colonial sentiments—upon which a common interest could be established. Anticipations of a rapid rise in the material standard of life were in the nature of things often bound to be disappointed. Population growth alone can eat up gains laboriously achieved. Besides, there are inevitable setbacks and frustrations in the best-laid economic plans.

There are also setbacks on the political level. A false hope encouraged the United States, after the war, to suppose that economic progress would necessarily be associated with the establishment of liberal regimes. Rapid economic progress, especially where capital must be in large part self-generated, has often involved centralized planning and strong governmental intervention in all phases of the economy. In different parts of Asia, national disappointment in the speed of economic progress is postponing the development of vigorous institutions based on consent.

The difficulties of the period would have been great enough in any case. They have been bitterly intensified by the incorporation of the massive population of China within the Communist camp. A democratic China might have provided a secure base around which a free Asia could organize itself, growing in strength and independence, in the capacity for self-government, in economic well-being and social progress. Any such hope has disappeared. Now the difficult task confronts us of helping shape a free Asian order without China, in the vast extended semicircle along the seas and oceans.

These setbacks must be faced up to. Yet, there is much that the United States can do in this vast area, if it devotes itself seriously to the task without being discouraged by the effort required or the difficulties encountered. The Communist Chinese are exerting their pressures throughout the region, perhaps varying the relative emphasis they place upon the military factor but still with a full spectrum of political, economic, and military means of action. We must similarly integrate and harmonize these elements in our own policy. The past tendency for American military and nonmilitary policies to be set independently and often at odds with each other can no longer be justified as being caused by the unavoidable confusion of the postwar emergency.

We are entering a period of widespread political ferment and change in which the experience in Latin America is likely to be duplicated in the more dangerous areas close to Soviet and Chinese military pressure. There is great need for facing the intricate question of how we can demonstrate a concern for the broader interests of the people without becoming identified with regimes not based on the popular will and likely to be displaced.

Our economic aid has been limited in its social and political results because it was often subordinated to military purposes. We must think our way through the obstinate problems of how to make reasonably sure that this aid serves the prime purpose of the growth of the economy so that the underdeveloped people will not awake some years hence to discover that their growth rates are still unsatisfactory, that our various forms of assistance have been used for short-range benefits. These countries, as their true interests manifest themselves, will surely want constructive and enduring advantages from aid and other resources.

On the military side, there is a similar need to find better ways to help bring these countries to a point where they are capable of defending themselves. The policy of common defense needs a firmer political base. In the long run, it will succeed to the extent that it is built on the growing self-reliance and increasing maturity of these peoples. Hungary and Tibet have opened the eyes of peoples throughout this area; these new attitudes can create the underpinning of new policies.

In general, our concern is to help build independent self-governing states, standing on their own feet, finding their needs satisfied within broad regional arrangements and institutions. Our judgment as to our capacity to help economically must not be warped by calculations that, while purporting to estimate what we can bear, really yield to concealed soft assumptions about the importance of carrying on as usual. In calculating the amount of our help, we should place primary emphasis upon the resolution of the particular underdeveloped country to face its own needs and commit its own resources to meet those needs and upon its ability effectively to absorb assistance and put it to fruitful use. Our determination must be to do whatever is necessary to supplement maximum self-help and mutual aid on the part of the underdeveloped countries in question, when the objective is so transcendently in the interest of freedom.

When the people of these underdeveloped countries face the facts concerning their own need, accept their responsibilities, and do their part, the evidence indicates that the amount of aid required will be of a magnitude that the United States can and should accept.

These general recommendations apply to the Asian perimeter as a whole. At any point along this great crescent the Sino-Soviet imperialists may choose, as in the past decade, to create new pressures. Our policies must be shaped to specific cases, but with the broad principles outlined above continually operative.


## Japan

A special emphasis needs to be placed upon Japan. The United States looks upon Japan as a partner in securing the defense of the

Pacific and in rendering important forms of assistance to a number of economically less advanced countries of Asia. Fortunately, Japan has emerged successfully from the period of the war and occupation, democratically organized, with its population increase brought under control and its trade directed into new channels. It cannot be forgotten, however, how large is the stake of the Soviets and Communist Chinese in diverting Japan from its present orientation. Chinese trade policies in Southeast Asia, directed against the efforts of Japan to find markets adequate to its vast export needs, are but one part of the intense pressures exerted by the Communists. Communist strategy sets a high priority on undermining Japan's present position and ultimately obtaining its adherence to the Communist camp.

Japan's need for exports together with its efficient, highly organized production can make it appear to United States industry as a strong and even dangerous competitor. It is sometimes forgotten to what an extent Japan also provides a major market for U.S. goods. Even more important than this, however, is the degree to which the free world counts on Japan in the world-wide struggle. The partnership in great objectives must not be subordinated to rivalry in the area of trade.

## India and Pakistan

At the other end of the long arc stand India and Pakistan, two nations whose fates are inextricably interwoven with each other and, taken together, engage vital American interests in the prospects for a new world order. Sharing the same subcontinent, the two are confronted on the north by powerful Communist neighbors, ideologically hostile to efforts to create two great free and independent nations at their threshold. Here, if anywhere, it must be proven that peoples can lift themselves rapidly into the modern age without submitting to the oppressions of dictatorship.

India has not sought, nor is willing, to align itself with the United States. This attitude need cause Americans little concern; the American stake is in India's continued independence and its ability to build a strong nation through constitutional means. If this goal is to be reached, India must make substantial economic and social advances under the most difficult circumstances. Large-scale assistance of many kinds from outside its own borders will be needed, including both intergovernmental assistance and private investment. It takes no talent for prophecy to suggest that it would be tragically shortsighted were the United States not to be ready to assist India's own resolute efforts to effect steady progress toward a better existence for her hundreds of millions of peoples.

Pakistan, a member of the Central Treaty Organization, has been somewhat closer to the United States than has India, at least through official relationships. The partition of the subcontinent presented Pakistan with severe problems: the nation bifurcated, normal economic channels disrupted, a lack of trained administrative and professional competence. But the country has marked potential. The United States is already committed to assist in its realization. The next years will be crucial in showing whether political and economic progress can be achieved.

To the extent that the United States can influence the situation, we must be concerned with the direct relations between India and Pakistan. Until the two have placed their relations upon a normal basis and can deal with each other in full co-operation and confidence, severe limits are placed upon the effectiveness of external aid to either or to both. The inflammable issues that stemmed from the partition period have not been quenched; we support the readiness of the United States to use its good offices in whatever way may be useful or acceptable. Our own policies should accept as fundamental the necessity for good relations between India and Pakistan, and action involving one should be seriously weighed in the light of its effect upon the other.


## THE MIDDLE EAST

No part of the world has presented American policy with more baffling complexities than has the Middle East. A mere reminder of the principal threads in the tangled skein will help to explain why this should be so.

The area lies across the lines of communication between Europe and the Far East. Historically it has been the home of three of the world's great and dynamic religions. It attracted the attention of world powers and threw the area into the cauldron of outside rivalries long before the discovery of its rich natural resources.

More recently, nationalist movements fed by dynastic and personal rivalries have insisted that the remnants of Western political and economic domination be eliminated. Finally, recent initiatives of the Soviet Union to penetrate the Middle East and to bring it under Communist influence suggest a desire in Moscow to create along Russia's southern border a group of dependent states similar to the satellites of Eastern Europe. In this complex of pressures, the Western powers have been unable to work out a common approach to a new relationship with the Middle East.

Sweeping demands for social and economic improvement are the more explosive because of the extremes of wealth and poverty characteristic of much of the area. Governments themselves have, for the most part, been unable to develop a strong and efficient administrative apparatus through which to get on with the public business and win the confidence of their peoples by steady progress. Critical shortages of trained personnel exist in all fields of social and economic improvement, and educational systems are not yet geared to produce them in the numbers and skills required.

Fierce tensions were created by the establishment of the state of Israel against the bitter opposition of the peoples and governments of the surrounding area. These tensions have made it impossible thus far to find solutions for such distressing and immediate problems as the Arab refugees, the ease and freedom of sea, air, and land communications in the Near East, and the reopening of rational trade channels and patterns at the eastern end of the Mediterranean. The same tensions have beclouded American relations with the Arab world and have offered easy opportunities for the Soviet Union to fish in troubled waters.

Competition for influence and leadership within the region has impeded regional co-operation and joint action. Underlying common interests are forgotten or set aside during periodic clashes among personalities or governments, a tendency undoubtedly encouraged by a variety of outside influences.

In thinking about these and other complications in our relations with the Middle East, Americans need not suppose that they are wholly without assets upon which to build a viable long-term approach. Geography alone suggests that the United States is capable of disinterestedness, and it is doubtful that there is any significant opinion in that area that the United States has imperial designs of its own upon the Middle East. On the other hand, the peoples of the Middle East live in the shadow of a powerful and aggressive neighbor to their north. They cannot escape the hard fact that in the absence of a change in Soviet policy, their independence requires a confrontation of Soviet power by the United States. Below the political level, the American and Middle Eastern peoples have been in friendly and mutually beneficial relationships in many directions: in science and scholarship, education, letters and the arts, in trade and commerce. These relationships have survived many vicissitudes and have laid a foundation of understanding and respect that is of considerable consequence.

In such a complex and difficult situation, it is good sense to "be ourselves." It is especially important not to become discouraged if simple and straightforward moves such as the "Baghdad Pact" and the Eisenhower Doctrine fail to meet the situation. Being ourselves means calling upon the long-range determinants of American policy for guidance. Applied to the Middle East, it means that we can make it clear that our weight is in support of security of the people of the region against aggression, direct or indirect—whether from outside the region or by one state against another within the region. It means that we are prepared to assist these states in becoming economically and socially viable and that our assistance is available without the price of military or political alignment with us and our Western allies. It means a quiet influence in support of policies and practices that will win the approval and support of the peoples of the area. It means a friendly and helpful role, if called upon, to assist in resolving outstanding issues which set neighbor against neighbor in the Middle East.

Open channels of trade and communication are a part of traditional American policy. So is the encouragement of countless relationships beneath the level of political action in a wide range of mutually beneficial educational, cultural, and humanitarian activities. Here effective action may consist of many quiet steps in detail, in which nongovernmental agencies—schools and colleges, foundations, and business enterprises in particular—can play a most important part, pursued in each country with patience, persistence, and sophistication.

In the case of the Middle East, style may be as important as the substance of policy. We can be helpful without being importunate, firm without being provocative, courteous without being patronizing or craven. We can afford to be patient in the face of rebuff and dignified in the face of minor irritation. Our first task is to maintain the respect of the people of the area; with their respect, many opportunities will present themselves for action that will gradually shape up a new relationship more workable than any we have experienced in the postwar years. We need not be nervous about the ability of the Soviet Union to win the Middle East by persuasion; we must be alert to their efforts to win it by other methods. Our panel is convinced that the United States and the nations of the Middle East have solid common interests upon which to build and that common aims can show the way to fruitful co-operation.

## THE AFRICAN CONTINENT

In terms of political, economic, and social factors, Africa presents a continent of great mass and population, with the greatest variety ethnically and geographically; it is undoubtedly the most rapidly changing area in the world today. By 1958, when the countries of South and Southeast Asia had found their new nationhood, most of the continent of Africa still lived within the framework of colonial systems. Two years have seen immense transformations, and the timetable of the years immediately ahead is crowded with the emergence of still other free countries. It would be impossible for such rapid progress not to be complicated by strains or for questions not to have arisen as to whether the shaping of free institutions can keep pace with the aspirations of peoples so much in a hurry.

The United States, apart from traditional ties with Liberia, has not in the past thought of itself as playing a role on the African continent. Indeed, it was only in 1958 that a separate Bureau of African Affairs was established in the State Department. But as the flood of nationalism swelled, it was impossible, as it would certainly have been undesirable, for the United States to exclude itself from a part in the great transformation of the African continent. Today, the United States is in the position of encouraging by practical, on-the-spot measures the emergence of a new political order. It has an equal interest in seeing the era of colonialism pass and in seeing that disorder and violence do not succeed it. Peaceful change is easier to achieve in those areas of Africa where nationalism is not accompanied by racial conflicts. At best, we must keep our hopes in line with the realities of a situation where immense difficulties and obstacles exist.

The nationalist movements in North Africa have provided one

of the severest tests for American policy makers. The war in Algeria seemed inevitably to be more than a French domestic concern. Relations with a principal NATO ally could not but suffer as virtually the whole French defensive force was drained off to feed the seemingly endless struggle in North Africa. Until General de Gaulle indicated a way out of the impasse, successive French governments proved unable to bring the fighting to an end or to propose an acceptable political solution. Since the General's offer of September 16, 1959, offering a choice of several paths, including independence, to the Algerians, a common Western approach to this major problem has seemed possible. Such an approach is facilitated by the liberal nature of the new French Community, in which all the participating countries have freely chosen their part and within which they preserve control over their internal affairs. With these developments and with the liberalization of the regimes in the French trust territories, Togoland and the Cameroons, France can claim to have made, with Great Britain, a statesman-like adjustment to new conditions.

The American attitude at this juncture must be one of sympathy and encouragement for the new nations of Africa. It must be sensitive to the degree of pride they feel in their new independence; it must seek to know better the many able leaders who are arising in Africa and in turn seek to make the United States and its purposes better known to them. These new nations require help in creating a viable economic life. They need facilities for education and public health, aid in the development of agricultural and natural resources as well as of industrial enterprises. The new leaders look both to governmental financing and to private investment. The United States must take account of these needs and seek in every feasible way to aid the new countries in meeting the expectations of their peoples.

It is inevitable that the Communists should look to this area, perhaps with the same strategic objectives that twenty-five years ago they held in relation to China. Racial tensions, economic underdevelopment, nationalistic seethings, and the residues of colonialism provide a tempting ground in which to work. Because of Africa's immense importance, both politically and strategically, the United States cannot afford to be detached or complacent.

The aim of the United States must not be to seek to align these new countries in a military alliance or to ask their commitment to the Western cause. It must be, rather, by common efforts to help further their advance along the road of political and economic freedom. Its aim must be to see that they are permitted to develop their lives and institutions in peace, with the assistance they desire and, in the light of their own efforts, are entitled to expect. It would be a tragedy, indeed, if Africa were to emerge from a century of colonialism to become a battleground in the cold war. That it may pass into an era of peace, free to develop in its own way, is the basic objective of American policy in this area.

# VI.  Elements of a New World

In a world changing rapidly, it is important to discern the next phase as well as to grasp the fundamentals of the present one. In this section of the report, we put down some of the big things that seem to be happening. They set the stage for the problems with which the next phase of foreign policy must deal. They are capable of being affected in their impact and in the speed of their development by deliberate choices of policy.

## DECLINE OF THE NATION-STATE

The nation-state as it was conceived in the sixteenth century and as it has existed throughout the modern age is now transforming itself. In this report it has been necessary to talk in terms of nations as if they were still the solid entities, watertight and sovereign, that traditional theory describes. In fact, they have not been that for a long time. The growth of the modern world has seen the interdependency of nations and communities increase to a point where independence, at least in the sense of self-sufficiency, is seriously eroded. If the United States were to be confronted with the necessity of existing apart from the trade of the world, apart from its intellectual and spiritual currents and the support of allied and kindred nations, it would quickly realize that independence can be pushed too far.

The modification of the nation-state has been confused by the fact that the aspirations of peoples all over the globe are today finding expression in the slogan of nationalism. What animates these peoples is a resolve to emerge rapidly and conclusively from the era of colonialism. They are going somewhere, but it is a real question whether they are going where they think they are. Many

of them simply would not possess in any circumstances the prerequisites of self-sufficient nationhood. They certainly do not possess
them in a day when even the most firmly established states find
many insufficiencies within their own borders and a constant necessity to enlarge the definition of their interests. In a deep way,
emerging states seem to recognize the inadequacy of their avowed
goal. Even while they affirm their nationalism they grope toward
those larger groupings in which alone they can hope to find their
needs met.

The new nationalism may thus be a halfway house. It may
provide a point in the line of the rapidly evolving development of
the former colonial peoples. But it is not a resting place where
men can hope to build viable communities for themselves and for
their children.

The eating away of the national idea has been brought about by
a world-wide economic system the essence of which makes it impossible for a state to find sufficiency within its own borders. It
has been brought about also perhaps most dramatically by new
developments in weapons and warfare. In classic theory the essence
of the state—in addition to economic self-sufficiency—was its de-
fensibility. It comprised a territorial expanse internally pacified
and outwardly defended. Order within and a reasonable security
against invasion from without: these were the opposite sides of
the coin of nationhood. Smaller nations have long had to accommodate their thinking to the fact of vulnerability, but the development of air warfare blurred the significance of borders for large
states as well. Even then it was possible in theory to stop the
airborne invader over the frontier. The coming of the missile age,
and with it the seeming impossibility of keeping the homeland
from being penetrated, will complete the process that is making
the modern nation an open and exposed, rather than a tightly
bounded, territorial unit.

In another way the new weapons have accelerated the erosion
of nationalism. The technological skill and financial resources necessary to develop these weapons and to produce suitable delivery
systems reinforced the tendency toward a bipolar world—a world,
that is, with two superpowers in juxtaposition to each other. Even
without atomic weapons, the United States and Russia would no
doubt have found themselves thus opposed, with a superiority
of power dwarfing other nations. In the nineteenth century,

Tocqueville already discerned that outcome. But for the past decade this bipolarity has been linked with the new weaponry, and in that period the two superpowers have as by an irresistible force transformed not only their own nature but the nature of the states and nations grouped around them.

American security is now meaningless apart from the security of the free world. From our point of view, the American territory remains as an inner citadel, but for all practical purposes the United States' defense area is far wider. Within these boundaries of the free world, other nations have kept their integrity and freedom; but their own responsibilities for defense have been transformed. They have been conscious, moreover, of varying degrees of mutual constraints and interdependency.

As for the relations of the countries within the Communist orbit, subjection has been the normal course. Yet it would be a mistake to ignore how the Soviet leadership has been compelled by the forces of nationalism and self-determination to grant varying degrees of autonomy. The satellite countries present something less than a uniform subjection. Khrushchev's hints (in Leipzig, March 7, 1959) of a new commonwealth structure for the Soviet bloc deserve attention.

If the bipolarity of the past decade diminishes significantly, the relations between states will once again alter. But the effects of recent historical experience will not be lost. The nations will still find themselves linked in regional groupings of various sizes and varying degrees of integration. It will be difficult for them to affirm the kind of independence that they possessed, at least in theory, up to the division of world power between the United States and the Soviet Union.

The combinations that will then become possible are suggested by the richness of international life that has grown up, to some extent unnoticed, in the past decade and a half. Nations have not only been finding new affinities within the overarching structure of the two great superpowers; they have also been working out new relationships as a consequence of economic and technological forces. The nation-state in its existing form has not permitted certain vital functions to be adequately or efficiently fulfilled. Markets have not proved large enough. Sources of raw materials and credit have not been organized on a sufficiently broad or stable base. Accordingly, we have seen developing a wide variety of institutions reaching across the old borderlines. Sovereignty has been relaxed in specific fields, but experience is proving that by voluntary pooling of efforts for certain ends, the nations are not diminished in any essential way, but rather gain an enhancement of what they have. Real power is increased as the meaning of sovereignty is reinterpreted.

Among the institutions that have been thus created are co-operative undertakings for specific, limited purposes, such as the European Coal and Steel Community, Euratom, the European Common Market, and the beginning of comparable arrangements elsewhere, as in Central America; arrangements to stabilize price and distribution of certain commodities; and finally, monetary and credit arrangements as in the European Payments Union, the International Bank for Reconstruction and Development, and the International Monetary Fund. Nor should it be overlooked that, outside of governments, the modern corporation is carrying on a considerable part of the world's economic activities, inevitably assuming functions that cut across boundaries, and playing an important though little-noticed role in internationalizing the economic substructure.

Discernible in many areas is a tendency for nations to involve some parts of themselves in different groupings or associations. Thus the Western European countries have for purposes of defense been part of an Atlantic community, while for economic purposes they have been part of a European community. Certain of these countries have further sliced off specific economic functions—such as the production of coal and steel or the development of atomic energy—forming from the segments new communities, that do not engage the entire nation-state. These new communities, carved out of the existing sovereignties, have their own capitals, their own civil services. Such developments are bound to increase. We are on the threshold of what will undoubtedly be a vast and many-sided institutional growth. What we have seen already is enough to suggest that the nation-state, as traditionally conceived, is no longer the sole possible unit of political power.

In general, it may be said that the less complex social structures tend to form themselves into groupings that maintain something of the character of traditional alliances—though even here with an interdependence born of twentieth-century needs—while the mature social and political organisms of the Western world tend to group themselves by functions, with overlappings and inter-mixtures that are often striking in their ingenuity.

These developments within the nation-state system offer diplomacy in the second half of the twentieth century tools of great flexibility and promise to work with. Americans have been traditionally concerned with community building—though too often they have proceeded uncritically on the assumption that the example of their own union can be duplicated in entirely different conditions. They have now a rich field in which to test their experience.

## ARMS AND DIPLOMACY

The shape of foreign policy has been profoundly affected by the developments in weaponry brought in with the atomic bomb and now the missile age. In a previous passage we have indicated the way in which these new weapons have heightened the tendency toward bipolarity, concentrating great power in the two nations that have been able to develop them to their fullest extent. We have indicated also how the relationships of other countries to these great powers have been affected; how, indeed, the very nature of their national existence has been altered.

There are other major ways in which the new arms have affected foreign policy. The support that these arms and our over-all military strength have brought to our diplomatic objectives scarcely needs to be stressed. The atomic bomb, while it was a United States monopoly, provided a shelter beneath which the free world could organize for defense; through dangerous years it afforded an effective counterpoise against the threat of Soviet manpower. With the monopoly broken, a new and delicate equilibrium—"the balance of terror"—has come into being. The nations have, as a result, been preserved from general war through a decade and a half despite the persistence of aggressive Soviet designs.

In subtle ways, through the same decade and a half, the nature of these new weapons has affected the atmosphere and conditions of diplomacy. The extraordinary destructiveness of these weapons has made it increasingly difficult to translate their force into a practical instrument of policy. The greatest Communist gains, including the communization of China, were achieved in the immediate postwar period when the United States possessed a monopoly of these weapons and therefore, in theory, a vast superiority of power. That power was not effectively converted into pressure in support of diplomatic aims. In the case of the United States, even when it had monopoly of the atom bomb, public opinion imposed severe restrictions upon its use. As a deterrent to all-out war, massive retaliation may well be a sound concept; but the frightfulness of the weapons makes the retaliatory threat less credible when it is applied to situations of "nibbling," of local aggression or subversion. The very lack of credibility may tempt the other side to move at a lower level of force, thus creating a situation in which we feel compelled to respond with equal or greater force.

Atomic weapons and the military doctrine to which they gave rise can cause new difficulties in maintaining our alliances. These weapons have been recognized by all countries concerned as providing an essential underpinning for NATO. Yet the inequality of power resulting from the fact that they have been in the possession of two nations of the alliance and not of others has inevitably caused strains and has required special care to maintain mutual understanding and confidence. While the bomb was a United States monopoly, Europeans tended to fear lest the United States use it too readily; when Russia broke the monopoly, the fears were expressed lest the United States be slow to use it in case of aggression against them for fear of exposing its own shores to Soviet atomic power. The uneasiness generated among Europeans by these separate fears—each understandable in the particular circumstances—has tended to work against the development of Atlantic unity.

The overhanging presence of atomic weapons has, besides, tended to make change and adjustment in the international order difficult to effectuate. The threat of a nuclear holocaust has made the use of force subject to great risks. This might conceivably be a gain if, with force inhibited, diplomacy were able to take charge. But with the balance so precarious and the results of upsetting it so potentially catastrophic, diplomacy, too, becomes hesitant. At key points, such as Korea and Berlin, we have witnessed what has been called "a slowing down of history." In a world where everything else is speeded up and underlying social and economic developments move at an unprecedented rate, these situations remain fixed.

The major powers have thus not worked out anything more than a crude and dangerous way of living with the new weapons. Yet the world is now faced with the proliferation of these weapons to other countries. If matters are left to take their own course, we shall first probably see an enlargement of the nuclear club, with France being first in a course that other technically advanced countries will follow. There is hope that at this stage the newer nuclear powers may use their prestige and influence to achieve the enforcement of some kind of order. It would be over-optimistic, however, to assume that this effort will be successful in preventing the spread of the bombs.

It is necessary, therefore, to foresee the deadly weapons coming into the hands of a number of nations. What the world order will consist of, if there are then no controls or limitation, it is difficult to imagine. At the worst, the possession of these weapons will give power of catastrophic destruction to a number of nations, while giving security to none. Irresponsible assertions of power will become a real and fearful danger. The chances for error or for deliberate creation of false appearances will leave the world in a state of unappeasable anxiety.

## CONTROL OF ARMS

As men look into the future, it is impossible for them not to be sobered by the burden of arms seen lying upon the nations. The realization that man has devised weapons capable of destroying life on this planet casts a shadow over the whole human adventure. The material costs of armaments do more than merely cause postponements of benefits to which peoples feel entitled after long efforts and great technological advances; they distort society by diverting scientific and other talents. These costs will mount as weaponry becomes constantly more technically refined, yet without any compensating assurance of security. The chances of error or miscalculation become the greater as resources are concentrated on weapons of growing complexity and compressed time scale.

Since World War II the United States has taken an active part in international efforts to reduce the risk and the burden of armaments through mutually agreed limitation. Its proposals of 1946 to achieve international control of nuclear energy were rejected by the Soviets, and the difficulties of the task have unfortunately increased through the ensuing years. Nevertheless, the United States can point with some hope to agreement on basic principles worked out through the channels of the United Nations. In addition, direct negotiations have been established between the United States and the Soviets on prevention of surprise attack and the suspension of nuclear weapon tests.

The United States' approach has in general been for worldwide arms control, calling for a step-by-step reduction in armaments, coupled with control and inspection. The hope has been to reduce armaments by stages, make disclosures, and establish inspection, beginning with the least critical stage and progressing to demobilization of our most effective arms and disclosure of our most sensitive secrets only after confidence has been gained through experience in the less critical preceding stages. Agreement with the Russians has been difficult because they propose sweeping disarmament measures without accepting inspection adequate to verify compliance.

The abolition of arms has been once more proposed by the Soviet government. Whether the proposal is serious is open to doubt. Substantial disarmament has long been an objective of United States national policy, provided it is accomplished with real assurance that the security of the world will be improved in the process. Recent Soviet statements have apparently placed more emphasis on inspection and control than did their early proposals. Negotiations must test whether there are sufficiently significant changes in the Russian position to make it possible to move toward a mutually acceptable plan for disarmament.*

It seems important to point out that there are deep and perhaps crucial differences between the Soviet approach to disarmament and that of the United States. The Soviet leaders maintain that the way to reduce tensions and enmities is through disarmament. The United States maintains, on the contrary, that effective disarmament measures can only come about as concomitant political settlements reduce the tensions. The Soviet spokesmen seem to be saying that only when nations no longer have the means to fight wars will they lose the incentive to fight. They are suspicious of systems of inspection and control, which would cause them to lose, during the interim period of disarmament, the strategic advantages

* Written in December 1959.

of secrecy. It must be admitted that they possess this advantage to a far larger degree than the free countries of the West. Moreover, the Western emphasis on political settlement takes into account that substantial disarmament would greatly enhance the use of externally supported revolution as a Soviet weapon of expansion.

We reiterate, therefore, that we believe political accommodations must accompany effective disarmament; we maintain that these settlements, with the relaxation of tensions they bring, should make possible a sound system of inspection and control. For this reason we deem it of the utmost importance to push forward a search for political arrangements that can allay the fears both of the free world and of the Soviet leaders and satisfy the legitimate quest for security. It is sobering to recall that on more than one occasion the United States has unilaterally reduced its arms below the level of safety without first negotiating arrangements to protect its general security.

At the same time, negotiations in the field of disarmament must be unremittingly pursued, taking advantage of every political or technological development that may offer a fresh line of inquiry. We urge that the United States pay greater attention to sustained studies of the arms problem. Negotiations in this field have become so complex and so involved with rapidly changing military, technological, and political factors that the first requisite is a clear understanding of what national policy should aim to achieve. There are matters of great subtlety and complexity involved in programs of monitoring and inspection in all aspects of arms limitation. The knowledge of what actually adds to security is not easily acquired and will not remain constant.

The amount of effort that has gone into this kind of study has been negligible compared to the effort which has gone into military matters or other aspects of our national security and international relations. The United States has tended to go into international negotiations with inadequate preparation and with rapid turnover of personnel officially engaged in the problem.

There are also required, this panel submits, thoroughgoing studies and experiments to improve our capacity to detect, to monitor, and to inspect, including studies in techniques of hiding and concealing atomic blasts. A group within the government should be in a position to give continuing attention to such problems, under a directive to explore every alternative. It is important that, wherever possible, such studies be made public, for without them public discussion of disarmament could become meaningless or even dangerous.

Disarmament, nevertheless, is not merely a matter of technology. Persistent and unremitting efforts to achieve step-by-step control and reduction of arms should not blind the United States to the really fundamental issues involved. If the control of arms becomes effective on a broad scale, it will almost certainly be because international institutions will have developed greatly in scope and authority over the coming years. Machinery for inspection and control (particularly if countries not now possessing atomic bombs agree not to manufacture them) will make heavy demands upon the international organization. In addition, the adjudication of disputes under international law must be expected to advance along with the lessening reliance on arms. The armaments that now present so heavy a material burden and so deep a cause for anxiety many thus, in the long run, prove to be one of the powerful forces impelling the world toward order and law.

## EMERGENCE OF A NEW POWER STRUCTURE

A world situation characterized by the rivalry of two superpowers, the United States and Russia, will almost certainly not last. This report is written in what may well prove, when men can look back, to have been the twilight of bipolarity. The preeminence of these two great centers, with their scientific skills, their advanced technology, their large highly organized populations, seems for the time being to be part of a continuing and even natural scheme of things. It is, on the contrary, highly unnatural and is surely destined to be impermanent.

The transformation of the existing structure is coming about through factors we have already noted. The rise of a united Western Europe and of a highly organized China are the most obvious signs that the polarizing forces existing in the postwar period are beginning to abate. But if we look beyond the 1960s into the remaining decades of the twentieth century, we are bound to feel that the shape of things will have been altered in all kinds of ways that are impossible to foresee except in broadest outline. The rapid progress that the underdeveloped countries have set as their goal—and that they must attain if they are not to slip backward into chaos worse than the poverty from which they are emerging —will begin to tell in the scales of world power. The new sources of energy that the industrialized countries stand ready to put at their disposal will have given them capacities that, in the normal course of development, would have been wholly beyond their reach. Taking over forms of technology and organization laboriously worked out over centuries in the Western world, some may be able to leap over decades of experimentation and discovery to stand in the ranks of the modern world.

It is difficult to make predictions in this area partly because the nature of strategic power is undergoing a transformation, and we do not yet have enough experience to assess the results. Many elements that formerly gave a nation a power status may have the opposite effect in the missile age. Thus, invulnerability has been a source of power; Great Britain's immunity to invasion was the basis of its first greatness. But seas and distances, however significant, will not provide immunity in future wars. Moreover, industrialism itself, with the concentration of population and resources that goes with it, may prove a severe handicap. How can one compare the strategic power of a small industrialized country, for example, with that of a relatively less developed nation where wide lands and scattered populations provide no easy targets? We actually do not know the answer to such a question, but the very fact that it can be seriously asked indicates how far the power situation is beginning to alter.

Nor do we know as yet what will be the effect on relative power of the increasing populations of Asia and, to a less extent, of other underdeveloped areas. The assumption is often made that the weight of nations in the world scale is roughly related to their population. This is highly questionable, especially where population growth is not due to any inherent ferment or vigor but to medical advances drastically reducing infant mortality.

Power in a confused and negative sense may conceivably accrue to crowded nations. A capacity for mischief may well increase beyond any capacity for effective or constructive action. Lacking adequate resources and in a state of political instability, such nations may form part of a restless, jostling mass, condemning the age to violence and disorder. In such an environment, seething population growth could provide a ferment easily mistaken for power, and hordes of manpower could be a crude asset in warfare.

Those countries that are bringing population under control, as Japan has been doing, may in the last analysis be most likely to form significant power centers in the decades ahead. A high degree of national purpose and education on an increasing scale are among the elements that can help bring population into balance and make a higher standard of well-being possible.

Whatever the precise effects of new forms of military power or of population trends, the rising power of Asia and eventually Africa is plain to see. The solidarity at Bandung was the beginning of a political consciousness that casts long shadows into the future. Self-determination of the African peoples, as expressed at Accra, is a rapidly growing force. The world stage will be immensely enlarged as these new peoples and continents play a larger part. The international order as it existed before World War I, in some ways more efficient and highly organized than anything we have been able to construct since, was fashioned on a small scale, with the old states of Europe managing between them virtually all important matters. That day has passed. Only slowly, however, are we grasping the implications of a world in which forces hardly yet measurable and peoples still in political infancy form essential elements of the total structure.

The picture of the United States held at least unconsciously in the minds of Americans is that of a large continent, endowed with virtually unlimited resources, enjoying an easy power, and favored with a comfortably large and growing population. That picture will change in the decades ahead. In comparison with the vast, amorphous new regional groups now obtaining political expression, the outstanding fact about the United States may come to seem its compactness. Notable among its characteristics will be a high degree of skill, elaborate organization, a refined technology. Its conviction of self-sufficiency will be replaced by awareness of how greatly it is dependent on its relations with other countries for essential materials and for a supporting atmosphere in which it can breathe and be itself.

Education (discussed in another Special Studies report, *The Pursuit of Excellence: Education and the Future of America*) will become an increasingly important element of our national strength. Not the power of masses but the power of intelligence—

groups schooled to excellence, disciplined and tempered in the exercise of widely decentralized responsibility—will be the source of such authority as America wields in that day.

## DANGER OF A NEW DIVISION
## OF THE WORLD

In such a new configuration of states and peoples, the United States will have a long-range objective that until now has been implicit rather than expressed. That objective will be to make sure that the world does not decline into a new bipolarity, this time more durable and more fearful in its implications, because based on color rather than on ideology. Ideologies can be transformed with time; color lines are fixed, if not permanently, at least for very many generations. The cold war with Russia is bitter to live with; but worse would be a rivalry in which men found themselves pitted against each other on lines of race or color.

Our present period is one in which race and color have assumed an undue significance as peoples in all parts of the world demand, by violence if necessary, an end to colonialism. It is understandable that national independence became confused with hostility between white and nonwhite; it is unfortunate that this confusion diverts attention from the militant imperialism of our own century led by Moscow and Peiping.

### United States as a Mediating Force

In building toward the future the imperative principle must be that race and color not be accorded artificial significance. The United Nations and its specialized agencies demonstrate the irrelevance of race in most human concerns. So do the Organization of American States and the Commonwealth of Nations, the Colombo Plan and American economic and technical assistance programs.

America's own interests and the role it is called upon to play in all parts of the world require it to work toward the removal of race and color as significant factors in a new world order. This is the reason why, from the point of view of foreign policy, the settlement of our own race problems in the United States is of such paramount importance: not because we merely want a propaganda victory in the cold war, but because we risk, except as we do solve them, disqualifying ourselves from the role demanded of us as a reconciling and mediating force in world politics. The United States throughout its history has shown itself capable of maintaining at home a free association of diverse nationalities; such a present-day example as Hawaii provides a lesson in the relationship of Eastern and Western peoples from which we ourselves can learn and an example that points the way to rational human relationships.

## Importance of U.S. Economic Growth

The gulf between East and West will be bridged, also, to the extent that the United States makes plain its participation in the economic forces that are manifesting themselves in all parts of the globe. As a people we want the less industrialized countries to know that we are involved with their growth. We want them to feel that we share their aspirations for a better life. Our own capacity for economic advancement is therefore a matter of supreme importance. It must be a demonstration of what can be accomplished under freedom. More than that it must provide a part of the resources from which the development of other countries is derived. Even if we could afford recessions or unemployment from the domestic point of view, we cannot afford them from the point of view of our long-range international interests.

The rapid expansion of the American economy is held by the panel—as set forth in Report IV on the domestic economy, *The Challenge to America: Its Economic and Social Aspects*—to be of utmost importance. Here we stress its relevance to the international scene.

It is commonly assumed that the United States can continue to surpass the Soviets in all areas if the challenge is forced out into the economic field. Perhaps for the first time in our history we cannot make this assumption unless we do something about it and do it thoughtfully, carefully, and consistently. Internally as well as externally, we face today larger demands on our economy than ever before. The attainment of maximum growth with high employment and relative stability of the price level requires a balance that is not easily achieved in a democracy. The balance will have to be maintained in the face of powerful domestic and international forces tending to disrupt it.

To move from an average rate of real growth of approximately 3 per cent to a rate of 4 to 5 per cent is a percentage increase of 30 to 60 per cent. This rate of improvement of collective efficiency in a free society will require us to have a better economic understanding and a willingness to make present choices with a long-term gain in mind if the delicate balance between the rate of growth and price-level stability is to be maintained.

The capacity to sustain economic growth depends in the American economy on maximum initiative and administrative flexibility. By these means we must insure such essential factors as a long-range supply of basic raw materials, adequate energy and fuel resources, competent manpower at all levels, the vitality and relevance of our educational processes, the consuming habits of the public, and a responsible attitude toward distinguishing between the more and the less important.

It is also evident that the United States has not found the means to maintain full and expanding production in the face of failures of agreement between management and labor. Stoppages in major industries, whatever their root causes and their domestic costs, have a grave impact upon the capacity of the United States to fulfill its task in world affairs. The problem is one that merits the highest priority and demands statesmanship from both management and labor.

The challenge before the United States is not merely to keep ahead of the Soviet system. We are not engaged in a sporting competition but in a deeply significant effort to make American production count as a constructive factor on the world scene. Only as we develop our full economic potentialities can this country have the resources, the flexibility, and the confidence that will make possible our leadership in the economic transformation of the globe, narrowing the gap between the rich and poor nations.

The economic progress of the hitherto underdeveloped countries generates in itself forces that could cause the United States to draw back and to pursue defensive policies. From the outbreak of World War II until the economic revival of other advanced countries in the 1950s, competition on the world economic stage was suspended. Such competition must be once more accepted as a fact of life. The world economy is now entering a new phase where price, quality, service, and other elements of true competition challenge the American economy to new standards of efficiency. This will be underscored as industrial progress occurs in countries that have not formerly been factors in the world markets.

The recent tendency for American exports to decline in relation to imports and the significant symptom of the drain on United States gold indicate how the world economic system is changing. The United States will need to make adjustments to such a developing situation; the important thing is that these adjustments be made in a way that does not thwart economic growth elsewhere in the world. The degree of our support of defense establishments in other countries can well be re-examined now that many of these countries have achieved a substantial economic revival. But the main answer to such a symptom as the drain on gold is not in policies of withdrawal or protectionism; it is in maintaining efficient standards of production and enlarging our rate of growth.

The long-range interest of the United States is in economic growth throughout the world. It wants the continuing prosperity of its allies in the advanced Western countries; more than that, it wants the other areas of the world to develop both agriculturally and industrially to their fullest potentiality. Measures taken by the United States in response to domestic economic situations must be looked at carefully in the light of such impediments as they may create to the progress of others.

The United States, in short, is challenged so to conduct itself as to bridge over in every possible way the potential cleavage between East and West. It is deeply concerned that East and West not draw apart through lack of understanding or through failure to see clearly the underlying interests that are held in common by the two great sectors of the globe. The way we order our life at home is an important factor in weaving the broad unity; so are our specific relations with individual countries. We can hope for bonds of friendship and ties of interest with the East; we must not let emotion or differences of ideology close the door to such possibilities of better relations with the Chinese people as may arise in years to come. Standing for freedom and for the essential dignity of man, the United States cannot see itself cut off from any continent or country.

# VII. The Democratic Process as a Vital Force

The great choices and decisions to be made in foreign policy over the next decades must be decisions arrived at by the democratic process. That seems an elementary requisite. Foreign policy becomes increasingly important and preoccupying in the national life; it touches more and more every aspect of domestic politics; it comprises by far the most significant of all the matters with which a nation must deal. If the citizens feel excluded from full and active participation in this field, they may be said to have renounced their basic rights and duties.

## THE PUBLIC AND FOREIGN POLICY

The proposition that the people have a large role in this area has not been easily accepted either in fact or among the philosophers of democracy. It has often been maintained that the citizens of a democracy are not capable of the kind of choices that foreign policy involves—however capable they may be of managing their own affairs at home. The kind of wisdom required in foreign policy, it has been argued, is basically different from the wisdom required in domestic choices. The people, according to their critics, know only what affects them—"where the shoe pinches," as it has been put in a homely simile. They are aware how a tax falls, how a law works when it is applied to actual circumstances. But in foreign policy, it is said, the results are remote and indirect; the situations involved are not understood instinctively, as a neighbor knows the character of a neighbor.

It is argued, further, that the foreign policy of a nation is not something that can be debated and arrived at by public opinion.

It is fixed by objective and largely unalterable facts. Choice and desire enter into it but slightly. The people can support it once it has been defined and revealed. They cannot "make" it in any real sense.

We cite these arguments, but we are convinced that they cannot be applied to the situation today. Granted all the difficulties of having the popular will enter into situations where far-off conditions and little-known facts must form the basis of decision; granted the high degree of objectivity and consistency that is required in effective foreign policy—still it seems incontrovertible that the citizens of a democracy have a genuinely creative role to play in this area. We know from American experience how often in great matters they have been ahead of their leaders in willingness to see the facts and to accept the course required of them. We know how the world has been drawn together by immediacy of communication and the tightly woven web of common interests. Almost no domestic issue today can be discussed without relating to the needs of foreign policy. The citizen who decides wisely in regard to what concerns himself and his own needs must be capable of wise decision, also, in regard to matters beyond the reach of firsthand experience.

As for the argument that foreign policy should be a revealed body of objective fact, self-evident once the experts have pronounced it, we do not accept that doctrine within the concept of foreign policy stressed in this report. Value judgments enter into foreign policy at crucial junctures. The ideals of the citizenry must constantly inform and guide it, or it loses its effectiveness and inherent power.

## THE ROLE OF LEADERSHIP

The real problem with regard to participation of the citizens comes, it seems to us, from significant failures and misconceptions in regard to leadership. Public opinion cannot operate in a disorganized and inchoate way on foreign policy; it cannot operate at all on certain phases of it, notably that of negotiation. What leadership must do—and what it has too often failed to do—is to determine the issues of public discussion. It must create the frame of reference within which popular choices take place and indicate the directions in which they lead. To say that there must be debate does not mean that everything must be debated all the time. For debate to be fruitful, policy questions must be posed in ways that permit relevant public judgments.

The promulgation of the Marshall Plan provides, we suggest, an example of the interaction between leadership and public opinion at its best. The public could not have been expected in such a case to take the initiative. That was done at the highest levels of the government by officials acting in concert with both experts within the government and the leaders of the democratic community. The public was presented with the basic facts and with the recommended course of action. Its judgment was sought on the great issues. In the long and complex negotiations with the prospective Marshall Plan countries, however, the public recognized that the determining role must be played by responsible officials acting in its interests.

If the role of leadership is not adequately fulfilled, public discussion is left with little other function than attack or criticism. Foreign policy inevitably has its failures; its results must often be long deferred or unknown. There is thus ample opportunity for partisan attack, and this will be taken advantage of if policy does not have deep roots in the public mind.

Effective leadership alone can counter the tendency to fatalism and indifference in issues related to war and atomic weapons. The popular inclination has been to leave these matters to experts or scientists, or to a President whom they trust to "take care" of them in the last resort. The people have not seemed able to convince themselves that these issues are manageable, preferring to ignore rather than grapple with such vague and terrifying obscurities. Yet in fact there is no essential difference between issues of this kind and any other. They have been made by men; they must be solved by men. What has made them seem different is that there has been public discussion with too little information for dealing with such large issues.

The obligation to give the facts upon these matters and others rests on the leaders today with a weight that has not existed previously. In most epochs, and certainly in the formative periods of American democracy, the public official and the citizen were presumed to be acting on the same basic knowledge. The gap between what the outsider and the insider knew was small or non-existent. That is not so true any longer. The government may have fewer relevant "secrets" than is commonly supposed, but it is possessed of information more voluminous and detailed than the average citizen can possibly appraise or absorb. The roots of the democratic process are weakened where the citizen gets the feeling that he is unable to form an intelligent judgment.

Thus there has come into the practice of democracy a genuinely new duty, too rarely grasped in its full implications. This may be called the duty of candor. What was formerly a private virtue of the responsible leader has become a grave public necessity. Its exercise is to be demanded by a citizenry that knows its own rights. It is a duty lying upon the leaders of a modern democracy as heavily as the reciprocal duties of attention and awareness lie on the citizens.

Candor in regard to atomic weapons or other grave matters is often identified with a policy of scaring the citizens out of pleasure-seeking and complacency. But this is only a small part of what we mean by candor. The essence of it is a full and frank unfolding of knowledge and its analysis *in relation* to the policy alternatives that are feasible and in the realm of acceptability. The democratic process is not necessarily furthered when, for example, bald figures are released upon estimates of the number of casualties in an atomic bombing of the United States. Such information by itself may merely inhibit the responsible functioning of public opinion. Democracy begins to be fulfilled only when the country's leaders present such problems as the level of conventional armaments or civil defense in all their dimensions and at the same time make recommendations for action. Then the problem becomes comprehensible. It can be faced, it can be debated, and a tolerable solution can be reached.

We have said that there are comparatively few real or relevant secrets withheld from the public. Nevertheless, there has grown up a tendency toward secrecy within certain elements of the government, and this has helped create in the public a feeling that it is cut off from vital information. Admitting necessity for secrecy in certain military and diplomatic affairs, we feel that when there is doubt the balance must go in favor of revealing information. The open world that this report makes one of its basic objectives can hardly flourish if there is an unnecessary tendency toward restrictions at home. The freest possible intellectual exchange means, among other things, exchange between the government and its own citizens.

## THE PUBLIC AND NEGOTIATIONS

The importance of the kind of leadership that sets the framework of debate is particularly important because of the long negotiations in prospect between this country and the Soviets. These negotiations are essential. They will provide, it may be hoped, opportunities for genuine accord as time and circumstances bring the interests of the two countries into conformity at limited but important points. But such negotiations, protracted and continuous, could give a dangerous bias to the foreign policy of the United States unless led with firm convictions and backed by an enlightened public opinion.

The danger, as we see it, is that negotiations carried on by professional diplomats (as they must be) and conducted (as again they must be) with a certain measure of sustained privacy will decline into a sterile bargaining. In such circumstances, substantive goals tend to be forgotten. Moral convictions begin to fade. Then one of two things happens. Either the negotiations become hopelessly stalemated, with propaganda their only function; or else a settlement becomes in itself an objective, regardless of its content and consequences.

Long-range negotiations without substantive goals give to the adversary the opportunity of setting the terms and inviting the other side to meet him halfway. The terms may be exorbitant, and their reduction in the course of diplomatic bargaining may still leave the agreement quite unrelated to justice or good sense. It may also leave it unrelated to stability. The latter point may be the more difficult to grasp, for stability often seems to rest with the other side's feeling satisfied. But there can be no satisfaction, no repose, and no peace where the Communist side has the feeling that it can set high terms and invariably get a good portion of what it asks for.

The need for substantive goals is particularly true because of the difference—too often unnoticed—between negotiations among friendly powers and negotiations with a power implacable in the pursuit of its own interests. Among friendly powers common objectives can be assumed; the problem of negotiation is a technical one; namely, to achieve a goal upon which all are agreed. But in such a situation as prevails when the United States faces the Soviet government across the bargaining table, the latter has its own clear long-range aims. Unless the United States representatives are equally lucid about their objectives and purposes, they will find that negotiations are fruitful neither in reaching accord nor in avoiding the sacrifice of important interests.

A slow attrition of interest can be avoided only when the national objectives are clearly defined, when the debate is initiated by responsible leadership and carried forward through the processes of a vigorous public opinion. This may be considered taking the initiative on foreign affairs. It is indeed the way in which the initiative is really meaningful: not as a propaganda device for embarrassing the Soviet government but as a means of putting the discussion in a frame of reference that protects and tends to enhance our own largest interests. The goals can thus become a matter of public knowledge and profound national conviction. The steps in the negotiations, meanwhile, can be surrounded with the privacy that is essential to serious and responsible dealings between nations.

## AGENCIES OF FOREIGN POLICY

It can be said, therefore, that the public has not been excluded by the emphasis of the modern state upon foreign policy. On the contrary, it has been given a newly indispensable role. In perceiving that it is not expected to intervene everywhere and at every point in diplomatic maneuvers, the public can gain confidence and scope so as to intervene decisively where its judgment and moral perceptions are required. It is then in a position to set goals, to choose between alternatives—above all, to give to negotiation the substantive content without which it becomes sterile or dangerous bartering. Only when it has seen afresh, in an age of great issues, the nature of an effective foreign policy can the public be in a position to sustain the personalities, agencies, and institutions through which foreign policy is conducted.

In a mature democracy, the Department of State and the Foreign Service require a degree of popular support that has not been regularly forthcoming. The stereotype of a Foreign Service officer as a man in striped pants who trades secrets at cocktail parties has, happily, been modified in recent years. But the public does not yet have a full sense of the skill, dedication, and often selflessness that are asked of representatives in this field. It still does not set as high a value as it should upon the role of these officials.

A democracy cannot afford to provide them with careers—in terms of opportunity for promotion and in terms of pay—that fall short of the highest careers of public life. The barring of top diplomatic posts to men not endowed with private wealth must be corrected. Ample salaries and allowances for living and entertainment are provided out of public funds by nations far less rich than the United States. The primary quality for appointment should be excellence, and means must be found to assure that excellence is not barred for any reason.

The challenges that should bring the best men into the parts of the government concerned with foreign policy must be operative, too, in many fields of private activity. The positive foreign policy that this report has stressed cannot be effectuated unless men and women in large numbers are prepared to undertake the hard work, and often the considerable personal sacrifices, that foreign assignments entail. Or let us say, rather, "that foreign assignments should entail." For too often it has been supposed that tasks in the service of the nation can be carried out lefthandedly, with no real effort to enter into the lives and the thoughts of other people, without speaking their language or knowing their history and their culture. Such a notion could only have arisen among a people that had not been drawn fully into the making of foreign policy and did not understand its significance in the modern world.

The same basic lack of comprehension that has deprived the Foreign Service of vital support has acted, also, to make the Secretaryship of State an almost impossible office in this country. The public has tended to be mistrustful of the Secretary of State, whatever his political party or whatever the actual policies he has pursued. It has condemned him to spend a disproportionate amount of his time and energies in explaining and justifying his course. It has thus exacted a toll of his vital spirits and of his capacity for objective thinking, which can ill be spared in the harsh contest with the Soviets.

These results have come about in part, we believe, because the right relation between public participation and official leadership had not been clearly enough worked out. The public has felt itself excluded from its full and rightful share in foreign policy. It has vaguely supposed that the Secretary of State was usurping its prerogatives—shaping a policy not readily comprehensible and not in line with its largest interests. Hence its suspicion and its ever-ready disapprobation.

The American Secretary of State has had his relations with the public further complicated, and his role in shaping of policy weakened, by the heavy and often conflicting demands which in recent years the office has exacted. The Secretary of State has tried to be an administrative officer, to carry on detailed negotiations in different parts of the world, to be a trouble shooter at various spots of tension, to be the country's representative at innumerable international conferences and its spokesman in the major debates of the United Nations. He is accountable to Congress and to the public through press conferences and constant questioning by Congressional committees. Finally, he is in constant negotiation with powerful domestic agencies in the fields of military power, economic development, and information. It has been difficult, in the midst of all this, for the Secretary of State to give to over-all policy that continuous thought and attention that diplomatic strategy requires in a world so essentially interrelated, where every problem touches every other.

We believe it is of the utmost importance that the task of the Secretary of State be defined so as to permit concentration upon policy at the highest level. As a result there would be restored to diplomatic representatives on the spot the responsible function they have been in danger of losing. The Secretary of State, meanwhile, would be in a position to identify and explain to the public those large issues for which popular judgment and support are vital.

## EXECUTIVE-LEGISLATIVE CO-OPERATION

In addition to the office of Secretary of State, the relation between the executive and legislative branches needs to be reconsidered. The outlook for American foreign policy must take into account the special complexities of the American constitutional and political system. It was deliberately devised to provide a large measure of individual freedom in the citizen's relation to public power. Although it has proved itself capable of considerable adjustment, its primary characteristics have survived, and Americans would not wish to revise it in any fundamental way. The separation of powers between the federal and state governments and the checks and balances within the federal government itself have two major consequences in the conduct of foreign relations. The first is that the United States can act effectively and persistently only upon the basis of a broad consensus among both citizens and public servants; the second is that the processes by which we arrive at national policy and specific decisions are complex, slow, and unsophisticated.

There is reason to believe, nevertheless, that there is serious concern in both the executive and legislative branches as to whether the federal government is properly organized to conduct the nation's business in the foreign policy field during, say, the next quarter century. But neither the Executive nor the Congress, acting alone, is likely to be able to effect significant improvement. The problem encounters sensitive questions of constitutional prerogative on both sides, and it is asking too much to expect those who have been entrusted with these prerogatives to yield them lightly. Nor is there in the American scene a recognized collection of wise and experienced men whose advice on such matters would elicit the respect and attention of the public and its official servants.

The panel believes that there would be merit in the establishment of appropriate arrangements and procedures, by agreement between the Executive and Congress, for joint study and action on the organizational and procedural aspects of foreign policy. What is needed is a serious and thoughtful consultation on constitutional arrangements between the executive and legislative branches. The panel believes that such a joint study should consider improvements that do not involve amendments to the Constitution because it is convinced that significant improvements can be effected within the existing basic law. The form of the appropriate arrangements and procedures—whether through the creation of a Joint Commission or otherwise—the assignment of tasks, and the action to be taken upon recommendations would require negotiated agreement, on a nonpartisan basis, between the Executive and the Legislature. There are obvious difficulties, but the panel believes that they are small when measured against the necessity for more effective procedures in the conduct of our foreign relations in the years ahead.

# VIII.   On Entering a New Phase

In the affairs of nations there are moments when the substance of things undergoes a subtle change. Events and upheavals that shake the surface may have already occurred; but men suddenly become aware of forces at work on a deeper level. They sense instinctively that henceforth the direction of things will be altered.

This panel is convinced that such a change is now coming over the international scene. It is bound to affect the foreign policy of the United States. That policy, we believe, is entering a new phase, keyed to themes and interests that have not yet received general recognition.

The precise formulas and policies of this phase cannot in the nature of things be immediately discerned. A whole generation will be concerned with working out these policies—finding the means to deal effectively with the cold war in which we are now necessarily engaged and to proceed to measures adequate to cope with a world stage enlarged and made more complex by emerging forces and peoples coming newly into their own. The task of statesmanship in the next decade must be to define with fresh clarity the purposes that the United States wishes to achieve. To this end it must reinterpret existing policies as well as devise new ones.

This process is already overdue.

Fourteen years have now passed since the end of World War II. This is a long time, if not in terms of history at least in terms of the life of a generation. When a similar period had passed after World War I, the United States was approaching the end of the Harding, Coolidge, and Hoover eras and was embarking on the New Deal. Those who were coming of age in the thirties will bear witness to the fact that World War I did not then loom very large in their minds. The fight over the League of Nations seemed, for instance, a remote historical event. The generation now entering college must find it hard to concern itself in any more serious way with episodes so important and so comparatively recent as Yalta, the civil war in China, or the Czechoslovakian coup; at best these are historical incidents, remote from personal experience.

This is not to say that the problems of World War II have been liquidated or to suggest that the experience of those who have lived through the trials and controversies of the last two decades is not an indispensable ingredient of policy. It would be all too easy for those who come onto the stage at this time to minimize the difficulties of dealing with the Soviet dictatorship, to give too little weight to the long train of deceptions and frustrations that has made American negotiators of necessity tough, suspicious, and insistent on guarantees of compliance. Yet, not inconceivably, new points of common interest, as well as new symptoms of danger, could reassert themselves. Understanding will require of Americans not only alertness but a living knowledge of history.

A public is now being formed that looks beyond the unsolved problems of a past generation. The interests of this new public are with the present; its emotional detachment from the problems of World War II and its immediate aftermath is found to affect the tone of the future. If that is true in our own country, it should not be overlooked that the same thing is occurring in other countries as well.

Invariably in such a change-over of generations the old subjects of controversies persist, but somehow the words—and even the issues—begin to cloak a new meaning. The best minds among the older generation perform the exceedingly difficult task of using old phrases while maintaining a clear understanding that the underlying substance has altered. Younger men, for whom the changed meaning tends to be the one chiefly grasped or understood, have the more difficult obligation to keep alive the awareness of continuity. As the residues and overtones of the earlier condition begin to fade, a new condition takes shape. It is more radically new, more fundamentally different than the content of public discourse would by itself indicate.

Many problems now under discussion date from the end of World War II. But beneath the surface new factors and conditions have since come into play. Men and women on both sides of the

Iron Curtain find themselves thinking in terms of the present and the future, though the arguments are cast in the form of precedents going back many years.

While old things thus develop new purposes and meanings, some genuinely new things enter the world situation. A generation that thinks in terms of the vast distances of space cannot but have a somewhat different outlook upon some of today's insoluble problems. The stubborn and familiar issues of the postwar era must appear in a fresh perspective to men who are to look upon the round globe from the void that surrounds it. Gradually, almost imperceptibly, a new perspective may thus take hold of the human mind, changing the atmosphere in which all decisions are reached.

Many additional developments are afoot that contain within themselves the possibility of redirecting the stream of international events. We are at the point where several revolutionary developments merge and overlap. Scientific progress, the industrialization of hitherto underdeveloped countries, the growth in populations combine to give their special cast to affairs. New regional and international structures, as well as new situations within the Communist world, are unfolding rapidly.

In the light of these conditions, the American people cannot afford to let short-range considerations preoccupy them to the exclusion of a long view and a total perspective on world problems. To deal courageously with the problems of the cold war and still to see and act beyond them—this, we submit, is the need of foreign policy today. It is the basic challenge before us all. The United States has been jolting along from crisis to crisis, viewing foreign policy as a rather unpleasant device for warding off threats all over the world. Bold action has too often been conceived as little more than putting Russia in a superficially embarrassing or awkward position. The fateful rivalry of the cold war may persist for a long time; nevertheless, this is an incident in a far greater world drama. We cannot escape—and indeed should welcome—the task that history has imposed on us. This is the task of helping to shape a new world order in all its dimensions—spiritual, economic, political, social.

There is the challenge. There also is the hope and the practical possibility. The men and women of our generation should know they have the chance to do something daring and creative. They are not prisoners of history; they do not have to walk a treadmill without alternatives or choices. They do not have to reconcile themselves to the loss of any value they hold dear. They can, on the contrary, hold reasonably in their minds the most ancient and the newest of all earthly visions: a peaceful world with justice and well-being for all.

# Report II

# INTERNATIONAL SECURITY: THE MILITARY ASPECT

(First published January 6, 1958)

# Introduction by Panel II

This report is the result of a group effort by Panel II of the Special Studies Project of the Rockefeller Brothers Fund, Inc. Although not every member subscribes to every detail, it reflects our substantial agreement.

We were charged with exploring the military aspect of international security, the strategies most likely to achieve this end, and the challenges in this area which may face the country during the next ten years. We have been meeting since November 1956. We have had the benefit of many specially prepared papers, and we have heard testimony of numerous experts.

It is our judgment that all is not well with present United States security policies and operations. The over-all United States strategic concept lags behind developments in technology and in the world political situation. In major respects, defense organization is unrelated to critically important military missions. Systems of budgets, appropriations, and financial management are out of gear with the radically accelerating flow of military developments. The United States system of alliances must be adapted to constantly changing strategic requirements. The United States is rapidly losing its lead in the race of military technology.

We are convinced that corrective steps must be taken now.

We believe that the security of the United States transcends normal budgetary considerations and that the national economy can afford the necessary measures.

Our panel therefore hopes that the most important result of recent Soviet advances in the field of earth satellites may be that they will serve to spark a deep review of the basic attitudes and policies affecting the security of our country and of the free world.

For the United States lag in missiles and space machines, however worrisome, is a symptom and not a cause. It reflects our national complacency over the past dozen years. It is vitally important to the United States to calculate its security requirements on an integrated and long-range basis, and to set about correcting all deficiencies.

FRANK ALTSCHUL, vice-president, Council on Foreign Relations.

GENERAL FREDERICK L. ANDERSON, former Deputy U. S. Special Representative in Europe.

KARL R. BENDETSEN, vice-president, operations, The Champion Paper and Fibre Company; former Under Secretary of the Army.

DETLEV W. BRONK, president, Rockefeller Institute; president, National Academy of Sciences.

GORDON E. DEAN, senior vice-president—nuclear energy, General Dynamics Corporation, and former chairman, Atomic Energy Commission, was a member of this panel and of the Overall Panel until his death on August 16, 1958.

JAMES B. FISK, executive vice-president, Bell Telephone Laboratories, Inc.; former director of research, Atomic Energy Commission.

BRADLEY GAYLORD, chairman, The Pennroad Corporation.

ROSWELL L. GILPATRIC, partner, Cravath, Swaine & Moore; former Under Secretary of the Air Force.

TOWNSEND W. HOOPES, J. H. Whitney and Company.

ELLIS A. JOHNSON, director, Operations Research Office, Johns Hopkins University.

COLONEL GEORGE A. LINCOLN, professor, Social Sciences, U. S. Military Academy.

*HENRY R. LUCE, editor-in-chief, *Time, Life, Fortune*.

*GENERAL JAMES McCORMACK, vice-president, Massachusetts Institute of Technology, served as chairman of the panel until October 1957 when illness forced him to withdraw from that position.

FRANK C. NASH, U. S. Delegation to General Assembly of the UN, and presidential consultant on overseas base study, was a member of the panel until his death on December 11, 1957.

LAURANCE S. ROCKEFELLER, president, Rockefeller Brothers, Inc.

ARTHUR SMITHIES, Department of Economics, Harvard University; former economic adviser, Office of Defense Mobilization.

*EDWARD TELLER, professor of physics, University of California, Berkeley; associate director, University of California Radiation Laboratories.

T. F. WALKOWICZ, aeronautical engineer.

CARROLL L. WILSON, president, Metals & Controls Corporation; former general manager, Atomic Energy Commission.

JOHN F. FLOBERG, served as a member of this panel until his appointment as a member of the Atomic Energy Commission in June 1957 after which date he did not participate in the deliberations of the group or the drafting of the conclusions.


This report was prepared under the direction of Dr. Henry A. Kissinger, associate director of The Center for International Affairs, who was director of the project until June 30, 1958.

* Also Overall Panel members.

# I.  Framework of the Study

The world is living through a period of swift and far-reaching upheavals. Standards and institutions that have remained unchanged for centuries are breaking down. Millions who have hitherto passively endured their place in life are clamoring for a new and more worthy existence. Western Europe, the fountainhead of our civilization, has lost its position of dominance in world affairs. Across the great land mass of Eurasia and on the continent of Africa, new nations are rising in the place of colonial empires.

Mankind is yearning to realize its aspirations in peace. But it is faced by two somber threats: the Communist thrust to achieve world domination that seeks to exploit all dissatisfactions and to magnify all tensions; and the new weapons technology capable of obliterating civilization.

The United States has thus been placed in a fateful position. Our whole tradition impels us to desire peace. Relatively invulnerable behind two great oceans, we have until the end of World War II asked little of the world save to be free to work out our destiny undisturbed. But we have been forced to realize that our security is inextricably bound up with the safety of the rest of the free world and that freedom everywhere depends on our strength and resolution. Force alone will not supply the answer to the hopes of humanity. Yet our strength, effectively mobilized, can help bring about a framework of security in which these aspirations may be realized in freedom and without fear.

Looking at the world from the perspective of our past isolation and recent nuclear supremacy, perhaps the most difficult thing for us is to accept the reality of our peril. Other more exposed nations have had to learn to live over a period of centuries with the awareness that their existence might be imperiled by foreign attack. It is a new experience for Americans.

A new technology of unprecedented power and destructiveness has placed *all* nations of the world in dire peril. The largest "conventional" bomb of World War II—the famous blockbuster—had an explosive power of 20 tons of TNT. The first atomic bomb had an explosive power equivalent to 20 thousand tons of TNT, a thousandfold increase. Today, weapons with an explosive equivalent of 20 million tons (20 megatons) have been tested, and there is no theoretical upper limit: it is possible to construct weapons of almost any explosive power.

As the weapons have become more powerful, their speed of delivery has grown ever faster. Soon* missiles will be able to travel intercontinental distances and wipe out whole cities in one blow. A blow on fifty of our most important metropolitan areas would bring under attack 55 per cent of our population and 75 per cent of our industry. Moreover, if the fireball of a nuclear weapon touches the ground, it sucks up particles of earth and buildings and deposits them downwind as radioactive material. The area of this "fallout" would depend on meteorological conditions, but it could cover an area of 10 thousand square miles, or the size of the state of New Jersey. A successful attack on fifty of our most important urban centers would produce at least 10–15 million dead and 15–20 million injured from blast and heat and another 25–35 million casualties from "fallout" or a total of 60–65 million dead and injured.

What gives this weapons technology its ominous quality is that it is in the hands of a Communist movement which has proclaimed for over a generation now—the last time in the Moscow declaration of all Communist states on November 16, 1957—the irreconcilability of its system with that of the free world. Of course "peaceful coexistence" has reappeared periodically as a Soviet slogan. But, as used in Soviet propaganda, it has in the past been primarily a device to disarm intended victims. After World War II, it did not stand in the way of Soviet domination of the satellite orbit and the breaking of the most solemn wartime pledges regarding respect for freedom and independence of Eastern Europe. It did not stop

* Written in January 1958.

the Berlin blockade, the Greek civil war, and the Korean aggression. After the Geneva "summit" conference, "peaceful coexistence" did not restrain the Soviet Union from fomenting a crisis in the Middle East or from brutally suppressing the Hungarian revolution. In 1957 it did not keep the Soviet Union from threatening nuclear attacks on Norway, Denmark, and Turkey. Both their doctrine and their internal dynamism will impel the Soviet Union and Communist China to try to encourage every dissatisfaction and to fill every vacuum. Should we ever allow the U.S.S.R. and Communist China to attain strategic superiority, we can be certain that subsequent events will be brutal. And the power of these states, particularly of the U.S.S.R., has been growing both absolutely and relative to the United States until today it constitutes a grave threat.

The willingness and ability to resist aggression is the best guarantee for peace. Until there occurs a change in Soviet attitudes, everything depends on the steadfastness of the United States and other free nations and on the willingness to act resolutely in the face of continuing peril and ambiguous challenges.

# II. The Nature of Our Strategic Problem

Ever since our unilateral disarmament at the end of World War II failed to produce the peace we desired so earnestly, the United States has been forced to engage in a military effort unprecedented in our history in peacetime. Even so, it has still proved inadequate to the challenge we confront. The sporadic nature of our effort has been caused by many factors, including the nature of our historical experience. Tradition impels us to believe that peace is the normal relation among states. As a result, we have conceived it to be the task of our military policy to assemble overwhelming power to "punish" the disturber of the peace—the aggressor. Also, aggression is best understood when it is an unambiguous and clear act. Because, in the past, many other states were threatened before the danger to our security became explicit, we have been able to count on other countries to hold a forward line while we rallied our physical, moral, and psychological resources. Thus, our remoteness from the other major centers of world affairs has enabled us hitherto to rely on relatively small forces-in-being and to mobilize our resources only *after* a war had started.

Many of these ideas have been overthrown by technological developments since World War II and by the emergence of the United States in the forefront of world affairs. Soviet policy has coupled an attempt to develop overwhelming power with a strategy of deliberate ambiguity. The ambiguity resides in advancing by steps so small that the risks of resisting any given advance always seem out of proportion to the objective, or masking the aggression so that the Soviet move appeals to what the free world considers as "legitimate" methods of political warfare. As a consequence, the recognition of aggression has often proved as difficult as finding the means to resist it. A symptom of the difficulty is that a

United Nations committee charged with the task of defining aggression felt itself forced to abandon the effort.

At the same time that the forms of aggression have multiplied and become more ambiguous, we have lost the safety indicators of a more secure past. We can no longer think of our military effort as designed for a conflict that we enter only after other nations have run the initial risks, as was the case with our participation in World Wars I and II. Since no other nation any longer has the strength to resist alone, the safety of the non-Communist world will depend on our ability, psychological and military, to engage our forces promptly and decisively in case of aggression.

The importance of forces-in-being is magnified by the changed significance of industrial potential. As long as the destructiveness of weapons was relatively limited as compared to the complexity of their means of manufacture, victory in war could be achieved only through a quantity of equipment too large to stockpile before the outbreak of hostilities. Massive production of armament during the course of a war was thus a vital element of national strength, and an attack on production facilities was a highly effective strategy. But with the rapid and overwhelming destructiveness of modern technology, each major power will, in the absence of a massive and reliable defense, be able to disrupt the production facilities of its opponents with relatively few weapons in a matter of hours. Industrial strength is therefore a military asset only to the extent that it can provide armaments before the outbreak of war.

Thus our military problem, with which this particular panel is exclusively concerned, has four aspects:

1. We require a growing industrial, technological, and scientific base in order to achieve a state of continual readiness for the long haul. Without an adequate industrial plant, we will not be able to produce the ever-increasing variety of weapons required for our protection. Without an expanding pool of scientific talent and a steadily rising level of scientific activity, we shall not be able to maintain our security in a situation where the real armaments race is in the laboratories.

2. Scientific development by itself is ineffective strategically, however, if it cannot be translated rapidly into operational weapons. Great importance therefore attaches to two kinds of lead time: first, the interval between the drawing board and operational

weapon; and second, the rapidity with which weapons are manufactured. A lag in either category is certain to create a strategic weakness.

3. At the same time, long-range programs and balance cannot become ends in themselves. However powerful we may be potentially, our strategic effectiveness in any given crisis depends on our active forces supplemented by any quickly mobilizable reserve capabilities. Given the power and destructiveness of modern weapons, we cannot count on an extended period of mobilization prior to the outbreak of hostilities.

4. But however vast our over-all strength, it may still be ineffective in meeting certain challenges if it cannot be applied with discrimination. With the development of the Soviet nuclear stockpile and the means to deliver it, we can no longer rely on our capability to deliver crushing retaliation on the Soviet homeland as the deterrent to *all* types of aggression. For with the growth of the Soviet capability to inflict a massive blow on the United States, there exists the great danger that the Soviet Union will seek to use its nuclear striking force as a shield behind which to expand by more limited means. Thus the adequacy of our military establishment will be determined by its ability to discharge two distinct though related tasks: one, to discourage an all-out attack through the existence of a powerful, instantly ready retaliatory force, and, two, to react effectively to limited aggression through the ability to make our response fit the challenge.

These four factors—the importance of a growing industrial base, the crucial role of lead times, the increasing significance of forces-in-being, and the necessity of a versatile military establishment—impose on policy makers an unparalleled problem of choice. It is further complicated by the explosive rapidity with which technology is developing. Almost up to the outbreak of World War II, a weapons system would be good for nearly a generation; the equipment of U.S. ground forces, for example, changed very little between 1919 and 1940. Today a weapons system begins to be obsolescent when it has barely gone into production. The B-17 "Flying Fortress" remained in operational use for eight years; the B-36 intercontinental bomber was obsolescent in less than five years; and the B-52 jet bomber is beginning to be outdated even before all wings of our Strategic Air Command are fully equipped with it.

Moreover, all weapons are becoming increasingly costly. A new submarine costs ten times as much as its World War II counterpart. A B-52 wing is four times as expensive as the B-36 wing it replaces. Each new weapons system costs more than double its predecessor, which it replaces at shorter and shorter intervals.

This technological race places an extraordinary premium on the ability to assess developing trends correctly, to make and back decisions firmly, and to be prepared to change plans when necessary. It also places the side that is on the defensive at special disadvantage. The aggressor need prepare only for the war he proposes to fight. But the side that is militarily on the defensive must gear its planning and procurement to the possibility of an attack at any moment. We must therefore take care to see that no important strategic weakness exists at any given point of time.

The basic problem of American strategy then is the ability to make effective choices. This will depend on the courage and sense of purpose of our leadership, the effectiveness of the organization of our government, and the spirit of our people.

# III.  Developing Power Trends

The outstanding characteristic of the strategic situation is a military technology in a state of spectacular change. Starting with World War II scientific research has produced military equipment and new patterns of military operations at an ever-accelerating pace. Four trends appear to be of particular significance.

1. Weapons technology will become increasingly complex with a corresponding increase in the difficulty of choosing the most effective combination of weapons. The atomic bomb of 1945 has been outmoded by a broad range of highly developed weapons both large and small. The original nuclear weapons required a large aircraft and crew. Equally powerful warheads have been reduced in size and simplified to the point where it will soon be possible to employ them effectively in antiaircraft rockets. And with the increasing capacity for the production of fissionable materials, nuclear and thermonuclear weapons have become available in very large quantities.

The outlook is even more portentous than the achievements of the recent past. Aircraft will be capable of cruising at several times the speed of sound, of bombing from altitudes of a dozen miles and more, and of carrying air-launched missiles so that they need not pass directly over heavily defended target areas. New high-energy fuels will give them greatly increased range and performance.

Within a very short time, a major role in both offense and defense will be played by missiles. It will be possible to produce missiles of almost any desired range, from very short distances analogous to traditional artillery to intercontinental ranges of five thousand miles or more. Because these weapons require less extensive installations than airplanes, it will be possible to disperse and protect them more easily, and they will therefore be less vulnerable to surprise attack.

Earth satellites are a special adaptation of missiles that explore a new frontier in outer space and that will have important military applications.

Submarines, already extremely powerful weapons, will be even more important as nuclear propulsion comes to play an ever greater role. They can imperil our harbors and our sea communications with friendly nations. As a platform for missiles they can pose a constant threat of a sudden, devastating blow from unpredictable directions.

These are not dreams of the far distant future. Many of these weapons are in existence now; even the most remote among them is attainable within the time frame of this report by both the United States and the Soviet Union. Many of them will be in the hands of several nations.

2. The rate of technological change will increasingly complicate the tasks of the defense relative to the offense. Both offense and defense will improve—and improve enormously. However, foreseeable new offensive weapons such as intercontinental ballistic missiles—sudden in action, massively destructive, difficult to destroy either before launching or in flight—will greatly aggravate the problems of strategic defense and enormously increase its costs.

3. The U.S.S.R. will continue to gain in over-all military strength greatly aided by Communist China and some of its other allies. Although the rate of growth of these countries may slow down, the economic superiority of the West will become less and less significant militarily at our present levels of effort. By sacrificing the civilian sector of its economy, the Soviet Union has caught up with the United States in major fields of technology. In certain areas assigned high priority by the Kremlin, the Soviet Union has surpassed us qualitatively as well as quantitatively. Unless we greatly increase the pace and level of our military effort, the Soviet Union will achieve superiority in other fields as well.

4. The concept of "scarcity" in nuclear weapons will disappear from the calculations of the United States, the U.S.S.R., and to a lesser extent Great Britain. The United States, the U.S.S.R., and Great Britain will continue to increase the number and variety of their atomic weapons. Other countries will in due course have their own atomic arms, if on a more limited scale.

## SOVIET CAPABILITIES

Ever since World War II, the United States has suffered from a tendency to underestimate the military technology of the U.S.S.R. When the Soviet Union produced its first long-range bomber, we comforted ourselves with the belief that it was simply a copy of our B-29. When it developed jet engines, some dismissed this achievement as due to the imitation of a British design. When our atomic monopoly was ended, we treated it more as a reflection on our security methods against espionage than as an indication that our technological lead was inherently transitory.

In the meantime, the Soviet Union has demonstrated that its achievements in the immediate postwar period were far from accidental. Today Soviet science is at least equal to our own in many strategically significant categories. In the military field, the technological capability of the U.S.S.R. is increasing at a pace obviously faster than that of the United States. If not reversed, this trend alone will place the free world in dire jeopardy.

The result of the Soviet concentration on military technology is an impressive and rapidly growing military establishment, which already poses a very serious threat to the free world. The generally accepted facts with respect to it can be summarized as follows.

The Soviet ground forces, far larger numerically than our own, are being reorganized and re-equipped for atomic war. New rockets and missiles capable of carrying nuclear warheads add to their atomic capability. New tanks, artillery pieces, and light weapons give them a powerful conventional strength. Vehicles and communications equipment have been markedly improved. In addition to these substantial forces-in-being, the U.S.S.R. possesses a vast and readily mobilizable reserve.

The Soviet Union now has the second largest navy in the world and since World War II has produced more vessels of every type, except aircraft carriers, than the United States. The Soviet Union has long concentrated on submarines. A fleet of well over 400 is already in operation. This number is greatly in excess of the German force which severely menaced Allied surface shipping during the early years of World War II. There is no doubt about the capacity of the U.S.S.R. to develop naval atomic power plants or to adapt ships and submarines to launch short- and medium-range missiles; in fact, Soviet leaders have pointedly discussed the vulnerability of the United States to such attacks. The magnitude of the threat becomes clear when it is realized that 43 of our 50 largest cities and 85 per cent of our industry are located within 500 miles of our coasts. Missile launching submarines are the Soviet equivalent of our overseas air bases.

Soviet air defense is based on a good radar detection and tracking system, supported by a large number of all-weather interceptor aircraft, an increasing proportion of which is supersonic. Ground-to-air missiles are a major element of the air defense system.

Over the last ten years, the U.S.S.R. has not only maintained the largest number of planes in the world but has progressively re-equipped its air force with new and modern aircraft. The Soviet Union now produces many aircraft at least as advanced as our own—and produces them in large numbers. Moreover, the Soviets have demonstrated their ability to manufacture modern electronic equipment and to master the techniques required to guide and direct defensive and offensive aerial operations.

The Soviet weapons program has given high priority to the development of rockets and missiles. A medium-range ballistic missile capable of reaching Japan, Taiwan, and most of Western Europe from Communist bloc bases is already operational in limited quantities. Missiles of intercontinental range will soon follow.

From what is known of the present Soviet stockpile of nuclear weapons, it is inferior to that of the United States, but it is already large and growing rapidly. Soviet nuclear attacks against the United States of great severity are possible now; within a few years the U.S.S.R. will be capable of delivering massive air and missile attacks against all major targets in the non-Communist world. In short, Soviet military strength poses a major threat to all countries of the non-Communist world.

## U. S. CAPABILITIES

As compared with the U.S.S.R., the United States now has these military advantages:

Our democratic structure is more stable and commands wider popular support than the Soviet system of dictatorship, which can resolve policy differences only by periodic purges.

We have a superior industrial base and production know-how, which, providing we apply it with a clear sense of direction, should enable us to assign high priority to a greater variety of projects than the U.S.S.R.

The system of alliances in which we participate is superior in integrity and strength and in the cohesiveness that comes from free association to the Soviet system of forced satellites. Moreover, our allies are stronger domestically, industrially, and in technical and scientific potential.

We have superior operational experience in the use of long-range manned airplanes. Our location coupled with our system of advanced bases favors us geographically.

We have superior and more flexible naval power, especially surface naval power.

We have more atomic weapons and a greater variety of them.

Some of these advantages must be qualified, however, and others are only temporary. For example, our long-range bomber force is always in competition with improving defenses. And our advantage in training is transitory because missiles will increasingly take over missons heretofore performed by manned planes. Moreover, some U.S. forward bases will continue to be exposed to the instability of the areas in which they are located, and all of our air bases at home and abroad are vulnerable to surprise attack, particularly as Soviet missiles become operational.

Nor can we afford to take for granted an indefinite continuation of our present superiority at sea. The aircraft carrier, around which our naval power is built, is vulnerable to nuclear attack, though protected to some extent by its mobility. It also faces a problem of limited refueling facilities, particularly for its aircraft complement. The unresolved naval weakness is the inadequacy of our antisubmarine capability. Moreover, our submarine fleet has not been given the attention its potential warrants.

Another point of present U.S. military advantage is in the number and variety of atomic weapons. But the U.S.S.R. is closing the gap, and because of the destructiveness of nuclear weapons numerical superiority tends to become less important after a given point, at least for certain purposes. It is therefore crucial to develop a notion of "adequacy" for each military mission so that we do not drain resources from some vital tasks by maintaining an excessive capacity in others.

Thus it appears that the United States is rapidly losing its lead over the U.S.S.R. in the military race. For perhaps the next two years, we still possess a superiority in strategic striking power, and any Soviet attack on us would meet a crushing reply. But our position a year or two hence depends on decisions that must be taken immediately. Unless present trends are reversed, the world balance of power will shift in favor of the Soviet bloc. If that should happen, we are not likely to be given another chance to remedy our failings. It is emphatically not too late, however, if we are prepared to make the required big effort now and in the years ahead.

# IV. Missions

The various challenges with which we may be confronted tend to overleap the traditional boundaries between the military services. With modern weapons the distinctions between the missions of the three services based on land, sea, and air warfare have lost a great deal of their validity. The criteria by which any future wars can be distinguished will turn on the nature of the conflict, the issues in dispute, and the geographical area of hostilities rather than on means of locomotion.

Among the possible challenges we may confront, three stand out most starkly: all-out war, limited war, and a kind of war new to the twentieth century and highly developed by the Communists—the disguised or obscure war concealed as internal subversion or take-over by coup d'état or civil war.

## ALL-OUT WAR

Of the threats to our security, all-out war is the most overwhelming. It can be defined as an attack of such magnitude that our survival would be directly and immediately at stake. It is therefore the ultimate war, in which no inhibitions would apply as regards the use of weapons.

For this reason the purpose of our capability for all-out war is above all to prevent war from breaking out; it is effective to the extent that it deters a sudden onslaught on us. At the same time, our capability for all-out war is the essential prerequisite for more discriminating applications of our power. Since the growth of the Soviet nuclear stockpile, the capability to conduct all-out war does not protect all our security interests. But it does preserve our ability to protect these interests by means less drastic than all-out war. Limited war, for instance, can be kept limited only if an opponent must consider expansion of the war too risky. Preparedness for all-out war must therefore be the first charge on our military establishment.

The basic requirement for all-out war is a retaliatory force so well protected and numerous that it can overcome any defense. For the next two or three years, this will be largely composed of manned planes; later, missiles will continue to play an increasingly important role. The hard core of this striking force, whether based at home or overseas, must be continuously alert, fully armed, and as secure as we can make it against destruction or neutralization by surprise attack.

The second requirement for all-out war is an active and passive defense system capable of protecting the bulk of our striking force, no matter what the scale of any foreseeable surprise attack, and of reducing the effects of a blow against our centers of population and industry.

Active defense seeks to blunt the enemy attack by providing warning to likely targets and by destroying as many attacking vehicles as possible. The speedier the enemy delivery system, the more rapid must be the reaction time of the active defense. The more powerful the offensive weapons, the higher must be the percentage of "kills" achieved. Thus, the protection of our retaliatory force and of our civilian population both require that a major and increasing effort be made to strengthen our active defense. Should the U.S.S.R. achieve an effective air defense before we do, our retaliatory force would correspondingly diminish in value. Conversely, a strong active defense on our side would reinforce the deterrent to surprise attack.

As attacking vehicles become speedier and weapons ever more destructive, increasing attention will have to be paid to passive defense, often called civil defense. Its task is to reduce enemy damage as much as possible. This can be accomplished through shelters, dispersal of industries and air bases, and the stockpiling of critical supplies. A nation which has succeeded in protecting its population at least to some degree is in a stronger psychological position than an opponent totally vulnerable to attack. In the age of the long-range missile, the known ability of a society to withstand attack through passive defense will become an increasingly important deterrent.

Preparedness for all-out war therefore depends on a combination of three factors: (1) a retaliatory force so powerful and well protected that, no matter what the scale of the enemy attack, an aggressor must always contend with a return blow which will inflict an intolerable amount of damage; (2) an active defense that can assure survival of at least a sizable portion of the retaliatory force and that is able to limit the disruptive effects of an enemy blow on our population and economy to the smallest possible proportions; (3) a passive defense which affords some protection for our population and economy.

The importance of defensive measures is that they force the enemy to increase his investment of resources in his offensive effort without adding to its strategic effectiveness. The value of a powerful retaliatory force is that it can deprive the aggressor of the fruits of a surprise attack. The task of strategy is to decide on the relative emphasis to be given to offensive capabilities and to active and passive defense and on the "mix" which will provide the greatest degree of deterrence.

In looking at the strategic equation for all-out war, there is reason for serious concern. Our retaliatory power, on which we have heretofore relied as the major element of our security, is imperiled by Soviet advances in the missile field and by the inadequate dispersal and protection of our Strategic Air Command. Our active defense designed against manned planes will have to be redesigned for the missile age. Our civil defense program, and that of our allies, is completely inadequate. A substantially greater effort is therefore required in order to insure an adequate system of deterrence.

## LIMITED WAR

Unfortunately, the capability to deter all-out war does not exhaust our strategic problem. For no matter how vast our over-all strength, we face the dilemma that the magnitude of the total does not assure its sufficiency in any particular situation. Even if we succeed in deterring all-out war by the threat of total annihilation, our country and the rest of the free world remains in peril. For we cannot expect to counter limited military challenges by the response appropriate to all-out surprise attack.

Until the development of a Soviet nuclear stockpile and the means to deliver it, our retaliatory force could serve as the major deterrent to Soviet aggression. But as the Soviet capability to attack American cities increases, our reluctance to engage in all-out war will grow proportionately. If all-out war becomes our only counter to aggression, the Soviet Union may be enabled to use its strategic striking force as a shield behind which to achieve limited advances, confronting us in each case with the alternative of yielding to what will seem a marginal Soviet gain or of precipitating a world-wide holocaust.

As a result, though all-out war is our greatest danger, it does not represent the most likely threat. The distinctive feature of limited war is that its outcome does not involve or seem to involve national survival. It is precisely for this reason that we have had such difficulty in coming to grips with it. For any peripheral Soviet move raises doubts whether this particular encroachment warrants a final showdown. A major difficulty is our lack of mobile forces capable of intervening rapidly and of restoring a local situation before matters get out of hand.

The forces designed to deter all-out war will, of course, also be useful in preventing or stifling limited war. It would be dangerous, however, to rely too heavily on the principal deterrent—our strategic striking force—to fight limited war. Since the chief sanction against the expansion of a limited war resides in a crushing capability for retaliation, the deterrent force must be kept in a state of the highest readiness particularly during periods of limited conflict. An aggressor who could inflict substantial attrition on our strategic striking force in a limited war would gain an advantage however those particular military operations ended.

It is therefore imperative that in addition to our retaliatory force we develop units that can intervene rapidly and that are able to make their power felt with discrimination and versatility. For this task we require a modern sealift and an airlift capacity we do not now possess. Our mobile forces must be tailored to the gamut of possible limited wars, which may range from conflicts involving several countries to minor police actions. Limited wars may require a highly complicated weapons system including nuclear weapons. They may involve conventional forces capable of assisting friendly governments to resist border incursions.

The effectiveness of our power thus depends on our unmistakable ability and willingness to oppose force with force at whatever level of intensity may be required. We do not now possess the necessary versatility.

## PROBLEM OF "CONCEALED" AGGRESSION

We must not make the mistake of assuming that even a diversified military establishment can protect us against the total range of our dangers. To begin with, force by itself is useless without the resolution to use it if need be. A great deal therefore depends on our psychological and political readiness. An effective policy must not only find the means to prevent adverse changes in the strategic balance, it must also be able to determine what changes to resist.

For our security can be imperiled not only by overt aggression but also by transformations which are made to appear, insofar as is possible, as not aggression at all. These "concealed wars" may appear as internal revolution or civil war; they may be instigated by outside forces or merely exploited by them. Greece has furnished one example; Vietnam another; the Middle East still another. One of the greatest threats to the security of the free world is gradual Soviet infiltration and domination of vital areas through steps each of which is so small and seemingly so insignificant that it does not seem to justify overt intervention.

These conflicts raise issues with which, in terms of our preconceptions and the structure of our forces, we are least prepared to deal. The gradual subversion of a government by concealed foreign penetration is difficult to deal with from the outside, even though the fate of millions may depend on it.

As a result, unless we have a clear understanding of our national purpose and close political ties with other nations of the free world, we shall find ourselves paralyzed in the face of upheavals which may gravely imperil the safety of the whole world. We must also realize that non-overt aggressions present issues that are deliberately and intrinsically unclear. To ask for certainty in these situations is a prescription for inaction. Nor is it possible in advance to determine the nature of the conflict or every United States response. The problem in its deepest sense is not military but political and will therefore be treated more fully by Panel I.

It should be our aim to prevent such situations from developing. When they do become acute, we may have a choice only between evils. Our security and that of the rest of the non-Communist world will then hinge importantly on our willingness to support friendly governments in situations that fit neither the soldier's classic concept of war nor the diplomat's traditional concept of aggression.

# V. The Problem of Nuclear Weapons

No one can look at the prospect of nuclear war with equanimity. It is with us not by our wish but because of Soviet hostility. The world knows that the United States will never engage in preventive war. But in resisting aggression we cannot in advance forego weapons that technology makes available to all who seek them, including those who might attack.

In dealing with the use of nuclear weapons, we come up against the hard fact that the choice is no longer entirely our own. Whatever we may decide, the Soviet Union may choose to conduct its aggressions with nuclear weapons. The introduction of nuclear weapons by an opponent would immediately raise the question of our reaction. Would we be prepared to respond with all-out war? And if not, we would be forced into a limited nuclear war under the worst possible circumstances: in the confusion of battle and without adequate psychological preparation.

Thus, against a nuclear power we must always be prepared to fight a limited nuclear war. Even when we decide to use conventional weapons, we would not dare to do so without a nuclear establishment ready at hand. And in a war in which the U.S.S.R. is a direct participant, nuclear weapons will have to be used almost of necessity. Confronted with their use, the huge Soviet conventional armament becomes obsolescent. In their absence the Soviet Union will have the choice of seeking to prevail with its preponderant ground army or to introduce nuclear weapons at a moment of maximum difficulty for us.

The use of nuclear weapons has been the subject of much debate. It is argued by some that the use of nuclear weapons marks the dividing line between all-out and limited war. Others maintain that even if there should be an intention to keep the war limited, neither side would accept defeat without resorting to every weapon in its arsenal.

Modern technology has created a spectrum of weapons, however, which makes it unreasonable to draw such rigid dividing lines. Some "conventional" weapons are more powerful than the lowest-yield nuclear weapons. Very powerful nuclear weapons can be used in such a manner that they have negligible effects on civilian populations—as high-altitude explosions over purely military objectives, for example. Relatively low-yield weapons or "conventional" bombs used against population centers can have devastating consequences. Whether a war produces more or less devastation depends on the manner and discrimination with which *any* modern weapon, nuclear or otherwise, is employed. Morality does not depend on the type of explosive but upon the use to which the explosive is put.

As for the argument that neither side will accept defeat short of having exhausted every means at its disposal, it would not seem to make any difference whether the war started as a conventional or as a nuclear war. A power unwilling to accept defeat in a nuclear war is not likely to be more prepared to accept defeat in a conventional war. This particular argument tends to run counter to every experience since World War II. If we keep our retaliatory force in a high state of readiness, it can be expected that both sides will look for reasons to limit, not to expand, the war. The Korean War was limited because of the fiction that the Soviet Union was not a direct participant and because neither the United States nor the Soviet Union wished to precipitate a general war.

We would also do well to recognize that since World War II it has been primarily the U.S. nuclear stockpile and delivery capability that has stood in the way of Soviet domination of the world. That the Soviet Union is well aware of this is shown by its persistent "ban the bomb" propaganda. Even a United States-Soviet equality in nuclear weapons will not change the fact that nuclear weapons complicate the tasks of an aggressor and reduce the significance of Soviet numerical superiority in conventional forces. The argument for not renouncing the use of nuclear weapons is that it represents our best chance to maintain the peace and to eliminate the Soviet advantage in conventional forces. The willingness to engage in nuclear war, when necessary, is part of the price of our freedom.

# VI. Defense Organization

Because of the tremendous significance of the affairs which center in the Department of Defense, all studies of the national security inevitably concern themselves to some extent with the organization and methods of the Pentagon. This concern is not new. It has been a preoccupation of successive administrations since the creation of the original National Military Establishment ten years ago. It has been the subject of numerous studies which have found the organization of the Department of Defense inadequate to its task and constantly outstripped by a rapidly evolving weapons technology.

Detailed organizational recommendations lead quickly to arguments outside the scope of this panel's undertaking. We have therefore confined ourselves to identifying the critical areas of weakness and to advancing several broad principles which should guide the development of specific organizational changes. It seems to us that the major defects in the present organization are inherent in its structure. They cannot be removed by modifying it. They will be further aggravated by the passage of time. These defects are three in number:

1. The roles and missions assigned to the individual military services have become competitive rather than complementary because they are out of accord with both weapons technology and the principal military threats to our national safety.

2. The present organization and responsibilities of the Joint Chiefs of Staff preclude the development of a comprehensive and coherent strategic doctrine for the United States.

3. The Secretary of Defense is so burdened with the negative

tasks of trying to arbitrate and control interservice disputes that he cannot play his full part in the initiation and development of high military policy.

These points will be discussed in order.

## PROBLEM OF ROLES AND MISSIONS

The range and destructiveness of modern weapons have tended to overleap the traditional boundaries among the services. As a result, our effort to develop an integrated national strategic plan has been beset by interservice rivalry. This rivalry is not due fundamentally to "parochialism" on the part of our military leaders; it is built into the present assignment of roles and missions.

Ten years ago, whatever else was hoped for in the new defense organization, one result was expected by the public: that through joint planning by the Chiefs of Staff, supplemented when necessary by the authority of the Secretary of Defense, there would be a co-ordinated and harmonious development of our potential in all three media of operations: land, sea, and air.

Such has not occurred. With the advantage of hindsight, it is now clear that the organization itself doomed this important goal. For the assignment of roles and missions among the Army, Air Force, and Navy has become increasingly inconsistent with the new technology. Heretofore, the Army has been assigned the task of winning a war on land, the Navy has been charged with control of the seas, and the Air Force has been responsible for dominating the sky. Thus the method of transportation by which a weapons system moved determined which service controlled it.

Until the development of long-range air power, the division of functions based on methods of locomotion worked relatively smoothly because it reflected the actual tasks each service had to perform. Each service was therefore able to develop its own strategy and to develop under its own control the weapons required for achieving its mission. But the revolutionary advances in technology have made the traditional division of functions increasingly obsolete. Given the range and destructiveness of modern weapons, the present assignment of roles and missions forces each service to duplicate the efforts of some other service. Thus one service, the Navy, operates in all the media—sea, land, and air. Other missions are shared by two or more services, such as tactical air support. There are three services with air power and two with armies; the Air Force is responsible for co-ordinating air defense, but the Army is responsible for the air defense of specific targets. And there are three separate service war plans with the common tendency of reducing the reliance on other services as much as possible.

Thus the division of functions, which worked without fundamental frictions until the end of World War II, has led to bitter conflict in the nuclear air age. It is inherent in the philosophy and training of each service that it should see in any developing enemy threat predominately those elements that its own particular organization seems best adapted to counter. And each service by a natural rationalization judges the proper balance of forces to be the one that maximizes its own role.

A duplication of weapons systems and a wastage of scientific talent are inevitable. This prevents us from drawing the full benefit from our military expenditures and forces our policy makers constantly to arbitrate among sharply conflicting advice. New weapons are placed into the strait jacket of obsolescent missions instead of missions being reshaped to conform to an evolving technology and to new military problems.

Conversely, the present organization may neglect certain vital tasks. An example is the problem of airlift for the ground forces. To provide such facilities is an Air Force responsibility. When budgets are tight, the Air Force is understandably reluctant to favor this mission at the expense of its primary task of defeating the enemy in the air, especially against the background of growing Soviet strength in planes and missiles. On the other hand, the Army is prevented by our mechanistic assignment of functions from developing and operating the transport aircraft required to move forces swiftly to the combat zone.

## JOINT CHIEFS OF STAFF

Except for the Chairman, the members of the Joint Chiefs of Staff are the senior officers of the military services. Therefore, even with the best will in the world, they cannot avoid being advocates of a service point of view. The position of each reflects a lifetime of dedication to his service. He is primarily the product of its training schools and its environment. Since he is responsible for the future of his service, its status and morale must be one of his chief concerns.

Thus, under the present organization, most of the decisive pressures on the Joint Chiefs of Staff organization are produced by the individual services, and the Joint Chiefs of Staff functions too often as a committee of partisan adversaries engaged in advancing service strategic plans and compromising service differences. Too little in present arrangements permits the Chiefs of Staff time and opportunity to think spontaneously or comprehensively about over-all strategic problems. The result is that our military plans for meeting foreseeable threats tend to be a patchwork of compromise between conflicting strategic concepts or simply the uncoordinated war plans of the several services.

## ROLE OF THE SECRETARY OF DEFENSE

The organization of the military establishment into three competing services and the aggravation of this difficulty by ill-defined and sometimes obsolete roles and missions have shaped the role of the Secretary of Defense in ways not foreseen when the office was created in 1947. To a considerable extent, these conditions have confined him to the essentially negative functions of arbitration and control. He has become the referee in disputes over policy issues originating in the services or in the Joint Chiefs of Staff. It is the essence of a referee's position that disputes reach him only *after* positions have hardened. The Secretary of Defense has, in consequence, found it difficult to play the positive, creative role required of the Cabinet officer who, together with the President and the Secretary of State, formulates high policy for foreign and military affairs.

In exercising the functions of arbitration and control, the Secretary of Defense and his staff have become overwhelmed with many administrative tasks that, were it not for deep-seated interservice rivalry, could be better handled by the individual services. This condition is reflected in the ever-increasing number of Assistant Secretaries of Defense and the heavy emphasis of the Secretary's office on financial controls at the expense of strategic doctrine. Financial controls are no doubt essential. Nevertheless, a principal objective of any reorganization plan should be to create conditions in which the Secretary of Defense can give a

more effective lead to the initiation and formulation of broad
military policy, while delegating to the substructures of the defense organization a substantial portion of his present administrative burden.

## RECOMMENDED CHANGES

The foregoing analysis indicates that the difficulties described
are *inherent* in the present organization of the Defense Department and that they cannot be removed merely by adjustments
of the existing structure. The obstacles to correcting these deficiencies are formidable indeed. Yet the growing complexity of
modern technology, the foreseeable rise in the cost of maintaining
weapons systems, and the interdependence of foreign policy and
military capability make it clear that our future security—which
is to say, our survival as a nation—will require a far more efficient
system for military planning and military decisions.

To remedy the central weaknesses, the following changes are
recommended.

Roles and Missions:

1. The military departments should be removed from the channel of operational command. The existing military departments
should cease to be responsible for carrying out particular combat
missions. Henceforth, their responsibility should be to provide
support in matters of recruitment, training, research, procurement,
and supply for unified operational commands (to be described
below). Relieved of their responsibilities for strategic planning
and combat operations, the service chiefs and their civilian superiors could concentrate on tasks of management and logistics.

2. All of the operational military forces of the United States
should be organized into unified commands to perform missions
that are called for by our strategic requirements. No foreseeable
conflict will fit the category of land, sea, or air battle. Therefore,
unified commands, each composed of appropriate land, sea, and
air elements and assigned a particular mission, are essential. Each
unified command should be composed of the appropriate elements from each military service brought together under a single
commander. As units complete their training within the existing
services, they would be assigned to a functional command. The
units assigned to each of the unified commanders should be

organic to his command and not simply placed under his operational control temporarily. Each unified command would be, in effect, a combined force with its own mission and trained to carry out a distinctive task.

The composition and mission of these unified commands should not be frozen by legislation. They should be determined from time to time in the President's discretion, so that they remain abreast of technology and of the tasks an evolving strategy will require. The conduct of all-out war may be one mission; continental defense another; limited war still another.

In such an organization, officers could more easily transcend the confines of service loyalty and address themselves more objectively to strategic problems. With each functional area representing a clear strategic mission, the requirements of self-interest and of strategic doctrine would be much more in harmony than now.

The Joint Chiefs of Staff:

3. The Chairman of the Joint Chiefs of Staff should be designated Principal Military Adviser to the Secretary of Defense and the President. The Chairman of the Joint Chiefs is the only member who can give his full-time attention to problems of over-all strategic doctrine. It is therefore logical that he be the Principal Military Adviser to the President and the Secretary of Defense instead of the Joint Chiefs collectively. The Chiefs of the several services would continue to serve on the Joint Chiefs of Staff but only as advisers to the Chairman and with particular responsibility for the areas of logistics, training, and procurement.

4. The staff of the Joint Chiefs of Staff should be organized on a unified basis and placed under the control of the Chairman. The Chairman should be in a position to shape strategic planning. One major obstacle is that officers on interservice staffs and committees are negotiators rather than planners and tend to represent the point of view of a service rather than an over-all approach. A unified staff under the direct control of the Chairman would remove many of the service pressures on the members of the staff. The organization of the unified staff would be analogous to that of the functional commands. It would assist the Chairman in his capacity as Principal Military Adviser to the President and the Secretary of Defense in strategic and operational planning.

5. All officers above the rank of Brigadier General or equivalent

should receive their permanent promotions from the Department of Defense and would become officers of the Armed Forces of the United States. This change is essential in order to derive the full benefits from recommendation 4. For effective over-all planning, it is vital that we develop a group of top officers who throughout their careers have been encouraged to transcend the thinking of any one service. The procedure recommended here would retain the specialization necessary to command specific units and the morale that goes with membership in a service. At the higher levels, however, where the requirement is for an over-all view, the primary loyalty of all high-ranking officers would transcend service boundaries. Since entry into this group would be the goal of most if not *all* officers throughout their careers, junior officers would know that their future would depend on their ability to take a broad view, rather than on the ability to defend the point of view of their service on interdepartmental committees. When a higher rank within a service seems required by circumstances, a temporary appointment should be made.

The Authority of the Secretary of Defense:

6. The line of operational command should be from the President and the Secretary of Defense to the functional commanders through the Chairman of the Joint Chiefs of Staff in his capacity as Principal Military Adviser. Any modern war requires swift reaction, and this can be achieved only if there are a minimum number of organizational layers. Since the present division of functions among the military services often represents no distinguishable strategic task, the separate military departments should be relieved from responsibility for the unified commands as recommended above. Rather, the unified commands should be under the Principal Military Adviser to the President. This proposal recognizes that the Secretary of Defense is the deputy commander in chief. His position in the line of command would preserve civilian control over the armed forces.

7. The line of logistic command should be from the President through the Secretary of Defense to the Secretaries of the three military Departments. This recommendation is an application to logistics and the recruitment and training of manpower of the previous recommendation.

8. The Secretary of Defense should be given authority over all

research, development, and procurement. He should have the right of cancellation and transfer of service programs together with their appropriations. He should also be given a direct appropriation for the conduct of research and development programs at the Defense Department level. One of the outstanding characteristics of the present period is the basic relationship between strategy and technology. When technology was relatively stable, the technical aspect of military planning usually involved problems either of procurement or of engineering. But today, with technology developing at an explosive rate, the direction of both research and development is a primary strategic concern. As a result, another war may well be won or lost in the laboratories and on the drawing boards. As long as the Secretary of Defense cannot shape the direction of research and development or of procurement, his role will be the essentially passive one of arbitrating disputes formulated elsewhere. Where so much depends on keeping up and staying ahead in the technological race, it is essential that our weapons development reflect a clear sense of direction and not a series of compromises.

## PROBLEM OF LEAD TIMES

Lead time—the interval between conception and execution—has never been more crucial. The best plans will be fruitless if they cannot be carried out rapidly. The best production apparatus will be ineffective if it requires too long to produce the necessary implements of defense. A nation can achieve a basic advantage if it is able either to develop or to produce weapons more rapidly than its opponent.

One of the major weaknesses in our strategic posture has been our inordinately long lead times. They have been produced in part by the cumbersome machinery in the Department of Defense. In part they have been caused by a quest for perfection in development and by its corollary, which is an overconcern with the avoidance of mistake. As our government has grown, it has followed the familiar course into a system of rewards that favors caution and mediocrity. Punishment for inaction is rare, but retribution is swift and harsh for measures that were imaginative, risky, and failed. It is especially important that this pattern be reversed in a situation that is inherently uncertain and where great achievement is inseparable from great risk. It is essential that we compress our lead times, and the recommendations in this report should help in this direction. At the same time, there has to be a greater flexibility and willingness to run risks in research, development, and procurement.

## STRATEGY AND PSYCHOLOGY

Another great weakness in the organization of our national government is the absence of a clear focus at any single point to assess the psychological impact of our actions. Whatever the wisdom of the decision not to engage in a race with the Soviet Union in the space satellite field, it does not appear that the psychological reaction of other nations to a Soviet "first" in this field has been given sufficient weight. Yet the more revolutionary the developments of technology, the more their significance depends on the interpretation placed on them. Since very few of the modern weapons have ever been used in wartime, their impact on policy reflects what people think with respect to them. It is therefore essential that within our national government there exist a mechanism to assess the psychological impact both at home and abroad of our actions in the military field as in others. This is a problem far transcending the organization of the Department of Defense and will be dealt with at greater length in the reports of other panels. It is mentioned here only because a section on organizational remedies would be incomplete without it.

## CONCLUSION

Implementation of the recommendations in this section would provide a unity and coherence now absent from our defense organization. They are the primary means to achieve economies in our defense structure because they will permit a better utilization of resources and eliminate the present duplication of functions.

# VII. Alliances and the Role of Force

Within the framework of Articles 51 and 52 of the United Nations Charter, the United States has since the end of World War II entered into a wide variety of mutual assistance agreements with other states. These range from the sweeping multilateral defense arrangements of the Rio Treaty of Reciprocal Assistance to a number of bilateral agreements with individual nations. Our armed forces overseas are reminders of our determination to carry out these commitments.

## BASIS OF THE FREE WORLD
## SYSTEM OF ALLIANCES

Strategically, the system of alliances in which the United States participates is invaluable in the over-all world balance of power. Overseas bases provide advanced observation and warning posts against possible Soviet aggression. They bring the retaliatory forces closer to possible targets, thus adding to the deterrent by making the counterblow more certain. The advent of missiles will not reduce the importance of alliances. To be sure, missiles will increase the vulnerability of all free world nations. On the other hand, intermediate- and short-range missiles can reach almost all of the U.S.S.R. from present free world territory. The geographic relationship is such that intermediate-range missiles in the hands of our allies or on their territory have strategic significance similar to that of intercontinental missiles in the hands of the U.S.S.R. And the shorter range the missile, the more mobile its launching site and, therefore, the less vulnerable it is to Soviet surprise attack.

The significance of alliances has been further increased by the growth of the Soviet nuclear stockpile. As long as the United

States possessed an atomic monopoly, the chief significance of alliances was in providing advance notice of the American intention to resist a Soviet move against countries covered by security arrangements. At the same time, as long as the chief deterrent to Soviet aggression was the United States predominance in retaliatory power, there was an understandable reluctance on the part of our allies to make a major military effort. As long as it was believed that the issue of a war would be decided elsewhere, few of our allies saw much significance in making a large military contribution. The reliance on an all-out strategy tended to run counter to our desires for building common strength.

But with the growth of the Soviet nuclear stockpile and the means to deliver it, *all* members of the alliance have an equal interest in removing any Soviet illusion that it might use its capability for all-out war as a shield behind which to expand by more limited means. They also share an interest in keeping any war that does break out to the smallest proportions. This is possible only to the extent that local resistance is feasible. Alliance arrangements can provide local forces to deter or check aggression. They can strengthen the local will to resist because they guarantee that a threatened country would not stand alone. The efficacy of the alliances in which we participate may not only determine the issue of a war; they are good insurance against such wars breaking out in the first place.

## ALLIANCES AND THE UNITED NATIONS

The United Nations remains the greatest symbol of man's hope for peace and the most comprehensive organization working toward it. It has proved its ability to act in a number of situations from Korea to Suez. It is an indispensable forum for expressing the hopes of humanity and an effective institution for pursuing agreed ends.

Still, it would be idle to pretend that under present circumstances the United Nations can replace regional alliances, the need for which was foreseen in the Charter. The Soviet veto in the Security Council prevents effective action by that body in all situations where Communist powers are parties to the dispute. And these are precisely the cases that present the gravest threat to the security of the world. Moreover, many other dangers may see the United Nations paralyzed either by Communist intransigence or by disputes among UN members extraneous to the issues actually at stake. Thus while we should strive to resist aggression through the widest possible expression of the consensus of humanity, we cannot permit the world to be dominated by hostile totalitarian nations simply because these have been able to hamstring the machinery of the United Nations. Until United Nations action is taken, we should try to act in concert with the widest grouping of nations attainable as provided by Article 51 of the Charter. The system of free world alliances thus is not an alternative to the United Nations but its complement; it is the only means for collective security where the processes of the United Nations may be blocked or its action rendered ineffective.

## PRESSURE ON THE ALLIANCE SYSTEM

To assert that alliances are important does not imply that all is well with them. On the contrary, it is essential that we recognize three sets of forces tending to weaken our system of alliances: the fear of Communist military power, the ambiguity of Communist tactics of aggression, and the lack of a strategic concept offering reasonable prospects of protection to our allies.

Our allies are faced with a situation in which, at one and the same time, the danger of war seems less imminent and the fear of the consequences of war grows greater. In Europe and in Asia, the Communist bloc is steadily improving its military capabilities, including nuclear weapons and delivery systems. Against the threat of nuclear attack, many of our allies have little defense of their own. The concern—assiduously fostered by the U.S.S.R.—that the use of even the smallest atomic weapon would involve enormous destruction may weaken the will to resist of many allies, in and out of NATO.

A correlative force contributing to the reluctance of many countries to make a substantial military effort is the growing cost and complexity of modern weapons. This imposes a heavy burden on frail economies, and it requires skills and facilities that some of our allies do not have. The attainment of a capability to deter or check local aggression is made much more difficult. In many cases, the ability to resist locally is actually decreasing, while the need for it has become greater than ever.

Aggravating the other pressures on our alliance arrangements is the concept of aggression which underlies them. Existing treaties essentially are concerned with open attack by armed regular troops and do not cover a whole range of Communist aggressive techniques, from economic strangulation to slow take-overs by Communist-guided and Communist-armed fifth columns. As a result, the Communist bloc has learned that if it keeps its challenges sufficiently ambiguous and below the level of intensity that the non-Communist world considers to warrant major military measures, we and our allies may prove unable or unwilling to take effective action. Korea, Indochina, and the Middle East deserve close study with this problem in mind. Confronted by an ambiguous threat, even a group of nations whose interests are very similar often find it exceedingly difficult to achieve an effective concerted response.

## ALLIANCE STRATEGY

One of the major problems faced by our alliance policy is to devise a military strategy equally meaningful both to us and to our allies. In view of its manifold commitments, the United States has been understandably reluctant to commit itself to defend specific allied territories locally. Instead, we have largely relied on our retaliatory force, supplemented by mobile sea and tactical air power, to deter aggression of all kinds. While the allies of the United States have joined together on that basis, none has ever given up the strong desire to see its own homelands protected from invasion or devastation.

This difference of viewpoints has meant that, with the partial exception of NATO, the alliances in which we participate are not based on a military strategy equally congenial to all partners. The lack of an agreed strategy has resulted in weaknesses, indecisions, and contradictions at all levels of our security arrangements. It has led to endless difficulties in formulating and implementing U.S. base agreements and military aid programs. There have been disagreements concerning military requirements and programs. And there has been a reluctance on the part of our allies to make or to meet specific force commitments, partly because the function those forces would perform has been so vague. Moreover, our strategy is largely atomic, those of our allies generally non-atomic, except those of Great Britain. Thus, as nuclear weapons and delivery systems play an ever greater role, present allied forces will become less capable of making major military contributions to other than internal security missions.

The United States must therefore make a concerted effort, together with its allies, to develop and implement plans that meet the joint security requirements of *all* partners. If allied forces are to be capable of acting in concert with U.S. forces, we will have to assist in their transformation and development. This does not mean that all allied elements must inevitably be equipped along the lines of comparable U.S. units. To the maximum degree possible, both the types and levels of equipment should be adapted to the particular security requirements of our allies. But we must establish a measure of harmony between the tactical doctrine of our allies and our own and equip the respective forces accordingly.

The free world is faced with a major task of strengthening and re-equipping its forces at a time when both rapidly changing technology and, in many parts of the world, decreasing popular support for military programs combine to make the job extremely costly and difficult. It is probable that the United States will have to provide—either directly or indirectly—substantial quantities of equipment needed by our allies or else see their political stability decline along with their military strength. Increased consultation will be of great significance in removing the sense of impotence of many of our allies, produced by unfamiliarity with modern technology and by a feeling of being left out from decisions which affect their fate.

The proposed military measures are by no means the sole means of maintaining the vitality of the system of free world alliances. They must be supplemented by positive programs for political cohesiveness, for economic and technical co-operation, and by other measures discussed more fully by various groups of the over-all study project of which this panel is but one part.

# VIII. The Special Case of NATO

Of the alliance systems in which we participate, the two most important are the Inter-American Treaty of Reciprocal Assistance and the North Atlantic Treaty Organization. NATO is militarily the most highly developed of our multiple alliances. It covers an area of great cultural and economic significance to both East and West. As in the case of our Western Hemisphere allies, it embraces nations with whom we share a common spiritual and cultural heritage.

In order to appreciate the military importance of NATO, we need only to contemplate our situation were Western Europe in Soviet hands. The Communist bloc would then have an industrial potential at least equal to our own. It would lie astride the world's main communications lines. It would flank and engulf the Middle East. It would be able to manipulate the manpower, factories, and cultural prestige of Europe to dominate Africa and infiltrate South America.

## WEAKNESSES OF NATO

Western Europe is deeply affected by the revolutionary changes taking place all over the world. Its position in world affairs has been altered by the emergence into nationhood of many of its former colonial possessions in Asia, the Middle East, and Africa. At the same time, for a variety of reasons, the sense of urgency on which NATO was founded has declined, and a number of rivalries and irritations between NATO members have been revived. The dispute over Cyprus was permitted to fester to the detriment of NATO; France has withdrawn most of her NATO units for action in North Africa. The Anglo-French adventure in

Egypt and our reaction to it weakened NATO ties, while the British White Paper on Defense for 1957, the issuance of which was hastened by the debacle at Suez, foreshadows sharp reductions of British military power on the continent.

Sentiment toward neutralism, or at least toward a more passive adherence to the alliance, has been growing in some NATO countries. Many factors contribute to this psychological retreat from a nuclear reality in which they have no part, including the relative weakness of our NATO partners as compared to the Soviet Union and the United States. But perhaps the most pervasive reason is the reaction to the consequences of nuclear warfare. This anxiety has two aspects: on the one hand, Europeans recoil from the damage and destruction they believe would result from the use of any sort of atomic weapons; on the other, they are beginning to question whether the growing Soviet nuclear stockpile will not make the United States reluctant to risk devastation of the American mainland in order to protect Europe.

Nevertheless, whatever the disagreements within NATO, the U.S.S.R. has demonstrated the significance it attaches to NATO by its incessant efforts to disrupt it. The disagreements indicate, however, that in order to continue to play a major role in the protection of the free world, NATO will have to be adapted to the new conditions created by an evolving technology. It will have to find new means of political and economic collaboration and a new expression for its military strategy.

## NATO STRATEGY

Since 1954, NATO planning has been based on the assumption that in any major war NATO forces would use nuclear weapons from the outset. Accordingly, NATO strategy calls for the maintenance of two components: a shield of local tactical forces and a sword of nuclear retaliatory forces. The shield component of NATO has a double purpose: it provides sufficient tactical forces in Western Europe to discourage or contain local aggression, and its presence notifies any possible antagonist that aggression with which these forces might not be able to cope would trigger the second component of NATO strategy, the sword of strategic striking forces carrying nuclear weapons.

Three factors have served, however, to cast serious doubts upon this strategy:

The first is the Soviet development of a large-scale air-atomic capability. This has led to speculation that the "sword" of NATO —the strategic air forces of the United States and the Untied Kingdom—may not be unsheathed in the event of Soviet aggression on Europe for fear of a devastating attack on the United States and the United Kingdom.

The second factor is that recent trends in United States military policy, and perhaps even more in British military policy, have done much to discredit the NATO effort to build forces capable of resisting locally. Both countries have emphasized the massive deterrent rather than the shield force. Thus our European allies are placed in a position where they feel they can no longer rely on the retaliatory force to deter every form of war while that element of power is being stressed at the apparent expense of forces needed for their local defense. This is compounded by the facts that the retaliatory forces are not under NATO command, that of the tactical forces only the British and the Americans possess nuclear weapons,* and that the opposing Soviet forces are daily increasing *their* capabilities to wage both strategic and tactical nuclear warfare. Under these circumstances, many Europeans may well regard aggression as posing solely a choice between occupation and destruction.

A third factor making for instability is the reverse of the above: a tendency on the part of some NATO allies to seek to escape their dilemmas by a policy of disengagement and neutralism. There is an understandable temptation to depend for deterrence on the military effort of a stronger power and to rely for protection on a war fought elsewhere. The strategic striking forces in the exclusive possession of the United States and the United Kingdom tend to produce a feeling of impotence inhibiting a major effort.

## RECOMMENDATIONS WITH RESPECT TO NATO

The problem of NATO is therefore one of will as much as of power. All partners must realize that henceforth security can be enhanced only by a sharing of risks and capabilities. And they

* Written in January 1958.

should all be placed into a position where they are able to contribute responsibly to their own security.

To be sure, the ultimate answers to the problems of NATO may be found in the realm of policy and not of strategy. NATO, to survive, must generate a common sense of political, economic, and social purposes. Many of the difficulties of NATO are aspects of East-West relations in general; others are produced by situations outside of NATO area proper. Panel I deals with the political problem at greater length and Panel III with the economic and social factors. Nevertheless, an alliance designed to provide protection against aggression can survive only if it is able to develop a common military strategy in which all partners can play a role. If it cannot adapt itself to new conditions, it must of necessity become sterile.

Fortunately, there are two factors that seem to offer possibilities for a viable common strategy. The first of these is the disaffection in the Soviet bloc, so vividly illustrated in the cases of Hungary and Poland. This reduces the combat value of satellite forces and makes even more precarious the already tenuous line of communications between the Soviet forces in Central Europe and their home base.

The second and more important factor is the availability in quantity of tactical nuclear weapons. The battlefield advantage accruing to tactical defensive forces, through preparation of positions, prior determination of target areas, and stockpiling of both nuclear and conventional munitions, offers hope that even relatively small but highly trained NATO forces could hurl back a local attack and blunt major aggression. It is perhaps too early to say that this is possible; it is crucial that we re-examine our present concept of the capabilities required to defend Western Europe in addition to the threat of strategic retaliation on the U.S.S.R.

Thus a prime element in the new strategy must be a significant strengthening of the NATO shield forces. The ability to resist local incursions will remove one temptation to aggression. The knowledge that an attack will meet with substantial local resistance provides an additional deterrent to Soviet encroachments. The United States must pursue with conviction this task of strengthening the shield forces, for it is equally in our interest to see that a conflict arising in Europe, either by design or by miscalculation, does not inevitably result in all-out war. But however earnest our effort to strengthen the shield forces, it will be unavailing unless our allies are prepared to make a substantially greater contribution both in forces and in the spirit with which they approach the *common* task of defense.

A corollary of this central problem of establishing an adequate NATO shield is to provide within Europe—controlled by Europeans—an atomic and missile capability that will substantially reduce Europe's dependence on United States and British strategic air power. This is necessary to restore the declining power position of NATO vis-à-vis the U.S.S.R. and to give reality to the European sense of participation, which is a basic ingredient of the will to resist.

A strong NATO shield is all the more important because one of the purposes of the growing Soviet naval threat is undoubtedly to bring about a situation where the Soviet Union may be able to disrupt sea communications between us and our NATO allies by submarines and by mining European harbors. In such a situation, the willingness to resist a simultaneous Soviet invasion will depend importantly on the forces available in Europe and under NATO control.

## ROLE OF THE UNITED STATES

To accomplish these objectives will require the following of the United States: first of all, we must pool with our allies scientific and technical information and assist in mobilizing the research and development capability of NATO both in the civilian and the military field. The history of science suggests that such pooling would in the long run be of special importance to the United States, which throughout its history has drawn heavily on the intellectual resources of Europe.

Second, we must strive for a true military interdependence which closely ties together the United States and the other NATO powers.

Third, we must acknowledge the necessity for maintaining in Europe for an indefinite period a strong contribution to the shield forces.

Finally, we must provide those of our allies that desire them with nuclear weapons and delivery systems, as well as with some of the other complex equipment of modern war. A step in the direction of these objectives was taken at the NATO Council meeting in December 1957.

It would be unrealistic to say that such policies will be either cheap or without risk. But the cost and risk of being without them would be greater still. A strong, self-reliant Europe must always be a major American concern. Such a Europe, continuing along its present path toward greater unity, is a major force for peace and can play an ever greater role in the future evolution of free society.

# IX. Civil Defense

There are few problems of the atomic age with which the United States has had greater difficulty in coming to grips than civil defense. Because of our historic invulnerability to direct military attack, we have treated civil defense as a minor adjunct to our over-all strategy, both in terms of planning and in the resources allocated to it.

The full civil defense problem is well beyond the scope of this report and has been the subject of a special study in the government. The technical possibilities of defending our cities and homes, the costs, the impact on our national psychology and ways of working and living present a complex of considerations deserving detailed and separate examination. Nevertheless, the connection between civil defense and the other elements of our national security requires a general evaluation of the subject.

If relations with the Soviet bloc ever reach the showdown stage, the edge of difference, which may be very fine, may well depend on the strength of the competing wills. This in turn is likely to reflect the relative vulnerabilities. It is an oppressive thought that such circumstances might in fact occur, but it would be irresponsible to suggest that they are impossible. Courage in crisis, if it is to be effective and continuing, must rest on confidence and hope.

Deterrence, in short, depends on a combination of power and will. The factor of power requires a retaliatory capability sufficient to overcome any enemy defense and as invulnerable as possible to surprise attack. The factor of will may hinge importantly on a reasonable combination of active and passive defense measures. An enemy who felt confident that he could disrupt and disorganize our society while preserving the substance of his own might be tempted to launch an all-out blow. Conversely, the ability to afford reasonable protection to our population may enable us to act with firmness and resolution in times of crisis. In the age of the ballistic missile, the known capability of a society to withstand attack will become an increasingly important deterrent.

Civil defense will not be easy, and it can never be complete. Protecting against massively destructive weapons is an enormous problem. A 20-megaton thermonuclear weapon, which is by no means the largest available, with a radius of surface destruction by blast and heat of between 5 to 8 miles, will inevitably have devastating consequences.

Difficulty does not mean impotence however. While it may be impossible to protect the population against the blast and heat of an atomic explosion, protection against radioactive fallout and other contamination appears to be much more feasible. Equally important is increased understanding on the part of our people about the effects of modern weapons. This will enable us to respond with discipline and effectiveness to a surprise attack, and it will discourage such a move because an aggressor would no longer be able to gamble that a sudden attack might disorganize our society.

It is possible to state certain general principles in relation to the development of any civil defense program:

1. Civil defense must be considered as part of the over-all U.S. strategic posture. It must be faced forthrightly. It should be part of our defense planning and included in our over-all strategic plans. Cadres charged with supervising civil defense activities, both in possible pre-attack and the post-attack phase, must be developed and trained immediately. The expense involved should be in addition to existing military outlays.

2. The American people need to be told more clearly the dimensions of the damage that would be inflicted on us by a sudden attack and about the measures to reduce its effects. Any civil defense program must have as a prerequisite a program of public information supported by the federal government and carried through at all levels.

3. A civil defense program should be integrated with the construction program needed for the normal development of our expanding population and economy.

An effective civil defense program can be separated into three stages:

1. To provide warning, where possible, and information about radiological levels. This requires an attack-proof radiation-level monitoring system and an attack-proof radio-net to broadcast instructions during and after an attack.

2. Protection against fallout. It has been estimated that half of the casualties of a large-scale atomic attack or between 25–35 million might result from radioactive fallout. A fallout shelter program could prevent such a calamity by reducing casualties substantially.

3. Protection against atomic blast and heat. This is a major problem particularly in our big urban concentrations. This panel has heard testimony about the utility of deep shelters. The subject is of such complexity, however, and the costs are so very large that this report cannot go further than to commend such a program for careful study. If indeed it proves feasible, it will add greatly to our security as a nation.

The major difficulty with civil defense has been our failure to treat it as an integral part of our defense planning. The first step will have to be to construct an attack-proof radio-net and to begin on a program of fallout shelters. Fallout shelters are more feasible than blast shelters because they are easier to construct and because the population does not need to enter them until *after* an enemy attack has in fact occurred. Thus in most areas a warning time of 45 minutes could be counted on. The shelter program should be carried out with a maximum degree of co-operation with local and state authorities.

In addition to the protection of the population against fallout, provision should be made for the post-attack period. It will be highly important to plan on centers of administration and government. Stockpiling food supplies and industrial reserves in safe places will prevent famine and enable the early resumption of economic activity. At the same time, a continuation of organized activity will be aided by the greatest possible degree of dispersal of industry. It would be too costly to disperse existing industrial installations, but tax incentives could be provided for the location of *new* facilities away from main concentrations.

While engaging in a civil defense at home, we must be prepared to assist our allies in similar efforts. Nothing would demonstrate better our basic concern for the security of our allies than a readiness to co-operate in the protection of their populations.

The main feature to note with respect to civil defense is that it is overdue. It does not make sense for the free world to engage in a major military effort without at the same time protecting its most important resource: its civilian population.

# X. International Tensions and the Reduction of Armaments

## ARMS AND THE PROSPECTS OF PEACE

The destructiveness of modern weapons has focused the hopes of mankind as never before on the attainment of a stable peace. Considerable attention has been paid to the effort of reducing tensions through the reduction and control of armaments.

This panel, as all Americans, considers the achievement of a peaceful world the primary challenge before mankind. The United States disarmed unilaterally and drastically immediately after World War II; it refused to take advantage of its atomic monopoly; it acted patiently and moderately in the face of constant Soviet provocation. Even after the Greek civil war, the Berlin blockade, and the Korean War had caused us to undertake a substantial rearmament program, we have responded to every seeming relaxation of tension by reducing our military establishment, sometimes even below the point of safety. In fact, many of the difficulties described in this report are due to this tendency.

The desirability of easing international tensions therefore does not require argument. It would be highly irresponsible, however, to raise hopes that cannot be fulfilled or to hold out prospects that on closer examination prove to increase our peril. However dangerous the multiplying armaments, the illusion of security brought about by a spurious agreement to disarm would be a poor substitute for vigilance based on strength.

Genuine, enforceable, inspected reduction of arms is an objective on which all Americans are agreed. Yet we must realize that of all the outstanding issues, disarmament is the most difficult problem to settle directly. There are many other problems such as

German unification or Soviet subversive activities in the Middle East, which, if resolved, would greatly ease tensions and thus almost automatically bring about a reduction of arms. We will make disarmament negotiations more realistic if we face their inherent difficulty frankly and if we are not seduced by Soviet slogans, which in the past have used these negotiations as a means to disarm their intended victims.

The nature of disarmament must be understood if peace and not slavery is to result from efforts to attain it. It has several meanings, all of which hide great complexities: the reduction of forces, the control of arms, the prevention of surprise attack, and the end of bomb testing. Each will be considered in turn.

## REDUCTION AND CONTROL OF ARMS

Reduction of forces is bound to be difficult to negotiate because it seeks to compare unlike quantities. What for example is the relation between the United States Strategic Air Command and the ability of Soviet ground forces to overrun nearby countries? How does one compare an aircraft carrier to an armored division? If the United States disbanded its Strategic Air Command, it would take a decade at least to reconstitute. The Soviet Union can demobilize parts of its vast army and still retain the ability to reassemble it from reserve components at very short notice.

Moreover, the Soviet Union is not likely to accept a reduction of forces that curtails its ability to control the satellites and to play a major role in areas like the Middle East. But forces sufficient to accomplish these tasks are also sufficient to imperil all the powers on the Soviet borders. A reduction of forces that leaves unimpaired the Soviet ability to overrun its neighbors will not diminish the basic security problem of the non-Soviet world.

A reduction of armaments is not meaningful unless it contains safeguards against violations of the agreement. But effective control has been complicated by the increasingly rapid advance of technology. Scientific research and development can decide the armament race. Hence no reduction in standing forces, however scrupulously carried out, can protect a nation against a technological development that drastically changes the strategic balance. The fact that so much of the armaments race occurs in laboratories makes control and inspection more and more complex. It is difficult to find something when one does not know what it is one is looking for.

Many control schemes that would have been effective had they been accepted at the *beginning* of a given scientific development become meaningless when that range of technology is fully developed. Thus acceptance by the Soviet Union of the United States Baruch-Lilienthal plan of 1946, which proposed the control and inspection of the production of fissionable material, might have practically eliminated the possibility of nuclear war. In the meantime, so much fissionable material has been produced and it is so easily hidden that no control scheme could completely guarantee against a violation. And the spread of fissionable materials through the peaceful uses of nuclear energy will complicate the problem even further.

## PROBLEM OF SURPRISE ATTACK

Because a controlled and verifiable reduction in forces has proved so complicated, a major emphasis of disarmament efforts has turned to the prevention of surprise attack. It is often argued that an inspection system that reduced the danger of surprise attack also would remove some of the urgent strains from international relationships.

There is no doubt that the danger of surprise attack contributes to the tensions of the nuclear age. But with evolving technology it is questionable whether aerial inspection will significantly reduce the element of surprise. The high state of readiness required of strategic striking forces means that they need no noticeable mobilization to launch their blow. As the speed of planes increases, warning times will be progressively reduced. And in the age of the intercontinental ballistic missile, the maximum warning time afforded by even a perfect inspection system will be half an hour, the period of time the missile will be in transit. Under such circumstances, even a foolproof inspection system will tell largely what is already known: that the opponent possesses the capability to launch a devastating attack on very short notice and with a minimum of warning.

But if aerial inspection can no longer protect against surprise attack, it can reveal an almost equally grave threat from hidden installations. Even a partial inspection system, operated by the UN, would protect the world to a degree from hidden military capabilities. But more than this is unlikely from aerial inspection. Much as we would like to be more optimistic, we cannot see how present vigilance could be reduced or insecurity be removed by any aerial inspection system now in prospect.

## PROBLEM OF WAR LIMITATION

This study has considered various suggestions for preventing the catastrophe of an all-out war caused by miscalculation or the spreading of small wars. It seems doubtful that ground rules for the conduct of limited war could be established by mutual agreement, since in order to undermine the will to resist, the Soviet Union has every interest in painting the consequences of resistance in the direst terms. Nevertheless, it would seem wise for the United States to include on the agenda of disarmament negotiations concrete proposals to limit to the smallest necessary dimensions such wars as may be forced on us. Even should the Soviet Union reject our proposals, they would serve to clarify our intentions and make less likely a war caused by miscalculation. Even a unilateral declaration that gave an indication of some of the steps we propose to follow to achieve the goal of reducing noncombatant casualties, such as a decision to use only weapons without substantial fallout effects, would give an opponent a strong incentive to follow suit.

The value of unilateral declarations is proved by the experience of World War II. Neither the Soviet Union nor Japan had ratified the Geneva convention of 1929 with respect to the treatment of war prisoners. Yet on June 27, 1941, the U.S.S.R. informed the International Committee of the Red Cross of its decision to adhere to the convention, and within a week of the outbreak of the war, Japan announced that it would abide by the Prisoners of War convention. Though violations undoubtedly occurred, this indicates that both countries saw an advantage in projecting themselves before the world as subscribers to rules of war. Clear United States declarations, firmly adhered to, might provide a similar framework for mitigating the consequences of modern war.

## THE ISSUE OF TESTING

Despite the vital importance of nuclear weapons to our survival, it would be irresponsible to be blind to the hazards inherent in their use. An indiscriminate and all-out use of existing nuclear stockpiles would bring about an extremely serious level of radiation on the entire planet.

The growth of nuclear stockpiles on both sides has been aptly described as the "balance of terror." It is a condition that some have incorrectly interpreted as a static, unchanging, nuclear "stalemate" or "standoff." Nothing could be further from the truth.

Nuclear deterrence is immensely complicated, since each new scientific advance, if applied by one side and not the other, is capable of overturning the strategic equation. In a dynamic situation, we must continually strive to improve our technological position lest an accumulation of advances by an aggressor ultimately confront us with overwhelming strength. It is this situation that should cause us to be extremely wary about ending nuclear weapons testing.

It has been proposed to start disarmament by an agreement to stop tests of nuclear weapons. It has been claimed that such a ban would be self-policing. Nuclear tests are said to be a hazard to the health of all people and of generations yet unborn; and they are represented as leading to ever more horrible weapons.

Unfortunately, a nuclear test is easily recorded or monitored only if no serious attempt is made to keep it secret. If a nation wants to hide its tests, observation will become very complicated and uncertain. To be sure, secret tests require considerable effort. But the Soviet Union has never spared resources in order to secure a military advantage. On the other hand, our history and our free society make it certain that we will respect the international obligations that we undertake.

As to the medical danger, there is much evidence to indicate that past tests have had a much smaller effect on public health than other biological effects to which mankind is constantly exposed. The accumulated radiation from weapons tests is only an insignificant fraction of the dosage to which most Americans are exposed from X-rays. To be sure, exposure to *any* additional radiation should be avoided. As in the case of X-rays, what is involved, however, is a balancing of risks. The dangers of continued weapons testing must be weighed against the hazards inherent in conducting them. If an end of weapons testing weakened the deterrent and made a war more likely, or more catastrophic, we would have brought on what we most wished to avoid.

As long as the production of fissionable material continues, an end of weapons testing would probably ensure that any future war would take the most extreme form. It would have to be fought with weapons in their present state of development, and past tests on both sides have concentrated on the most powerful devices. Conversely, since the most destructive weapons have already been tested, further tests will enable us to use nuclear arms in a more discriminating manner. By increasing our capability for limited war, this will add to the deterrent to local aggression. At the same time, continued testing may enable us to reduce radioactive fallout to the point where we will become increasingly able to confine any war that may be forced on us to our opponent's war machine. And it may make possible the development of nuclear antiaircraft or antimissile weapons to protect our population against enemy attack.

Thus, a ban on weapons testing without adequate inspection and without an end to the production of nuclear weapons would be beneficial only to the side prepared to violate the agreement. Our strong desire for peace and security should not induce us to buy the semblance of one at the expense of the other.

## PROSPECT OF PEACE

A world from which the threat of war has been removed would correspond to the deepest desires of American society. But peace cannot be attained by wishing for it. It requires patience, understanding, and determination. We must always stand ready to negotiate on the issues that divide the world, including disarmament. But until the Soviet Union has shown a greater willingness to settle these disputes on terms other than her own, it would be dangerous for us not to be wary of a power that has brutally suppressed Hungarian freedom, fanned the flames of violence elsewhere, and constantly threatens the world with rocket and nuclear attacks. As soon as the Soviet Union shows a sincere willingness to help in the construction of a peaceful world order, it will be able to count on an eager American co-operation in any disarmament effort.

# XI. Budget for National Security

Achievement of the objectives of our national security programs in the years ahead hinges on the availability of financial resources and the manner in which they are applied. There is grave reason for concern with respect to the inadequacy of recent levels of military appropriations as well as with respect to the workings of the budgetary process.

## THE BUDGETARY LEVEL

Programs of great importance to U.S. security now suffer from insufficient funds. Several reasons have brought about this state of affairs. When the Korean War ended, it was natural that an effort be made to reduce military expenditures. But the execution of the reductions has had serious consequences, which did not become evident for some time because of a backlog of unspent appropriations. For example, the momentum of the Air Force build-up continued until unspent appropriations from 1952 and 1953 ran out. Similarly, Army procurement was financed well into 1956 from pre-1954 appropriations.

The result has been a serious imbalance in our military preparedness. Recent budgetary ceilings could be maintained only by a reduction of forces in all services, a process which has been slowly going on for the past three years. The budgetary squeeze affected not only force levels, it also slowed down our research effort in many fields, causing us to lose ground to the U.S.S.R.

Recent military expenditures are therefore insufficient to maintain even our current force levels. And events have made clear the inadequacy of these levels. This panel has noted these major shortcomings in our strategic posture:

## Strategic Forces

1. Aircraft procurement to modernize existing units will have to be authorized into the 1960s. Otherwise, a gap in ready forces between the latest types of manned aircraft and the operational stage of ballistic missiles seems unavoidable. We cannot risk obsolescence of present weapons before new ones are ready.

2. At the same time, we should press for the most rapid development and procurement of operational intermediate-range and intercontinental ballistic missiles.

3. The base structure of the Strategic Air Command, long out of phase with other elements in its program, should be made less vulnerable to surprise attack through dispersion and other protective measures.

4. Accelerated research and development support should be provided for all key programs, including missiles and advance reconnaissance systems.

5. The SAC alert time should be reduced. As the Soviet strength in missiles increases, the maximum warning time available will probably not exceed 20 minutes. It is therefore essential that as long as we rely on manned planes, the Strategic Air Command achieve a 15-minute alert time.

6. The establishment of a retaliatory system based on missile-launching submarines should be expedited.

## Active Defense

Today, the U.S.S.R. can attack the United States with a strong bomber force. In a few years it will be able to attack with a stronger bomber force, submarine-launched missiles, and intercontinental ballistic missiles.

Whichever side first achieves a strong defense will be in a strong psychological position. The stronger the active defense, the more it reduces the threat of the opposing strategic striking force.

Our early warning and antimissile defense systems therefore require greater attention.

## Forces for Limited War

To provide the mobile units essential for limited war, additional troop lift should be authorized in the form of both modern aircraft and modern ships.

The Army should be permitted to speed up the modernization of its weapons and of its division structure.

## Navy

Antisubmarine warfare requires additional funds. The program of equipping both surface and underwater ships with missiles of various types should be accelerated. We require a large number of modern, nuclear-powered submarines.

## Personnel

With the complexity of modern weapons, the importance of a highly competent professional force has never been greater. But despite recent increases, present pay scales are inadequate to retain the skilled officers and men necessary to an effective and economic military establishment. Neither are we attracting a sufficient number of the best of our youth to military careers.

## Civil Defense

A start should be made without delay on a program of fallout shelters and related warning and communications equipment.

## Mutual Assistance

The re-equipping of allied forces, particularly in NATO, with modern weapons should be speeded up.

## THE LEVEL OF EFFORT

The above deficiencies in our strategic posture can be removed only by substantially increased defense expenditures. These increases will run into billions of dollars and must rise substantially in each of the next few years. This panel does not possess the data to determine the precise budgetary level. The best testimony it has heard indicates that the deficiencies noted above will require successive additions on the order of $3 billion each year for the next several fiscal years. This figure does not cover the necessary increases in mutual assistance programs and in civilian defense. Because we must maintain our present forces, particularly of manned planes, even while we go into production on new weapons, such as missiles, the cost of military programs will continue to rise with no leveling-off likely before 1965.

This is a heavy burden, even though its effects will be cushioned by the expected growth of our gross national product. The impact of defense spending on our national economy will be discussed by Panel IV. It is worth noting here that the proposed increases in expenditures will be ineffective or reduced in value if national policies permit any important reduction in the purchasing power of the dollar.

The price of survival, then, is not low. This panel is convinced, however, that the increases in defense expenditures are essential and fully justified provided that the greater expenditure is coupled with increased efficiency. We can afford to survive.

## THE BUDGETARY PROCESS

An increased defense effort will not be fully effective unless it is accompanied by the organizational changes outlined in Section VI. These in turn can be prompted by improvements in existing methods of presenting the budget.

The budgetary process could be greatly improved if military budgets were prepared and presented in more discriminating terms. The present method of preparation does not give the President, the Secretary of Defense, Congress, or the public a clear indication of what the funds requested will accomplish in terms of military missions or effective units. As a result, it is natural for Congress to make reductions by percentage cuts across-the-board without the opportunity for a full examination of the effect on strategy and military missions.

Complete budgetary reform may not be immediately feasible. However, a start can be made toward a system that corresponds more closely to a coherent strategic doctrine. It should not be too difficult, for example, to restate the presentation of the service budgets so that instead of the present categories of "procurement," "operation and maintenance," "military personnel," etc., there would be a much better indication of how much goes, for example, to strategic air, to air defense, to antisubmarine warfare, and so on.

Another highly desirable change is to transform the present one-year budget cycle to two years. Under present rules, the top personnel of the services spend a great part of six months of every year preparing, justifying, and revising the budgetary requests of their departments. Much of the next six months are consumed in testifying before Congressional committees and otherwise defending the service budgets as approved by the President. If the budgetary process would extend over an entire Congressional term, the energies of key personnel could be directed toward strategic doctrine and over-all management. At the same time, Congressional control would be more meaningful because the examination of requests could then be more careful.

# XII. Conclusion

No aspect of America's problems presents a deeper challenge than the field of national security. It is not only because the technical problems are so complex, though an accelerating technology will test severely our wisdom and our ability to make choices. Nor is the economic challenge the most complicated one we face, though the price of security in the nuclear age is high and likely to increase. It is not even the field of strategic doctrine that presents our deepest problem, though military strength is sterile without a doctrine for employing it.

Rather our long-run difficulty resides in our approach to the problem of the role of force. We like to believe that reasonable men can settle all disputes through good will and compromise and that power should be invoked only as a last resort. We therefore tend to think of diplomacy and force as successive and separate phases of national policy. Unfortunately, the position in which we find ourselves does not permit such absolute distinctions. In a revolutionary period, the ability and willingness to use force may in itself provide a factor of stability. To a world threatened by aggression and infiltration, American strength and resolution are essential if there is to be a guarantee of security.

To be sure, this may not always be apparent in the public declarations of other nations. To countries primarily concerned with domestic development, foreign aggression may seem unreal and the measures required to resist it may appear as irritating interruptions of more primary tasks. But while we should have full understanding for the psychology which produces these reactions, we would be wrong to gear our policy to it. Force will not solve the problems of this period, but the resolution to use it if necessary may afford the breathing spell in which nations can work out their own destiny without foreign interference. We must not forget that the neutrality of many nations is possible only as long as we are strong, just as for a century and a half the British Navy made possible our American neutrality. Many of our most vocal critics would be deeply troubled were the protection of our military strength suddenly withdrawn.

Power is a fact whether it be ours or that of the Soviet Union. Its existence cannot be ignored. The dilemmas that it imposes cannot be wished away. Yet the destructiveness of modern weapons confronts us with a moral dilemma. The extensive and indiscriminate use of modern weapons in war runs counter to our deepest sense of private and public morality. We should seek to prevent war and to limit it, if it breaks out, to the smallest area, terminate it as rapidly and decisively as possible, and conduct it with the minimum loss of life. Yet in a conflict between despotism and freedom, it would be immoral were we to shrink from an adequate defense of the values for which we stand. The very shrinking may serve to precipitate armed conflict.

We are engaged in the phase of a global struggle that has come to be known as the cold war. In this report we have tried to set forth measures that we feel are imperative in the interest of national security. We consider them essential if we are to reduce the likelihood of war and to make sure that if in spite of all our efforts war should be forced upon us, we shall not be overwhelmed by it.

The cold war poses a twofold dilemma. In our desire for peace, we must not overlook the importance of power in maintaining it. But once we have recognized the role of force we must forever beware that it does not become an end in itself. The more drastic the consequences of modern war, the more we must make certain that we are true to the principles the defense of which alone justifies resort to force. These are facts that we must never forget in the middle of the cold war.

When the security of the United States and of the free world is at stake, cost cannot be the basic consideration. The cold war cannot be won and a "hot" war cannot be avoided without a major effort. This is clearly not a time for complacency; it is just as clearly not a time for hysteria. *What is required throughout the country is an attitude of sustained and informed determination.* If this report makes a contribution to the emergence of such an attitude, it will have served its purpose.

Report III

# FOREIGN ECONOMIC POLICY FOR THE TWENTIETH CENTURY

(First published June 16, 1958)

# Introduction by Panel III

This report seeks to outline a structure for a free world that gives effect to the interdependence of nations and that makes possible the achievement of the aspirations of its peoples. We believe this to be the economic challenge of the mid-twentieth century.

We live in a period that has the task of rebuilding an international order and of establishing new international economic relationships. While we have devoted considerable attention to the Soviet threat, we have not derived the justification for our foreign economic policy from it. A structure cannot be built primarily on motives of negation. Its sole justification cannot be merely to prevent an expansion of the Soviet sphere.

We are convinced that it is not sufficient to construe the end of foreign policy simply as the procurement of military security. It is not enough to base foreign economic policy on the need for meeting emergencies requiring instant action; in fact, one of the purposes of a sound policy is to prevent emergencies from arising. Nor is foreign economic policy important simply because of United States reliance on foreign resources—considerable as this is. The free world confronts a deeper challenge than mere survival. The impetus behind our efforts must always be the things we believe much more than those we reject. We should consider our efforts not as an act of benevolence but of partnership. The challenge is therefore to our sense of purpose and to our values. The heritage of freedom and the tradition of faith in human dignity depend on our response.

This report is the result of a group effort by Panel III of the Special Studies Project. Although not every member of the panel subscribes to every detail, it reflects our substantial agreement.

*MILTON KATZ, director, International Legal Studies, Harvard Law School. Former Ambassador and chief in Europe of the Marshall Plan; chairman and U.S. member, Defense Financial and Economic Committee under NATO; U.S. representative, Economic Commission for Europe; U.S. executive officer, combined Production and Resources Board; chairman of Panel III.

* ADOLF A. BERLE, JR., senior partner, Berle, Berle and Brunner; former Assistant Secretary of State and Ambassador to Brazil.

*CHESTER BOWLES, former Ambassador to India and former Governor of Connecticut.

HARLAN CLEVELAND, dean, Maxwell Graduate School of Citizenship and Public Affairs, Syracuse University; former assistant director for Europe, Mutual Security Agency.

* JOHN COWLES, president, *Minneapolis Star and Tribune*; chairman, *The Des Moines Register and Tribune*.

FREDERICK H. HARBISON, director, Industrial Relations Section, and professor of economics, Princeton University.

STACY MAY, economist.

DAVID ROCKEFELLER, vice-chairman, board of directors, The Chase Manhattan Bank.

MAX WESTON THORNBURG, foreign industrial consultant.

FORREST D. MURDEN, Ford International; special assistant to Mr. Henry Ford II; former economic adviser to the U. S. Delegation to the United Nations; secretary to Panel III.


William F. Butler, vice-president, Economic Research Department, The Chase Manhattan Bank, and Richard N. Gardner, associate professor of law, Columbia University, were consultants to the panel in the preparation of this report.

* Also Overall Panel members.

# I. The Challenge

The world's present disorders often seem as a series of unrelated crises. Actually they reflect disintegration of a whole system of relationships, which once provided nations with some measure of stability both in politics and in economics. Enormous transformations in human aspirations, in the structure of societies, in science and technology, have reshaped events at unprecedented speed.

All over the world, social and economic conditions taken for granted for centuries have come to seem intolerable. Economic and social growth have become matters of primary concern everywhere. These aspirations for growth, if they are based on respect for national and human dignity, can become the basis of a new and more enduring world community.

The challenge, then, is to build a new structure that will make possible the fulfillment of the basic purposes of humanity. The well-being and the prosperity of every nation will depend to an increasing degree on its participation in a complex of nations designed to satisfy awakening human aspirations. No country—not even the United States—can meet the expectations of its people or continue to grow merely by developing and using its own resources alone. The free world must devise the institutions for a world community in which free societies may flourish and free men have the opportunity to realize their potentialities as human beings.

There is every reason why Americans should take the lead in meeting this challenge. Our own development has been marked by a belief in growth and in the use of this growth to enhance individual well-being. This belief reflects our own deepest aspirations. Our task now is to project more effectively our historic concerns to the world scene. For values, if they are meaningful, transcend national boundaries. Our participation in world economic and social progress is important from the point of view of our own economy and that of the free world. It is crucial from the point of view of our survival and the survival of freedom everywhere. Such participation is imposed by our deepest beliefs.

It is imperative that we become clear about the nature of our responsibilities. We have lacked a clear vision of free world institutions, which make the increasing interdependence of societies a source of mutual strength. Now such vision is essential. In the absence of a comprehensive and well-defined purpose, our actions have often seemed fitful and have not always been meaningful. The challenge, therefore, to our foreign economic policy is to develop a concept for an international structure within which the basic human objectives can be realized, to understand our responsibilities with respect to it, and then work steadily toward achieving it.

# II. The Nature of the Problem

A sound United States foreign economic policy must be based on accurate assessment of the world in which it must operate.

## DISINTEGRATION OF THE NINETEENTH-CENTURY POLITICAL SYSTEM

The central political fact of our time is the disintegration of the international system that dominated world affairs almost until the outbreak of World War II. Until the turn of the century, thirteen empires ruled the world. The neutrality of the Western Hemisphere—as of many regions today—depended on the existence of an equilibrium maintained by other states. This balance of power saw to it that most transformations were relatively minor; they did not threaten or seem to threaten the survival of the states composing the international system.

The nineteenth-century international system, for all its failings, provided order, rationalized administration, and arrangements for economic exchange. It supplied a form of answer to the increasing interdependence of societies. Europe was the world's principal manufacturer and the principal user of raw materials. She was the world's primary banker and source of capital. People, goods, and money moved with relative freedom from country to country; and Europe's banks financed the exchange of goods. The gold standard maintained by a central banking policy of the principal powers made for a kind of common currency.

The internal stresses of the imperial system began to be apparent in the nineteenth century and became conspicuous in 1914. World War I led to the collapse of the German, Austrian, Turkish, and Russian empires. By 1955, most of the remaining imperialist systems had dissolved. The nineteenth-century system of empires, as a means of maintaining world order, arranging world economics, and settling international disputes, has collapsed.

Twenty new sovereign nations have come into being since the end of World War II. More will undoubtedly emerge in the next decade. While fulfilling their aspirations to national sovereignty, these nations face new problems. At a moment when the pressures of the contemporary period impel greater and greater interdependence, the newly independent nations are driven or tempted to erect self-sufficient economies, which tend to restrict the broad markets essential for industrialization. One system of organizing the international order has been destroyed without replacement by another. The diverging forces of nationalism must be balanced by converging forces seeking to bring about a free association of nations so that political, social, and economic co-operation can transcend national boundaries. Simón Bolívar, the great Latin American liberator, expressed this principle of interdependence of free nations more than a century ago. He saw that as the young republics of the Western Hemisphere achieved their independence, some new system of free association would be needed.

Twice within a generation the United States has been instrumental in bringing a world organization into being: the League of Nations in 1919 (though we refused to join) and the United Nations in 1945. In both instances the impetus was the belief that the interdependence of nations, demonstrated in two catastrophic wars, had to find an institutional expression. In each case high hopes were not fully realized because the formal institutions of the world organizations were designed to achieve more than the consensus of existing shared aspirations was prepared to support. The emergence of revolutionary dictatorships in Germany, Italy, and Russia after World War I and the pressures of Communist expansionism since the end of World War II frustrated many hopes. The existence of a group of powers seeking to undermine the free world has thus far prevented the United Nations from giving effective expression of a consensus of humanity.

This international organization has been hampered in many of its functions by the schism between the Communist and the free world. This has not decreased the importance of striving to realize its potential. But it has increased the importance of other group-ings, regional and functional. After World War II, Europe dra-matically led the way toward new groupings such as the European Coal and Steel Community, the European Atomic Energy Com-munity (Euratom), the European Common Market (Euromart), and the European Payments Union. The same process has begun to take place elsewhere.

Multinational structures, regional or functional, require con-tinuous and imaginative attention, as well as political institutions based on common goals, if they are to succeed. The structures must become a primary concern of American policy, for in this development, national interests and idealistic hopes can converge. Provided we have the vision and courage, solutions and institutions can evolve into a great design. The twentieth century is attempt-ing to replace national and international systems of the nineteenth century; it must seek to do so with more understanding of its goals, so that human ideals and practical requirements can both be achieved.

## THE WORLD-WIDE SOCIAL REVOLUTION

Until the end of the eighteenth century, mankind accepted the view that poverty and want were no more to be questioned than illness and death. In the pyramid of each society—it was assumed—some would be born to wealth or power; a very few might rise to it. But for the mass of mankind, a man's station was fixed by tradition. The vast majority could hope at best for subsistence.

In the late eighteenth century, the inevitability of this social order was challenged and with it the validity of the political sys-tems that maintained it. The philosophers of the Enlightenment proclaimed the doctrine of the *political* equality of all men; the British, French, and American revolutions created institutional expressions of these beliefs. During the next century most nations of the Western world—with the notable exception of Russia—followed suit.

The concept of equality was not at first extended to economics. On the contrary, the economic life of society was considered to be outside the sphere of governmental action. The advocates of po-litical reform saw their task in sweeping away the old mercantile system and the regulation of enterprise by government charter.

It was thought that the absence of political restraint would automatically produce economic well-being.

Within a generation, to the original eighteenth-century postulate of political liberty was added the concept that economic liberty—in the sense of freedom from economic oppression and from extremes of want—was a necessary condition for the preservation of political liberty.

The industrial revolution gave substance to these ideals. Mass production drastically reduced the costs of manufactured articles. More efficient methods of distribution stimulated wide consumption. Mass media of communication contributed to creating common patterns of taste. Over the years the notion that industrialization could first end extremes of want and then bring about a more or less general condition of well-being became increasingly plausible. Universal suffrage gave impetus to this belief in Western Europe and the United States; expanding world trade spread it all over the globe.

Economic possibility was translated into urgency under the impact of the great depression of the 1930s. Many governments were forced to intervene to a greater extent in the economic life of their people. It came to be generally accepted that the government shared in the responsibility for the alleviation of distress and for preventing excessive fluctuations in economic conditions. This movement gained added impetus through the two world wars. Modern war brought with it the need for sustained and conscious governmental direction of the economic effort. There was, in addition, a widespread tendency to seek to maintain the needed productive effort and patience in the face of suffering by bright hopes for a peacetime world.

As a result of all these factors, there came about by the end of World War II an almost universal demand for a better standard of living to be achieved through political action, if purely economic efforts proved insufficient. In the United States, where the gap between aspirations and reality was smallest, this demand was at its mildest—but it was unmistakably evident in such concerns as legislation for full employment, veterans' pensions and education, and a renewed impulse toward racial equality. In other nations, where the gap between reality and aspirations was larger, demands took on increasingly revolutionary overtones—the revolution of rising expectations became a dominant current in contemporary affairs.

America cannot stand aloof from this revolution. It was produced in the first place by the liberal doctrines of the West, of which we are ourselves a product and an example. It was made possible by a system of industrialization that has been coupled with growing social responsibility. Unless their future offers a realistic prospect of economic growth and social betterment, many nations will prove receptive to schemes that promise economic and social progress at the sacrifice of other great values.

## THE LESS DEVELOPED NATIONS: RISING EXPECTATIONS AND POPULATION GROWTH

The social revolution is particularly pressing in the less developed regions of the world. There, many nations are seeking to achieve, in a generation and under extremely difficult conditions, a development that took a century in the now industrialized states. Industrialization is impossible without either domestic savings—that is, a measure of sacrifice in the present for the sake of the future—or foreign investment. Generally it requires both. Yet the areas where the gap between aspirations and reality is greatest are also the very countries in which it is typically most difficult to encourage domestic savings or where conditions are often too unsettled to attract foreign investment.

Similarly, these countries also frequently lack the social and political institutions that are essential for sustained growth: adequate medical and educational facilities, power and transportation, efficient government services. Finally, the regions most in need of capital also are often handicapped by the absence of a tradition of enterprise, a trained labor force, or an adequate market system.

Attaining rapidly a higher level of economic and social well-being goes far beyond increasing a given level of capital investment. The experience of the Marshall Plan with respect to the relationship between economic well-being and political stability is not necessarily applicable to other areas. In Europe the institutions of democracy had grown up over centuries; the administrations were competent; the national consciousness was well developed. The danger to these institutions was the gap between economic reality and the hopes of society. An improvement in economic conditions could therefore be expected to have a stabilizing effect. It did not transform the social order. By improving the conditions of life, it restored confidence in the political framework.

The situation is more complicated when political and social revolutions are occurring side by side, as in the case of many of the newly independent nations. Here, the overthrow of the colonial rule involves at the same time the collapse of the existing political framework and often of the social framework as well. As a result, economic, social, and political institutions must be built anew, side by side. The process of transition in most of the newly developing countries involves an attempt to replace the disintegrating colonial or indigenous feudal rule with new institutions. Moreover, we need to recognize that to the extent economic development is successful, it may well have politically unsettling effects. Many traditional institutions become obsolete. New patterns of organization—economic, social, and political—are required. As the economy expands, its demands for talent will multiply. An increasingly wide base of education becomes necessary.

The world-wide social and economic revolution is made even more acute by the explosive increase in the world's population. Ever since 1650, the world's population has been increasing at an ever-accelerating rate. From 1940 to 1955, for example, the annual percentage increase was twice the rate of the period between 1850 and 1900. Since the base of the population is growing, the rising percentage increase involves huge numbers. In the short space of thirty-five years, between 1920 and 1955, the total increase in the world's population was greater than the entire world population of 1750. If the rate of growth between 1900 and 1950 is maintained, the world's population will increase by at least a third in the next generation, or by about one billion. In recent years, the rate of growth has been even greater.

Among the causes of this increase are advances in public health and related factors, which have produced a startling drop in the mortality rate and extension of life expectancy, while the birth rate has remained relatively constant. The impact of this increase is particularly pronounced in the less developed countries, where population growth often threatens to outstrip gains in productivity. A number of these countries face the paradoxical situation in

# GROWTH OF WORLD POPULATION
## in millions of persons

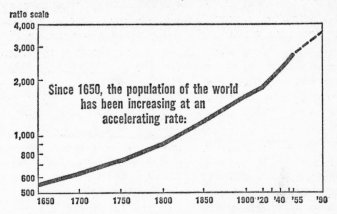

ratio scale

Since 1650, the population of the world
has been increasing at an
accelerating rate:

4,000
3,000
2,000
1,000
800
600
500

1650  1700  1750  1800  1850  1900 '20 '40 '55  '90

## Rates of growth have varied widely among countries:

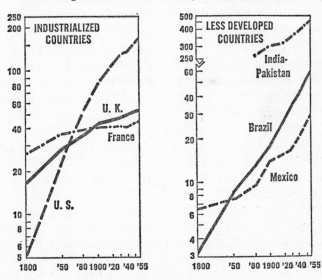

**INDUSTRIALIZED COUNTRIES**

250
200
100
80
60
40
20
10
8
6
5

U. K.
France
U. S.

1800  '50  '80 1900 '20  '40 '55

**LESS DEVELOPED COUNTRIES**

500
400
300
250
60
40
30
20
10
8
6
4
3

India-Pakistan
Brazil
Mexico

1800  '50  '80 1900 '20  '40 '55

Sources: W. S. Woytinsky and E. S. Woytinsky,
*World Population and Production;*
United Nations Statistical Office

which the standard of living may drop despite a considerable increase in the gross national product.

This experience differs from that of similar periods in Europe and the United States. Because in Europe the greatest increase in population occurred only *after* a considerable amount of economic development had been achieved, it was possible not only to absorb the growing labor force but also to increase the standard of living. The United States had the advantage of virgin regions so that increases in population led to the settlement of new lands and the development of natural resources. In Europe and the United States, economic development and population growth therefore tended to reinforce each other.

It is different, however, in most of the currently less developed regions, with the exception of much of Latin America. The relation of population to resources in most contemporary agrarian nations is much less favorable than was the case in Western Europe in the eighteenth or early nineteenth century or in North America at any time. It is therefore extremely difficult in many of the less developed countries to raise national income to keep pace with population growth, much less to improve the standard of living. Thus these countries will have to increase their production very rapidly simply to maintain existing living standards.

The restlessness produced in a rapidly growing population is magnified by the predominance of youth. In Algeria, for example, the age group under twenty-five represents 61 per cent of the population and in Burma 55 per cent, as compared with 43 per cent in the United States and 38 per cent in France. In a comparatively youthful population, impatience to realize rising expectations is likely to be pronounced. Extreme nationalism has often been the result.

No assessment of the contemporary scene can ignore this mushrooming increase of population and the awakened aspirations of the less developed areas. They are possibly the greatest incentives today for speeding up the development of resources, the growing industrialization and power development, the expansion of educational opportunities for young people. The challenge is political, social, and spiritual, as well as economic. Unless economic growth goes hand in hand with the creation of institutions that safeguard respect for human dignity, industrialization will have merely succeeded in creating more efficient means of oppression. The ultimate worth of economic development will be determined by the convictions and purposes of men.

## THE INDUSTRIAL NATIONS
## OF THE FREE WORLD

The transformations of the postwar period challenge not only the less developed regions. Many of the industrialized nations are undergoing painful adaptations to positions of diminished power and influence. This requires psychological adjustments that may be even more difficult than economic adaptations. In the light of the magnitude and intricacy of the task, it is remarkable how much has been accomplished. Western Europe, at first hesitantly but with gathering momentum, has sought to compensate for a decline in its political influence overseas by strengthening its own internal relationships. Japan has established new political and economic relationships to replace the former imperial pattern.

Major problems emerge. The great industrial complex of Western Europe supports a dense population at a very adequate living standard despite an insufficient base of agricultural land, fuel, and raw materials. For the most part, it fabricates largely imported raw materials and sells overseas enough of its output to cover the food and fuel deficits and to pay for the raw materials. For this sector of the world, high levels of international trade—assured supplies of fuel and materials and ample markets—are essential. Japan's position is similar but even more acute. Her living standard is the highest in Asia although the relationship of population to resources is far poorer even than Europe's.

The crucial political importance of these areas can be taken for granted. What cannot be taken for granted is an international structure in which their economies can continue to flourish. Western Europe's industrial pre-eminence was gravely weakened by World War I and the great depression, and transformed beyond recognition by World War II. Europe's economic security today depends on two indispensable factors: (1) her own intellectual and technical vitality and economic enterprise; and (2) an international structure that will enable Europe to have access to foreign markets on fair terms and adequate supplies of materials if Europe can offer reasonable value in return for them.

Whatever doubts may have existed in the immediate postwar years as to Europe's technical vitality, economic enterprise, and political inventiveness have been laid to rest by the extraordinary record of the last decade. Once catalyzed by Marshall Plan aid, the European economy has moved from strength to strength. German recovery is widely acclaimed as a miracle, but similar miracles have been achieved in Britain, France, Italy, Austria, the Low Countries, and Scandinavia. Japan, supporting an enlarged population in a much smaller homeland, has also made an extraordinary economic recovery.

Nevertheless, the economic situation of the industrialized nations remains precarious. If Asian, Middle Eastern, and African nationalism, exploited by the Soviet bloc, becomes a destructive force, European supplies of oil and other essential raw materials may be jeopardized. Moreover, the Soviet Union is increasingly resorting to economic warfare designed, it would seem, to disrupt Western trade through systematic market raids.

Also, while the acute dollar shortage of the immediate postwar years has been alleviated, total United States exports of goods and services still exceed imports by $6.6 billion. The difference has been made up by United States private investment abroad, economic assistance programs, its expenditures overseas for military bases, and by troop pay spent abroad. Even so, the demand for American goods has so far outstripped available dollar supplies that there has been continuing recourse in various countries to import quotas and exchange controls. Free convertibility for the major nondollar currencies has yet to be achieved. The growth of foreign gold and dollar reserves has still to reach a point where liquid balances could readily cover normal fluctuations in international trade and financial conditions.*

Even the precarious balance is dependent on sustained growth of the American economy and on American foreign economic policy. The dollar reserves of our industrial allies could be reduced below the essential minimum by any one of three developments: a prolonged recession in the United States; a curtailment of foreign assistance programs; or a shift of the United States away from its Reciprocal Trade Agreement policy.

* Written in June 1958.

A great deal depends therefore on developing an international structure which reflects the interdependence of countries, large and small, industrialized and less developed. Europe and Japan, together with the United States, supply most of the machinery and equipment and capital investment required by the less developed countries for their industrialization. The less developed countries in turn supply an increasing percentage of the raw materials and commodities required by the industrialized nations. It is necessary to establish a structure that gives effect to this partnership. An essential component will be an increasingly liberal United States trade policy, which will permit other nations to sell in American markets.

## THE COMMUNIST THREAT

The world-wide social revolution, the pressure of rising expectations, the problems of population growth, and the readjustment of industrial societies are a sufficient challenge by themselves, but they are given particular urgency because of the existence of a militant world-wide Communist movement, centered in Moscow and Peiping, eager to exploit all dissatisfactions and to organize all grievances. Whereas the impetus of the revolution of rising expectations derives from the liberal values of the West, that of the Communist empire is built on a negation of these values. While giving lip service to democratic ideals and concepts for over a generation, Communist leaders have stubbornly maintained their implacable hostility to the free world.

Their irreconcilability has been maintained through all the fluctuations of Soviet policy. It was characteristically affirmed in Khrushchev's report to the Supreme Soviet in November 1957, when he said: ". . . we, of course, have no intention of asserting that there are no contradictions between socialism and capitalism. The ideological differences are irreconcilable. They will continue to exist." Even periods during which Soviet leaders proclaim a doctrine of peaceful coexistence have never had more than a tactical significance—to encompass more surely the downfall of the free world. The "spirit of Geneva" did not stand in the way of Soviet maneuvers to magnify Middle Eastern tensions. The moral outrage of the world did not prevent the brutal suppression of the revolt in Hungary. The Soviet and Chinese Communist leaders are not concerned with fulfilling individual human aspirations. They see their task in exploiting or even generating grievances and in maximizing dissatisfactions.

The insidiousness of the Soviet strength derives in part from their skill in *appearing* all over the world as defenders of the very values that have given us our strength: freedom, human dignity, and national sovereignty. To be sure, these terms have a different meaning in Communist vocabulary, but the difference is often not understood until too late. At the same time, the success of communism's attempt to steal the vocabulary of freedom could come about because the concepts of freedom, human dignity, and social justice are too often used without a sense of inner conviction in the free world. No more important task confronts all nations of the free world than to give more concrete meaning to the values they profess.

Another source of initial Soviet strength resides in part in the difference in time scale between tasks of construction and efforts of disruption. The challenge before the free world is to bring about a new international order. To fulfill aspirations, to build for economic and social growth, to bring about a new international structure based on consent requires patient and sustained efforts, the results of which are rarely immediate. To fan dissatisfaction, on the other hand, to sharpen tensions, is relatively simple and can be done rather quickly. Even in the best of circumstances and with the wisest policy, it will not be an easy matter to overcome the Soviet policy of disruption and negation carried on under the constant threat of growing Soviet military might and its policies of subversion.

The Soviet Union has recently begun an increasingly aggressive program of economic penetration into a few countries that have been assigned high political priority. The period was ushered in by Stalin's last theoretical pronouncement, an article in *Bolshevik* in October 1952. In it he argues that the expansion of the Soviet sphere was bound to accelerate the disintegration of the capitalistic economic system. As the market available to the free world shrank, Stalin said, the competition among the capitalist states would grow ever fiercer. It was the task of communism, so the argument ran, to aggravate tensions by keeping up unremitting pressure and by disrupting economic relationships within the free world as much as possible.

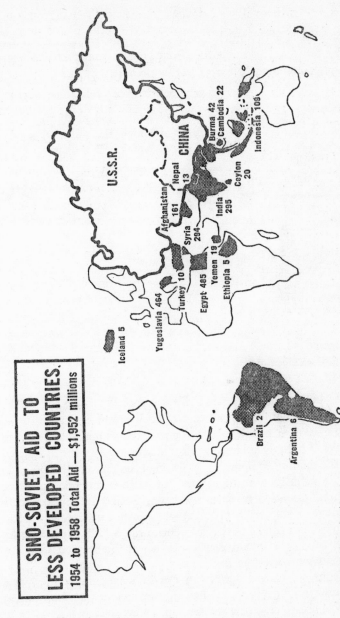

SINO-SOVIET AID TO
LESS DEVELOPED COUNTRIES.
1954 to 1958 Total Aid — $1,952 millions

U.S.S.R.

CHINA

Burma 42
Cambodia 22
Indonesia 109
Nepal 13
Ceylon 20
India 295
Afghanistan 161
Syria 294
Turkey 10
Yemen 19
Egypt 485
Ethiopia 5
Yugoslavia 464
Iceland 5

Brazil 2
Argentina 6

Source: U.S. Dept. of State

## Soviet Aid

Sino-Soviet aid promised (only a small part has been delivered) to the less developed countries from January 1, 1954, to February 1, 1958, amounted to $1,952 million as follows:*

|  |  | Millions of Dollars |
|---|---:|---|
| Egypt | 485 | (of which 250 military) |
| Syria | 294 | (of which 100 military) |
| Yemen | 19 | (of which 3 military) |
| India | 295 | |
| Afghanistan | 161 | (of which 25 military) |
| Indonesia | 109 | |
| Nepal | 13 | |
| Ceylon | 20 | |
| Burma | 42 | |
| Cambodia | 22 | |
| Yugoslavia | 464 | |
| Turkey | 10 | |
| Ethiopia | 5 | |
| Other | 13 | |
| Total | 1,952 | |

* U. S. Department of State.

The political intent behind this program is apparent from the figures. For example, 44 per cent of total Soviet assistance to the Middle Eastern countries was for military equipment. The percentage of military aid in this program is even larger if it is realized that the military equipment has already been delivered while probably no more than 10 to 15 per cent of the economic assistance has been disbursed to date. Moreover, Soviet assistance is concentrated geographically in areas that promise a maximum political return: almost half of Soviet aid went to the Middle East. Another 24 per cent went to Yugoslavia with which the Soviet Union was then striving to restore relations.

Credits are extended with an eye to maximum political and psychological effectiveness. They are usually announced on formal political occasions. Their volume appears deceptively large because even though the credit may extend over a five to ten year period, it is the *total* amount of the loan that has been publicized. Soviet loans are usually accompanied by the offer of technicians. And they are often extended for projects that have maximum conspicuousness.

## Communist Bloc Trade

The question of United States policy toward Soviet bloc trade is a very real one that must be faced realistically. The Communist nations have not in the past participated in any substantial degree in world trade, partly because of the nature of their economies, partly because of political reasons. Although the Soviet bloc produces about 25 per cent of the world's goods and services, as a whole it accounts for only about 10 per cent of world trade. It is interesting to note that trade with the Soviet bloc in 1956 accounted for less than 3 per cent of the $49 billion combined import and export trade of the less developed free world nations.

More recently, however, the Soviet Union has been engaging in a vigorous program to expand its trade with the newly developing regions. Although most of the publicity has concerned recent trade overtures made by the U.S.S.R., the latter's volume of trade with the less developed areas is considerably smaller than that of its satellites or even that of Communist China. But regardless of which segment of the Soviet bloc is making the trade overtures, they are being used in a concerted effort to disrupt the historic ties between these less developed countries and the industrialized nations of the democratic West. The objective is clearly one of economic and political domination.

Through an ever-increasing number of trade and clearing agreements with countries in Asia, Africa, and Latin America, the Soviet bloc has been bidding on a barter basis, with machinery, equipment, cement, aluminum, or other processed materials and supplies, for surplus agricultural products or industrial raw materials. As a result, the volume of Soviet bloc trade with the free world has shown considerable expansion. Although Soviet trade accounts for only a minor fraction of the total foreign trade of the less developed areas as a whole, it has had a considerable impact on the relatively few countries upon which it has been focused.

### TRADE OF VARIOUS COUNTRIES WITH
### COMMUNIST BLOC—1956

| | Exports to Communist Bloc | Imports from Communist Bloc |
|---|---|---|
| | (Percentages are of total exports or imports of each country) | |
| Egypt | 34% | 14% |
| Yugoslavia | 24 | 23 |
| Burma | 14 | 19 |
| Turkey | 20 | 15 |
| Iran | 17 | 10 |
| Ceylon | 11 | 9 |
| Syria | 8 | 4 |
| Pakistan | 6 | 0.3 |

Source: U. S. International Cooperation Administration.

To most of the above countries, trade with the Soviet bloc has assumed proportions that indicate a continuing degree of dependence rather than a casual or transient bargaining incident.

It is important for us to recognize that trade competition from the Soviet bloc has not had, and for many years to come probably cannot generate, the capacity to supply a substantial portion of import needs and export outlets of the less developed countries. The competition that it offers is essentially political. Piecemeal competition, on a selective basis, fits readily into its political strategy of gaining a foothold in the less industrialized nations, one by one. The economy and resources of the Soviet bloc are ample for such purposes and for a considerable expansion beyond what it has so far attempted.

It is probable that this competition will be intensified. Since the particular offers will be designed to accomplish political rather than economic ends, they need not necessarily be restricted to exchanges that are mutually profitable. To be sure, the willingness to maintain terms that are economically disadvantageous to the U.S.S.R. would disappear once the ties of dependence had been forged. But once the ties exist, they can be used to increase further the economic dependence of the less developed world.

Thus, the Soviet trade offensive is a powerful weapon to achieve economic domination and political penetration, particularly as long as it can be conducted on a bilateral basis. Small countries that find themselves depending upon the U.S.S.R. for a large portion of their import supplies and export outlets may well find themselves caught in a vise far more restrictive and controlling than any colonial system of the past.

The free world can withstand the impact of the Soviet geopolitical trade offensive, if it organizes itself to do so. The more highly industrialized nations of the free world are linked to the less developed nations by a two-way trade of goods that totals more than $35 billion annually or almost thirty times the amount of trade between the less developed countries and the Communist bloc. By building appropriate international institutions on the solid basis of existing mutual interest, the free world can perpetuate an advantage that lies *overwhelmingly* on its side.

## Exchange of Leaders

Coupled with their trade programs is an increasing emphasis by the Soviet bloc on the exchange of technicians and other personnel. During 1957, 2,000 Soviet bloc technicians were working for periods of one month or more in 19 less developed countries in Asia and Africa. Roughly one third were military technicians. The others (1,375 or more) were civilian technical specialists. The supply of Soviet talent available to be sent abroad is increasing rapidly. The Soviet Union is currently graduating more scientists and engineers than the United States. The U.S.S.R. has no difficulty in inducing personnel to serve abroad; it settles this question by command. Its emphasis on five-year language training helps to insure that most Soviet personnel in foreign countries speak the language of the areas to which they are assigned. Moreover, living conditions for these specialists abroad are more comparable to those to which they are accustomed at home than is the case with American personnel.

At the same time, a growing number of people from free world Asian countries are being brought to the Soviet Union or China for academic study, in-service training, and guided tours. In 1957, over 2,000 such technicians, professional people, and students went to Soviet bloc countries for study and indoctrination. A series of agreements have been negotiated to increase this number. All these factors combine to make their psychological impact an increasingly potent force.

## Conclusion

While the Soviet threat in the field of foreign economic policy is potentially formidable, it must be seen in its proper perspective. It is menacing to the degree that the cohesion of the free world is inadequate.

The selective economic program of the Soviet Union is politically effective primarily to the extent that weak countries must face the strong Soviet economy alone. If these countries are part of larger groupings, they will be able to resist pressure more easily and negotiate on a more nearly equal basis.

The Soviet effort is impressive primarily because the free world has failed to develop a workable structure within which the industrialized and newly developing regions can co-operate in fulfilling the aspirations of their peoples. We must contribute to the growth and cohesiveness of the community of free nations, not merely because we wish to prevent an expansion of the Soviet sphere, but because we want to co-operate in bringing about a new international system dedicated to peace, to human dignity, and to respect for national independence.

## UNITED STATES TIES WITH THE WORLD ECONOMY

In 1956, total United States private investment and economic assistance abroad, excluding all military assistance, amounted to over $6.6 billion. As a result, in 1956, foreign countries were able to obtain $6.6 billion more of goods and services from this country than the United States purchased from them through commercial transactions. In addition, foreign holdings of gold and dollars increased by more than $500 million.

This compares with a flow of development loans from the Soviet bloc to the free world nations valued at about $200 million in 1956—3 per cent of the United States figure.

The following table presents *net* United States private commitments abroad (including reinvested earnings) and *net* United

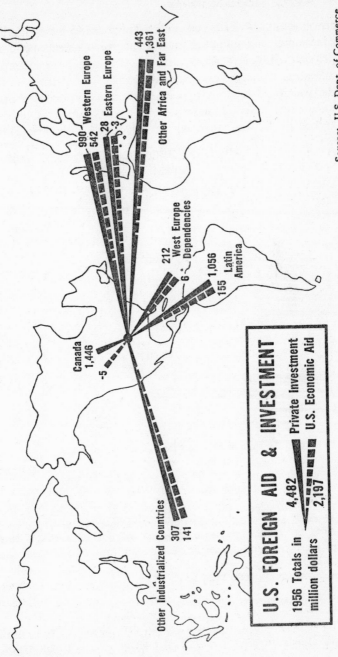

U.S. FOREIGN AID & INVESTMENT

1956 Totals in million dollars

Private Investment 4,482
U.S. Economic Aid 2,197

Western Europe 990 / 542
Eastern Europe 28 / -3
Other Africa and Far East 443 / 1,361
West Europe Dependencies 212 / 6
Latin America 1,056 / 155
Canada 1,446 / -5
Other Industrialized Countries 307 / 141

Source: U.S. Dept. of Commerce

States government grants and credits. The statistics differ from the conventional presentation in the balance of payments accounts, which omit reinvested earnings and net out a variety of transactions representing money flows in both directions. The statistics in the table, which are derived from official accounts, present a more representative order of magnitude of recent United States performance in this field than do the balance of payments figures.

## U. S. GOVERNMENT ECONOMIC ASSISTANCE AND NET PRIVATE COMMITMENTS ABROAD—1956

### (Millions of U. S. Dollars)

|  | From U. S. Private Sources | From U. S. Gov't | Total from U. S. |
|---|---|---|---|
| 1.  To Free World Industrialized Countries | 2,743 | 678 | 3,421 |
| a.  Western Europe | 990 | 542 | 1,532 |
| b.  Canada | 1,446 | – 5 | 1,441 |
| c.  Other | 307 | 141 | 448 |
| 2.  To Newly Developing Countries: | 1,739 | 1,519 | 3,258 |
| a.  Latin America | 1,056 | 155 | 1,211 |
| b.  Western European Dependencies | 212 | 6 | 218 |
| c.  Independent Countries of Asia, Africa, and Middle East | 443 | 1,361 | 1,804 |
| d.  Eastern Europe | 28 | – 3 | 25 |
| Total—All Areas | 4,482[a] | 2,197[b] | 6,679 |

[a] $2.8 billion in the form of net direct investments by U.S. enterprises, including reinvested earnings; $1.2 billion net portfolio investments in foreign securities and short term loans; and $500 million net remittances of private individuals and philanthropic organizations.

[b] $1.7 billion net nonmilitary grants, including about $1.0 billion of defense support aid—i. e., economic assistance to nations co-operating in the free world defense effort. Three of these countries are included under the Western Europe heading and nine under independent countries of Asia, Africa, and Middle East.

Net short term assistance totaled $0.5 billion.

Source: U. S. Department of Commerce

Almost $4.5 billion of the total United States commitments was privately furnished. United States government grants, credits, and public sales of surplus agricultural products for local currencies (to be used for local economic development) netted about $2.2 billion. In addition, the International Bank for Reconstruction and Development made disbursements of $332 million during fiscal year 1957; and the United States government contributed $15.5 million in 1956 to the United Nations Technical Assistance Program.

Of the total United States capital flow—government and private —$3.3 billion went to the less developed areas in 1956. In addition, the International Bank for Reconstruction and Development made development loans of $184 million to these areas; and Western European capital contributions are estimated at $1.3 billion ($800 million from government sources; $500 million from private capital flows). Thus, the newly developing economies of the free world received almost $5 billion from the industrialized West, compared to $200 million from the Soviet bloc.

The foregoing statistics refer to the *flow* of funds during a single year, 1956. These flows served to augment the *total value* of the investment capital provided through flows of foreign investment over the years. While statistics are not fully available for total free world foreign investment, it is noteworthy that the total value of United States investment abroad at the end of 1956 is estimated at over $49 billion, of which $33 billion was furnished by private sources.

We have been particularly negligent in giving proper weight to the constructive role played by private capital flows. From the tabulation we have presented, it will be seen that over all these are running at a rate that is more than twice the volume of United States government economic assistance, and in the newly developing economies it is of comparable magnitude to the United States government effort. Furthermore, in recent years private foreign investment has been expanding rapidly and broadening its base both geographically and in industrial diversity. Yet it is too often written off as having only secondary importance as an instrument for forwarding economic development in the less industrialized economies. It is our conviction that private investment can carry abroad the dynamism that has characterized the United States economy more effectively than any other means at our command. We should give far more effort than we have in the past to finding ways of encouraging its maximum use for achieving world economic and social development.

In addition to commitments in the financial field, the United States initiated in Latin America the concept of technical assistance some fifteen years ago and has pioneered its development throughout the world in the past decade. At the end of 1957, there were almost 5,000 United States specialists on government assignment in the less developed areas: 381 in Africa; 2,066 in the Far East; 1,529 in the Near East and South Asia; and 883 in Latin America. Most of them were working on agricultural, health, and education programs. Increasingly, technical assistance experts are being sent abroad in the fields of industry operation, transportation, and public administration. The number of nationals from less developed countries who in 1957 were receiving training in the United States under our technical assistance program totaled almost 4,000; and many others received similar training under private auspices.

Thus the effort of the free world industrialized countries, and particularly of the United States, in the less developed regions has clearly been of major significance. Their capital contributions represent about one fourth of the total capital accumulation in these countries. Of the total trade of the newly developing areas, about 75 per cent is with free world industrialized nations; about 25 per cent is with the United States alone.

Nevertheless, the fact must be faced that the present level of total private and government capital flows from the industrialized free world is not nearly enough. Nor is its distribution sufficiently well balanced. Except for a few places, economic growth in the less developed areas is hardly keeping pace with population growth. It is far from sufficient to give a sense of steady progress in raising individual living standards to the peoples of these areas. Since the rate of capital accumulation for the less developed areas is only about $17 billion annually, the additional amount needed to provide a margin between static and genuinely dynamic progress is well within the resources of the industrial free world.

# III. A Twentieth-Century Economic Structure for the Free World

## THE INTERDEPENDENCE OF NATIONS

The cardinal feature of the contemporary world is the ever-growing interdependence of nations. The less developed nations need the industrial equipment and consumer items of technologically advanced nations and markets for their primary products. The industrialized nations depend on these sources of raw materials and food, and they require markets abroad for their manufactured products. Both require markets larger than any individual nation can provide. Because of the weight of the United States economy, perhaps the major contribution we can make to world growth is the maintenance of the vitality, growth, and stability of our own economy.

In the nineteenth century, though the interdependence was somewhat less, the economic cohesion of the world was greater. There was a relatively free flow of goods and money across national boundaries. The movement of peoples was easier. The economic system united by the gold standard worked, however, at a level of economic and social well-being that is no longer acceptable. Nineteenth-century economic and social conditions were accepted partly because it was thought that the resources of the world did not permit much improvement and partly because no higher level had ever been known. Similarly, sharp fluctuations in economic activity, employment, and price levels were regarded as inevitable and acquiesced to with resignation.

None of these conditions holds true any longer. The nineteenth-century system of economic exchange has been disrupted by growing ideas of protectionism and by emergency actions during two wars and a depression. The economic and social conditions of the nineteenth century are no longer acceptable to the peoples of the world. No country will any longer passively submit to market adjustments that, however small from the perspective of the over-all world economy, would shake the economic, social, and political structure of weaker countries. In all free societies, peoples expect their governments to achieve social goals considered outside the scope of government in the nineteenth century. Throughout the world, there exists a conviction that modern science and technology can bring about a fuller and more meaningful life. All nations have a joint interest in a dynamic and growing world economy.

In field after field it has been demonstrated that the small production unit bound by the limits of a restricted market simply cannot compete. Science and technology have developed products that need to draw on materials that are not available within any one narrow geographic area. Not even the widest existing political boundaries are large enough to accommodate or contain the reach of competitive production as it is organized in today's world. For the smaller nations, the modern economic organization that is now a general aspiration is beyond realization unless there is a framework of economic law and accommodation that runs beyond the boundaries of existing political sovereignties.

Any effort to fulfill the aspirations of the peoples of the free world must include institutions that take account of this interdependence. Since World War II, a number of institutions have been developed, many of them representing an effort to create communities that permit the nation-state to enjoy the benefits and assume the responsibilities of participation in a larger complex. These include:

1. The European Coal and Steel Community and now the European Atomic Energy Community. Here segments of the economies of the European powers concerned have found their way into communities that exercise many of the functions formerly carried out on a national basis. Sovereignty appears divisible. Community of action may exist with respect to some functions and not with respect to others. This offers possibilities of cooperative effort barely suspected in the nineteenth century.

2. Communities based on a common market, for example, Benelux (the earliest), comprising Belgium, the Netherlands, and

Luxembourg, and now the European Common Market. Another community of this type is being developed in Central America, composed of Costa Rica, El Salvador, Honduras, Nicaragua, and Guatemala. At the same time, there is discussion of such a structure for the Latin American economies as a whole. Over the years another kind of multinational economical and political grouping has grown up in the British Commonwealth.

3. Market and commodity agreements, looking toward price stabilization and orderly distribution of certain commodities. The United States at various times has entered into multilateral arrangements with respect to specific commodities; for example, sugar with Western Hemisphere producers.

4. Monetary and credit arrangements, as illustrated by the European Payments Union and, on a larger scale, the International Monetary Fund.

5. Corporations whose operations extend through many nations. In order to be effective, these corporations, through which a considerable and essential part of the world's economic activities is carried on, must be able to compose diversities, adjust conflicts of interests, and adapt their operations to the needs of the countries within which they operate. In doing so, they represent a further example of a multinational solution of common problems.

These arrangements, however useful, have grown up on an *ad hoc* basis to meet specific needs. Such organic growth is vital and should continue. However, a structure adequate to the aspirations and opportunities of the twentieth century requires a more comprehensive outlook and a longer-range purpose. Henceforth, the nations of the free world should make a deliberate effort to determine their common objectives and to create institutions that give effect to them.

Moreover, while strengthening the cohesion of the free world is important for its own sake, it is also the most effective means for meeting the Soviet economic offensive. A reinforced political and economic structure of the free world can prevent the domination of weaker economies by the Soviet bloc. For it is not trade as such with the Soviet bloc that concerns us but the possibility of the political domination it creates.

The task of increasing the economic cohesion of the free world obviously transcends the economic realm. The nineteenth-century economic structure was closely related to the imperial system of political organization. The economic structure of the twentieth-century free world must be related to associations of free nations working together in the common interest. As with all great tasks, the goal of constructing a new political and economic structure for the free world must be perceived clearly before intermediate steps can be effective.

The details of an economic structure for the free world involve a great deal of technical study. In this report we shall consider the following broad aspects:

1. The United States and world economic growth.
2. Regional arrangements.
3. Functional arrangements.
4. Liberalized trade arrangements.

## THE UNITED STATES AND WORLD ECONOMIC GROWTH

Basic to world economic growth is an expanding and vital United States economy. We produce 35 per cent of the world's goods and services. Our exports and imports constitute 16 per cent of the world's trade. Relatively small fluctuations in our imports can have a major effect all over the world and catastrophic consequences for weaker economies geared to a few commodities. A United States recession can have a violent effect on other free world countries. Conversely, an expanding and reasonably stable United States economy is essential to world growth. A growing United States economy will import more goods from abroad, thus providing dollars for economic development. It will create additional resources for foreign investment.

The importance of the United States as a market and as a source of supply is fundamental. In fact, perhaps the greatest single economic contribution the United States can make to the free world, and hence the greatest responsibility of the United States, lies in efforts to promote the growth and stability of the American economy. The measures to achieve an expanding and healthy American economy recommended in the report of Panel IV, *The Challenge to America: Its Economic and Social Aspects*, are essential to world economic development.

## REGIONAL ARRANGEMENTS

Policies to promote the vitality of our economy are only the beginning of our task. They must be taken concurrently with measures which make the interdependence of nations a source of mutual strength. It is impossible for the United States to deal creatively with 80 sovereign nations solely on a bilateral basis. The most natural multinational arrangements are frequently regional. In many parts of the world, geography combines with common history to provide the basis for common objectives and fruitful co-operative efforts.

We have had a special experience with regional arrangements, both domestically and within the Western Hemisphere. Domestically, we have benefited from the stimulus of a large trading area. The United States is composed of regions as diverse in their geographic and economic characteristics as many groups of nations elsewhere in the world. Mutually beneficial trade exchanges are nevertheless achieved between areas as diverse as the manufacturing Northeast, the agricultural Central states, and the desert and mountain areas of the Southwest. It is clear that the development of each region would have been less rapid if each section of the country had maintained its own currency, separate tariffs, and its own system of capital investment.

Partly because of our domestic regional system, the economy of the United States is larger than the combined economies of Western Europe and Latin America. The strength and durability of the North American economy is greatly enhanced because it has at its disposal a large geographical area unimpeded by the barriers set up elsewhere by fragmentation into sovereign nations.

Moreover, in the history of the Western Hemisphere, participation in regional arrangements has found expression in the joining together of the American states in a free association in the common interest of all. Gradually, and at times painfully, a community of nations united by similar aspirations for the welfare and dignity of their citizens has evolved. This association has been based on six principles: juridical equality, nonintervention, consultation, common objectives, common action, and mutual security. The path of development of these principles has not always been smooth and even. Yet the nations of the Western Hemisphere have made notable, and continuous, progress toward a political structure for a free association of nations. They have been less successful in the development of common economic objectives and institutions.

The United States should encourage the formation of regional arrangements if they are designed—as they should be—with due regard to the general growth, cohesion, and interdependence of the entire free world. Regional arrangements of the kind here considered do not imply regional autarky. Their aim is the progressive elimination of barriers within groups, not the erection of new barriers between groups.

It is not possible to describe the precise form regional arrangements should take in all parts of the globe. They may involve joint efforts to achieve economic development, common markets, and free trade areas or functional arrangements like the European Coal and Steel Community. Fully developed, they imply a joint accord on monetary and exchange arrangements, a common discipline on fiscal matters, and a free movement of capital and labor. We believe that this regional approach has world-wide validity. Because the particular adaptation will be different for each region, the structure will have to be worked out by each region through consultation. We feel the United States should encourage the development of such regional structures in all areas of the free world. We have tried to develop the outline for Western Hemisphere unity in Section V as an illustrative case.

Regional arrangements can spur world economic development. They can make possible more rational international economic relationships. Instead of large numbers of states dealing with each other bilaterally, large trading areas can regulate their relationships to bring about the greatest mutual benefit. In addition, such arrangements will permit weaker economies to withstand more effectively the impact of selective trade offensives by larger states, such as the Soviet bloc.

At the same time, regional arrangements impose a responsibility on the participating nations. They must not substitute protectionism of a larger unit for the national trade barriers they replace. Regional arrangements should be considered a step in the direction of freeing world trade. We should not only encourage regional economic groupings but strive for increasingly free relations *among* these groupings. Such a policy will be essential not only to promote world economic development but to promote our own trade interests.

For, once regional trading systems are fully developed, we shall no longer deal with units whose economic strength is dwarfed by ours. A fully integrated common market in Western Europe, for example, would represent trade interests larger than our own. It is therefore highly important that we adopt more coherent, consistent, and responsible trade policies than we have practiced in the past. We not only need an extended Reciprocal Trade Program, but ultimately we must be prepared to make bolder commitments if we are to be effective in negotiating with Europe directly or with other areas against Europe's trade bids with them. We have to subscribe fully to international bodies like the Organization for Trade Cooperation and to meet a reasonable need for commodity stabilization.

In striving for regional arrangements, we should remember that they depend importantly on political vision and initiative. Regional arrangements can give content to the hopes and aspirations of humanity seeking to encompass a greater community. Clearly the actual details will require careful technical exploration. What is needed immediately is a determination to move in the direction they imply. Regional arrangements are no longer a matter of choice. They are imposed by the requirements of technology, science, and economics. Our course is to contribute to this process by constructive action. It will emerge through us, and we can participate in its benefits, if we are wise; it will come into being in opposition to us, if we are timid or turn our backs on the aspiration to human betterment, which is the source of our strength.

## FUNCTIONAL ARRANGEMENTS

Regional arrangements by themselves cannot supply the entire structure of a free world economy. Some problems and opportunities cut across regional lines; other should be dealt with on a world-wide basis. Three of the most important functional challenges—the problem of primary commodity products, the new vistas of science, and the role of international financial institutions—will be discussed here.

## Special Problem of Primary Products

Most of the countries in the less industrialized areas of the world derive the bulk of their foreign exchange earnings from primary products exports. Collectively, close to 40 per cent of their exports are agricultural food products; close to 25 per cent are petroleum and other fuels; and the remainder are industrial raw materials, either agricultural or mineral. Since the pace of their general economic development depends so importantly on the amount of foreign exchange available for the purchase of industrial equipment from highly industrialized economies, the price of primary products and the demand for them is of vital significance to many newly developing economies.

The demand for primary products and their terms of trade in international markets have been, in general, highly favorable since 1939. In 1957, however, the prices of most export foodstuffs fell, and prices of industrial raw materials declined even more sharply. Industrial raw materials prices now average about 20 per cent below their levels at the end of 1956. Meanwhile, international prices of manufactured items have continued to climb. The result has been a sharp drop in the buying power of countries that generally are ill-equipped to stand the economic and social consequences of such disruption. In many of them, partially completed development projects are imperiled. In others, the entire economy faces a drastic decline.

Prices for individual commodities have fluctuated far more than the broad averages. Since many of the less industrialized countries count upon one or at most two or three export commodities for the major portion of their foreign exchange, they are concerned with particular rather than general price movements. In Brazil, Haiti, Guatemala, Colombia, and El Salvador, coffee exports account for from 70 to 80 per cent of total foreign trade earnings. From 1953 to 1958, coffee prices (quarterly averages) advanced over 60 per cent and fell again to 1953 levels or below. More than half of Bolivia's export earnings come from tin and over two thirds of Chile's from copper. Export prices for copper advanced 65 per cent above their low point in 1953 and fell off 56 per cent by the first quarter of 1958. Tin prices advanced 33 per cent above their lows in the third quarter of 1953 and fell off 14 per cent by the last quarter of 1957. For Vietnam, Indonesia, and Cambodia, exports of crude rubber bring in from 30 per cent to 50 per cent of foreign exchange earnings. Since 1953, rubber prices in world trade have fluctuated between 100 per cent above and 20 per cent below the 1953 average. The impact of price swings of such dimension is often devastating upon economies that are exceptionally dependent upon the sales of the commodities involved.

It is not surprising, then, to find an insistent demand on the part of countries so situated for international agreements designed to mitigate the extreme fluctuations that cause so much human suffering and that introduce so large an element of uncertainty into their economies. Such demands have been increasing, as the recent downturn of the terms of trade for primary products has created balance of payments difficulties that seriously threaten the capacity to preserve economic, and even political, stability.

Clearly, this is a major problem for the economy of the free world. To be adequate to its responsibilities, the economic structure of the free world must find a way to prevent excessive instability. Its meaning to many of the less developed countries will reside in its ability to discharge this responsibility.

The task, however, is exceedingly complex, technically. There are obvious difficulties in attempting to substitute international control mechanisms for the free market operation under which supply and demand are adjusted to each other through price changes. The United States experience with its own agricultural support programs demonstrates both the formidable expense of guaranteeing prices, when the supply of given commodities exceeds effective demand, and the extreme difficulty of controlling supply of agricultural products even within a single country that has been building an elaborate governmental administrative machinery over many years.

Often the proposed remedies are of doubtful practicality. The few international programs that have been tried have failed to produce results that conclusively demonstrate their effectiveness. Since 1953, an International Sugar Agreement has been in effect under which quotas for sugar production and exports are assigned as a means for stabilizing prices. But between the first half of 1956 and the first quarter of 1958, world sugar prices rose by more than 80 per cent and fell off again by 40 per cent from their peak in the second quarter of 1957.

There is another international agreement for wheat, under which exporting countries agree to ship a fixed minimum amount at not more than a stipulated ceiling price, and importing countries agree to purchase fixed minimum amounts at not less than stipulated floor prices, with the market operating freely so long as prices hold within the agreed-upon limits. This agreement may have exerted some moderating effect upon price fluctuations in the international wheat trade, but the evidence is far from compelling. World wheat prices in the first quarter of 1958 were 17 per cent under the 1953 average.

A third international agreement, governing tin, has been in effect only since the middle of 1956. It calls for a buffer stock arrangement to cushion both shortages and surpluses. Experience to date has been too limited to permit adequate appraisal of its effectiveness. The Suez incident introduced a strain upon normal operations. Tin shipments from the U.S.S.R., a nonparticipating nation, have further unsettled the market. On a quarterly average basis, tin prices fell 14 per cent from the fourth quarter of 1956 to the fourth quarter of 1957.

In view of our own experience with agricultural price supports and the less than convincing achievements to date of international control experiments, the United States has been reluctant to give support to new commodity stabilization proposals of international scope. But the situation in a number of countries is now so acute and the outlook ahead so grim that immediate action is required to avert crises and to deal with these problems on a long-term basis.

We have the duty to explore all means for averting economic collapse in many areas of the free world. Since it is improbable that any workable commodity stabilization programs could be agreed upon in time to meet the needs of certain crisis situations that may be immediately upon us, these should be dealt with through the extension of international credits. The International Monetary Fund can help through its regular procedure for extending credit to ease short-term balance of payments adjustments. Bilateral credits, such as Export-Import Bank loans, will undoubtedly be needed to complement the Fund's efforts.

For the longer term, it is essential for the major industrial nations to put more effort and imagination into the exploration of procedures that will reduce the instability of primary producing nations. Ways must be found to keep violent fluctuations in commodity prices from producing economic crises and interfering with economic progress.

No panaceas will be offered here for a problem that is very complicated and that must be dealt with largely on a case by case basis. But in order to make our line of thought tangible, we would suggest consideration of the following two procedures:

An agreement for commodities like coffee and cacao, for which there are no practical means for controlling supply, might be worked out by the producing and consuming countries to deal with surplus stocks and to hold price fluctuations within certain bounds. Just as agreements limit the allowable daily price fluctuations on certain commodity exchanges, longer-term agreements might limit the fluctuations within a given year to a stated percentage, say 10 per cent, above or below the average price for the given product in the previous year. If demand were greater than supply, most of the year's shipments would move at the ceiling price, and prices for the following year would be set at the 10 per cent range above or below the given year's ceiling. If supply exceeds demand, the base on which the range was set would move gradually downward. Enforcement would operate through custom authorities at either end. If such an arrangement could be administered, it would have the virtue of damping down the violent swings of commodity prices while still allowing long-term price trends to work toward an adjustment of supply to effective demand.

A second procedure would be to use international credits to cushion the impact of necessary adjustments in commodity markets on producing nations. This would involve longer-term balance of payments credits than are presently granted by the International Monetary Fund. The objective would be to enable nations producing raw materials to maintain imports of the machinery, equipment, and materials essential for development in periods when export earnings are low. Thus, the necessary adjustment of supply to demand could be accomplished without slowing the pace of general development. The credits would be repaid after the adjustments had been completed and prices moved higher. Safeguards would be needed to make sure that the credits would, in fact, facilitate necessary readjustments in commodity production rather than merely delay them. Both the International Monetary Fund and regional payments unions could be used in this manner, although their resources would need to be greater than the amounts needed for shorter-term credits.

It may be that other and better ways of serving similar purposes can be devised. Our firm conviction is that the urgent problems of primary commodity products should be dealt with and that it is not beyond the capacity of technically competent men of good will to find better ways for meeting them than operate today.

## Vistas of Science and Technology

No field requires international co-operation more and makes its benefits more generally available than that of science. Scientific knowledge has never been confined for long by national boundaries. The co-operative efforts of the international community of scientists have tended always mutually to support each other. The advances of science can be translated to benefit all of humanity.

In the field of science, international co-operation on a world scale is most readily conceivable. In many areas it is essential if progress is to be made at all. Since each country is judged by its day to day contribution, accomplishment rather than propaganda will count. The experience of world-wide co-operation might then extend into other fields.

The United States should, therefore, seek to develop a series of agreements, looking toward the stimulation of scientific interchange and the fostering of scientific progress on a world scale, such as the International Geophysical Year. The Communist nations should be invited to participate. Unlike other agreements which to be effective depend on nations not doing certain things, scientific co-operation has the advantage of permitting the achievement of positive ends through positive actions. If, however, some or all the Communist nations refuse to join, the United States should proceed with whatever countries care to join on a free world basis.

In fields like the following, international agreements and co-operation are essential if significant progress is to be made because the problems are broader than national boundaries:

## Oceanography

A large percentage of the world's food supply already comes from the oceans. But the exploitation of the oceans is comparable to a nomadic stage of agriculture on land. No systematic attempt is made to farm the seas or to modify life in them. Eventually we may be able to breed fish as we now breed cattle or to grow plankton to increase the world's food supply.

## Development of an Agriculture Using Irrigation by Sea Water

The use of sea water has been most frequently discussed in connection with the problem of extracting the salt, thereby making the water suitable for irrigation. The cost of this procedure appears at present to be prohibitive. On the other hand, salt water can support life. In fact, it is the original cradle of life. Crops might be developed that could thrive under salt-water irrigation. This could make a significant contribution to the economy of some arid regions.

## Meteorology

Meteorology has developed rapidly during the past few decades. This is due partly to the great amount of information that has been gathered by airplanes everywhere in the world. It is also due to improved computation techniques. High-speed electronic machines can today correlate and digest data with sufficient rapidity so that the complex process of weather prediction can be carried out before the results become obsolete. For really good weather prediction, global data is necessary. Therefore the natural agency for meteorological work is an international one. If it becomes possible to interfere actively in the big processes of the atmosphere, the results are likely to transcend national boundaries. The problems that will then arise must be handled on an international basis. They may well turn out to be insoluble if the development leading up to weather control has been carried out by uncorrelated national efforts.

## Medical Research

World health must be a major concern for a community of nations dedicated to the well-being and fulfillment of the individual. Moreover, in many areas of the world endemic diseases hamper economic development by sapping the vitality of the people. An international effort to encourage medical research is of great importance.

## Peaceful Uses of Nuclear Energy

The cost of electricity from nuclear sources is uncertain, and for our national economy nuclear energy may be unattractive for some time to come. However, the materials required for the production of nuclear energy are light and easily transportable. Therefore, power from nuclear energy could be made available throughout the whole world at a relatively uniform price. This will have important consequences in places like Europe and in many other areas where fuel costs are high.

# Role of International Institutions

The world possesses a most impressive array of international institutions concerned in one way or another with economic and social problems. There are highly specialized bodies, such as the International Air Transport Association, which are concerned with international consultation on technical matters well within the resources and political consent of the nations concerned. There are organizations concerned with the co-ordination of international trade: the General Agreement on Tariffs and Trade provides an informal meeting ground for negotiations on trade restrictions, and the International Monetary Fund has given assistance in helping individual nations overcome specific crises in the balance of payments.

In the field of economic and social development, the array of organizations is most remarkable of all. There are the United Nations and its specialized agencies for food and agriculture, for health, for refugees, for special aid to the world's children. There are technical assistance programs through the United Nations

Technical Assistance Administration, through regional programs, such as the Organization of American States and the Colombo Plan, and through bilateral arrangements under the United States International Cooperation Administration and other agencies of the United States government. In the financing of international investment, the International Bank for Reconstruction and Development and the International Finance Corporation exist side by side with investment programs in the British Commonwealth of Nations and the nations of the Soviet bloc. But all are overshadowed by the volume and variety of investments provided under country aid programs of the United States International Cooperation Administration, the United States Export-Import Bank, and the potential of the new Development Loan Fund.

The very multiplicity of these institutions concerned with international development poses obvious problems of co-ordination. The lack of a clear and coherent central purpose, of a well-understood framework of world order, is the main trouble. Matters of organization also require attention. Co-ordination is required on the level of individual country development plans. One of the most important forms of assistance to the newly developing lands can be in helping them take maximum advantage, within their own national purposes, of the complex of opportunities available to them in the way of outside assistance. For problems of development that cross the political boundaries of nations, regional development banks and organizations may prove a most fruitful method of relating regional needs to the various forms of international assistance available. Some of our aid can be most effectively channeled through the existing institutions of the United Nations. In addition, consideration could profitably be given to the establishment of an International Development Authority to provide added impetus to world-wide economic growth.*

## TRADE POLICY

Ultimately the vitality of the economy of the free world will reveal itself in a high level of international trade. Here much depends on United States policy.

* Written in June 1958.

Before policy with respect to our foreign trade can be formulated, it is requisite that the broad outlines of world trade structure be understood.

In 1956 the total value of goods moving in international trade, exports and imports combined, totaled approximately $206 billion, or about 18 per cent of the world's total production of both goods and services. If the international trade in services, shipping, tourism, banking, and insurance were added, the degree of interdependence in the world economy would be seen to be considerably higher still.

The degree to which the countries in any given area are dependent upon the maintenance of trade with the outside world is better indicated by comparing the combined imports and exports of each with the total value of goods and services it produces. We then find that the trade of Western Europe and of the other industrialized free world nations, excluding the United States, averages about one third of their total national product. For the less industrialized group of free world nations, the percentage is even higher, at about 37 per cent. For the Communist bloc as a whole it is 7 per cent, and for the U.S.S.R. only 5 per cent.

An understanding of these basic elements of the over-all world trade pattern is essential to the formulation of a constructive United States commercial policy. We must take account of the fact that, comparatively, the impact of fluctuations in the level of United States imports and exports upon the economies of other countries is greater even than the considerable effect of such fluctuations upon our own economy. Within the free world trading system, United States exports account for 20 per cent of all exports, and its imports for 14 per cent of total imports. But in terms of our domestic economy, combined imports and exports represent only about 8 per cent of annual output. This relatively small—although, as we shall see, highly significant—proportion that foreign trade bears to our own total output often leads us to underestimate, and indeed to misunderstand, the importance of that trade to *other* nations. What is a small item on our import list may be a major source of revenue for an exporting nation, as for example our imports of Swiss watches, Scotch whisky, or Latin American coffee and copper. Thus, a small fluctuation in the level of United States imports or exports may have a major

# WORLD TRADE WAS $206 BILLION IN 1956
## (EXPORTS AND IMPORTS COMBINED)

$206 billion

THE COMMUNIST BLOC ...

U.S.S.R., China, and
Eastern Europe

$21 billion

THE FREE WORLD

$185 billion

Australia    New Zealand

Industrialized Countries

$136 billion

Western
Europe

U. S. & Canada    Japan    South Africa

Less Developed Countries

$49 billion

Middle East

Latin
America

Africa

South Asia

Sources: United Nations Statistical Office;
Communist Bloc (1957) estimated

impact on the economies of other nations—including many in whose political and economic stability we have a deep concern.

Despite its relatively small percentage weight in our over-all economy, a vigorous and expanding foreign trade is essential for the vitality of our economy. We import half or more of a wide variety of metals and minerals essential to United States industry. Three fourths of our newsprint is imported, all of our natural rubber, 18 per cent of our iron ore, and over 15 per cent of our petroleum.

Between 9 and 10 per cent of all the durable goods produced in the United States is sold abroad. Significantly enough, these sales provide the margin between profit and loss for a large segment of American industries. Exports represent from one fifth to one third of the total sales of American production of civilian aircraft, textiles, steel and rolling mill machinery, and sewing machines. They represent 19 per cent of all motor truck and bus sales, 16 per cent for diesel engines, 14 per cent for agricultural machinery, and 11 per cent for machine tool production. American farmers depend upon foreign markets for the sale of 20 to 40 per cent of their wheat, rice, cotton, rye, barley, hops, grain sorghums, soybeans, leaf tobacco; and the same is true for domestically produced calfskins, fats and oils, dried fruits, and processed milk.

Even this does not exhaust the United States dependence on foreign trade. For 1957, the total value of United States goods and service exports totaled $26 billion. But the total sales of 2,500 branches and subsidiaries of United States companies located abroad were estimated at $32 billion, and at least 40 per cent of these were sales in international rather than local markets. About 4.5 million workers, or 7 per cent of the entire United States labor force, are directly dependent upon foreign trade for their livelihoods. Foreign trade provides more direct employment in the United States than the automobile, steel, chemical, and textile industries combined.

Against the background of this degree of interdependence between the United States and other areas, it might be expected that the foreign commercial policy of the United States would be encouragement of exports and imports to the utmost, if only from the point of view of our most immediate economic self-interest. When we add the vital importance of expanding production and trade for all of the other nations of the free world, it would appear that the case for a liberal trade policy should command virtually unanimous national agreement.

Yet it is clear, from the debates over the renewal of the Trade Agreements Act and the President's authority to reduce tariffs, that this is not so. The case for a freer trade policy must be repeated year after year and the same arguments must be refuted each time. Nearly everyone recognizes the advantage of a liberal trade policy. But it seems that we hesitate to pay the price it demands. Understandably, those who suffer by lower tariffs are reluctant about a freer trade policy. Yet economic wisdom demands acceptance of the fact that if other jobs, sales, and profits are to accrue from United States exports, we inevitably must be willing to accept the imports upon which payment for our exports depends. It is unavoidable that some of our imports will compete with segments of domestic production as do our exports in many of the markets in which they are sold.

Every serious study that has been made in this field to date indicates that the preponderant bulk of American industry is well able to meet such competition. Indeed, one of the most important arguments in favor of trade liberalization is that it will broaden competition and thus increase the competitive discipline that is a major safeguard against inflation. Especially when consumer demand in the United States is pressing against our capacity output, freer access of foreign producers to our market will help to keep prices from rising. Under any gradual progression toward tariff liberalization, the displacements are not likely to be on a broader scale or of deeper dimension than those that are continuously occurring through domestic competition within and between industries.

The major fault of United States commercial policy, in recent years at least, has been its failure to provide assurance of direction and continuity. Judged by current world standards, our prevailing tariff levels and commercial policy procedures are not unduly restrictive. But our market is so large and so generally competitive that it requires a sustained and expensive effort for foreign business interests to establish a foothold in it. Relatively few have the resources or the fortitude to make the effort when they are faced with the possibility or even probability that our rules will be changed if they are successful.

We therefore believe it essential that the Reciprocal Trade Agreements Program be made a permanent part of our national policy. There should also be a broadening of presidential discretion to allow for consideration of broad domestic and foreign policy interests. Escape clauses, peril point provisions, and even defense essentiality procedures should be reconsidered so that the criteria for decision is based upon the whole balance sheet of national policy instead of items of short-run advantage and disadvantage. Beyond the Reciprocal Trade Act, the United States should use its influence in bringing about an increasingly free world trade. The regional groupings described earlier, if properly conceived, can be an important step in this direction. We need above all to be clear about this aim, and we require sufficient resolution to adhere to it.

Thus our trade policy necessarily becomes a central part of our foreign economic policy and must be considered on this plane. Without a policy of vigorous promotion of multilateral trade, our larger foreign economic policy cannot promote a just and workable international order or forward our own aspirations for growth.

# IV. Special Problems of the Economic Development of Less Developed Countries

The interdependence of nations implies that any lagging part of the world economy holds back every other. Conversely, to the extent that the less developed regions participate fully in world economic growth, the entire free world will benefit. Markets will expand, both for raw materials and industrial products, and an increasing range of human aspirations will be satisfied. We cannot achieve a community of free nations if the disparities of opportunity for their peoples are so vast as to preclude any common experience. The ultimate objective of all economic development is the well-being and happiness of the individual and the basic unit of society, which is the family. The future peace of the world and the achievement of some of our deepest values depend on the sustained advance of the less developed countries in co-operation with the industrialized nations.

## GENERAL CHARACTERISTICS

The term *less developed* covers nations with an immense diversity of resources, social structures, political leanings, and economic conditions. It embraces countries under heavy population pressure, like India and Indonesia; societies that have an actual shortage of manpower for agricultural and industrial development, such as Iraq and certain parts of Latin America; countries with potentially vast and largely undeveloped resources, like Brazil or Rhodesia; and also countries with a meager resource potential, like Libya; societies that have effective central governments commanding popular confidence and support; and countries in which the structure of government and administration is rudimentary. Yet underlying a diversity of local conditions, which makes hazardous a rash generalization of operating policy, lie certain similarities of basic conditions.

Conspicuous among these characteristics is the wave of rebellion that has been sweeping over many of these areas. In the sources of this upheaval, there is a paradoxical element—for current revolutionary doctrines were introduced into colonial areas by the imperial powers themselves. These powers typically displaced existing ruling groups in populations that neither enjoyed nor expected direct participation in government. This enabled relatively small numbers from the conquering powers to establish their rule over vast dominions and millions of people. But they were not content with simply replacing an indigenous feudal ruling class. They brought with them doctrines of administration and popular participation in government that in time proved inconsistent with their own continued rule. The attempt to form coherent administrative units led to the consolidation of many areas for the first time in their history. For centuries before the appearance of the British, India had known only nominal unity of control. Similarly, Indonesia was nothing but a geographic expression until the Dutch found it more efficient to administer its many islands as a unit. At the same time, the colonial powers trained a group of indigenous leaders in their universities where they absorbed the ideals of the right to self-government, human dignity, and economic advancement, which had been the rallying points for the European Enlightenment.

Thus while colonialism exacted a human and political toll, it also represented one of the greatest conversions in history. As the ideals of the British, French, and American revolutions became diffused, partly through the very spread of colonialism, the seeds were sown for the destruction of colonialism itself. The more successful the teachings of the colonial powers, the more untenable grew their position. Almost without exception, the leaders of independence movements fought their rulers in terms of the rulers' own beliefs. They asked them to live up to their own principles. They did not seek to overthrow the political system of the West but to enter it.

The disintegration of the colonial systems is thus fraught with both promise and peril. Its promise resides in the community of values that produced it. This gives the basis for hope of future co-operative relations based on the principles of human dignity that inspired the colonial upheaval. Its danger resides in the fact that anti-colonialism, so heroic while in opposition to foreign rule, may turn out to be the only shared objective of a people, that it may be easier to find agreement on things to oppose than on constructive steps of development. The result may be nationalism impelled more by resentment than by positive aspirations.

It is deeply in the national interest of the United States that economic development in the less developed countries should take place in a manner that encompasses genuine national independence, peaceful international attitudes, institutions supported by the consent of their people, and respect for human personality. It is also profoundly in their own interest that these countries should pursue their goals in this manner. This harmony of interest, if understood and given effect through operating policies, can be a great source of hope and strength for the free world.

Economic development can both foster and profit from the concept of a new structure for the economy of a free world described earlier. The United States and the other industrialized nations cannot underwrite the separate aspirations of some forty less developed nations. However, through a structure of multinational groupings, the industrialized nations can work together with the less developed countries in a joint effort to achieve their common objective of a dynamic and growing world economy.

It is essential that sights be set high. The total capital investment in the less developed part of the free world came to $17 billion in 1956 compared to $146 billion in the industrialized part, even though the population of the less developed countries is almost twice as great. An increase in capital flow to the less developed areas could have vast economic consequences, providing adequate political and social structures exist. A farsighted effort of world economic development, boldly executed, would yield enormous returns in individual well-being and in a sense of common purpose.

Judged by the magnitude of the opportunity before us, we have fallen far short. The scale of our effort has been insufficient. The co-ordination of private and public activities has been inadequate. The institutional and social aspects of economic development have too often been neglected, together with the conceptual framework into which these essential elements fit.

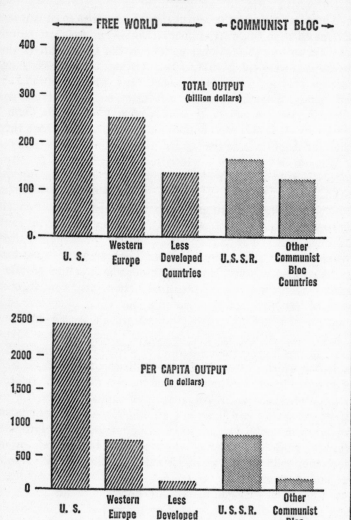

# WORLD OUTPUT OF GOODS AND SERVICES
## 1956

← FREE WORLD → ← COMMUNIST BLOC →

**TOTAL OUTPUT**
(billion dollars)

400 —
300 —
200 —
100 —
0.

U. S. | Western Europe | Less Developed Countries | U.S.S.R. | Other Communist Bloc Countries

2500 —
2000 —
1,500 —
1000 —
500 —
0

**PER CAPITA OUTPUT**
(in dollars)

U. S. | Western Europe | Less Developed Countries | U.S.S.R. | Other Communist Bloc Countries

# ESSENTIAL ELEMENTS IN ECONOMIC DEVELOPMENT

The similarities of the less developed countries must not leave the impression that the problems that arise in them call for uniform treatment. Nothing could be further from reality. While in their quest for a new life most of these countries may seem to have basically the same objective, their start is from different levels, the problems they face are different, and their progress is at different rates. A variety of local circumstances affects them in different ways, and the outside world affects them in widely differing ways.

The process of growth is conspicuously a process of change involving a great number of factors, each of which affects the others and is in turn affected by them. Many of these changes result from the processes of growth itself. Many others require the application of some new force that compels the change to take place. In assessing the development problem of a less developed country at any particular time, nothing is more important than to recognize the factors *critical* to the process of continued growth—requirements that must be supplied before the next step can be taken.

## Governmental Structure and Services

Economic and social development presupposes the existence of a responsible government reflecting the aspirations and hopes of its people. Without such a political structure and adequate enabling legislation, it will be impossible to develop the long-range objectives essential for growth or to impose the disciplines necessary to achieve them. Essential elements to the rate of advance, therefore, will be law and order with justice; the development of sound structure for taxes, customs, and budgets; plus an efficient, loyal, and trained civil service.

## Education and Trained Manpower

Attention must be given to the advancement of education at all levels. Well-developed plans for universal primary education are essential if people are to develop and preserve their own democratic institutions and well-being. In the final analysis the future of all nations depends on their wisdom as well as their vocational and technical skills. The quality and availability of educational facilities are therefore key factors.

High-talent manpower, a critical factor limiting capacity for economic growth, depends on development of secondary and vocational education, as well as university facilities in both liberal and specialized fields. In many countries the need for competent administrators, engineers, and skilled technicians of all kinds is as great, if not greater, than the need for capital. Indeed the operation of power and irrigation systems, railways, and factories, will lead to tragic waste of invested capital and excessively high costs of goods and services unless such talent can be developed.

Preparation for the assumption of the responsibilities of leadership cannot be mass produced; it is a slow, lengthy, and expensive process. Though it may take only a few years to build a dam, a steel mill, or a textile factory, many years are needed to produce a competent engineer or an able administrator.

The less developed countries require the assistance of the industrially advanced countries for staff, materials, and equipment for their technical colleges and universities. They cannot utilize machinery purchased abroad unless technicians are loaned to install it and to instruct local personnel in its proper utilization. They need help in establishing vocational schools, employment exchanges, and programs of job training. They will need to send abroad larger numbers of able young persons for study at technical institutions and universities in the industrially advanced countries. They require a wide range of consulting services for building their own industrial enterprises in addition to foreign enterprises operating factories within their boundaries. Thus, governments, private enterprises, consulting firms, universities, and foundations are in position to offer very strategic technical assistance. The future of the less developed countries may depend on the sources of this assistance and also on the philosophical premises upon which it is provided.

Accordingly, we recommend an approach to educational problems along the following lines:

1. An appraisal should be made of the problems and needs of development of high-level manpower in free world less developed

countries. In particular, it is important that each country or region assess its own problems and develop its own measures to meet them, as well as the extent to which it wishes outside assistance.

2. In order to determine high-priority programs of technical assistance in these areas, there should be a general assessment, in terms of impact and cost, of all present United States activities that are related to human resources development. The existing wide variety of private and public programs is an advantage rather than a shortcoming, for it provides opportunity for experimentation, latitude for individual initiative, and many avenues for co-operation by United States citizens. One shortcoming, however, is that there is no appraisal of the combined programs at the regional and country level with their relationships to over-all efforts in the area.

3. The United States should co-operate with the region or country concerned in the development of educational institutions of all kinds, particularly in the field of higher education. A major role in this task can be and is being played by private American foundations. But the task transcends private resources. It is a major field for government action.

4. Finally, there is need to develop specially trained personnel in the United States government, as well as in educational, philanthropic, and industrial institutions, serving abroad. In dealing with other nations and peoples, the need for personnel with language facility, knowledge and understanding of cultural and historical backgrounds is especially acute. Our capacity in this respect must be enlarged through carefully worked out programs of recruitment, selection, training, and tenure.

Business enterprises operating abroad, foundations, educational institutions, and various departments and branches of the United States government alike report the difficulty of attracting and keeping American men and women in overseas operations. In certain aspects, this difficulty may be compared with the difficulty to which so much attention has been called in attracting qualified men and women into teaching and into scientific research. This difficulty reflects the importance of a deeper national understanding with respect to world economic development and human betterment, so that our ablest people will feel challenged to contribute to it. The problem of values and incentives will be discussed in the Panel V report. Here we should like to affirm our belief that these needs represent opportunities for young men and women comparable in excitement and constructive promise to the challenge of the old American frontier.

## Public Health and Sanitation

Increased skill and productivity are also dependent on improvements in health and sanitation, as well as better nutritional standards. Too often the vitality of the peoples in the less developed areas has been sapped by the ravages of disease and famine. The elimination of endemic and debilitating diseases will make possible a more stable and reliable working force. Economic and social progress must go hand in hand with sanitation and health services, including care for women and children.

Modern medicine and science have made attainable the virtual eradication of such diseases as malaria, yaws, tuberculosis.

This area has received the effective attention not only of the World Health Organization but also of such regional health groups as the Pan American Sanitation Bureau. The work in public health was pioneered by the private foundations and has been supplemented in recent years by effective programs of co-operation on a bilateral basis through the various United States government technical assistance programs. A major contribution to well-being and development can be made by more effective planning and the co-ordination of existing services.

## Agriculture

As industrialization starts to take hold in the developing areas, it produces an accelerated movement of people to the urban centers. Unless modern technological and scientific methods are introduced, the dwindling agricultural populations will not be able to increase their productivity sufficiently to feed the rapidly growing national and urban population. To achieve this evolution in the rural areas requires a major expansion of government services in the fields of agricultural extension service and home demonstration. It also requires the availability of supervised rural credit, both short- and long-term, at reasonable interest rates.

The development of such services by government is a slow process. Yet experimental programs have been successfully carried out in many of the less developed countries. A balanced agricultural development is an essential corollary to industrial growth and a rising standard of living for the people of the nation as a whole. Once agricultural extension service, home demonstration, and supervised credit services are established, new scientific methods can be made available and effectively absorbed.

## Basic Public Works

Economic development requires a systematic expansion of basic public works in such fields as transportation, power, irrigation, and port facilities.

Because most of the less developed regions suffer from a lack of transportation, the typical pattern even within the borders of the individual nation itself is not that of an integrated economy but of a large number of isolated ones.

The lack of power has been a major deterrent in industrial development.

The lack of irrigation has been the cause of holding back agriculture essential for production of foodstuffs in arid regions, while contaminated water supply has been a serious health threat in the urban centers.

A lack of port facilities has seriously retarded the development of international trade and commerce.

These fields require intelligent, long-range planning, both nationally and regionally. The financing of such projects must be a major concern for the free world.

## FINANCING CAPITAL NEEDS

The capital needs of the less developed countries can be grouped roughly into three categories: basic services (public health and sanitation, education, agricultural extension, public administration); public works (roads, railways, harbors, irrigation works); and the production and distribution of goods and services. A variety of financial tools, public and private, is available to help meet such needs. Yet closer co-ordination is necessary and new institutions for specific needs must be devised.

As a general rule, the provision of basic services and public works in the less developed areas has been financed from government sources while production and distribution are private enterprise functions in a free economy. There are, of course, exceptions. One of our problems is to work out appropriate procedures for making the best use of all of our financial tools toward the general purpose of promoting economic development.

A substantial portion of the capital to finance public services and public works comes from tax receipts of individual governments. An additional source of financing available to governments lies in the sale of government securities to the public. In most cases, however, capital markets in these nations have been little developed and governments have been reluctant to place interest rates on their securities that will attract private savings. In most of the less developed nations, local sources of capital have been inadequate to finance the public works and public services needed to support rapid development.

While a great deal can and must be done to increase local savings and capital formation, the less developed nations will still need capital from abroad, just as the United States did in its early years. Thus, the problem is to increase the availability of both local capital and foreign exchange.

Productive projects that generate the means of repayment within a reasonable term of years usually have little difficulty attracting financing. Both our own Export-Import Bank and the International Bank for Reconstruction and Development, which has drawn almost half of its capital from the United States, are organized to make loans to sound industrial projects or to the basic public utilities upon which they depend. The International Finance Corporation, closely affiliated with the IBRD, is set up to assist private enterprise in the less developed areas through loans and what amounts essentially to an equity participation. Since it can share in profits, it can consider projects entailing a degree of risk that would preclude eligibility for Export-Import Bank or IBRD loans.

Despite the existence of these facilities, there are still many development projects of genuine merit that have difficulty in finding financing. It is often impractical to raise capital within a country to finance the local currency expenditures needed to build a plant or construct a railroad or electric power facility. It is particularly difficult, for example, for governments in financial straits to provide the capital needed for the flood control and irrigation portion of a multipurpose dam, even where the electrical utility that might be an integral part of the project would qualify for loan support from existing institutions if the rest could be financed. For instance, an important irrigation and power project might cost $300 million, but the earnings from the project would be only sufficient to finance a $250 million loan. Because of the political, social, and economic significance of such a project, it might be extremely important that it go forward. However, to loan the total amount involved would be to risk the possibility of default. What is needed in such a case is an institution that has the authority to make grants. A $50 million grant here would make the project a sound financial risk for an international loan from the International Bank or the Export-Import Bank. There are many such projects in the less developed areas that are being held up for the lack of this kind of facility.

It was to fill such gaps in the existing international credit structure that the Development Loan Fund was conceived as part of the United States program. It began operations in November 1957, with a modest appropriation of only $300 million. By the end of January 1958, it had received 161 applications from 27 countries totaling $1.3 billion. The Administration is seeking an additional appropriation of $625 million for fiscal year 1959 with future expansions contemplated.

The Development Loan Fund is designed to operate as a loan agency with exceptionally flexible scope and operating procedures. We are in agreement that it be incorporated as a permanent government corporate institution, and we recommend that it specifically be authorized to make grants. At least a portion of the United States grant and aid program should be handled through it. We also recommend that it be authorized to contract with American companies to produce goods and services abroad in areas where private capital will not go on its own initiative because of the risks involved.

The Development Loan Fund can operate with great flexibility. Its funds do not revert if they are not committed or spent by a fixed deadline, and repayments are used to replenish its capital. It can finance either private or government projects. Its maturities are adjustable and may run for as long as forty years. It can participate in earnings in the manner of the International Finance Corporation procedure, and it is not required to adhere strictly to the criteria of what is or is not bankable that governs the practice of existing agencies. It can guarantee private loans, help in the establishment or expansion of existing local development banks, and it can accept payment in local currencies when such a procedure is indicated. One of its prescribed responsibilities is to be responsive to situations considered important to our foreign policy interests.

It is essential to bear in mind that, in many cases, the difference between success and failure in the efforts of the less developed countries to achieve their goals, in a manner consistent with their genuine national independence and their growth in freedom, will be determined by the availability of sufficient capital investment or technical assistance from the outside. In such cases, it is in the national interest of the United States and the broad interest of the free world that appropriate means should exist to provide such capital or technical assistance.

The Development Loan Fund can add an important dimension and give increased effectiveness to our foreign economic program. It provides needed flexibility in the international financing field. Thus, the Development Loan Fund can participate with the International Bank for Reconstruction and Development, the Export-Import Bank, or private enterprise to carry through needed projects that could not heretofore be financed. For this reason, we believe that a considerable increase in its capital may be thoroughly warranted.

The Development Loan Fund should become the focal point in the United States government for United States effort in the international development field. This instrument may also help to establish regional development agencies where such agencies would have a constructive role to play in promoting the prerequisites of growth in many of the less developed areas. It could also work closely with an International Development Authority should such a multilateral development institution be set up.

The chart opposite serves to illustrate the possible relationship among international and United States government investment institutions.

ILLUSTRATION OF POSSIBLE RELATIONSHIPS
AMONG INTERNATIONAL AND
UNITED STATES GOVERNMENT
INVESTMENT INSTITUTIONS

United States Financial Institutions

*Export-Import Bank*—dollar loans to governments and to others with or without a government guarantee

*Development Loan Fund*—dollar and local currency loans to public or private enterprises; loan guarantees; equity participation through debentures; management contracts

International Financial Institutions

*International Bank for Reconstruction and Development*—self-liquidating loans directly to governments and loans with a government guarantee

*International Finance Corporation*—loans and equity-type capital to private enterprise

Regional Development Authorities

Participating Countries

## SIGNIFICANCE OF
## PRIVATE ENTERPRISE

### Encouragement of Private Enterprise

The discussion so far has been centered on the principal areas of government responsibility that importantly support and facilitate economic and social development. However, the driving force in a free country comes from the initiative, imagination, and willingness to assume responsibility on the part of innumerable individuals. The success and effectiveness of the totality of their efforts depend importantly on the climate, the framework, and the conditions under which they are able to operate.

Recognition must be given to two factors that work against their achievement—the lack of a tradition of the value of individual initiative together with the pressures of rising expectations tend to result in a centralization in government of economic and social forces. Therefore, a major conscious effort must be made to encourage the development of systems that permit the flourishing of these values within structures not necessarily identical with ours but that are compatible and make possible a common effort.

Two general approaches to the encouragement of private enterprise by national governments should be emphasized. The first relates to domestic policies to encourage initiative and enterprise and promote domestic saving and investment. Among the most important of such policies are those designed to check inflation and stabilize currencies. In many of the less developed countries, domestic inflation has been the chief enemy of growth. Steps to contain inflation, through the active use of monetary and fiscal methods, would make a most significant contribution to economic growth. An end to inflation would encourage savings, assure that savings would be channeled into the most efficient form of investment, and make possible the removal of the maze of direct controls that inhibit initiative and enterprise.

Taxation is another field in which national governments might take action to promote the growth of private enterprise. Tax structures should be reviewed to minimize impediments to growth.

## Role of Private Foreign Investment

The capital needs of less developed nations are so huge, relative to their resources, that rapid economic growth can be achieved only if local saving and public foreign investment are supplemented by an increasing inflow of private foreign investment. Such investment performs two key functions: it adds to the capital resources of the host nation, and it is the chief mechanism through which the managerial and technical skills and the creative and catalytic quality of foreign enterprise can contribute to the economic development of the less developed areas. Private capital from abroad, particularly from Europe, gave dynamic impetus to the expansion and development of the United States. United States captial has played an increasingly significant role in the economic and social development of other nations, particularly in the Western Hemisphere.

Private philanthropic capital can also play a constructive role in economic development. Such efforts can help directly by providing facilities for education, health, and similar purposes, and indirectly by supplying leadership in such fields as medical and agricultural research. Philanthropic activities are already making a significant contribution in Latin America, Asia, and Africa.

It should be the policy of the United States to encourage private overseas investment as a complement to programs of economic aid and technical assistance. However, private investment—with the exception of private philanthropic capital—will flow into foreign fields only if there is the prospect of a return commensurate with the risks involved. If the risks or uncertainties are too great, private enterprise will not enter many areas where it could make a great contribution. One of the preconditions for the fullest use of private enterprise is the development of the regional, political, and economic structures described in Section III—a framework that permits men, money, and goods to move freely to where they can play the most important role in world economic growth.

In addition, we recommend that the United States government take direct action to encourage the flow of private funds into international investment by providing appropriate tax incentives for foreign investment. At the very least, the advantage now provided to Western Hemisphere corporations of a 14 point reduction in the corporate income tax should be extended to the rest of the world.

## Co-ordination of Private and Public Activities

Our private and public activities in the international investment field have suffered from a lack of co-ordination. Two steps would help overcome this difficulty:

1. Facts should be collected covering all substantial private American capital investment presently taking place abroad. Information as to the projects and plans of American private companies carrying on overseas operations should also be collected. Such information would make possible the co-ordination of private and public activities for the maximum benefit of the less developed regions.

For example, in Honduras there is a forest reserve large enough to found a paper and pulp industry capable of supplying a large part of Latin America, and private companies have been interested in it. Co-ordinated with public projects—for example, road building—a higher rate of growth and development for an entire area might be obtained. Appropriate plans for co-ordination, including an accurate survey of existing private operations, can eliminate bottlenecks, which prevent further expansion, or can create facilities making new development possible.

2. The handling of intergovernmental loans, such as those made by the Export-Import Bank, could be made less time consuming and more productive. Programs should be developed to use appropriate combinations of private and public capital and thus magnify the impact of our contribution to economic growth. Regional development authorities may be most helpful in the development of such programs.

Another of our problems is to introduce the managerial and technical skills of private investment into areas where the normal standards for private investment decision would not induce such investment. Two approaches to this problem should be thoroughly explored:

1. To achieve certain objectives in these areas of high risk, it might be practicable and useful to make long-term, low interest

rate loans to private enterprise as a special inducement to go into such areas. This form of participation by the United States government might well make private investment practical and desirable. The Development Loan Fund has authority to operate in this manner.

2. Where even this type of loan would not induce private enterprise to go into these areas and where it is in our national interest to develop the production of certain types of goods and services there, another approach is possible. Rather than making an outright grant to state-operated organizations, the newly incorporated Development Loan Fund should be given authority to contract with American private enterprises to render certain services of a technical or managerial character abroad, just as is done under the atomic energy or defense production programs at home. In most cases, governments in these areas, which have in the past received grants, have been unable to get American companies to come in to perform these services.

The procedure would be for the United States government to negotiate agreements with the governments of the countries in question that would provide for such technical and managerial services contracts with American concerns. The agreement might also include an option for an ultimate participation by the contract firm in an equity position along with local investors.

Obviously, the feasibility and desirability of such arrangements would depend upon the facts and circumstances of the particular situation. The purpose would be to combine the objectives and criteria of a sound program of economic development with the utilization of the talents of enterprise and management and technical skills that might otherwise be unavailable.

## Framework for Investment and Enterprise

The long-range need of the United States and other industrial societies for an expanded production of raw materials and the availability of investment capital in these societies can be mutually supporting. This prospect assumes, however, a continued hospitality for foreign investment in other nations as well as forward-looking national policies on our part. Equally, in the less developed areas, cool and rational judgment based upon actual need has on more than one occasion been swept aside by fierce nationalism, by a bitter distrust of any arrangement that seemed to smack of colonial relationships, and by the confusion engendered by rapid growth and inexperience. In short, private investment can only take place in a world in which political and legal foundations are provided for economic activity.

The principle of contract finds expression in virtually every known legal system. The terms of statement vary: from the familiar doctrine of the binding obligation of contract in the Anglo-American common law and the civil law of the continent; to the Muslim principle, "Muslims must abide by their stipulations," derived from the injunction in the *Qur'an*—"O ye who believe, fulfill your pledges"; to the recognition of the binding character of vows and pledges in Chinese and Japanese law; to comparable affirmations in Hindu legal doctrine; to the *pacta sunt servanda* of public international law. These legal systems, national and international, represent a distillation of the experience of mankind. This varied and universal experience testifies to the need for legal institutions and procedures to vindicate the contractual rights of investors.

In collaboration with other nations, the United States must continuously seek to establish legal institutions and arrangements, national and international, that serve as the foundation for a dependable and productive flow of investment and trade in international economic life.

## LIBERALIZING INTERNATIONAL TRADE

Action to liberalize trade throughout the free world can provide important encouragement to the expanding production of goods and services by private enterprise. Without exception, the less developed nations, if they are to achieve maximum industrial and general economic development, need broader markets than can be provided within national boundaries. What is more, steps to liberalize trade broaden the scope of competition, thus providing incentives for more efficient production and distribution. And they reinforce efforts to contain inflation and thus favor the removal of restrictive controls. This calls attention to the importance of adopting the trade policy recommended in Section III.

## CONCLUSION

The free world can best demonstrate the vitality of its principles by making much more rapid progress in fulfilling the aspirations of its peoples. In these terms, programs of international cooperation to achieve economic and social goals can become an expression of the vitality of free societies and the values they represent. An imaginative program developed in advance of an emergency will be a symbol of moral purpose. A crash program formulated after a crisis will appear as an attempt to buy our way out of difficulties. Everything depends therefore on being clear about the kind of world we wish to bring about and being prepared to make much greater efforts, both materially and spiritually, in achieving it.

# V. The Western Hemisphere—A Test Case

Much of our discussion has of necessity been concerned with principles rather than with particular applications, which will vary with circumstances. Regional arrangements will have to be adapted to local conditions; functional arrangements will be affected by the specific needs that called them forth; economic development cannot be divorced from the particular situation in which it must take place.

For this reason, we have thought it appropriate to discuss one region in somewhat greater detail in order to illustrate the application of the free world structure described in this report to a particular case. In an important sense, Western Hemisphere relationships are a living example of our foreign economic policy. They derive from historic ties; they reflect a geographic fact; they can give expression to a profound opportunity. They can illustrate regionalism, functional arrangements, and problems of development.

It is imperative for the United States to co-operate closely with its Western Hemisphere neighbors in the solution of problems that necessarily are of common concern. Sober review and consideration of our longer-term economic and social objectives and relationships have been too long deferred.

Any serious reformulation of United States foreign economic policy must include as a major element careful consideration of our common objectives with respect to and our impact upon the neighbors to whom we are so closely bound. Even in Canada, where the development record of the economy has been outstanding, there have been recent rumblings. These reflect at least a sharp questioning of certain of our economic interrelationships and deserve immediate and serious attention.

For the United States, for Canada on our north, and for the twenty Latin American republics to our south, interhemisphere economic ties are the predominant factor in their respective foreign trade interests. About half of all the United States trade flow is within the hemisphere, almost equally divided between Canada and Latin America. Over 65 per cent of Canada's trade is with the United States and almost 50 per cent of Latin America's. Trade connections between Canada and Latin America are of small dimension on both sides, but they have a common concern in hemisphere development because their interests are closely bound to the United States economy that lies between them. Interhemisphere trade interests are today of far greater magnitude and far more important relatively than they were thirty years ago.

A comparable phenomenon has been occurring in the field of capital investment. Of the $22 billion of United States direct investments abroad in 1956, 33 per cent was in Canada and 33 per cent in Latin America. These investments are contributing importantly to the expansion of hemisphere industrial output and export earnings.

## CURRENT EMERGENCIES

Over the past quarter century, Latin American countries generally have made substantial, though unevenly distributed, economic progress. Rapid industrialization and a high level of export earnings have helped produce a per capita income increase of about 2 per cent per annum, even though the population growth in Latin America is the highest for any major area of the world.

In the past two years, however, Latin America's economic growth has slowed, in part because of sharp declines in prices of such important exports as coffee, copper, lead, and cotton. Rapid domestic inflation in a number of Latin American nations has served to complicate the problems of adjustment. As a result, we face a situation of serious economic deterioration—one that could lead to crises in a number of Latin American nations.

Export earnings have already declined substantially in Brazil, Chile, Colombia, Uruguay, Bolivia, and Mexico, while there have been lesser declines in other nations. This decline in export earnings is forcing drastic cutbacks in imports of machinery and equipment, fuel and raw materials. The result will be at least a slow-down in the rate of economic advance, and serious economic and political crises are possible. Such developments are of the utmost concern to the United States. Crises tend to lead to improvised solutions that are never as good as carefully considered measures that can be provided with proper forethought.

The acute problem is coffee, with current production running considerably above indicated demand and carry-over stocks very high. Continuing effort on the part of a number of the producing countries to support coffee prices, by holding exports at an agreed upon percentage below past shipment rates, is proving to be an expensive burden on national treasuries. Aside from coffee, demand and price fall-offs in copper, tin, lead, and zinc, intensified by the current recession* in the United States, may create sufficiently severe problems in certain other Latin American economies to justify emergency handling.

## AN INTER-AMERICAN CONFERENCE

The United States should participate in calling an Inter-American Economic Conference to which Canada would be invited.

The conference should be called as soon as possible for the joint consideration of and action on the following problems:

1. Finding workable procedures for moderating extreme price fluctuations in commodity trades that can importantly affect certain national economies.

2. Devising ways for the co-operative promotion of general economic growth and development to the end that individual living standards may show progressive upward trends throughout the hemisphere and including consideration of the establishment of an Inter-American Development Authority.

3. Working toward international agreement to set up a common market of hemisphere-wide scope or of regional common markets with merger as an eventual goal.

4. Establishing an Inter-American Payments Union to provide for the full convertibility of currencies among all nations subscribing to the above common market arrangement—interim or complete.

* Written in June 1958.

5. Facilitating other inter-American arrangements for co-operation upon common purposes and social objectives in such fields as education, low-cost housing, health, and technical assistance.

6. Assuring that all arrangements shall be so conceived and executed as to promote high levels of multilateral world trade and the general economic growth of the entire free world.

## COMMODITY AGREEMENTS

Since the problem posed by recent declines in prices of a number of commodities is immediately acute in certain Western Hemisphere nations, we believe that this is one of the first problems with which the Inter-American Economic Conference should cope.

Brazil, Haiti, Guatemala, Colombia, and El Salvador depend upon coffee exports for from two thirds to more than four fifths of their total export revenues; two thirds of Chile's exports earnings come from copper, and over half of Bolivia's from tin. Sugar, cotton, wheat, and meat are important foreign exchange earners for a number of Latin American countries. Venezuela is extraordinarily dependent upon oil exports; and to Ecuador, Panama, and three other Central American countries, bananas are of major significance. The peacetime markets for the latter two commodities have been relatively stable, however.

Measures to deal with the impact of surpluses and fluctuations of commodity prices on producing countries were set forth in Section III. We believe that the Inter-American Economic Conference should give urgent consideration to their implementation.

## PROMOTING HEMISPHERE
## ECONOMIC GROWTH

Although current emergency situations must be faced, the conference should give a major part of its attention to co-operative measures to achieve vigorous growth economies.

We have never organized ourselves, as a hemisphere, to give concerted attention to this task. The formation of an Inter-American Development Authority with capital contributions from all Western Hemisphere nations on some equitable formula, such as that which governs the Organization of American States contributions, could be the focus for co-operative action. There would be no lack of genuinely useful projects of broad regional significance once ingenuity is focused upon the objectives of fostering industrial and agricultural growth in a hemisphere of broad horizons and ever-increasing interdependence. We have scarcely begun to build the fabric of transport facilities that will clearly be needed if we do no more than follow the trends of intrahemisphere linkage that are forging themselves without benefit of conscious design.

## A WESTERN HEMISPHERE
## COMMON MARKET

One of the obvious items that should have high priority on the conference agenda is the development of new structural arrangements to promote trade and economic growth throughout the region and with the rest of the free world. This involves steps to work out a co-operative agreement with all the nations in the hemisphere to eliminate barriers to trade and investment and to ensure that the proceeds of growth are used to attain our common social and human objectives.

Latin American nations already are giving consideration to the regional application of common market arrangements for all of the twenty republics and for smaller groupings such as the Central American states. At present the intertrade among the Latin American nations amounts to less than 10 per cent of their total trade. This compares with a figure of about 50 per cent for Western Europe's intertrade. Historically, most Latin American economies have been oriented toward overseas trade with Europe or the United States. Trade within the area has been hampered by a lack of transportation and by tariffs, quotas, and inconvertible currencies. Therefore, any common market structures restricted solely to Latin American countries would start from a fragile base.

The Latin American economy however, has now reached a stage of development in which greater freedom of trade within the area would contribute to general growth. Industrialization in many nations is now outrunning local markets. Yet the barriers to trade are such that few industries in Latin America can serve more than a protected local market. In short, industry is bursting its seams, and it would be logical to widen the scope of industrial activity by removing present constraints. Any steps that Latin American countries take toward eliminating internal barriers and working toward broader regional development planning in harmony with the general economic growth of the free world deserve our support.

At the same time a broader approach is indicated. Serious consideration should be given to the advantages of working toward the establishment of a common market embracing the entire Western Hemisphere. We believe that this would contribute most effectively to a rapid and broad economic development in all nations of the Western Hemisphere. As is the case in the Western European Common Market, we might suggest a procedure to arrive at that goal over a period of, say, ten to fifteen years. This would permit time for the adjustment to the conditions of freer trade and exchange. The United States might well consider adopting a much swifter timetable on which it would free its own restrictions, and some special concessions of the infant-industry variety might be offered to nations lagging far behind in industrial progress.

Either of two general lines of approach might be followed. One is to move first to the development of regional trade arrangements among three groups: the Central American nations, the northern tier countries of South America, and the nations of southern South America. At the same time, a mechanism looking toward a common market area for the hemisphere might be established providing a timetable for the reduction of barriers to trade. The other is to move directly toward the ultimate and bolder concept.

No doubt the proposal of a common market will raise fears about impeding the industrialization of our South American neighbors. But the experience of Puerto Rico would seem to indicate that tariff barriers are not required to stimulate economic development; in fact, they may impede it. Puerto Rico is part of a common market with the United States. This has encouraged a greater degree of industrialization in Puerto Rico than anywhere in the Caribbean.

The experience of all less developed regions within the boundaries of sovereign states further supports the merit of this approach. The less developed regions of the United States, for example, have not been progressively impoverished. Rather, their participation in the same trading system as other areas has enabled them to attract an ever-greater share of industry.

## AN INTER-AMERICAN PAYMENTS UNION

A necessary complement would involve setting up an Inter-American Payments Union to provide full convertibility of currencies of all participants. Such a step is essential since currency restrictions and regulations can impede trade as effectively as tariffs and quotas. Thus, the development of a Payments Union must go hand in hand with steps to set up either a general or regional common market.

This fact offers an opportunity for the United States to assume constructive leadership. To make a payments union work, the participants must gain some direct advantage from it. The advantage such an arrangement would offer consists of making available to members drawing rights along the lines of the European Payments Union. The United States would supply the major part of the capital for the Payments Union and would be a part of it. Thus, the Inter-American Payments Union would be able to provide credit to cushion the adjustments entailed by shifts in the international economy. Such credits would enable nations to maintain their imports of materials, machinery, and equipment needed for economic development while carrying through the adjustments required to restore a high level of foreign exchange earnings. The credits extended by the Payments Union would be repaid in periods of high export earnings.

The details of the Payments Union would be worked out in negotiating the treaty setting up the organization. The objective should be to expand the area of convertibility throughout the hemisphere as a major step toward free world convertibility.

Adjustments to maintain over-all equilibrium in each nation's balance of payments would be made primarily through the exchange rate mechanism. To make the system work, multiple exchange rates would be abolished. If a nation is in persistent deficit with the Union, it would be required to adjust its exchange rate to restore equilibrium. At the same time, the managing body of the Payments Union would work, as the European Payments

Union has, to encourage member governments to adopt realistic monetary and fiscal policies.

An Inter-American Payments Union is an essential first step in broadening markets throughout the area. It would provide a tremendous impetus to economic development by making it possible for industries to serve the entire area, instead of individual nations. Thus, it could set in motion the sort of broad industrial and agricultural expansion that has been facilitated in the United States by the fact that there has always been one broad common market instead of forty-eight separate ones.

## WESTERN HEMISPHERE
## SOCIAL OBJECTIVES

An Inter-American Conference should consider also common efforts on the part of Western Hemisphere nations to further the important social goals that have been an inherent part of this hemisphere's cultural tradition.

In all our countries, the improvement of educational standards —primary, secondary, professional, and vocational—must be a compelling concern for all of us. We should also take more positive steps toward fostering a greater measure of hemisphere knowledge —its problems, cultures, values, and languages. A sufficient interchange of teachers and students would assure that the understanding would be more intimate and human rather than merely literary.

The foundation for mutually advantageous programs in the field of health already has been laid through the pioneer efforts of the Pan American Sanitary Bureau. The work in this field should be continued and expanded. Disease evades tariff barriers and has singularly small regard for latitude.

There are many other fields for which the possibilities of fruitful Western Hemisphere effort might be explored. Low-cost housing development is one that deserves exploration. In Lation America, as in Canada and in the United States, there is a flood of migration to urban centers inadequately equipped to deal with the problem. In this country, one of the measures that has helped has been the Federal Housing Administration program of mortgage insurance or guarantees. Without actual cost to the government it has mobilized funds for housing on a scale that would have been impossible without it. We should explore ways and means of developing co-operative procedures for dealing with urban housing problems throughout the hemisphere.

# VI. The Significance of Economic Growth for Attaining World-Wide Objectives

Experience supports three broad generalizations about economic growth:

First, it is not automatic. It requires a favorable climate. Some of the measures to provide such a climate have been set forth earlier in this report.

Second, even though we achieve a high rate of economic growth, we shall always face the problem of choice. The essential economic problem is that it is impossible to divide up more than we produce—some needs and demands will always go unsatisfied. And while the problem of choice must be posed as an economic matter, it cannot be resolved in purely economic terms. It is by the success with which a community uses the proceeds of its economic efforts to contribute to human, spiritual, and cultural development of its peoples that the community will ultimately be judged.

Third, steps to create a propitious climate for economic growth and to provide positive encouragement for growth can help immensely in dealing with the economic and social challenges facing the free world. A growing economy can absorb adjustments of a social, political, and economic nature which would prove unmanageable in a stagnant economy.

In economic terms, the immediate problem is to start the more than a billion people now living in the less developed areas up the road toward rising production and consumption while maintaining the growth of the industrialized areas. As we have pointed out, these two problems are intimately related.

## PAST GROWTH TRENDS

The economy of the free world has experienced considerable growth since 1948.

Manufacturing output per person has advanced 70 per cent since 1948. Specific examples of growth in the free world outside the United States in this period include increases in telephones in use from 23 million in 1946 to 50 million in 1957, in passenger cars from 10 million in 1949 to 24 million in 1957, in steel production from 72 million tons in 1949 to 144 million tons in 1957, and in petroleum production from 87 million tons in 1938 to 443 million tons in 1956.

Perhaps the most significant feature of this growth has been the resumption of general economic advance in Western Europe, following a period of virtual stagnation in output per person from 1913 to 1948. Western Europe has achieved an economic dynamism surpassing that of the period of growth in the century ending in 1913. Since 1948, gross product per capita in Western Europe has increased 40 per cent as compared with a rise of 20 per cent in the United States.

This growth in Western Europe has been accompanied by a tremendous upsurge in capital investment, a dramatic expansion of the middle income market, and a general acceptance of the idea that steps to encourage further economic growth are desirable. The fact that Western Europe's existing capital equipment—the value of all plant and equipment in being—may be less than half that in the United States for close to twice the population, points to the possibility of a long-term increase in capital investment in this area. The basic need for more investment in Europe provides a strong underpinning for the structure of world trade and development.

There has been some growth in per capita production in the less developed areas taken as a whole during the past decade. However, it has fallen short of that in the industrialized nations. While our statistical measurements leave much to be desired, it would appear that production has increased more rapidly than population in most nations in Latin America, the Middle East, Africa, South Asia, and Southeast Asia. There are some exceptions—in India, production may have about matched the growth in population after an extended period of decline in the level of living; and per capita production may have declined during the past decade in Indonesia, Chile, Haiti, and some other nations.

Nevertheless, the growth trend of the economy of the free world in the past decade undoubtedly has bettered that of the period before 1913 and is clearly above that of the 1913–38 period. To use exceedingly rough estimates, the total production of the economies of the industrialized free world may have moved ahead at an annual rate of 4 to 5 per cent in the past decade as compared with an annual advance of 2 to 3 per cent in the 1870–1913 period. This represents a considerable improvement in the performance of the economy of the free world in comparison with earlier decades.

As far as the less developed countries are concerned, their general growth trend was influenced by two important factors—one of which may prove transitory and one of which may prove of great significance in the longer run.

The first of the two factors is the fact that while prices of basic commodities rose much more rapidly after 1938 than prices of manufactured goods, many of them have fallen sharply in the past year, so that nations heavily dependent on exports of a single commodity face a significant reduction of export earnings during 1958.

The second factor is that many less developed nations have used a higher proportion of their increased international purchasing power of the past decade to finance imports of the capital equipment needed to support general economic development than in earlier decades when consumer goods dominated import patterns. This has produced a most significant shift in the general pattern of world trade:

1. In the pre-1914 period the typical pattern of trade involved an exchange of raw materials from less developed areas for consumer goods from industrialized areas—cotton and wheat were exchanged for cloth and flour.

2. Now the typical trade pattern involves an exchange of industrial raw materials or fuels for the machinery and equipment needed to support the general economic development of less developed nations.

3. Thus today's pattern of trade favors the general development of the entire world economy in a manner fundamentally different from the trade pattern of the nineteenth century.

## PROJECTIONS BASED ON PAST
## ECONOMIC GROWTH TRENDS

What would the world economy look like in ten or twenty years if recent trends should continue? In the present state of our statistical and economic knowledge, such a question can only be answered in the most tentative terms. International comparisons of economic statistics are exceedingly difficult to make in terms that are meaningful. Here are a few examples of the difficulties:

1. Statistical concepts and definitions differ importantly among nations. As an example, the statistical treatment of food produced and consumed on farms is far from uniform.

2. There is no satisfactory method for comparing levels of living as between different nations with scales of values that are not fully comparable—the choices between using any increase in purchasing power to buy an automobile as opposed to the basic necessities of food, clothing, and shelter may involve vastly different considerations.

3. Population projections are particularly hazardous. Too little is known about the factors influencing population trends to make anything more than very rough projections of populations in any area of the world.

Despite these very real problems, it may prove useful to attempt some projections of world production and population. While such projections cannot in any sense be considered as forecasts, they may help provide perspective on the general nature of the problems and challenges that may lie ahead. Their purpose is the modest one of showing the general dimensions of the economic prospects for the next ten to twenty years. Such projections are of course subject to modification as the world moves ahead in economic, social, scientific, and political fields.

If recent trends in the world economy should continue, we would see growth rates in total production of goods and services as shown in the chart, Recent Economic Growth Trends:

4 per cent in the United States

5 per cent in the other free industrial countries, including Western Europe, Canada, Japan

3 per cent in Latin America and perhaps 2 per cent in other less developed areas

6 per cent in the U.S.S.R., 3 per cent in the satellites, and 2 per cent in Red China*

If these growth rates are regrouped by broader categories, we get these results:

4.5 per cent in free world industrial nations
4.5 per cent in the Communist bloc
2.5 per cent in less developed nations

The following table projects these rates of growth in total production into the future and translates them into production per capita, using presently available population projections.

The broad conclusion that emerges from these projections of recent trends is that existing economic disparities among nations would widen. At recent growth rates in total production, output per capita in the free world industrial nations would increase 43 per cent in ten years and would double in twenty years. However, the increase in per capita output in the less developed areas taken as a whole would work out to only 14 per cent in ten years and 29 per cent in twenty years. Clearly, past rates of economic growth must be bettered throughout the free world, and particularly in the less developed areas, if we are to match the rising expectations of individuals everywhere.

It is also significant that the same rate of growth seems to characterize the Communist bloc as a whole and free industrial nations as a whole. Rapid growth in the Soviet Union is partially offset by the slower growth of Red China and the satellites, just as rapid growth in Western Germany, Canada, and Japan is combined with a slower growth in the United States, the United Kingdom, and some other nations. If these trends continue, the *relative* economic strength of the two groups will not change significantly.

A widening disparity between the industrialized and the less developed nations would make the attainment of a peaceful community of nations increasingly difficult. A great deal depends therefore on the ability to speed up the rate of growth of the less developed regions.

* Written in June 1958. The growth rate for Red China was probably understated at that time, although the lack of reliable data makes any estimate difficult.

# RECENT ECONOMIC GROWTH TRENDS

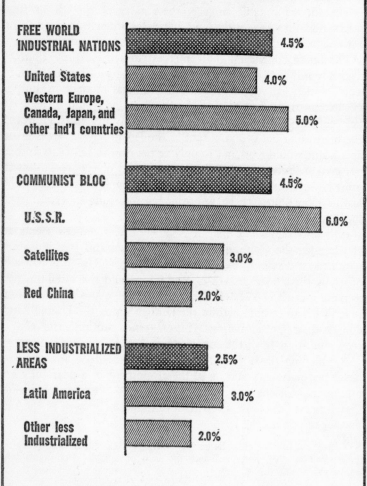

## AVERAGE ANNUAL INCREASE IN GROSS NATIONAL PRODUCT

**FREE WORLD INDUSTRIAL NATIONS** — 4.5%

United States — 4.0%

Western Europe, Canada, Japan, and other Ind'l countries — 5.0%

**COMMUNIST BLOC** — 4.5%

U.S.S.R. — 6.0%

Satellites — 3.0%

Red China — 2.0%

**LESS INDUSTRIALIZED AREAS** — 2.5%

Latin America — 3.0%

Other less Industrialized — 2.0%

Figures compiled in 1958.

PROJECTIONS OF WORLD POPULATION AND PRODUCTION

Assumptions: GNP grows 4.5 per cent in the free world industrial countries; 2.5 per cent in the less industrialized countries; 4.5 per cent in the Communist bloc.

| Area | Population (millions) | | | Total GNP ($ billions) | | | Per Capita GNP (dollars) | | |
|---|---|---|---|---|---|---|---|---|---|
| | 1956 | 1966 | 1976 | 1956 | 1966 | 1976 | 1956 | 1966 | 1976 |
| Industrialized Free Countries | 640 | 696 | 761 | 742 | 1152 | 1789 | 1159 | 1655 | 2351 |
| Less Industrialized Free Countries | 1132 | 1278 | 1451 | 134 | 172 | 220 | 118 | 135 | 152 |
| Communist Bloc | 910 | 1018 | 1148 | 284 | 441 | 685 | 312 | 433 | 597 |

Sources: United Nations Statistical Office; U. S. International Cooperation Administration

## NEEDS AND POSSIBILITIES FOR
## FUTURE GROWTH

What can be done to accelerate growth throughout the free world? The process of economic growth is extremely complex, involving as it does not only economic matters but also social, psychological, and political forces. Yet, as has been indicated earlier, one obvious economic difference between industrialized and less developed nations is the higher rate of investment in the former. In recent years, in Canada, Western Germany, and the U.S.S.R., where gross investment has run to 25 per cent or more of gross national product, GNP has grown at an average annual rate of more than 6 per cent. In the United States, the United Kingdom, and Latin America, where the investment ratio has been 15 to 19 per cent, average annual growth in GNP has been 3 to 4 per cent. In Asia, the Middle East, and Africa, investment has averaged 10 to 15 per cent of GNP, and the growth rate has been no more than 1 to 2 per cent.

It would be a profound mistake to draw the conclusion that the only secret of growth is an investment ratio of 25 per cent of GNP. A great many other things are involved in growth: effective governments, social attitudes, a high rate of saving that supports investment, a willingness to accept change, the training of scientists, business managers, and workers to use new capital. Yet there seems to be empirical evidence to support the conclusion that the development in a society of institutional arrangements that make it possible to devote a large part of GNP to investment is an indispensable factor in achieving a high average annual growth rate.

Consequently, one of the important tasks is to create conditions under which the rate of investment in the less developed areas can be increased from its present level of about 13 per cent of GNP as rapidly as possible. If this can be done in a political and social atmosphere that favors growth, these areas might achieve a rate of economic advance comparable to that of recent years in Canada, West Germany, and Japan.

To illustrate the significance of rapid growth, consider what might happen if total output in the less developed areas were to increase at an average annual rate of 6 per cent: per capita production in the less developed areas might rise 59 per cent in ten years and 151 per cent in twenty years—as against only 29 per cent in twenty years under recent trends.

The attainment of these goals would lift the average level of living in the less developed countries to that achieved by the industrialized nations in the early 1900s, with the average in Latin America approaching that in Western Europe in the 1920s. Moreover, the very qualities of dynamism involved in such a rapid pace of economic advance would lead to an ever-broadening sharing in the fruits of economic growth in a manner that would contribute to the ultimate purpose of our society. In short, the significance of rapid economic growth is that it would enable the peoples of the free world to face the future with hope. It is to this objective that the measures recommended in Sections III and IV are directed.

## INCREASING THE LEVEL
## OF INVESTMENT

In 1956, the less developed areas invested $17 billion in plant and equipment, housing, roads, schools, and other forms of capital. More than one fourth of this total represented the contribution of foreign investors—through a direct flow of private and public capital plus the reinvestment of earnings and depreciation funds. Thus, foreign investment has a vital role to play, and the measures recommended in Sections III and IV to encourage a greater flow of such capital throughout the world are essential.

The essential responsibility, however, remains that of the country itself. It is vital to encourage an upsurge in domestic capital investment of the less developed nations financed largely by their own domestic savings. This can be done although the effort required will be great. Even in areas with a low growth rate in total output, policies to channel the proceeds of growth into investment can accelerate the rate of economic advance. This works to the advantage of everyone in the community.

In other words, even a poor economy faces the choice of consuming all of the increase in its output (an increase which may run to 2 to 3 per cent per year) or devoting some of it to investment. If it is consumed, growth ceases. But if part of it is invested, the flow of goods and services is thereby increased for the indefinite future. That this process is one of the great bargains available to the world's consumers is shown by what has happened in the United States and in other industrialized nations. Living standards have increased because our institutions were so set up as to channel a part of the increase in output into capital investment.

What can be done to produce these benign results in the vast areas of the world where investment is now insufficient to support a rapid rate of economic growth? There are no simple answers, and no short cuts. An attempt to double the rate of investment in less developed areas in a short period would result in major economic and social changes.

In the long run, however, there is no reason why this cannot be accomplished. Yet economies cannot be turned upside down overnight without creating stresses and strains. Any attempt to raise the rate of investment in the less developed areas by massive international loans or grants would very likely prove disruptive if attempted in too brief a period.

An increasing flow of international capital—private and public —can assist in the development process, and it may be peculiarly important in initiating the cumulative and self-sustaining process of growth. The main and continuing impetus to investment must come through the encouragement throughout the free world of saving and investment together with initiative and enterprise, high levels of multilateral trade, and through the development of a broader understanding of our common purpose. We must, in short, develop a new vital international economic structure.

By doing so, the world can accelerate its economic growth and development. Important though such an accomplishment would be, it would solve only part of the economic and social problem. In a society dedicated to the fulfillment of the individual, the *uses* to which production is put are all-important.

## USES OF GROWTH

Ultimately the difference between societies is not only in their ability to achieve growth but more fundamentally by the uses to which this growth is put. This is shown in dramatic fashion when one compares the uses made of production in the free world with those of the Communist bloc. Such a comparison is presented in the table opposite. While it should be emphasized again that

## USES OF PRODUCTION—1956
(Billions of U. S. Dollars)
Percentages of total GNP)

| | GNP | | Investment | | Military | | Supply of Civilian Wants | |
|---|---|---|---|---|---|---|---|---|
| | Amt. | % | Amt. | % | Amt. | % | Amt. | % |
| Industrialized Free Nations | 742 | 100 | 146 | 20 | 59 | 8 | 537 | 72 |
| United States | 416 | 100 | 77 | 19 | 42 | 10 | 297 | 71 |
| Western Europe | 251 | 100 | 50 | 20 | 14 | 6 | 187 | 74 |
| Canada | 30 | 100 | 8 | 26 | 2 | 7 | 20 | 67 |
| Other Industrial | 45 | 100 | 11 | 24 | 1 | 2 | 33 | 74 |
| Less Industrialized Free Nations | 134 | 100 | 17 | 13 | 4 | 3 | 113 | 84 |
| Communist Bloc | 284 | 100 | 60 | 21 | 53 | 19 | 171 | 60 |
| U.S.S.R. | 162 | 100 | 44 | 27 | 42 | 26 | 76 | 47 |
| Satellites | 65 | 100 | 10 | 15 | 5 | 7 | 50 | 78 |
| Red China | 57 | 100 | 6 | 11 | 7 | 12 | 44 | 77 |

# USES OF PRODUCTION : 1956

## FREE WORLD INDUSTRIAL NATIONS

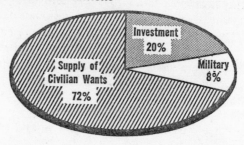

## U.S.S.R.

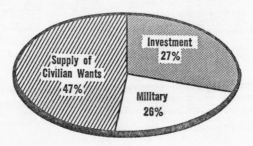

## LESS INDUSTRIALIZED AREAS

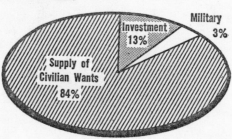

international statistical comparisons are subject to many reservations, the conclusions that emerge from the table in so striking a fashion have general if not precise validity.

It must also be stressed that the figures in the last two columns of the above table reflect the percentage of the gross national product that is devoted to improving current living standards, regardless of whether the goods and services are privately or publicly supplied. The figure is arrived at by subtracting from the gross national product military expenditures and capital investment, which, whatever its merit in increasing future output, does not satisfy current consumer needs.

In these terms the greater concern for the individual of the free system is plain. Seventy-two per cent of the output of the industrialized free world is devoted to the current welfare of the citizen, while the Soviet bloc makes available only 60 per cent, and the U.S.S.R. only 47 per cent. This is due largely to the fact that the U.S.S.R. devotes 26 per cent of its production to military uses as against 10 per cent in the United States.

Economic growth is not an end in itself. The growth achieved by the Soviet Union has involved the sacrifice of so much that it has been of little benefit to the individual citizen. The economic growth of the free world is a reflection of its concern for the individual, and its meaning resides in the possibility it affords for individual fulfillment. This must be the ultimate impetus behind our effort and the goal to which it must be directed.

# VII. Conclusion

This report has sought to outline an economic structure that may assist us, together with the other peoples of the world, to fulfill the universal aspiration to individual fulfillment and economic and social advance. To achieve this goal many specific recommendations have been made. Implementation of these recommendations will, we believe, greatly strengthen our nation and the free world.

A final concern of this report is an intangible problem: the attitudes of the American people and the vision of its leadership. The free world structure described in this report will not be meaningful unless it expresses a true sense of the community of all people. The measures required to attain such a structure cannot be carried out unless there is an informed public opinion accompanied by both concern and courage. One of the chief obstacles to an effective United States foreign economic policy has been the absence of an adequate public awareness of our stake in world economic and social progress; nor has our leadership been effective in bringing it about. There exists no vocal constituency for foreign economic policy as for so many other aspects of national policy.

As a result, foreign economic policy has all too often become simply a response to a series of separate crises. Specific measures to meet each such crisis tend then to be discussed and evaluated in terms of a particular issue alone, a procedure that accentuates the difficulties of each situation and obscures the over-all relationships.

Nothing is more important, therefore, than to bring about the conviction that a sustained and imaginative foreign economic policy, directed to the human aspirations we share with all peoples, is crucial not only for our self-interest but for the peace and well-being of the entire world. The history of America has seen an expansion of our concerns. Our task now is to project these concerns abroad, to make of the interdependence of all nations a source of mutual strength and vitality, to understand that the well-being of mankind is truly inseparable.

The rewards are great. They lie in a community of nations that support each other in realizing common hopes and in solving common problems. Every individual has a personal stake in the solution of the problems and the realization of the aspirations of his fellow men in ways that will preserve the great traditions of initiative and freedom. A community of sovereign nations bound together in service of this common goal is man's best hope for peace.

Report IV

# THE CHALLENGE
# TO AMERICA:
# ITS ECONOMIC AND
# SOCIAL ASPECTS

(First published April 21, 1958)

# Introduction by Panel IV

This report is the result of group effort to assess the potentials of our social and economic system and the responsibilities and challenges that will confront it in the next ten to fifteen years. In brief it is an effort to measure our capabilities, during that period, against our needs and aspirations. Although not every member of the panel subscribes to every detail, it reflects our substantial agreement.

As this report is published, we are undergoing an economic recession, a period of adjustment that should bring into sharp focus certain fundamentals. We have prided ourselves on the dynamism of our competitive economy. We have insisted that its freedom was the condition of its vigor. We have become aware of the interdependence of our well-being and that of the rest of the free world. Our economic and social system must demonstrate it vitality by the energy and courage with which it deals with its current problems

But beyond the immediate, even more fundamental tasks await us. We must accelerate our rate of growth. We must improve our educational system. We must expand our social progress in response to changing needs. We must strengthen our free institutions so that growth liberates the inner forces of individual development. Attaining these objectives implies a material cost as well as the marshaling of will and effort. Panel II outlined a security program, the fulfillment of which will require substantially higher expenditures over a period of years. The same is true for the nation's educational requirements formulated by Panel V. Our assignment was therefore to act as an auditor of the nation's economic potential—to add up the prospective claims in various fields covered by other panels and to compare their total with an appraisal of national productive capacity.

We are convinced that, even if our most hopeful projections are realized, new aspirations will produce new needs. The condition of our optimism and the impetus behind our growth is that our goals must always outrun present achievement.

\*THOMAS B. McCABE, president, Scott Paper Company; former chairman, Board of Governors of the Federal Reserve System; chairman of Panel IV.

\*ARTHUR F. BURNS, president, The National Bureau of Economic Research; professor of economics, Columbia University.

WILLIAM F. BUTLER, vice-president, Economic Research Department, The Chase Manhattan Bank.

LOWELL T. COGGESHALL, dean of the Division of Biological Sciences, University of Chicago; former special assistant for health and medical affairs, Department of Health, Education, and Welfare; president, Association of American Medical Colleges; president, American Cancer Society.

J. NORMAN EFFERSON, professor of agricultural economics and dean, College of Agriculture, Louisiana State University.

\*LESTER B. GRANGER, executive director, National Urban League, Inc.

\*DEVEREUX C. JOSEPHS, chairman, New York Life Insurance Company.

DEXTER M. KEEZER, vice-president, McGraw-Hill Publishing Company and director of Economics Department.

FRANKLIN A. LINDSAY, consultant, McKinsey & Company, Inc.

JOSEPH A. LIVINGSTON, financial editor, *The Philadelphia Bulletin*; former economist, *Business Week* and War Production Board.

STACY MAY, economist.

ROSWELL B. PERKINS, Debevoise, Plimpton and McLean; former assistant secretary, Department of Health, Education, and Welfare.

*ANNA M. ROSENBERG, public and industrial relations consultant; former Assistant Secretary of Defense for Manpower and Personnel.

EUGENE ROSTOW, dean, Yale University Law School.

J. CAMERON THOMSON, chairman of the board, Northwest Bancorporation.

*FRAZAR B. WILDE, president, Connecticut General Life Insurance Company.

BAYLESS A. MANNING, associate professor of law, Yale University; secretary of Panel IV.

This report was written primarily by the panel members themselves with the assistance of the staff. The panel especially appreciates the generous help of distinguished consultants from the fields of economics, business, labor, health and welfare.

* Also Overall Panel members.

# I. The Challenge of the Future

A great opportunity confronts the American people. If our economic system lives up to its opportunities, we can achieve an unprecedented degree of well-being for our citizens while making an increasing contribution to the world economic progress, which is indispensable for a lasting peace. The next decade and a half can thus enable us to approach the realization of a cardinal American ideal: a world in which every individual can lead a life of dignity, freedom, purpose, and fulfillment.

The past performance of our economy has been impressive. Over the seventy-five years before World War II, we doubled our national output about once every twenty-four years. Since World War II we have been growing at an even faster pace: at an average yearly rate that promises to double our output every eighteen years. It is the conviction of this panel that even our recent rate of advance can be bettered if we understand the rewards of growth and are prepared to make the necessary effort.

Economic growth is meaningless if its benefits are not generally shared. Actually a revolutionary upswing in the distribution of income and an extraordinary rise in social services have accompanied our increased productivity. Millions of families and individuals have steadily shifted from lower to higher brackets. Six out of ten families today are to be found in the bracket between $3,000 and $10,000. In 1947, about one fourth of all consumer units had more than $5,000 per year income; nine years later the proportion had risen to about one third, in terms of constant dollars. Moreover, the American people have always demanded and achieved not only increased incomes but more creative social action, better education, increased protection against economic vicissitudes, useful public works.

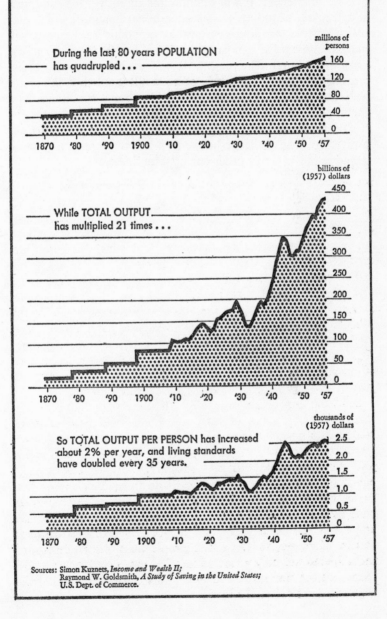

# THE ECONOMIC GROWTH RECORD

millions of
persons

During the last 80 years POPULATION
has quadrupled ...

160
120
80
40
0

1870    '80    '90    1900    '10    '20    '30    '40    '50    '57

billions of
(1957) dollars

While TOTAL OUTPUT
has multiplied 21 times ...

450
400
350
300
250
200
150
100
50
0

1870    '80    '90    1900    '10    '20    '30    '40    '50    '57

thousands of
(1957) dollars

So TOTAL OUTPUT PER PERSON has increased
about 2% per year, and living standards
have doubled every 35 years.

2.5
2.0
1.5
1.0
0.5
0

1870    '80    '90    1900    '10    '20    '30    '40    '50    '57

Sources: Simon Kuznets, *Income and Wealth II;*
Raymond W. Goldsmith, *A Study of Saving in the United States;*
U.S. Dept. of Commerce.

Thus, as our productivity rises so will the opportunities for individual fulfillment. It will multiply the incentives for enterprise. It will enable us to improve our educational system. It will permit us to increase our protection against economic hardship. It will make possible rising standards of national health. It will open new vistas of cultural achievement. It will enable us to devote increasing resources to giving hope to millions all over the world who are striving to improve their economic conditions, and thereby the freedom and dignity of their lives. The greater the rise in our productivity, the greater the possibility of realizing our aspirations. The challenge before us is whether our purposes can generate the effort to fulfill our opportunities.

# II. The American Economic Heritage

To meet the challenge of the future, it is important that we understand the elements that have shaped our social and economic environment. Some of these were accidents of history and geography. We had the advantage of a richly endowed territory. Two great oceans protected our shores while opening highways of commerce, and we had the good fortune of developing a largely unexplored continent with little interference from the outside world. Vast resources spurred the hope of great rewards and promoted intense competition and great efforts. An influx of peoples from all over the world provided the dynamism of new ideas and a constantly refreshed impetus toward development. But the mere presence of these factors was not enough. To a considerable extent the growth of our economy was the result of *tradition* and *attitude*.

From the beginning, a religious strain has permeated American society. A severe, self-denying ethic expressed the philosophy of a society seeking to develop a wilderness and encouraged attitudes of hard work, thrift, competition, and a dedication to one's worldly calling.

While the religious background contributed to the dynamism of our economy, it also infused the American system with a conviction that the pursuit of gain was not an end in itself but had to be justified by the use to which the gain was put. Thus our Puritan ancestry has been one of the forces importantly involved in the evolution of the American social consciousness. This strain of self-imposed accountability has been a persistent note of our society. It has produced the recognition—sometimes tardy and reluctant but never totally lacking—that the ultimate justification of our economic system is measured not merely by the private pocketbook but by the general welfare.

As a result, our national attitudes are a blend of individualism and social consciousness. The belief that a person or enterprise is entitled to the maximum rewards achievable by energy, vision, and competitive striving is powerful. But it is tempered by a concern for the underprivileged and by a faith in equality of opportunity. Similarly, the idea that a man's income and assets are his own, to be used as he wishes, is real but limited by considerations of social responsibility. The precise combination of individual rights and social responsibilities has changed over time and has always been a constantly evolving process. The reconciliation or compromise remains, and will probably always remain, one of our great challenges.

A second vital characteristic of the American economic system has been an absence of a feudal heritage. Except for the tragic racial problem stemming from the institution of slavery during this nation's formative years, there has been a lack of rigid class consciousness. The idea of an inferior or superior class of men is repugnant to the American ideal. Traditionally, ours has been one of the very few countries in the world where a man was proud of his humble ancestry and where his advancement typically depended on his ability rather than on his social background.

This basic outlook on men as individuals gifted with inherent worth has prevented American social and economic disputes from turning into irreconcilable conflicts. To be sure, our nation has not escaped economic and social discriminations and antagonisms. Yet the idea of a struggle to the finish has not been characteristic of our social disputes. Change has been sought *within* the economic and political system rather than in overthrowing it. The principal factors that have contributed to the development of this overriding consensus stem directly from our lack of a feudal past. One is the extraordinary mobility, social and geographic, that has invigorated our society. Another has been the gradual and fruitful development of labor-management relationships. Still another has been our capacity to absorb millions of new Americans, coming from every nation on earth, and to offer to them an environment in which their personal aspirations could take root.

A third source of vitality in the American economic system has been the democratic political framework, based on the concept of freedom and individual responsibility, within which the system has operated. In effect this has meant that the will of the people determined not only the political but also the economic framework. It has resulted in the constant adaptation of the economic system to the political wishes of the electorate. There has been a strong thrust toward equality of opportunity. Privilege and entrenched power, private or public, have been the constant targets of the popular will and have never been permitted to assume such proportions as to jeopardize the democratic texture of our society.

Closely related to this is an important characteristic of American society: its practical approach. Americans wanted education, health, freedom, and a higher living standard; they wanted an efficient credit mechanism, adequate electric power, and modern transportation; and they wanted the measures and policies that would yield these results. In general they did not want government in business or detailed regulation of economic life. But if the desired result called for either, Americans chose to do what seemed necessary.

The result of these attitudes and traditions has been an economic system in which private initiative, competition, public responsibility, and moral convictions have formed a singularly dynamic combination. To be sure, without the resources of a continent and our insulation for over a century from major foreign wars, the degree of expansion that the American economy experienced might never have taken place. But no discussion of our economic growth is complete without including the extraordinary role played by our *aspiration* to growth and by our belief that our aspirations could be realized by the economic and social system we knew. In the driving energy with which we assailed the wilderness, planted our cities, and developed our economy, there was a quality of impetuous vitality and hopefulness. The building of America was not only a matter of economic motivation. It was above all a tremendous human adventure.

# III. Policies to Promote Growth

The adventure of the American economy is a continuing reality. The dynamism that has produced the present level of well-being holds out the promise of a still more challenging future.

Our nation is dedicated to economic growth. It is also dedicated to full employment.* Each of these goals is a means to the other. In an economy where the labor force grows, capital accumulates, and technology advances, growth is necessary for the maintenance of full employment. And protracted failure to maintain full employment would, in turn, undermine the incentives to invest that are essential to growth.

We want to achieve rapid growth and full employment in a free and private economy. The freedom of the economy is fundamental to other freedoms we cherish. And the essentially free and competitive character of the economy is a vital condition for its growth. The freedom of millions of businesses to decide what and how to produce, for sale in competitive markets, stimulates a vast flow of enterprise and inventiveness, all of it being constantly tested by the efficiency with which it satisfies the desires of consumers.

The freedom of workers to choose occupations and to bargain for the fruits of their labor produces a strong motivation for the individual worker to improve his own capacities and for workers to co-operate with management in the introduction of better production methods. And the free choices of consumers define the purposes for which the productive process operates.

* Full employment means that employment opportunities in the nation as a whole are adequate and that unemployment is confined to a relatively small number of people who are without work for a relatively short period while they adapt to the available employment opportunities.

The way in which our free and private system works is importantly affected by public policy, which must indeed preserve it, create conditions for its success, and generate a climate of confidence. But the basic motivation and direction come from individuals in the private economy.

## ECONOMIC STABILITY

Rapid growth, full employment, a free economy—these three are consistent with each other and contribute to each other. But wise policies are required. An economy of growth is an economy of change and adjustment. An economy, like other organisms, does not grow at an even rate, in total or in its various parts. It will usually reveal some firms, areas, and industries growing very rapidly, some less rapidly, and others declining. The declines, as well as the expansions, are part of the necessary adjustment to the process of growth.

When the declines in major sectors of the economy coincide in time, economic activity as a whole recedes. Recession contains within it the danger—not the necessity, but the danger—of a cumulative downward spiral. If wages and profits decline and future prospects darken, individuals and businesses will cut their purchases, which will curtail production, employment, wages, and profits further and lead in turn to still further contraction.

Recognizing the importance of permitting adjustments in particular sectors of the economy, we must still seek to moderate their impact on individuals and to prevent the particular adjustments from cumulating into a general spiral. Business and labor must act constructively and with boldness. The government also must be prepared to stimulate and assist recovery.

While the problem of recession occupies our attention today,* in the long-term perspective we face another grave danger to growth—inflation. As a nation, we are deeply conscious of the consequences of failure to maintain full employment. We know the privation, insecurity, and anxiety it brings to those who suffer its chief impact. And we can see the economic loss of possible production.

But even after two decades of rising prices, the evils of inflation

* Written in April 1958.

are not understood sufficiently. Inflation also takes a human and economic toll. Persons with relatively fixed incomes, which includes most aged and dependent persons, typically suffer most. If inflation is protracted, everyone loses. Protracted inflation weakens incentives to save and misdirects economic effort. The pressures of inflation tempt many individuals and businesses into rash and unsound investment planning, with the grave danger of economic and social collapse.

Anti-recession and anti-inflation policies must thus be seen as two sides of the same coin. Firm and effective action in either direction cannot be marshaled unless there is confidence that action in the opposite direction will be equally prompt and bold when the trend turns.

Our problem is to walk a tightrope between inflation and recession. There are two necessary conditions for success in this endeavor. One is flexibility and reversibility in policy. The other is political maturity—the willingness to accept actions that are necessary to combat either inflation or recession, putting the national interest above the private interests of any special group.

## The Current Recession

The immediate economic task is to stop the current recession and bring about recovery. In combating the recession, however, we must not overlook nor disregard the basic strength of the American economy. Conditions today are structurally different and sounder than they were in the 1920s. But we must not be complacent. We should make the present setback the occasion for a step forward toward our over-all objective of stable growth. Wherever possible, measures to deal with the current recession should be in the direction of effecting permanent improvements in our economic structure. We need not only to take steps to promote an early recovery but also to take actions that will prepare us better to deal with future recessions.

Effective policy in the current recession requires simultaneous action on two fronts: private and public measures that create jobs, and public measures that cushion the impact of the recession upon the unemployed.

## Private Measures to Expand Employment

Jobs in this country arise fundamentally from a process in which people spend income earned in production for the purchase of goods and services, the production of which creates income. In this private employment-generating process, the businessman has a key role. His decisions about what to produce, how to sell it, and how to price it have great influence upon how much people buy and therefore upon how many people are employed. Moreover, the businessman's own investment in plant and equipment is a large and especially dynamic part of the total market for goods and for labor.

The vigor and imagination of the American businessman in developing new products, merchandising them effectively, and pricing them within the reach of consumers, plus his courage in making investments for future expansion, have been basic to the long-run growth of employment. The American businessman has today an unparalleled opportunity and challenge to exercise these talents. In spite of the increase in unemployment, consumer incomes for the nation as a whole are still high, and accumulated savings are higher than ever. Consumers have shown their willingness to buy when offered attractive values. Funds for investment are available at lower cost than a year or two ago. And as will be shown in the last section of this report, the long-term outlook for our economy is one of demands exceeding our capacity to produce.

Some businessmen are now demonstrating that by introducing new products, by selling aggressively, and in giving better values, they can expand their volume, increase profits, and provide more employment. Many businesses, keeping their eye on the real facts and prospects of the economy, are proceeding to carry out their long-term investment programs. There is an opportunity for many more to profit by these examples. It therefore is imperative that businessmen lead the way by exercising their traditional vision and courage in dealing with the current situation. They should not cling to old practices or rigid price policies or wait passively for government action or for the other fellow to blaze the trail for them.

We commend business organizations that urge businessmen to take advantage of the great opportunities that lie ahead.

## Federal Tax Reduction to Expand Employment

Of the anti-recession measures available to the federal government, tax reduction can be effective in the shortest time. Properly designed, it can have an immediate impact on both consumption and investment.

This panel believes that a tax cut would help overcome the current recession and expand employment. The precise amount should be determined by the Administration and Congress in the light of the best information available when the tax cut is made.

This panel also believes that any tax cut should be consistent with the long-term goals of tax reform. We therefore urge that the following principles be followed and implemented in the tax cut:

1. A tax reduction program should affect all taxpayers and stimulate individual and corporate enterprise, with the objective of creating more jobs.

2. The reduction in tax rates should be confined to a change in rates of personal and corporate income taxes. It should benefit individuals throughout the income scale, without favoring any special interests or eliminating any large group from the rolls.

3. The tax reduction should have no time limit specified in advance. Rather it should be conceived as an initial step in a permanent tax policy that regularly lowers taxes during recessions and that restores them to necessary levels once full employment is regained. When an increase in taxes is required, this also should be done in a way consistent with the long-term goals of tax reform.

In addition to the general tax reduction, we recommend another stimulus for the creation of jobs. Business firms should be allowed to depreciate at a more rapid rate capital improvements begun in a reasonably short period, say within the next twelve months.

## Accelerating Public Works

Major emphasis has been placed on tax reduction because it can have an immediate impact. The amount government can do quickly by expanding public works is very limited. The long lead time between the planning and execution of public works calls attention to the importance of creating the permanent shelf of projected public works that will be discussed below.

To combat the current recession we recommend that the government continue its efforts to accelerate public works projects already under way. Only useful projects that can be quickly started—say within three months—and completed within a reasonable period—say another twelve to eighteen months—should be initiated as part of the anti-recession program.

## Monetary Policy

The first important step taken to counter the recession—in the fall of 1957—was to reverse the policy of monetary restraint. In a series of moves, including reduction of reserve requirements, the Federal Reserve has put the banks in a position to expand their loans and investments. This has resulted in a greater availability of credit and a reduction of interest rates, thus creating conditions favorable to investment by businesses, present and prospective home owners, and state and local governments.

We urge the Federal Reserve System to move further: to increase the supply of money and credit as long as the economy is declining. This should produce lower interest rates and greater availability of credit, thus encouraging the creation of new jobs.

## Unemployment Compensation

While making every effort to create more jobs, we must cushion the impact of the recession on the unemployed. The unemployment compensation system is already doing much to reduce economic hardships. It also provides a major support to consumption expenditures and thus helps to buttress the economy. Unemployment compensation payments, however, have run out for many people and will run out for more.

Experience in the current recession underlines the need to improve the system of unemployment compensation. A program of permanent improvements will be discussed below. Such steps, however, are unlikely to bear fruit in time to help many of those now unemployed. Therefore emergency action must be taken. We agree that temporary federal supplements to unemployment compensation under state systems are necessary.

## Top-level Policy Guidance

Effective anti-recession policy requires decisive, continuous action reflecting a balancing of conflicting considerations and choice among alternative instruments. The same is true of anti-inflation policy and is more than doubly true of the real problem, which is to avoid both recession and inflation.

It is therefore necessary that the federal government be organized in such a manner that the question of what remedies to apply and how to apply them can be answered quickly and decisively.

During the current recession the President, under his own chairmanship, has been holding periodic meetings with a group composed of the Secretary of the Treasury, the chairmen of the Federal Reserve Board and of the Council of Economic Advisers, and the President's Special Assistant on Economic Affairs. This group follows in detail all economic intelligence relevant to the formulation of anti-recession policies and measures.

We believe that this is a step in the right direction but that consideration should be given to broadening the representation of the group to include the Cabinet officers especially concerned with foreign affairs and the human aspects of our economy. The implications of stability are broader than fiscal and monetary considerations and should benefit from the counsel of those who have direct responsibility for representing such interests. There is need, we think, for an informal advisory committee, thus broadly constituted, to meet at the call of the President, and under his direct leadership, at such intervals as may be necessary to consider and advise on stabilization policy, either anti-recession or anti-inflationary as appropriate.

The effectiveness of the program set forth above to combat the current recession will depend on prompt action in the application of the proposed remedies. Delay may make necessary the application of massive measures later on. A piecemeal approach will deprive otherwise sound policies of their full impact.

## Long-term Anti-Recession Policies

The current recession should spur an over-all improvement in our instruments for achieving growth with stability, which will help us to deal constructively with any threat of recession or inflation in the future. Not only that, but by building today for a better future, we will strengthen the confidence that must be the basis of a vigorous and sustained recovery.

### Improving the Unemployment Compensation System

The current recession has underscored the importance of a permanent improvement in our unemployment insurance programs. For one thing, the present system does not cover some 12 million workers. For another, the duration of benefits is too short. Thus, unemployment insurance tends to fail at the precise point when a prolonged downturn makes it most necessary. Finally, the extent of the benefits is insufficient. In terms of a percentage of the over-all wage, insurance benefits have in fact declined since they were first instituted in the 1930s.

This panel has endorsed, above, the temporary federal supplements to unemployment insurance benefits. At the same time we recommend the following permanent improvements:

1. Extension of the insurance system to include all or most of the 12 million employees not now covered.

2. The increase of insurance benefits to cushion more adequately the loss of wages during unemployment and provide purchasing power to counteract recession.

3. The lengthening of the maximum duration of the benefits to something like thirty-nine weeks.

Finally, we recommend that the permanent improvement of our unemployment insurance system be coupled with better administration in the interest of preserving incentives to work.

### A Shelf of Public Works Plans

In no aspect of anti-recession policy do short- and long-term considerations more critically affect each other than in the construction of public works. Many months necessarily elapse between the planning of public works and the actual expenditure of funds. Thus if they are initiated only after the onset of a recession, they may fail to reach the construction stage in time to check the downturn, or conversely, if an upturn has already occurred, such projects may then become a stimulus to inflation. Therefore, it is essential that needed public improvements be planned and stock-piled, in advance, for ready use as counter-recession measures when needed.

To undertake such a stockpiling of public works requires a long-range and continuing study of the public investment needs of our nation over the next decade. Such a study should put high priorities on clear public needs such as urban redevelopment, schools, hospitals, and highways. Not all types of public works lend themselves readily to use as countercyclical measures, and determination of priorities will be influenced by that consideration. By and large, to be useful as anti-recession weapons, public works should be the kind that can be quickly initiated and completed within a period of twelve to eighteen months.

Stockpiled public works plans should also include provisions for acceleration and deceleration as the economic situation may require. A shelf of such projects is especially important at the state and local levels, where they can be related directly to local needs and conditions and where purchases of goods and services are much larger than federal nonmilitary purchases.

In summary then, we recommend:

1. A long-range and continuing study of the public investment that will be needed over the next decade, together with the development of specific plans for public works that can suitably be fitted into a countercyclical program.

2. Enabling legislation should, whenever and wherever possible, involve a provision for two-way flexibility so that public works can be speeded up to combat recession and slowed down if inflation threatens.

## Economic Statistics

To develop sound economic policies we need the best possible economic intelligence.

One of the great dangers of attempting to minimize economic

fluctuation is that we will take action either prematurely or too late and that the type and extent of action will not be closely related to the economic threat. We cannot hope for perfection in these delicate matters of timing and judgment. But the sensitiveness of our economic warning system can be considerably improved. We need better information on projected capital expenditures, on inventories, on construction work, and on consumer spending intentions—to mention only a few items. An additional $5 to $10 million a year for such government statistics would yield very high returns in the form of more reliable economic intelligence.

## Anti-Inflation Policies

In an economy dedicated to full employment and growth, it is necessary to be very alert to the dangers of inflation. Anti-inflationary methods are, in the nature of the case, unpopular. They all involve holding back some demands—by making it less easy to borrow or requiring higher taxes or lower government expenditures. It is true that these measures are designed to protect total *real* incomes, *real* product, and *real* benefits. But even if this is recognized, a difficulty would remain. Anti-inflationary restraints will affect different people differently. Therefore, it is always difficult to get agreement on any particular combination of anti-inflation measures.

### The Problems of Inflation

The problems of dealing with inflation are to a considerable extent the reverse of problems of overcoming recessions. The necessary condition for containing inflation is that money expenditures on goods and services should not rise faster than the real supplies available. The means for achieving this result include making money relatively scarce and expensive and maintaining a surplus in the federal budget.

Thus, the Federal Reserve has the important responsibility for using its powers to raise rediscount rates and reserve requirements and conduct open market operations in a manner that will place a rein on credit expansion. Government fiscal policy can also make a contribution to checking inflation; by collecting more money in tax revenues than it pays out in expenditures, government can reduce effective purchasing power and help relieve the pressure of a demand that is outrunning the supply of goods and services.

We have less than assured knowledge of the timing and magnitude of either monetary or fiscal action necessary to accomplish a given effect under given conditions. But we do know the direction in which both operate and that both can exert a potent influence. We are entitled to the assurance that government will use these powers when they are needed to curb inflation with no less vigor than when they are applied to counter recession.

Reasonable stability of the average consumer price level should be explicitly recognized as a high objective of national policy by a Congressional declaration, preferably through an amendment to the Employment Act.

It is frequently claimed that our economy has an inflationary

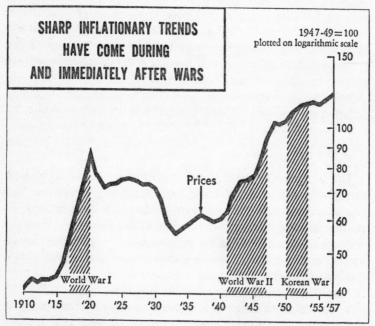

SHARP INFLATIONARY TRENDS HAVE COME DURING AND IMMEDIATELY AFTER WARS

1947-49=100
plotted on logarithmic scale

Prices

World War I   World War II   Korean War

Sources: U.S. Dept. of Labor;
         U.S. Dept. of Commerce

bias because of the tendency of wages and prices to rise even in periods of slack demand. Most of the inflation of the past twenty years, however, was associated with World War II and the Korean War, when demand was clearly excessive. Much of the rest of it came in the years 1955–57, and did not exceed the amount that historically has accompanied a vigorous cyclical expansion. Our experience with inflation when demand was neither excessive nor rapidly rising is too scanty to support fundamental conclusions about the inflationary bias of the American economy.

Yet we cannot deny that this problem of inflation, even in time of slack demand, may exist in the future. If it does, the nation would be faced with a choice to which there can only be one answer. Power to force inflation upon the nation as a whole cannot be left in the hands of private groups. If such power exists or comes into being, it will have to be restrained, preferably by the self-restraint of business and labor leadership.

## Steps to Control Inflation

There is much to be done in improving instruments for restraint of demand and increasing understanding of their use. But the general outlines of a program for the restraint of inflation are clear:

1. When the economy is at a full employment level, the federal budget should have a surplus of receipts over expenditures.

2. The adoption of two-way flexibility in public works programs recommended above will enable these expenditures to be used countercyclically.

3. The Federal Reserve should use its general controls to keep the supply of money and credit from rising too rapidly.

4. Business and labor must exercise restraint, the former in its pricing policies, the latter in its wage demands.

5. The explicit recognition of general price stability as an objective would contribute to better balance in public policy.

6. Tax policy reforms should take into account the use of taxes in combating inflation as well as recession.

7. Industry and labor should continue to seek out new production and construction methods to reduce costs and increase productivity as a positive approach against inflation.

## THE ENCOURAGEMENT OF GROWTH

It is the essence of an economy of growth that its frontiers are constantly changing. The frontiers of today become the familiar territory of tomorrow.

The full harvest of a growth economy can be reaped only in an environment that affords incentives. Initiative and enterprise, the willingness to save and invest capital, and confidence in the future are essential ingredients of a growth economy and flourish where constructive effort carries the expectancy of satisfying reward.

The basic factor that will determine this country's future rate of economic progress is the degree to which we keep alive the incentives upon which growth depends. Profit and competition are the mainsprings of business initiative and imagination, as well as the weighing scale of business competence. The expectancy of progressively increasing income, the raises that go with promotions in an expanding economy, and the prospect of achieving ownership status through an investment stake or even through independent proprietorship have been a vital part of our tradition.

The policies, private and public, to encourage long-term growth are the concern of this section.

### Government Responsibility for a Climate of Growth

Government policy and action influence the economic climate in a host of indirect ways quite apart from direct purchases of goods and services and fiscal operations.

The incidence of its tax structures can encourage or blight incentives. The same is true of its regulations governing domestic and foreign trade, its patent laws, the intricate fabric of its legislative and administrative dealings with business, agriculture, and labor. The way in which it administers its stockpiling programs and disposes of its surpluses, the management of its procurement policies, the extent and manner of its direct competition with private enterprise—all of these build or undermine an environment conducive to growth.

The matter of government attitude is scarcely less important than the letter of its laws. We are quick to recognize the presence or absence of a favorable or unfavorable economic climate in foreign countries but less aware of the limitations in the climate at home. Since the health of our private economy will determine our growth progress, it is incumbent upon us to see that our government provides a climate in which private incentives flourish.

Throughout most of this nation's history, the government's direct role in economic life was of relatively minor weight. In 1929, government expenditures for goods and services—federal, state, and local—absorbed only 8 per cent of the country's total output. The federal government's outlays, including expenditures for national defense, were outweighed by state and local government expenditures by a ratio of almost six to one.

The heavy burden of national security requirements combined with a variety of additional responsibilities with which government has been charged have increased the relative weight of government purchases in our economy to two and one-half times what they were in 1929. And within the government sector, federal expenditures are now over 40 per cent larger than state and local combined.

Today, government, through its spending and taxing measures, exercises an important influence upon the demand side of the national economy's ledger. But its role in contributing to the supply of goods and services produced is of relatively modest weight. The private sector of the economy produces most of what government buys, as well as almost all of the much larger purchases of private consumers and investors. Hence, our ability to service the expanding demands of our economy as a whole depends primarily upon the growth trend of private business and industry.

### Strengthen Competition and Remove Rigidities That Impede Growth

If we genuinely believe in the competitive system, we should be willing to abide by its rules. Chief among these is the requirement that businesses should compete. Each should stand on its own feet, justify its existence by its offerings in the market place, and sell on a price-quality basis against all competition. It similarly should be incumbent upon both business and labor to adjust to changes that promote the progressive improvement in productivity upon which increased living standards importantly depend.

The natural adaptation of a free economy is not always quick or complete. There is a tendency to seek protection against pressure for change. When this resistance takes deep-rooted forms or when it acquires legislative sanction, rigidities impede and distort the over-all advance.

The protective tariff is a leading example of a policy aimed at protecting industries against the forces of change. Our tariffs were originally intended to help new American industries take root. At present, however, our tariffs often serve to impede rather than to encourage the achievement of a higher national product and lower costs for the consumer. Since the economic health and rising living standards of the other nations of the free world depend importantly on their ability to trade with us, considerations of foreign policy are added to those of economic efficiency in urging tariff reduction.

This does not mean the wholesale reduction or elimination of tariffs. Grave damage could be wrought by tariff cuts indiscriminately applied. But there is a need for a tariff policy that moves steadily toward our goal of lower trade barriers. This could be coupled with provision to help redirect the resources and efforts of those industries and workers seriously affected by tariff reduction.

The report of Panel III on international economic and social objectives and strategy of the United States deals with this matter more fully and in more detail. Therefore we confine ourselves to a strong recommendation for the continuance of reciprocal trade policy, and we urge that it be administered so as to promote gradual and selective tariff reductions.

A second group of rigidities that impede economic growth are those caused by the formation of monopolies or collusive practices that reduce the invigorating stimulus of a genuine competition. Government must be alert at all times to maintain and strengthen competition throughout our economy. This was and remains the purpose of our antitrust laws. Yet in the enforcement of the antitrust laws a balanced flexibility must be attained. Their administration must be sufficiently flexible to adapt to the realities of change in business structures and operations, yet not so volatile as to risk a paralysis of responsible business activity because of uncertainty.

A third area in which a greater degree of flexibility is needed relates to the remaining instances of resistance to modernization and efficiency in production. Rules that require more labor than is needed for given jobs, the retention of outmoded equipment or processes, or any restrictions that interfere with the goal of expanding production with due regard to the welfare of workers are inconsistent with our national growth.

## Tax Reform to Promote Incentives for Growth

In 1957, government—federal, state, and local combined—collected in taxes the equivalent of 25 per cent of the nation's total output. About two fifths of this covered federal government expenditures for national security purposes.

One fifth (the so-called transfer payments) was collected by government from one group of citizens and paid out to others, as welfare payments, payments under the several social insurance programs, and as interest on government debt. The remainder went for the purchase of goods and services on government accounts, including payrolls of public servants. Thus, government at all levels collected in taxes 25 per cent of the national product and purchased 20 per cent of all goods and services produced by the economy on direct government account.

Clearly, government institutions determine the direction of a formidably large portion of total economic activity in the United States, and their tax takings are even larger. Before World War II, their tax takings were proportionately less than half as large. Yet our tax structure has grown haphazardly, with numerous changes in rates but without a serious consideration of how the incidence and rate structure were affecting the incentives that determine growth upon which ability to pay taxes depends. Systematic tax reform, at federal, state, and local levels, is long overdue. The prospect of a substantial future increase in over-all government expenditures, and hence of tax collections, in the years ahead makes this an even more urgent requirement.

As presently constituted, our tax system presents a series of important impediments to growth. The very high graduated rates in the personal income tax structure reduce the incentive and the ability to accumulate capital and put it to productive use. The failure to develop averaging devices presents an impediment to certain groups. The very high corporate tax rates and present depreciation provisions slow the growth of corporate enterprise.

If we are to have a more rapidly growing economy, we must seek ways to reduce or remove these impediments. Yet there is a wide diversity of opinion over the incidence and impact of various elements of our tax system and a deplorable lack of factual knowledge in this significant field. Before decisions can be made about the kinds of tax revisions that would serve to stimulate growth, it is necessary to learn more about the manner in which various taxes operate to impede growth.

Therefore, we recommend that a careful and thorough study be undertaken of our entire tax system—federal, state, and local. This could be done by setting up a tax commission, which might be under private auspices, along the lines of the recently created Commission on Money and Credit.

In our opinion, such a tax commission should devote major attention to the following four impediments:

## Problem of Capital Accumulation

Without private capital for investment, we would, as we know, lack one of the essential ingredients for our growth. But the special vitality of the American economy is based on more than the mere availability of private capital—it finds its wellsprings of vigor in the very possibility and the actual process of capital accumulation. It is this expectation and the process of realizing it that have given our society much of its uniquely buoyant thrust.

As our tax structure has developed, it has steadily become more difficult for those who start without capital to accumulate it. This is especially true of those who are dependent on salaries or those who elect to do business as sole proprietors or partners. For it is on individuals in these categories that our high tax rates—and particularly the high graduated rates on any increases in incomes —fall with devastating effect. At the same time, it is the able and energetic individuals in these groups that we must particularly encourage for the drive and imagination essential to growth.

The largest source of taxation in this country is the tax on individual incomes. Our strong reliance on income taxation reflects our belief that personal incomes are the best index of ability to pay, and we graduate our personal income tax because we believe that those with higher incomes have a greater relative ability to pay than those in lower income classes.

But experience strongly suggests that the nation would be better served by an income tax with somewhat lower rates that would apply more equally among persons with the same income. With personal incomes in excess of $340 billion we now levy rates starting at 20 per cent and rising to as high as 91 per cent in order to collect $37 billion.

At all income levels, there are entirely legal opportunities for people to avoid the stated rates. The reason these opportunities exist is that Congress has legislated special relief provisions believed to be in the national interest and designed either to soften the impact of the high rates on particular groups or to encourage particular activities. In some cases, the relief provisions were enacted many years ago when their revenue consequences were small. In most cases there has been no careful modern review of these exemptions, exclusions, credits, and preferential provisions to balance the loss of revenue they involve against the contribution they now make to growth in the economy as a whole.

There should, we believe, be a fundamental review of our income tax structure to determine its effectiveness in achieving its fundamental purposes of revenue collection and promotion of growth. Without such a comprehensive review, and the revisions in our tax laws that it establishes as necessary, the next decades will not see the fruitful economic growth that is possible and that the well-being of the people in America and the free world will require.

If our tax structure is equitable and promotes healthy growth, we will not find individuals spending disproportionate time and effort on earning incomes in ways that receive preferential tax treatment but that may no longer fully contribute to national growth and well-being. A distortion in incentives to work, save, and invest is tolerable and warranted only if it promotes a better allocation of resources and thus insures an even greater rate of economic growth for the nation as a whole.

## Income Tax Averaging

All taxpayers, individual and corporate, experience variations in income. Some, however, by the nature of their occupation, are more subject to such variations. This is true of creative artists and many professional people whose incomes have sharp peaks and valleys. It is also true of athletes and others who may crowd peak earnings into a relatively short span of years. The problem is compounded for self-employed persons who cannot set aside a part of their earnings, free of tax, under retirement plans to provide income in their older, less productive years.

Small business, too, is vulnerable to sharp variations in earnings. Small businesses tend to be less stable, to be frequently associated with more risks, and to have less depth and variety of resources to cushion and spread the normal risks of free enterprise.

Our present tax system unduly penalizes the taxpayer whose income is not evenly spread but concentrated in a relatively few years of high earnings. Greater equity and more incentive would, therefore, be achieved by a system that permitted the averaging of income over a period of years.

Provisions for income averaging are familiar in our tax system, and they take many forms—including, for example, tax loss carry backs and carry forwards, and provisions for spreading back certain types of income earned over a period of more than three years. The difficulty is that such equitable principles are not always consistently applied throughout the tax laws, and frequently they are not available to all taxpayers. The present situation should be corrected. It is discriminatory in its impact and tends to distort the form and manner of our economic growth.

## Depreciation Allowances

Depreciation allowances under the tax law greatly influence the extent and timing of capital investments by business. All capital outlays involve risk and uncertainty. The sooner a capital outlay can be expected to be recovered, the greater will be the willingness to invest in depreciable property and the greater will be the opportunity to secure funds for such investments.

The tax law in this country, in spite of some helpful liberalization in 1954, still may be too rigid and restrictive in its treatment of depreciation. More liberal depreciation allowances, properly safeguarded to prevent abuse when depreciated property is sold, would be an important reform.

## Moderation of Corporate Income Taxes

The present corporation tax rate of 52 per cent is the highest corporation tax rate in our history with the exception of wartime periods, when excess profits taxes were levied. High corporate tax rates encourage wasteful expenditures and promote tax considerations to a dominant place in business decisions. Excessive rates discriminate against equity financing and encourage debt financing, thus making business more vulnerable to decline in business activity. In short, the high corporate tax rate tends to distort and inhibit the vital contribution that business, through the use and investment of its capital, must make to our natural growth. Some moderation of the general corporate rate is long overdue.

Even with reforms, the impact of our basic tax structure will remain great. If our needs or our desires for public expenditure increase faster than our total economic growth, then our tax burden will be the heavier. Economic growth alone can keep that burden from becoming excessive. In any case, taxes will be a constant burden on the foreseeable future. It is the cost we pay for freedom and for the ends we choose to pursue under freedom.

We have identified four areas in which there is ground for believing that reform is needed and where, intelligently applied, it should promote higher national product and income to offset the effect of lowered rates. But we are fully conscious that a responsible position in this field requires a careful weighing of the effect of any changes on revenue requirements as a whole. We believe that no time should be lost in setting out upon this task.

## Public Expenditures in Support of Growth

Public expenditures in support of growth are a traditional and an essential part of our economy. Far from being a hindrance to progress, they provide the environment within which our economy moves forward.

As set forth in other sections of this report, we shall need, in

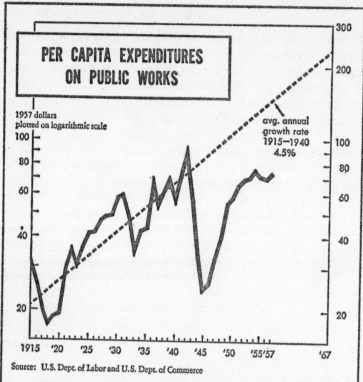

**PER CAPITA EXPENDITURES ON PUBLIC WORKS**

1957 dollars
plotted on logarithmic scale

avg. annual
growth rate
1915—1940
4.5%

300

200

100

80

60

40

20

1915  '20  '25  '30  '35  '40  '45  '50  '55 '57  '67

Source: U.S. Dept. of Labor and U.S. Dept. of Commerce

We need to increase expenditures on public works to support economic growth. In the period 1915-40, per capita expenditures in constant dollars on schools, roads, waterworks, and other public works rose at an average annual rate of 4.5%. In this manner, federal, state, and local governments provided the public assets needed by a growing economy.

Expenditures dropped sharply in 1932 and 1933 and, despite a massive effort by the federal government, did not regain their previous rate until 1936. This experience shows that public-works programs are slow to get under way.

Despite the sharp increase during the past decade, per capita expenditures on public works are no higher than they were two decades ago. Moreover, they have leveled out in the past few years. And total public-works expenditures have lagged behind the growth of total national output—the ratio to GNP declined from 4½ per cent in the late 1930s to 3 per cent now.

the next decade, a greatly expanded school system to broaden and improve education. We shall need urban redevelopment on a vast scale to lift the living standards and the social and cultural content of metropolitan life. We shall need more and better highways and improved modes of transportation to spur commerce, communication, and travel. We shall need better water supply and pollution control systems to meet domestic, industrial, and agricultural requirements. We shall need more health and hospital facilities, more basic and applied research, more recreation areas. The list is extensive and, as the final section of this report sets forth, estimates indicate an increase of almost 50 per cent in government purchases of goods and services by 1967.

If total national output grows at a comparable rate, then government's share in the total would stay at approximately the present level. Without such growth, however, these "social capital" investments will either have to be curtailed, or they will take a larger share of the national output, leaving a smaller share to the private economy. Since most of the dynamic thrust of our growth comes from private activities, there is danger that too large and too rapid a diversion of funds to public expenditure will react adversely on the entire economy.

Therefore, the very magnitude of prospective claims for publicly directed expenditures imposes upon us the obligation to exercise wise and vigilant discipline. We must see that wasteful government expenditures are eliminated and that less important public purposes are subordinated to those with higher priority. This poses a challenge to our political system as much as to our economic one. It raises questions of leadership, of government information policy, of the relevance of established institutions of government to new and difficult tasks. These subjects are dealt with in Report VI, which examines democratic processes and procedures.

Unwarranted public demands on government must be checked. Notable among these are numerous subsidies which have no place in a growing and prosperous economy.

Many of these subsidies have their roots in the 1930s or World War II and no longer serve the public interest. For example, the stockpile programs have been used to support the prices of some industrial raw materials rather than to store materials that may be needed in the event of war. Pensions to some veterans for nonservice-connected disabilities, as well as subsidies in other fields, also warrant re-examination. And the agriculture program should be redirected along the lines discussed elsewhere in this report in order to bring supply and demand into better balance.

## Government Monetary and Fiscal Policies
## Contributing to Growth

Since we have set forth our ideas on the responsible use of monetary and fiscal powers as stabilization instruments earlier in this section, it would be redundant to discuss here procedures already described.

It is appropriate, however, to point out that the moderation of the fluctuations in either direction not only serves to prevent serious hardships but contributes constructively to the growth process itself. The fear of inflation or deflation inhibits alike business and consumer decisions that make for growth and causes distortions in our economy that are not quickly remedied.

The lost ground incident to a serious decline may take years to make good. Even the current relatively moderate recession has cut gross national output by an annual rate of $25 billion, from the $450 billion level that we might by now have achieved on a steady growth trend to the $425 billion actual rate of the first quarter of 1958. Since government has been taxing at an over-all 25 per cent rate, this in itself means a $6 billion annual loss rate in government revenues if production for all of 1958 does not average above current levels. If a tax cut could importantly influence a prompt recovery that might not otherwise take place, it would be a good bargain for the economy as a whole and for the fiscal position of the federal government as well.

Quite apart from their specialized use as stabilization instruments, sound monetary and fiscal policies play a continuing role in supporting a growth economy. The flow of money and credit has to be geared to expanding demand, and its availability is a condition of expansion. Government expenditures, when budgets are generally in balance, contribute to over-all demand, as do private expenditures, without exerting an influence in the direction of either inflation or deflation.

## The Encouragement of Small Business

Basic to much of our past economic achievement has been our ability to encourage men with new ideas and new products to establish their own enterprises. Our great industries began as small-scale operations, and the majority of them are still less than 50 years old.

We still possess a very great reservoir of such economic initiative in the 4.2 million nonfarm businesses of our nation. This is the largest total in our history. Although there is a rapid turnover of some 300,000 to 400,000 of the smallest of these businesses—the figures indicate that there is no shortage of the spirit of enterprise in the business population. They may also indicate that managerial experience and competence is the most important factor in growth.

There is, however, a growing body of evidence that smaller and medium-sized businesses, and particularly manufacturing firms—

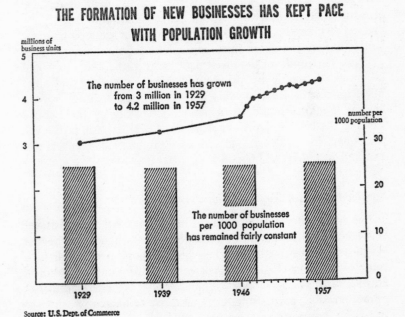

### THE FORMATION OF NEW BUSINESSES HAS KEPT PACE WITH POPULATION GROWTH

millions of business units

The number of businesses has grown from 3 million in 1929 to 4.2 million in 1957

number per 1000 population

The number of businesses per 1000 population has remained fairly constant

Source: U.S. Dept. of Commerce

even those that have successfully established themselves in their industries and have solid prospects for growth—have difficulty in obtaining financing for the expansion of their operations. There is also a probability that inadequate financing reduces the rate at which new firms are established.

The need is primarily for long-term equity or loan funds. As a result of the inability to obtain capital funds, the opportunity for establishing a new firm or for expanding an established firm is too often lost. Often the established firm merges with a larger enterprise that can command the necessary resources. The past few years have seen a wave of such mergers. Such a condition is neither conducive to vigorous competition nor to economic growth.

## Financing Mechanisms and Managerial Counsel

One of the means by which the growth of small business can be encouraged is to make available funds for expansion from sources outside the business and to help with expert management advice. One promising approach is the establishment of regional investment trusts—that is, "capital banks"—that can expertly appraise the prospects of firms seeking funds for expansion, make long-term investments in them, and advise them on management policies. The funds for the investment trusts in the long run would be provided mainly by private investors. Experience indicates, however, that success for this type of venture requires governmental sponsorship and participation, preferably by the Federal Reserve System, in providing part of the initial funds for the investment trusts. Possibly some special tax treatment on retained earnings would be justified.

## Special Impact of Taxes on Small Business

The factor that chiefly distinguishes the present difficulties of small business from that of an earlier day, when most of our existing large firms attained their leading positions, is the high rates of taxation. Eighty-five per cent of the nonfarm business entities in the nation today operate as unincorporated businesses (proprietorship, partnership, etc.), and the earnings of such businesses are taxed at the personal income tax rates. Since the small businessman and innovator must rely to a large extent on his own financial resources or on the resources of his family and close friends, high individual and corporate taxes that preclude large individual savings restrict the flow of funds to this vital segment of our enterprise system. In other words, they greatly limit the amounts that firms and their owners can save for re-investment from business profits. We recommend tax reforms to cope with this situation:

1. Provision should be made to extend the accelerated depreci-ation provisions enacted in 1954 to include business purchases of up to $50,000 of used assets in any one year.

2. The period over which business losses may be carried back should be increased from two to five years, in order to enlarge the opportunity for the small businessman to obtain an im-mediate tax refund in the event he sustains a sizable loss in one year after a series of profitable years.

3. Estates consisting largely of investments in small businesses should be allowed, subject to a reasonable interest charge, to pay estate taxes over a period of ten years in order to prevent forced liquidation of the businesses to discharge the overhanging tax obligation.

4. Serious consideration should be given to the introduction of more averaging into the income tax system as indicated earlier.

For example, corporations should be entitled to carry back and to carry forward unused surtax exemptions, just as they are allowed to carry back and to carry forward losses. This revision would permit small corporations to take full advantage of the $25,000 surtax exemption in every year even though their incomes fluctuate above and below this level.

## Role of Responsible Trade Unionism

Our labor movement has grown with our economy. Free col-lective bargaining has achieved recognition as an established part of our economic environment.

Honest, responsible trade unionism can give encouragement to growth by securing the full and willing co-operation of labor and management in the task of expanding national output. Since labor's role in economic growth is so vital, it is important to establish and maintain an environment that will call forth the most honorable, responsible, and imaginative trade union leadership. The further development of unionism along these lines imposes a great responsibility not only on the rank and file of labor but also on industry and government. Co-operation with responsible labor leadership should serve to stimulate the full contribution labor can make to growth and eliminate the forces that might take root in a strained and troubled labor movement.

## Natural Resources

Any serious effort to project our growth potential for the future must take account of our supply of natural resources. These are the bone and sinew of our economy, upon which all else— domestic and international—depends.

The drain on our traditional supplies of raw materials is prodigious. In 1900 our production of all raw materials exceeded our consumption by 15 per cent. By 1950 our consumption exceeded our production by 9 per cent. By 1975 our consumption will exceed our production by 20 per cent. It is estimated that our reserves of good U.S. iron ores—those containing more than 50 per cent iron—will have vanished in the next two decades. Only our reserves of poorer ores are still substantial, and it is to these lower-grade ores that we will have to resort through the development of new technologies, new plants, more efficient extraction processes, and more efficient use.

Here, the challenge to innovation and inventive thinking is immense. New technologies, more efficient extraction processes, new uses may open up new worlds. Even now we can discern the outlines of a future in which, through the use of the split atom, our resources both of power and raw materials will be limitless. But the theoretically possible is not yet within our grasp. Pending the necessary scientific and technological breakthroughs, we must face the fact that our supplies are not inexhaustible.

One resource which we must actively conserve is water. Already, demand is outrunning our supply in some areas and thus placing a limit on growth. In the last half-century the number of water users in American cities has doubled, while their use of water has increased fivefold. By 1975, the increase in our population, coupled with the growth of industries that require large quantities of water, will more than double the current rate of water consumption. The enormous amounts required by industry are illustrated by the fact that it requires 300,000 gallons of water to manufacture one ton of rayon, and the rayon industry in the United States turns out 600,000 tons of rayon a year. The nation's water problem, already serious in important areas, may well become, in the next ten to fifteen years, one of the most difficult issues facing our economy.

A solution depends partly on tapping new water sources, partly on more co-ordinated policies to bring about the more efficient use and re-use of existing resources, and partly on better protection of watersheds and reservoirs. The industrial use of water—which accounts for 30 per cent of the total—can be greatly economized: modern steel mills use only one quarter as much water per ton of steel as those built 20 years ago. In agriculture, as well, more efficient techniques can stretch water use. In the arid regions of the West, where losses through evaporation account for as much as 50 per cent of the total water in reservoirs, experiments are being conducted on means to minimize such losses by use of thin surface films and by use of floating covers.

Of even greater immediate urgency than an improved water technology is the need for institutions to manage and co-ordinate the development and use of water. The problems of the Connecticut River and the Colorado River are neither so similar that they can be easily handled by a single agency nor so localized that each can be adequately dealt with solely at the state level. Typically, water problems are regional problems and often can best be dealt with by specifically designed public agencies. The Port of New York Authority's handling of regional transportation problems is an example. In addition to these regional bodies, a degree of national policy formation and co-ordination, possibly centralized in one federal agency, is essential for such nationwide problems as water pollution and for research into technological problems of water conservation.

## An Expanding World Economy

An expanding volume of trade can make a most significant contribution to our general economic growth. The essence of trade is that both parties gain from the process—we exchange things we can produce most efficiently for products that can be

# OUR GROWING NEEDS FOR RAW MATERIALS
# PROVIDE EXPORT OPPORTUNITIES
# TO OTHER NATIONS

In 1900 we PRODUCED MORE RAW MATERIALS THAN WE USED and exported 15% of our output ...

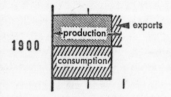

**1900**

By 1950, domestic PRODUCTION HAD FALLEN BEHIND NEEDS and 9% of materials were imported ...

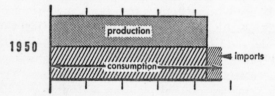

**1950**

Estimates are that by 1975 we will DEPEND ON IMPORTS for 20% of our needs.

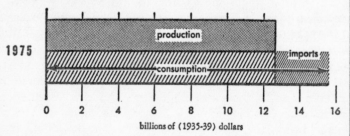

**1975**

| 0 | 2 | 4 | 6 | 8 | 10 | 12 | 14 | 16 |

billions of (1935-39) dollars

Source: The President's Materials Policy Commission, *Resources for Freedom*

produced most efficiently someplace else. In this manner we en-large the supplies of goods and services available in our economy by enlarging trade.

Our growing dependence on raw material imports highlights the importance to the future growth of our country of an expand-ing world economy. In the long run, the economic growth of the world will be best served if each country develops those resources which it can produce most economically. Where foreign oil and other mineral deposits can be discovered and developed more cheaply than those in the United States, both we and the rest of the world stand to benefit by their use.

At the same time, we can, through our international trade and investment, make an expanding contribution to the development of the world economy. Our imports provide dollars to other nations, and these dollars can be used to purchase from us the machinery and equipment needed to support economic develop-ment. Our private foreign investment not only provides funds for the purchase of capital goods but also provides technical assistance to producers in other nations. Our programs of technical assistance and mutual aid contribute to the development of a vigorous world economy.

Although these and other aspects of our international economic relationships are dealt with more fully in the report of Panel III, we wish to stress here the importance of expanding trade in promoting our general economic advance.

## Encouragement of Scientific Advance

The greatest single active force toward economic growth is scientific advance. It was the scientific and technological revolution of the seventeenth century that paved the way for the industrial revolution; the subsequent expansive history of capitalism has been stimulated by its successful incorporation of the brilliant and steady scientific discoveries of the eighteenth and nineteenth centuries; and in the twentieth century the unprecedented ac-celeration of scientific advance promises that we are only on the threshold of a new age of science.

The world may well be on the verge of a major revolution in available energy. Already the proven reserves of uranium and thorium, in terms of energy equivalent, are at least 1,000 times the world resources of coal, gas, and oil. Our own needs for energy from nuclear power are not immediately pressing, thanks to the availability of plentiful low-cost power from coal, oil, natural gas, and water. By the 1970s, however, the significance of nuclear power will not reside alone in achieving costs competitive with fossil fuels, but in the utilization of such power in stationary installations in order to conserve the known supplies of oil for other uses. In some tasks, such as earth removal jobs and mining, nuclear explosions may soon assume major significance. This could relieve some of our important shortages of raw materials.

Nuclear energy is not the only frontier at which we are now pioneering. Research in the physical chemistry of the cell opens new vistas not alone for health and for the extension of life but for the control of agriculture on a totally new scale. New advances in solid-state physics, in polymer chemistry, in the design of electronic equipment have resulted in astonishing extension of our boundaries of control over nature. We have begun to consider realistically problems—such as weather control and the exploration of space—that were unimaginable only a decade ago.

The translation of scientific advance into economic growth and advancement of human welfare is a task to which our system has in the past shown itself marvelously well adapted. But the encouragement of science itself is not a task which we have hitherto consciously taken upon ourselves to perform. Clearly our economic growth will reflect to an important and perhaps critical degree the effectiveness with which we stimulate free inquiry, the incentives by which we induce our potential young scientific talents to devote themselves to this field, and the quality we obtain in the whole of our education program. These are major problems for a free society to which the report of Panel V is addressed. Here we must stress their importance and set forth three basic guides to national policy in this area:

1. The nation should put primary emphasis on the broad potentials for economic and social growth inherent in scientific developments. The nation should not permit the pace, direction, or nature of its scientific effort to be limited either by possible military applications, important as they are, or by the fortuitous availability of shorter-run economic incentives to developmental activity by private industry.

2. Restraints on the free flow of basic scientific information,

always a temptation where military applications are in any way involved, should be resisted since it is through the free flow of such information that both scientific progress and economic and social growth are, in the long run, made possible.

3. When normal economic incentives are insufficient to bring about a high rate of scientific development, the government should be alert and resourceful to foster the desired activity by any one of the numerous devices, including grants, tax incentives, and long-term loans, that we have found in the past can be successful in enlisting private initiative and resources to meet a public need. In some cases, the necessary scope of scientific development is beyond the means of private enterprise or of institutions that depend on endowment and support from private funds. In these cases, the government should generously support the needed scientific development. Areas that might qualify for such support include atomic energy, space exploration, meteorology, oceanography, agriculture, and health.

# IV. Problem Areas in a Growth Economy

A dynamic economy must expect growing pains. No matter how dramatically its figures for gross national product may rise—there will always be areas where growth is uneven, distorted, or retarded. This may be the result of advancing technology, rigidities of organization, or obsolete laws and regulations. Whatever the cause, internal rejuvenation is needed to bring a dragging component of the economy back into the mainstream.

Growth itself generates imbalances. New developments in one field may produce obsolescence in others. Where flexibility and adaptability are lacking, the problems of adjustment may be quite severe. The pace of growth and scientific development in the years ahead will intensify the need for such flexibility. Steady discard of obsolescent plants and methods, steady and efficient provision of goods and services, steady adaptation of new discoveries and developments will be required. Where lags occur and assume proportions that affect total growth, comprehensive study and informed action will be needed to overcome them.

In the following pages, some of these areas are identified and discussed. In general they represent segments of our economy that are out of step with our present and potential needs and requirements. They do not represent problems so much as beckoning opportunities. By seizing on them with bold and imaginative programs that are geared to our needs and potentials, we can convert them into full and fruitful partnership in our growth economy.

## AGRICULTURE

Any consideration of our farm problems should be designed to bring agriculture back into a healthy partnership with our total economy.

Farming was once the major occupation of Americans. As recently as 1910, 35 per cent of our people lived on the land. Today, only 13 per cent live on farms, and each year a million more people leave the farms. A minority, comprising 2.1 million farms, now produce 91 per cent of the output of food and fiber and could produce more, while the majority, comprising 2.7 million farms, produce only 9 per cent. The result is a major imbalance in our economy, from which stem many complex and interrelated problems. Thus, the large number of farms with low production contribute to poverty in the United States. At the same time, federal expenditures for support of farm prices are a significant part of the federal budget. Efforts to dispose of our farm surpluses complicate and sometimes adversely affect our foreign relations. And most importantly, the standard of living of America—not alone of our farmers but of the whole nonfarm population—is affected.

Agricultural policy could be discussed in terms of any one of these problems. We shall deal with it, however, in terms of one basic fact—that the present operation of American agriculture is not efficient for the farmer, for the consumer, nor for the taxpayer. This may seem paradoxical at a time when farm techniques are increasingly productive. The 2.1 million most efficient farms now in operation are capable of producing all of the farm commodities we need at home, as well as an exportable surplus for the world. But by trying to keep 100 per cent of our farmers producing, we are acquiring large surpluses, while many of our farmers make a substandard living, and the incomes of the remainder are less than they should be.

It is clearly necessary to bring supply and demand into better balance, and this will involve adjustments. But there is a right and a wrong way to bring this about. The right way is to assist and expedite movement in an efficient direction. The wrong way is to provide relief that actually retards adjustment. Down the latter route lie ever-mounting costs which will cause those who were to be helped and the economy as a whole to suffer.

The causes of agriculture's major ills are clear in outline. Productivity in agriculture has been rising at an extraordinarily rapid pace in recent years. Consumption of farm products has risen at a far slower pace.

The national decision not to leave the process of agricultural adjustment entirely to the mechanism of the market has been wise. But the means selected by which the market process was supplemented—namely, by government purchases to support the prices of some agricultural commodities above the levels they would have reached in the market—has hampered, rather than facilitated, the needed adjustment. High, fixed price supports, adopted during World War II, were scheduled to be reduced within two years after the war. The reduction has been successively postponed however. The result has been overproduction, depressed markets, and lagging incomes, especially for the less efficient farmers.

For the price support program does little for the poorest farmers. It is estimated that the 2.7 million farms that sold less than $2,500 of product each averaged only $109 in benefits from price supports in the fiscal year 1956-57—far too little to bring those families up to satisfactory living standards. At the same time, the 1.3 million farms that sold $5,000 or more of product received an average of $1,993, with many individual support payments running into tens of thousands of dollars.

Thus the first flaw in the price support system is that it does little for the large portion of the farm population that genuinely needs help. A second objection to the present support program is that there is considerable doubt that even those farmers who presently receive the bulk of all support payments are really as well off as they would be without them. And the consumer pays for the program in two ways: higher taxes and higher farm prices.

The proper approach to a farm policy would be to concentrate efforts and funds on measures to assist the necessary readjustment of our whole farm sector. This involves encouragement and assistance, for those farmers who wish to do so, to shift to nonfarm occupations. They could, when necessary, be enabled to do this by selling or leasing their land to the government.

In a growing economy, a greater number of workers will be

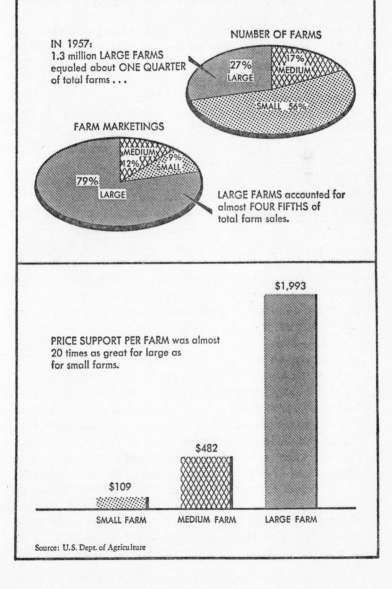

# SMALL FARMERS DERIVE LITTLE BENEFIT
# FROM PRICE SUPPORT

NUMBER OF FARMS

IN 1957:
1.3 million LARGE FARMS
equaled about ONE QUARTER
of total farms . . .

27%
LARGE

17%
MEDIUM

SMALL 56%

FARM MARKETINGS

MEDIUM
12%

9%
SMALL

79%
LARGE

LARGE FARMS accounted for
almost FOUR FIFTHS of
total farm sales.

$1,993

PRICE SUPPORT PER FARM was almost
20 times as great for large as
for small farms.

$482

$109

SMALL FARM

MEDIUM FARM

LARGE FARM

Source: U.S. Dept. of Agriculture

needed in nonfarm areas. Those who wish to transfer to urban employment could be given helpful reorientation and training, as well as assistance in finding jobs. Acquisition of marginal and submarginal lands could not only help reduce overproduction but would also add to the nation's forest, grazing, and recreation areas. At the same time, every effort should be made to induce industry to settle in rural areas, so that those who prefer rural living will not be dependent on farm income alone. Expanded programs of rural low-cost housing, road building, market development, soil conservation, and reforestation are also recommended.

About 600,000 of the nation's 2.7 million poorer farms are now part-time farms whose proprietors are already supplementing their incomes. Another 900,000 are really rural residences rather than farms. Therefore, the hard core of the transfer problem is limited to about 1.2 million farm units.

The objective for an agricultural support program for high production farmers is not to support their *prices* but to aid in reducing instability of income due to conditions beyond their control. This can be done by means of temporary loans based on normal market prices, self-financed crop and livestock insurance, and disaster insurance. The objective would thus be to insure against severe economic and natural hazards, not to induce, by means of a fixed price umbrella, production beyond the capacity of the domestic and international markets. Such a program would benefit not only the farmer but the consumer in terms of lower food prices.

In summary, we would propose:

1. A constructive farm adjustment program including:

    a. A program of encouragement and assistance to those farmers who wish to transfer to nonfarm occupations. Assistance should include technical and vocational training, counseling, and help in finding employment.

    b. Fostering of industrial development in rural areas to enable those who prefer rural life to attain better incomes.

    c. Lease or purchase through voluntary sales of uneconomic farmlands to curtail production. In order to be fully effective, this would require that entire farm units be taken out of production. Congress should clearly define the details of lease or purchase, including the use to which the lands would be put and the manner in which they would be administered.

2. Continuation and expansion of farm credit programs, soil and water conservation, self-financing crop insurance, and agricultural research.

3. The gradual withdrawal of price supports as surpluses are reduced and balance in production and demand is achieved.

We discuss agriculture here at some length, in part because of its essential nature and importance in our history and tradition. We also believe there is an extremely valuable lesson in the case of agriculture. There are other cases where economic growth and economic change have necessitated difficult adjustment to particular industries and regions. In the long view, the interests of our country, as well as our primary goal of individual human betterment, will be best served when we do not perpetuate the maladjustments but restore these lagging sectors of our economy to a dynamic place in our national life.

## TRANSPORTATION

Our vast transportation network is a vital component of our economy. Transportation services influence the growth and prosperity of our communities, industries, and whole regions of the country. Their costs are a critically important factor in the ultimate price of almost all goods and services. In times of disaster or wartime emergency, national survival may rest on efficient operation.

Both long- and short-term transportation difficulties could impair our economic health. Large segments of the industry are in financial trouble. Corrective measures long overdue must be taken if we are to prevent transportation from becoming an impediment to economic growth. They must take into consideration the extremely complex and highly diverse elements of modern transportation and should be approached in the light of shifts and changes constantly developing.

The total volume of freight moved in this country has been constantly growing and will continue to advance as population and gross national product increase. Inland waterways, including the efficient Great Lakes shipping, now carry 16 per cent of the total intercity freight traffic and, because of their low rates, are an important factor in new plant location. Nearly 19 per cent of intercity freight movement is handled by trucks, with regulated trucking accounting for only one third of this total. While the railroads still carry nearly half of all intercity freight, their portion of the total is decreasing.

The private auto handles about 88 per cent of all intercity passenger traffic with rail, air, and bus competing for the remainder. New superhighways and expanded federal highway plans will encourage the still greater use of privately owned cars. Local governments are now spending considerable sums for highways and parking facilities to provide for commuter traffic. These are some of the factors that contribute to the serious financial condition of some of the railroads.

Air passenger miles continue to climb. Inability to make adequate rate increases, however, has seriously cut into earnings and threatens the financing of forthcoming jet and turbo-jet equipment. Heavier traffic and anticipated use of jet aircraft make necessary additional government expenditures for new facilities and devices to meet safety requirements.

The general public has a paramount interest in a sound, efficient transportation system. Government policies and programs of direct and indirect assistance, regulation, and taxation intimately affect our national transportation system. City, state, and federal regulatory bodies are involved in management decisions. Federal regulation, however, is divided among three separately administered agencies: the Interstate Commerce Commission, the Civil Aeronautics Board, and the Maritime Commission. Each of these agencies has been charged with responsibility for regulating a specific branch of the transportation industry and for developing policies to assure its growth and sound operation.

Nowhere in the executive branch of the government is centered responsibility for formulation of over-all transportation policy. Since a wide overlap of competition does exist between the several transportation media, no genuinely coherent policy or system of regulation with respect to one can be worked out without regard to the competition offered by others.

We recommend, therefore, the creation of a single focal point within the federal government, a Department of Transportation, with broad powers to develop over-all national transportation policy designed to serve the best interests of the public.

We would also recommend as an immediate step a study to assemble more comprehensive and reliable data as to the productivity of various types of transportation with particular reference to the costs and advantages of each. In addition, such a study should determine, in the light of population growth, probable future needs, including those of defense.

The aim should be to develop over-all policy and procedures to bring about a rational use of the various modes of transportation, the general objective being to make available to the shipper the mode or carrier or combination that can do the most efficient job, cost and service both considered.

The extent to which the transportation industry is performing services either below cost or excessively above cost is a matter of major economic concern. Regulatory policies should clearly encourage and direct that services be priced in reasonable relationship to the cost of providing the service under economical and efficient management.

The present double standard of regulation as between common carriers on the one hand and contract and private carriers on the other is basically unsound, and a single standard of regulation should be developed where possible. In particular, the 3 per cent excise tax on freight transportation, which is not imposed on private carriers, is discriminatory and should be removed.

## METROPOLITAN AREAS

The metropolitan problem has been called the major domestic problem of our times. But the nation as a whole has not awakened to its gravity. The piecemeal approach to date is inadequate and self-defeating. Many programs now cancel each other out or have results opposite to those intended.

Since there is every reason to assume that urban or suburban living will characterize American life in the decades ahead, it is imperative that our metropolitan areas provide an environment favorable to economic growth and to the cultural and social enrichment of the lives of our citizens.

There is nothing essentially new about the metropolitan problem except its magnitude. A half century ago, our cities were expanding as a result of great migrations from abroad. Then, as now, people were drawn by the hope of getting a foot on the economic escalator, of sharing more fully in America's abundance. It was out of such hopes and aspirations that our country was built.

Today, many of those who have moved up on the escalator are leaving the central city for the suburbs, especially young families. The cycle is continuous, changed only by the fact that the dominant stream of in-migration is now from our own rural areas and offshore islands. More than 30 million Americans change their place of residence every year — most of them moving to or within the metropolitan areas.

Thus the big, complex problems of our metropolitan areas are really a reflection of the dynamism and vitality of our country. As such, we should welcome them.

At the same time, we must recognize the magnitude of the problems created by this process. The blight of slums is spreading through our metropolitan areas, and particularly in the centers of our cities, at a rate far in excess of our programs to remedy it. The problem is intensified by the fact that many racial minorities

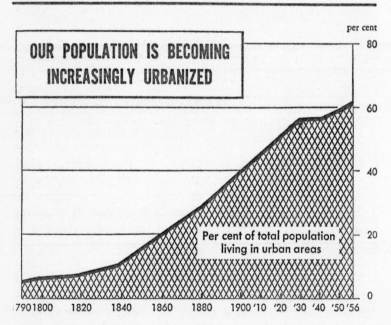

OUR POPULATION IS BECOMING INCREASINGLY URBANIZED

Per cent of total population living in urban areas

per cent

80

60

40

20

0

1790 1800    1820    1840    1860    1880    1900 '10 '20 '30 '40 '50 '56

Source: U.S. Dept. of Commerce

are confined to blighted areas. This is a situation that militates against both the self-realization of the individual and the healthy growth of the community. It is the blending, rather than the sealing off of minorities that has created our dynamism. Any movement that runs counter to that historic truth runs counter to the promise of America.

The investment required to make our cities attractive and healthy places in which to live has been estimated as running into the hundreds of billion dollars. Ten million substandard urban dwelling units would cost an average of perhaps $10,000 each to replace or rehabilitate. But one must add to this other necessary investments. Urban transportation is approaching the chaotic. Basic community facilities such as schools and parks are inadequate. The decline or leveling off of the tax base, which accompanies urban blight, creates acute financial problems for city officials; at the same time costs for health service, welfare, and fire and police protection are rising. Arbitrary and outmoded political and administrative boundaries and unresponsive state government prevent decisive community action. Where the metropolitan complexes extend across county or state lines, these problems are magnified.

The federal government has assumed important leadership; but far more needs to be done. There is a special need for co-ordinating federal programs, such as the housing and highway programs, which reach into urban centers and vitally affect their future. Since the governmental adjustments must also come through state legislation and with state assistance, their responsiveness and effectiveness will have a great, if not a decisive, bearing on the states' role in the future of our federal system.

States can stimulate and encourage areawide studies of metropolitan problems; they can enact legislation to facilitate solutions, on a regional basis, both intrastate and interstate, of such problems as transportation, water supply, and waste disposal. They can provide authority for credit operations, which will certainly be needed, for the tax base of localities frequently does not and cannot supply the "social" capital needed.

But it is also clear that the initiative for coping with urban growth, including urban blight, rests with the localities themselves and with individuals, official and private, who care about urban living and wish to preserve and enhance it.

Funds will have to be drawn from three sources: private capital, local and state credit, and federal credit. At present the ratio of private to public expenditures is running about five to one. It is evident a larger amount of additional government support will be needed, preferably through insurance and guarantees. The capital budgets of most large cities list many essential items for which there are no funds available within their financial capacity and legal restrictions. Such facilities as schools and hospitals, roads and transport, are silent but powerful partners in successful private investment, but where these social expenditures are cut off or fail to keep pace with needs, private operations rapidly cease to be profitable and soon become impossible.

To provide incentive to private capital, a number of policies involving every level of government are essential:

1. Increased governmental assistance will be needed to assemble plots of land for redevelopment and for the sale or lease of land to responsible private developers at a price or rental that makes private investment in new structures feasible.

2. Housing must be provided where needed for individuals displaced by urban renewal projects.

3. Adequate sanitation, housing, and zoning regulations should be established and rigorously enforced. Where closure is needed, relocation must also be arranged for.

4. New methods to encourage the flow of private investment into the field of urban renewal should be sought. Federal insurance and guarantees of mortgages have not been used as effectively in urban rental housing as in the case of single family homes in suburban areas; but they could be made to serve the objectives of urban redevelopment.

5. Nonprofit, co-operative housing can go a long way toward providing housing for families in the lower and middle income brackets. In New York City alone, approximately 20,000 families now live in nonprofit sponsored co-operative housing projects, and there are 10,000 co-operative apartments on the drawing boards. The successful results achieved by co-operatives are due to several factors, including acquisition of land at a fair price, direct loans from government agencies or government insurance, lower interest rates, and, in many instances, partial tax abatement from the municipality.

There is still unmet need, however, for middle income housing, particularly within the cities. The factors that have militated against the middle income group include building costs that rise faster than incomes; building codes and, in some cases, union rules that impose unnecessary rigidities in the cost structure; and inadequate credit, especially for the small contractor.

Beyond this group, there is a segment of the community now living in urban slums that will require public housing. Our public housing programs have created many problems. They have crowded low income families, and especially minority groups, into high-density, many-storied apartments, thus intensifying economic segregation while breaking down constructive neighborhood relationships.

Public housing programs need to be fitted together with the other elements of an urban program. A full-scale and integrated attack on this problem will yield immeasurable dividends, not only in terms of better cities but above all, in terms of enhanced human happiness and effectiveness.

In the next section, we shall deal with some of the social steps necessary to reach this objective.

In contrast to the cities, we have made far greater progress in dealing with housing problems in the suburbs, where the greatest population growth has occurred. The FHA and VA programs, plus the development of a national market for both guaranteed and conventional mortgages, have supported an impressive increase in home ownership. As of 1956, some 60 per cent of American homes were owner-occupied.

But the flight to the suburbs is not a solution to, but rather an expansion of, the problem of urban living. The metropolitan problem is indivisible. The suburbs and the central city are interdependent; their problems, including those of urban sprawl and incipient blight, differ only in degree. Hence, time only underscores the necessity of a comprehensive approach.

Aside from the physical regeneration of the metropolis, new governmental arrangements and accommodations must be developed to deal with this problem of urban growth. The metropolitan sprawl does not stop at city, county, or even state boundaries. It is generally intergovernmental, often interstate, sometimes international. Imagination and experimentation will be needed to develop the political structures necessary to provide the needed governmental services. Experience thus far indicates that there is no master plan that will serve every metropolis. But pioneer efforts, such as those in Dade County, Florida, and Toronto, Canada, where authority to provide areawide services has been transferred to a broader level of government, suggest the outlines within which solutions may lie. Experience also suggests that co-operation among existing governmental units, under existing authority, can often go far to meet these problems, and that this, rather than the creation of new layers of government, may be the most effective means of coping with metropolitan growth.

# V. Economic Growth and Human Welfare

## GAINS FROM ECONOMIC GROWTH

We have been dealing with the challenges of achieving economic growth. But economic growth derives its value only to the extent of better enabling the individual to pursue a life of dignity and to develop his own capacities to their maximum potential. Our purpose to translate economic growth into individual well-being is the touchstone of our dedication to the ideal of human dignity.

An expanding economy contributes to the welfare of individuals and their families in essentially two ways:

*directly*, through increased private earnings and through gains in health, welfare, and retirement programs developed by employers and employees; and

*indirectly*, by making possible the expansion of both private and public institutions and programs which have as their objectives the improvement of human well-being.

### Direct Benefits of Economic Growth

Human betterment is primarily achieved directly through increased individual and family income. The capacity to live in a better home, to buy more nutritious food, to provide better health care for one's family, to acquire life and health insurance protection, to widen educational and cultural horizons—these are all basic aspects of individual and family welfare that increased income can make possible. It is for this reason that individuals and families presently outside the mainstream of our economic growth must be enabled to the fullest extent possible to become more productive and thus participate in the general economic advance of the nation.

A healthy and expanding private economy means far more in

terms of individual and family well-being than any reasonable expansion of government services and social programs. In the period from 1929 to 1952, for example, a period of great expansion in government's participation in welfare programs, the absolute increase in purchasing power afforded to all workers through their regular wage and salary payments amounted to eight times the increase in social welfare payments made available from public and private sources combined.

The distribution of national income in 1957 showed about 70 per cent of it went to employees in the form of wages and salaries, about 11 per cent to the self-employed, and about 18 per cent to the owners of property in the form of corporate profits, interest on indebtedness, and the rental of real estate. The realization of the growth potentials we have found in our economy should double real wages in the next thirty years. This will make possible a tremendous advance in human welfare.

An increasing portion of earnings is being utilized for fringe benefit plans rather than for increases in "take-home" pay. These plans, either initiated by management or labor, or developed in collective bargaining, represent a growing element in the welfare of individuals in this country. By supplementing the retirement, death, and disability income benefits provided under government social insurance programs and by providing hospitalization and medical insurance, these private plans are playing a major role in enhancing human welfare. The benefits are not confined to cash payments. Medical centers, for example, are being established for employees and their families under employer and union sponsorship.

Encouragement should be given to the expansion of these plans and programs. They represent an effective means of putting economic growth directly to work for human welfare. A broader application of these plans depends in the first instance on the growth of our national output.

## Indirect Benefits of Economic Growth

There are certain aspects of human welfare that are not a direct concomitant of economic growth alone. Some areas of need require action through social *institutions,* as distinct from action by individuals or even by employers and employees. Medical research, for example, cannot be furthered by individual workers and their families nor even in any significant way by most employers. Similarly, education for all cannot practicably be provided through individuals or collective employer-employee action. Certain groups in society that have not been effectively integrated into our working economy also need special public attention. In these instances, we need *institutional* provision for channeling economic growth toward human betterment.

The social institutions to achieve this may be either private or public in nature, i.e., nongovernmental or governmental.

## Private Institutions

Private philanthropy in this country has been and will continue to be a very substantial factor in our social welfare structure. Its expenditures from contributions alone (exculsive of endowments) aggregate at least $6.7 billion annually and serve many functions that public institutions cannot. These expenditures, more effectively than governmental outlays, fit specialized and local requirements and can be quickly channeled toward new and pressing needs. Perhaps most important, private philanthropy has provided in many fields the leadership and pioneering spirit so essential to meet changing needs in human welfare.

Charitable contributions by individuals have risen to unprecedented levels. In addition, a fairly recent development in private philanthropy is the increase in corporate giving for education and for general welfare purposes. Corporate giving in the aggregate, however, averages only slightly over 1 per cent of taxable income, while the federal income tax law permits deductions for charitable purposes up to 5 per cent of taxable income. We should give every impetus to accelerating the upward trend of corporate giving in the next decade.

## Public Institutions

In many areas of human welfare, *government* action is clearly necessary as a complement to private action. Through the use of tax revenues and its legislative powers, government can assure that a portion of our increased national product goes to achieve those human welfare purposes that would not otherwise be adequately served.

Whether the institutions to promote human welfare are sponsored privately or publicly, they are dependent for their continued effectiveness on a growth economy. All over the world there are examples of social legislation and private welfare endeavors that remain "paper programs" or that badly fail of their objectives because the communities or countries that establish them are not sufficiently productive to support them. Our social welfare policies in this country must recognize clearly the fundamental importance of an expanding economy toward furthering human welfare.

At the same time, successful social welfare policies will help to advance our economy. A society characterized by rising standards of living, and by physical and intellectual vigor, and in which each person is helped to achieve his maximum potential as a productive human being, is important to maintaining a dynamic economy.

## Areas of Welfare Concern

Some of the basic elements of individual and family welfare that we shall examine are the opportunity for a good education, economic security, good health, and the opportunity to expand cultural horizons. We shall also discuss the special problems of the lowest income groups in our population and the welfare problems that have been created by the weakening of family life and the tensions of an urbanized society.

Reference to government programs will predominate. By this we mean to de-emphasize neither the role of individual action nor of private institutions. We intend rather to give special focus to those matters that present questions of *public* policy, as distinct from questions more appropriate for private decision. At all times, public policy should be so formulated as to encourage and foster expansion of individual and private institutional effort.

## EDUCATION

Educational opportunity is fundamental to the full development of the intellectual, spiritual, and material capacities of the individual, and universal free education is the key to equality of opportunity in this country. From the political viewpoint, universal education of a high quality is basic to the functioning of a truly democratic society. From the economic and social viewpoint, well-educated men and women are vital to the operation of an increasingly complex society. Business, government, science, medicine, social service—all are competing for the available supply of well-educated individuals. Thus the improvement of the entire educational structure of our nation is one of the most crucial needs of the next decade.

The effectiveness of our educational system and our utilization of manpower is the subject of the report of Panel V of the Special Studies Project. Here, however, we wish to stress the economic aspects of the problem.

At the present time a long needed re-examination by the American people of the content of our educational programs is under way. A general raising of goals and standards should result. This will require increased expenditures—primarily for the improved salaries needed to attract more talented people to the teaching profession.

Even meeting the standards of education that are now generally recognized as desirable requires much larger government budgets for educational purposes. At the higher education level, private giving—particularly through corporations—must be greatly increased to meet the demands that will be made in the next decade. To provide education for an increasing number of school-age children, for more average years per student, and to obtain enough teachers of sufficient quality to make this huge investment of student years worthwhile will probably require doubling by 1967 the $13 billion spent for education in 1957.

## ECONOMIC SECURITY:
## SOCIAL INSURANCE

Perhaps the greatest advance in raising minimum living standards in the past generation, aside from the consequences of high employment and economic growth, has been made through social insurance. Under social insurance systems, employers and, in some instances, employees and self-employed persons set aside part of their current income to support programs that protect against certain major economic events or hazards confronting individuals. These are, primarily, loss of income on retirement, during unemployment, and during periods of temporary or permanent disability.

Today the total cost of government social insurance plans—the largest of which are the Federal Old-Age, Survivors, and Disability Insurance system and the State Unemployment Insurance systems —and of veterans' pensions is over $15 billion. That cost is estimated to rise to $25 or $26 billion by 1967. Most of this increase is the result of increases in benefit payments already legislated and a numerical increase of the eligible age groups. Unemployment insurance now covers approximately 80 per cent of wage and salary workers. Over 57 million—about 85 per cent of all persons in remunerative activity—are covered by Federal Old-Age, Survivors, and Disability Insurance.* Another 5 to 6 million come under other federal, state, and local retirement programs, some of which are supplementary to OASDI; while an estimated 15 million workers now have supplementary pension coverage through private plans, and some are covered by private supplemental unemployment insurance plans.

It appears likely that the importance of income insurance will increase in the next decade and that it will cover more citizens more fully. It should be noted, further, that these programs are already demonstrating their effectiveness in stabilizing the economy.

No major change in the concept of our social insurance plans seems indicated, but a number of improvements of the present structure are needed, and most states need to fill the gap of temporary disability income benefits.

## Old-Age, Survivors, and Disability Insurance

With respect to Old-Age, Survivors, and Disability Insurance (OASDI), we recommend as a goal the reduction by successive steps in the present minimum age of eligibility for income benefits for extended total disability. Because disability benefits are new to OASDI, such liberalizations should be enacted only as they are found to be practicable in the light of actual experience.

* Some individuals or groups in special categories are eligible to participate in OASDI, but they or their employers have not elected to do so. Many of these are groups of employees of state and local governments and nonprofit organizations.

Essential to any such liberalization is the intensification of state vocational rehabilitation programs, so that those made eligible for disability insurance will be given the opportunity and incentive to regain a status of self-support and independence.

We are opposed to any general reduction of the retirement age under OASDI. Indeed, there are psychological as well as economic advantages of continuing in employment those workers who wish to work past age sixty-five and are able to do so. Also, a growing economy will demand the full utilization of the skills of many of these workers. Therefore, we recommend further study of means of adjusting the present retirement age to encourage continued employment after age sixty-five.

The wage "base" and the benefit structure of the OASDI system must be reviewed periodically with a view toward keeping benefit levels up to date in relation to prices and wages. By this we do not mean to advocate successive benefit increases not justified by changing conditions; but we urge a realistic recognition that the OASDI system is an evolving structure that, to be effective, must be kept current with economic facts.

## Unemployment Insurance

A second vitally important part of our social insurance structure—unemployment insurance—should be greatly strengthened along the lines recommended in Section III; namely, the extension of coverage, increase in benefits, and lengthening of their duration. Minimum federal standards should be enacted to encourage this improvement.

At the same time, state administration of the program should be strengthened by obtaining more skilled personnel, providing more specialized services, and establishing more co-operative and effective relationships with industry. Particular help should be given to middle-aged and older persons having difficulty finding jobs.

## Workmen's Compensation

Workmen's compensation has been a static field of social insurance in recent years and is often out of date in its awards and administration. Our best estimates of its coverage range from two thirds to four fifths of employees, and some of the omissions are serious. For example, agricultural workers who are not covered have higher than average injury rates as well as higher than average unemployment rates. Even though the long-range importance of workmen's compensation may decline with improved disability and sickness insurance programs, we recommend state legislative action to improve coverage and benefits. At the same time medical care and particularly *rehabilitation* should be given far greater emphasis as essential elements of workmen's compensation.

### Temporary Disability Income

The newest area of income insurance at the state level is temporary disability, or "sick pay" insurance. Such insurance provides benefits to compensate for wage loss during illness, up to a fixed number of weeks. Only four states have adopted plans of this nature. We believe that such plans are an integral part of adequate social insurance coverage, and we recommend that all states adopt temporary disability insurance systems.

### Private Plans

We have already referred to the importance of private plans supplementing government-sponsored retirement, life disability, and other insurance. Ways need to be found of extending such plans to smaller firms. Also continuing efforts and study should be devoted to enabling workers to carry some rights in private plans with them when changing jobs.

## HEALTH AND MEDICAL CARE

Health in its broadest aspects has an importance to our nation second only to our national security. The advances in this field during the past few decades have been remarkable. The gradual extension of the average lifetime offers ample evidence of the results of medical research, preventive medicine, and health education. The infectious diseases have ceased to be major causes of death; the hazards of childbirth have been largely overcome.

But the more rapid our progress is, the greater the necessity that we think ahead in the field of health. The broad national policies that such a "look ahead" suggests are outlined below.

## Medical Research

The toll of today's leading killing and crippling diseases, such as cancer, cardiovascular diseases, and mental illness, is staggering in both human and economic terms. In addition, many new types of health problems and opportunities are emerging today that demand intensive investigation.

The acquisition of new knowledge is basic to advancing national health. We recommend, therefore, continued expansion of our medical research programs as rapidly as the supply of scientific talent will permit.

As we step up medical research efforts, equal strides must be taken toward putting their results to use more rapidly. We recommend that public health authorities and private medical groups join in a study analyzing the extent of the time lag between the acquisition of new medical knowledge and its practical availability to the general public, identifying the causes of delay and delineating measures to reduce it.

## Medical Manpower

We are short of doctors in many parts of the country and also of many categories of medical specialists. The number of doctors should increase in relation to total population, whereas it appears now to be constant or declining in relation to population. We urge immediate steps to overcome this trend, including maximum possible utilization of the facilities of existing medical schools and immediate planning for the inauguration of new medical schools.

The existing medical schools are having serious financial difficulties. If private fund raising efforts and indirect government aids prove inadequate, we would recommend consideration of a federal-state program of assistance to the operational budgets of the medical schools.

Federal and state loan and scholarship programs, in addition to increased scholarship funds from private sources, commend themselves as a means of helping the student to overcome the high cost of medical education, which is not recouped by the student for many years. Similar measures to encourage the training of more professional and practical nurses should be continued and expanded.

## Medical Facilities

Subject to the limitations imposed by personnel shortages (particularly nursing and technical personnel), we need in most areas of the country more hospitals and other health facilities of many kinds. The increase in chronic disease and the needs of an aging population highlight the necessity for substantial expansion of facilities for long-term care, particularly of high quality nursing homes for the care of the aged with moderate impairments.

We recommend the use of a portion of available hospital construction funds for developing radically new types of medical facilities, such as hospitals permitting maximum self-help and community care centers offering diagnostic services and extensive outpatient treatment and homemaker services.

At the same time, modernization and rehabilitation of existing hospitals—particularly older ones in large cities—must be a major target of the next decade. We suggest consideration of low-interest state loans for this purpose.

## Paying the Costs of Medical Care

As medical practice has become more complex and specialized, it has become apparent that co-operative efforts among practicing physicians can enhance the quality of care given. The first question is how best to achieve this. The second is how to pay for high quality medical care so as to spread costs among a large group of individuals and families, and over years of high and low health costs for each individual or family. The increasing costs of hospital and medical care lend urgency to this question.

One approach, adopted effectively in some communities, is group medical practice, affiliated with a common hospital, and with essentially all costs prepaid by the subscribers through family health insurance premiums. The range of physician services covered by the fees should be comprehensive in scope. The resulting incentives tend to emphasize preventive care and early diagnostic services and to minimize unnecessary hospitalization. We believe that this group practice prepayment approach, although by no means suited to all communities, could be advantageously adopted by more communities.

Health centers established by industry and labor in connection with a place of employment also offer great possibilities for improved health care.

Irrespective of the form through which physician's services are provided, we urge as a major objective of prepayment plans over the next decade the coverage of doctor's and nursing care *outside* the hospital. Such coverage can serve as a real encouragement to early discovery and treatment of physical defects and illness, thereby resulting in better health and lower costs, and to shorter periods of hospitalization.

More people should be covered by the newer "catastrophic illness" plans, designed to help meet extraordinary costs of accident or illness over and above the costs met by a comprehensive basic plan. The cost of this protection, when spread over a large group, is relatively small—provided that the underlying basic plan is broad in the scope of services covered and encourages rather than discourages early use of diagnostic services and facilities.

For the present needy aged and for the "medically indigent" who cannot afford to pay for protection even under basic health prepayment plans, financing from general tax revenues—federal, state, or local, or a combination of the three—seems essential.

## LOW INCOME GROUPS

We have considered three basic aspects of human welfare: education, economic security, and health. The approaches we have suggested are applicable generally to the population as a whole. We shall now refer to certain special problem areas in our social structure—low income groups and groups particularly affected by the tensions of our complex and urbanized society.

Studies have indicated that there were in 1955 about 4 million families with a year's income of less than $2,000. These represented some 9 per cent of all the families in the United States. In addition, several million single persons were in a comparable income bracket.

Many in the low income category are in jobs for which the pay is below reasonable standards. We believe that the coverage of the minimum wage laws should gradually be broadened and that continuing study be given to the proper level of minimum wages with due regard for efficiency and productivity. We recognize the complexity of this problem and its implications for the expansion of employment opportunities in some industries and areas. Nevertheless, adequate minimum wage standards for *all* workers must be our ultimate goal.

Low earnings for regular, full-time employment are not, however, the primary cause of the distress of the majority of lowest income families. A large segment of our population is outside the mainstream of the economic growth of the nation as a whole.

Many in the low income category are aged persons, and opportunities for restoring them to an economically productive status are limited. The long-range solution for their problem is largely the maturing and strengthening of our Old-Age, Survivors, and Disability Insurance program. Many are physically or mentally ill or disabled; they can be helped through the combined force of improved social insurance, health and rehabilitation programs. Some, even in times of high employment, are unemployed for a variety of reasons; they can be helped by improved unemployment insurance and vocational counseling and retraining programs. Many are members of broken families lacking the support of a husband and father; here the long-range solutions lie largely in the strengthening of the role of the family in our society. Many are in rural areas and working on uneconomical farms; they can be helped by vigorous prosecution of an agricultural policy along the lines suggested in the previous section. Many are in areas of urban blight and can be helped by comprehensive urban redevelopment programs or, in the case of persons newly arrived in cities from rural areas, by efforts at preparation for urban life.

For the employable, there are sometimes specific impediments to movement into better paying jobs, such as discrimination in employment against minority groups. Indeed, herein lies perhaps the most dramatic example of waste of manpower in our economy. Other impediments are the costs of geographical movement to better jobs and lack of education or vocational training to meet the needs of our technologically advancing economy.

Where all else fails, public assistance must continue to serve as the ultimate economic backstop. Public assistance payments must be kept adequate to achieve the purpose of providing basic subsistence. At all times there should be vigorous pursuit of the objectives legislated into the federally aided public assistance programs in 1956—that of helping individuals on the relief rolls to achieve self-support and self-care.

In conclusion, the economic status of many low income families can be raised through programs focused specifically on their individual problems. While the initial leadership should come from the federal government, only through co-operative effort on the part of both public and private organizations can an intensive attack be successful. Launched perhaps through the selection of pilot communities, such help ought to be extended as its effectiveness is demonstrated.

## OTHER HUMAN WELFARE PROGRAMS

Financial dependence is a familiar and easily understandable but by no means the most serious manifestation of social distress. Some manifestations, indeed, have no constant relationship to the income factor but appear at all levels of economic well-being. These include, for example, broken family life, personal frustration, aberrant juvenile conduct, and intergroup tensions.

These problems are the most elusive and most difficult for society to combat. At the heart of many of them is a lessening in the force and meaning of family life as a result of a generally more complex, impersonal, and crowded society. Juvenile delinquency is one of the most serious and tragic examples of such a problem. Here, intensive casework of a highly individualized nature is essential. Similarly, in related areas, family counseling services, psychiatric social work, and community psychiatric services must all be expanded. Rehabilitation and retraining programs must be given greater emphasis. The question of finding new and satisfying opportunities for constructive activity on the part of older persons is an important area of concern for the next decade.

Crucial to any expansion of these types of individualized social services is the training of more social workers and counselors. We recommend that private organizations, states, and the federal government (through appropriations under a 1956 authorization) take steps to expand opportunities for social work education.

Special mention should be made of the question of racial discrimination and tensions, particularly in urban areas, which create barriers to the fuller self-development of individuals in minority groups. It is of little avail to prepare Negro or Mexican or Puerto Rican arrivals to the cities for better lives in the cities if the opportunities for realizing those lives are not offered to them. Racial prejudice runs counter to our basic moral beliefs and national purposes. There is no single cure; it is a matter that must be attacked by the imaginative use of every means at our disposal. Failure to cope with this problem would represent a serious indictment of our entire society.

## SPIRITUAL AND CULTURAL VALUES

As our economy moves toward higher levels of income, the basic wants and needs of individuals—food, clothing, shelter, economic security, and health—become increasingly satisfied. As a consequence, we have more income and leisure to attain intellectual and cultural objectives.

This report has dealt largely with the material and physical well-being of our citizens. But these gains will have only partial meaning unless they are accompanied by the fullest possible realization by the individual of his spiritual, intellectual, and cultural capacities.

Our democratic faith is a faith in the whole human being. We are concerned for the individual's life and health, his security and comfort; but even more we must be concerned for the fulfillment of his highest aspirations.

Of recent years there has been a growing realization that our opportunities and responsibilities call for a searching of the soul as well as of the mind.

Cultural interests and creativity are flowering in all parts of the nation. The American people are participating in the creation and performance, as well as enjoyment, of art, music, literature, drama, and the dance as never before. This is true in the small communities as well as in the great cities.

Viewed in historical perspective, civilizations are judged by their culture rather than by their might. The encouragement of spiritual and cultural growth is every bit as essential to our future as the nurturing of our material welfare. But it is a more subtle and delicate task.

To make the fruits of an expanding economy serve the noblest ends of man is our greatest challenge. Security and wealth must be intermediate, not ultimate, goals. Only as they serve as tools for the realization of our deeper spiritual aspirations will we as a nation achieve true greatness.

# VI. The Key Importance of Growth to Achieve National Goals

To govern, it has been said, is to choose. No more difficult choice is imposed upon any society than the use it seeks to make of its economic product. For there is one adamant limitation on our—or any other—society: it cannot, unless it literally consumes its own substance, put to use more than it currently produces. There is no such thing as deficit financing of total output. However vast its productive capacity, a nation is nonetheless limited in its choice of economic objectives by the compatibility of its total demands with its actual production of goods and services.

Even a rapidly growing economy faces the problem of choosing among alternative uses of its national product. Yet an expanding economy can realistically set its goals above its present capabilities by the margin of growth available to it. But then it must also determine the priorities by which its expanding output will be put to use.

It is this problem of choice to which this section is addressed. In previous sections we have looked at some of the things that need to be done if we are to achieve a high rate of economic growth and use our expanding production in a manner that will contribute to the attainment of the objectives of our society. Now we propose to try to strike a balance between these demands and our ability to meet them. This involves making a set of projections of possible demands and production in the period ahead. We have chosen for this purpose 1967 as a year not so far away as to be entirely speculative and not so close as to be predetermined by existing policies.

Obviously such a projection into the future is essentially an extension of certain trends of the past. It does not predict that given expenditures or a certain gross national product will in fact materialize. Rather it confronts us with the choices we will have to make *if* certain trends *do* materialize. Thus, the figures cited in this section are far from inflexible. The gross national product can go beyond its projection through a sustained national effort, or it can fall below it as the result of a sustained recession that is not effectively met. The main categories of demand may also vary considerably. But the projection indicates general base lines that are likely, and it serves as an illustration of the type of choices that may be open to our society over the time period of this report.

## PROJECTIONS OF GROSS NATIONAL PRODUCT

Before setting forth projections of what our gross national product could be in 1967, it may be useful to review past trends in our total production. From its earliest beginnings our economy has exhibited a strong growth trend. This does not mean that national output has proceeded in its upward path in a regular unwavering line. There have been ups and downs in activity associated with the swings of business cycles. But these variations have taken place around a trend of vigorous growth—after each period of contraction the economy moved ahead to set new records.

Our growth trend in the long period from 1870 to 1930 worked out to 3 per cent per annum. In the past decade we have been following a 4 per cent per annum upward trend. This record of growth lends confidence to the view that, if we act effectively and purposefully, we may reasonably expect a continuation of a growth rate of 3 to 4 per cent per year over the next decade and beyond. In fact, a growth rate of 5 per cent is possible if we realize fully our impressive opportunities for economic expansion. If the problems of growth are formidable, we have also found the impetus of our economy enormous.

Accordingly, we propose to examine the implications of three alternative projections of our growth over the next ten years. Our objective is to illustrate what might be accomplished if our growth pattern follows its historic rate, the postwar rate, or a still higher rate. In this manner, we hope to highlight some of the problems

# GROWTH TRENDS IN OUR ECONOMY

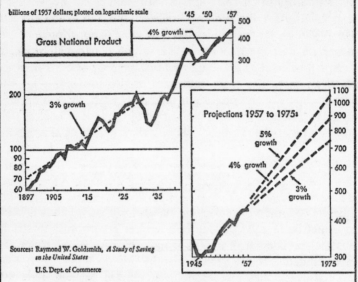

billions of 1957 dollars; plotted on logarithmic scale

Gross National Product

4% growth

3% growth

Projections 1957 to 1975:

5% growth

4% growth

3% growth

Sources: Raymond W. Goldsmith, *A Study of Saving in the United States*

U.S. Dept. of Commerce

Growth has been a dominant characteristic of the U.S. economy. From 1870 to 1930 total national output increased along an average growth trend of 3 per cent per year. The upward path was not smooth and even—there were fluctuations around the trend. Yet it is the growth, rather than the variations of business cycle, that is most striking in the record.

In the decade of the 1930s there was little or no growth in our production. With the onset of World War II, however, we mobilized our resources and achieved a growth rate of about 9 per cent per year from 1939 to 1945.

In the postwar period, total production has been following a 4 per cent annual growth trend. This performance reinforces the American faith in its growth economy as a means of providing the potential for doing what America wants to do.

The challenge is to better the 4 per cent growth rate in the future. By doing so, we can come close to meeting national goals.

of choice that we may face and to emphasize again the key importance of growth.

We start out with three projections of our growth over the next ten years:

| | Gross National Product | |
|---|---|---|
| | 1957 | 1967 |
| | Billions of 1957 Dollars * | |
| At the 3% rate of 1870–1930....... | $434 | $583 |
| At the 4% rate of the past decade.. | 434 | 642 |
| At an accelerated rate of 5%....... | 434 | 707 |

It should be noted that the difference between the 3 per cent and the 5 per cent rate is $124 billion by 1967, or a range of one fifth. As we shall see, this extra margin of growth can spell the difference between a static level of consumption with a minimum expansion of needed government services for a growing population on the one hand and a fuller realization of our national aspirations on the other.

To see how our rising national output can be used, it is necessary to make a set of projections of the various demands on our economy. In making these projections, we have drawn on the estimates made by other panels of the Special Studies Project of the costs of programs in the fields in which they are concerned. The projected cost estimates to meet our domestic social and economic objectives have been largely developed by this panel.

The projections of demands that follow are presented in two forms. First, we have attempted to make rough estimates of the minimum demands on our economy. These estimates represent what seems to be the least that must be done to approach the objectives set forth in earlier sections. Second, we present a higher range of very rough estimates to cover the cost of accommodating other programs to which we would assign very high priority. It should be re-emphasized that our purpose here is to illustrate some of the choices that may lie ahead, rather than to prejudge the selection among various programs.

* In this and all subsequent projections, 1957 prices are used, so that the dollar figures reflect changes in real output.

## PROJECTIONS OF GOVERNMENT
## PROGRAMS

We turn first to government programs, not because we believe they necessarily take first priority, but because we wish to assess the general impact on the economy of the various governmental programs that have been discussed by this and the other panels. One of the most difficult problems of choice we face is that of determining how much of our expanding income should be channeled into government programs and how much should be left to be used in furthering individual objectives.

In general, our national objectives would be best served by maximizing the area of individual choice. Yet it is important to consider carefully the relative advantages of increased government programs in key areas as opposed to increased private consumption expenditures. Such consideration would bring home the truth that government expenditures are not costless—in general, they subtract from private expenditures. Yet it would also emphasize the fact that certain government programs may contribute more to the general well-being than the private expenditures that have to be foregone—in this sense they are worth what they cost in taxes.

In any case, a first step in making this evaluation is to consider the general magnitude of the demands confronting our federal, state, and local governments. Detailed projections of these demands are presented in the table on page 325.

The reasoning underlying these estimates is essentially as follows:

1. Estimates of *National Security Expenditures* are based on the assumption that the international environment remains about as at present—major changes, favorable or unfavorable, would substantially affect a ten-year projection. A range of expenditures from $60 billion to $70 billion in 1967 is projected on the basis of the findings of Panel II. It is impossible to assess the magnitudes of economies that will be achieved through the reorganization of the defense establishment. As we shall emphasize later, even the lower estimates of national security demands constitute a burden on our economy that we support in the hope that we can achieve a world of peace. If that objective could be realized, the resources

now devoted to defense could be put to more constructive uses at home and abroad.

2. The low estimate increase in *Education* would accommodate a continuation of the past trend toward larger expenditures per

Projections of Federal, State, and Local
Government Expenditures
Billions of 1957 Dollars

|  | 1957 Actual | Range of Estimates for 1967 Low | High |
|---|---|---|---|
| National Security .......... | $ 46.0 | $ 60.0 | $ 70.0 |
| Defense Department ...... | 39.0 | 49.8 | 55.9 |
| Military Aid ............. | 2.3 | 3.0 | 4.5 |
| Economic Aid ............ | 1.7 | 2.7 | 3.7 |
| Atomic Energy*............ | 2.1 | 3.0 | 3.9 |
| Other ................... | .9 | 1.5 | 2.0 |
| Education (Including School Construction) ............. | 13.0 | 24.0 | 30.0 |
| Welfare ................... | 20.0 | 38.5 | 45.0 |
| Social Insurance and Public Assistance ............. | 15.5 | 31.0 | 36.0 |
| Health (Including Hospital Construction) .......... | 4.5 | 7.5 | 9.0 |
| Public Works (Except Schools and Hospitals) ............. | 9.5 | 20.5 | 27.0 |
| Roads**................... | 4.8 | 10.5 | 12.0 |
| Water Supply and Disposal .. | 1.3 | 2.7 | 3.5 |
| Urban Renewal .......... | 0.7 | 4.0 | 7.0 |
| Other ................... | 2.7 | 3.3 | 4.5 |
| Other ..................... | 25.5 | 27.9 | 31.0 |
| Agriculture .............. | 4.7 | 2.0 | 2.0 |
| Veterans ................. | 4.9 | 4.9 | 4.9 |
| Administration and Operation | 15.9 | 21.0 | 24.1 |
| Total Government Cash Expenditures ................. | $114.0 | $170.9 | $203.0 |

* Includes expenditures by the Atomic Energy Commission on civilian projects.
** $10.5 billion estimate for 1967 is based on current legislation.

pupil, whereas the higher figure would support a substantial improvement in our educational system. This subject will be treated more fully in the report of the panel on education.

3. A continuation of existing trends in the *Welfare* field would yield estimated expenditures of $38.5 billion in 1967. Increased emphasis on such programs as disability insurance, medical research, and broadening the scope of unemployment insurance could lift demands in 1967 to $45 billion.

4. Minimum demands for *Public Works* (other than schools and hospitals) result from a projection of trends during recent years. Such a program would provide funds to meet needs in the *Water Supply* field and to increase government expenditures for *Urban Renewal* from about $700 million last year to $4 billion in 1967.

If we were to provide public assets on a scale commensurate with the long-term trend, demands could easily exceed $27 billion a year by 1967. An accelerated program to rebuild our cities would be the item of largest increase in such an enlarged public works program.

5. Expenditures on *Veterans* programs are held constant. Estimates of the cost of *Agricultural* programs are substantially reduced, along the lines set forth earlier in this report. The costs of *Administration and Operation* are projected as rising about in line with total government outlays.

In casting up our approximate trial balance for the future, we begin with these expenditure projections for government. However, the expenditure figures must first be adjusted to allow for *Transfer Payments*. These are payments made by the government that do not make a direct claim on our production of goods and services. In effect, spending power is transferred from one group in the economy to another. Thus, transfer payments include most welfare items, interest on the various government debts, etc. If we deduct such transfer items from government expenditure, we arrive at the government's claim on production.

The amounts in each of these two categories are shown in the following table.

|  | 1957 | Range of Estimates for 1967 | |
|---|---|---|---|
|  |  | Low | High |
| Federal, State, and Local Government Expenditures | $114.0 | $170.9 | $203.0 |
| *Less* Transfer Payments | 27.6 | 43.9 | 50.0 |
| Government Purchase of Goods and Services | 86.4 | 127.0 | 153.0 |

Billions of 1957 Dollars

The key fact is that, even under the lower projection, government purchases of goods and services would rise more rapidly than would total national production at the 3 per cent long-term average rate of growth of our economy.

## PRIVATE INVESTMENT
## AND CONSUMPTION

To appraise the significance of this fact we must now look at the two main categories of private expenditures—private investment and consumption. In recent years of high employment, gross private investment—for business plant and equipment expenditures, for housing and other private construction, and for inventories—has stayed consistently close to 15 per cent of the gross national product. This offers a fairly reliable indication of the proportion of the national output that must be invested in order to maintain recent rates of growth. We have projected a moderate increase in the ratio of private investment to GNP on the assumption that private investment in urban renewal may rise from its present $3.5 billion a year to $12 to $13 billion in 1967.

In recent years private consumption expenditures have increased along a general trend that has yielded an average annual growth of about 2 per cent in per capita consumption. A projection of this trend to 1967 would yield a figure for consumer expenditures of almost $400 billion as against the $280 billion spent last year. Such a projection may not be a "minimum demand" in quite the sense that applies to some government programs—we must, for example, carry out the national security programs that are essential for our survival, and there is no question but that we can afford to do so.

Yet, as was stressed earlier, we cannot divide up more than we can produce. If there is a widespread agreement that a greater share of our production should be devoted to government programs, then private expenditures cannot keep growing at the rate they have in the past. This rule does not imply that we cannot choose to support certain government programs regarded as essential or that we must be content with any historic rate of advance in our economy. But it does require that we face up to the problem of making choices among the alternative courses available to us.

## STRIKING TRIAL BALANCES

Now that we have set forth various projections of possible trends in both production and demands, the next step is to cast up what might be termed a set of trial balances for our economy. Consider first what would be involved if we set the projections of low estimate demands against growth rates in production of 3 per cent and 4 per cent:

| | Billions of 1957 Dollars | | |
| --- | --- | --- | --- |
| | 1957 | 1967 | |
| | | GNP at 3% Growth Rate | GNP at 4% Growth Rate |
| Gross National Product .. | $434 | $583 | $642 |
| Less Low Estimates for Government Purchases of Goods and Services | 86 | 127 | 127 |
| Less Gross Private ...... Investment to Support Growth | 67 | 100 | 112 |
| Leaves Available for Consumption | 281 | 356 | 403 |
| Annual Growth Rate of Per Capita Consumption | — | 0.8% | 2.1% |

Tax revenues of federal, state, and local government should rise a bit faster than total output if tax rates are kept constant, because our tax system as a whole collects higher percentages from higher incomes. At the 4 per cent growth in GNP our present tax system would yield just about enough revenue to cover the projected low estimate expenditures, but there would be a substantial deficit with the 3 per cent growth in GNP. Under either growth rate, a decision to adopt the low estimates for government programs would imply a decision to forego general and permanent tax reduction, though this would not rule out reform of the tax structure.

## THE KEY IMPORTANCE OF GROWTH

The first basic conclusion that emerges from our analysis is the very great importance of maintaining a high rate of growth. A 4 per cent rate of growth would enable us to meet all the low estimate demands for government expenditures outlined in this report, cover the capital investment requirements, and give a growth in the annual rate of consumer expenditures equal to the recent past. But even with a 4 per cent rate of growth we will as a general rule be pressing against the margin of our capacity for at least the next decade. The threat of inflation will be ever-present, and vigorous anti-inflation measures may be needed. On the financial side, the likelihood of a long run need for increased government revenues underscores the urgency of our recommendations for reform of the tax structure.

A slowdown in our rate of growth to 3 per cent would naturally leave us in a more difficult position. The low estimate demands for government expenditures could either not be met in their entirety or could be met only by holding the rate of growth in per capita consumption to less than 1 per cent per annum. Moreover, taxes would have to be increased to achieve balanced budgets in periods of good business. Clearly we must better our historic growth trend if we are to meet the demands imposed by a minimal estimate of our needs.

A second conclusion is that even with the 4 per cent rate of growth our capacity would be far below our desirable objectives —which is to say, below our aspirations. Let us cast up an alternative trial balance using what we have projected as high estimate demands in place of the low estimate needs:

|  | Billions of 1957 Dollars | | |
| --- | --- | --- | --- |
|  | 1957 | 1967 | |
|  |  | GNP at 4% Growth Rate | GNP at 5% Growth Rate |
| Gross National Product .. | $434 | $642 | $707 |
| Less High Estimates for Government Purchases of Goods and Services | 86 | 153 | 153 |
| Less Gross Private ...... Investment to Support Growth ............ | 67 | 112 | 123 |
| Leaves Available for Consumption ........... | 281 | 377 | 431 |
| Annual Growth Rate of Per Capita Consumption ................ | — | 1.4% | 2.8% |

This projected trial balance, while necessarily composed of even rougher estimates than those in low estimate demands, illustrates the fact that our aspirations will exceed our capacities even if we match the relatively rapid growth rate of the past decade. This is as it should be in a free economy, where the ultimate purpose of production is to provide maximum opportunity for individual development. The simple fact is that the American people want a higher level of living, as is evidenced by their willingness to work hard to get it. Our aspirations will challenge our ability to produce goods and services as far ahead as anyone can see.

These projections also emphasize the fact that the high and rising level of defense expenditures is a major factor in holding back our progress on other more constructive fronts. We can afford the defense programs essential for survival. In doing so, however, unless we achieve a 5 per cent growth rate, we shall have to hold back otherwise desirable expenditures in the government field and keep the growth of private expenditures below a level commensurate with our aspirations.

If it should become possible to reduce defense expenditures substantially as the result of the attainment of our basic goal of a genuine and lasting peace that would favor the growth of freedom, we could come much closer to meeting our economic aspirations. Such a propitious turn of events would make it possible for us to accelerate desirable government programs, including aid to the developing nations around the world, and at the same time reduce taxes in a manner that could promote a substantial increase in private consumption and investment.

## THE PROBLEM OF CHOICE

A third major conclusion derived from the trial balance projections is that, even with a high rate of economic growth, the future will make heavy demands on our ability to make choices. While we can envisage an era of well-being far beyond present experience, it will not come about automatically. We will be able to achieve much in the immediate future and a great deal more over a period of time. But we cannot do everything at once. To seek to do too much too soon will increase our economic *problems* but not our economic *results*.

Thus, the immediate challenge is to our sense of values and to our self-restraint. We must decide between the essential and the desirable; we must choose among our aspirations those which carry the highest value. We must make our decisions of choice in the framework of a confident belief in our future ability to continue to progress.

We need, in short, a greater and more articulate sense of national purpose to guide us in this inevitable process of choice. This is in large measure a problem of promoting a broad public understanding of the problems and challenges that lie ahead. As an example, a more general appreciation of the values that could be secured by increased government expenditures for education or social welfare might well generate broad public support for such programs.

## THE NEW FRONTIERS

In making the choices that will confront us, we have the opportunity to adopt a series of measures that could give us a more rapid economic growth than the 4 per cent rate of the past decade—conceivably a 5 per cent rate. Our choices are not necessarily limited by past rates of expansion—they encompass the possibility that we can adopt policies that provide positive stimuli to greater output.

Earlier sections of this report have outlined steps that could promote economic growth. In summary fashion, policies were recommended to:

1. Provide a climate that encourages initiative and enterprise, saving and investment, and a broad confidence in our future growth and prosperity.

2. Use government's monetary and fiscal powers to contribute to growth.

3. Reform our tax system to reinforce incentives for growth.

4. Eliminate the rigidities that impede growth by reducing tariffs, strengthening the competitive vigor of the business system, and eliminating restrictive practices on the part of both labor and management.

5. Encourage the continued development of small business by measures to increase the flow of venture capital and by tax reform.

6. Provide needed urban redevelopment and such public assets as schools, roads, hospitals, and water supply systems.

7. Encourage the expansion of international trade and the development of the free world economy.

8. Stimulate efforts to develop the broad frontiers of science and technology by strengthening incentives and providing necessary educational facilities and funds for basic research.

Underlying all of these is our national commitment to an untiring search for peace and freedom.

The frontiers that are just beginning to be opened to us by science and research dwarf to comparative insignificance the historic American frontier of open, unused land. They are as unlimited as space and as the reach of man's inquiring mind. The power of the atom has been unlocked, but we have scarcely begun to harness it. The same is true of solar energy. Minerals have only been scratched from the outer skin of the earth's crust. The seas are as yet unfarmed. New structural materials, alloys, fibers, and foods are being invented almost faster than they can be tested and put to use.

We have other frontiers to open that may prove equally challenging. We are just beginning to understand the full potentials of international developments in a world in which distances are shrinking, barriers to trade are being reduced, and more than a billion people are living in newly-developing economies. We are inextricably a part of a free world economy striving for growth. That fact offers a major challenge and opens a great opportunity for our nation to work with the other free nations to promote economic growth and the broad use of its proceeds to support the maximum opportunity for the individual.

America has a notable record of responding to challenges and making the most of opportunities. With our growing population, our extraordinary record of rising productivity, the inherent dynamism in our free enterprise economy, there is every reason to face the future with full confidence that we shall measure up to the challenges that lie ahead.

Report V

# THE PURSUIT
# OF EXCELLENCE:
# EDUCATION AND
# THE FUTURE
# OF AMERICA

(First published June 26, 1958)

# Introduction by Panel V

Much of our present-day social achievement is manifested by group effort. It is our ability to marshal and unite the skills and abilities of thousands of individuals that makes possible the achievements of modern technology. It is a condition of modern society that we spend our lives in an atmosphere of collaborative effort.

But while the strength of co-operative effort is impressive, there is danger that we may misunderstand the true source of that strength. The danger is that we may forget the individual behind a façade of huge and impersonal institutions. The risk is that we will glorify science and forget the scientists; magnify government and ignore the men and women who discharge its functions; pin our hopes on education, business, or cultural institutions and lose sight of the fact that these institutions are no more creative or purposeful than the individuals who endow them with creativity and purpose.

Beyond the temptation to overlook the individual, there is another danger. This is the difficulty of giving free expression to creativity within an institutional atmosphere. We face the threat that our increasingly organized efforts will become increasingly routine; that the structures of science, government, and enterprise will become hard shells, resistant to growth and change, rather than flexible institutions capable of renewing and re-creating themselves.

Paradoxical though it may seem, society as a whole must come to the aid of the individual—finding ways to identify him as a unique person and to place him alongside his fellow men in ways that will not inhibit or destroy his individuality. By its educational system, by its public and private institutional practices, and, perhaps most importantly, by its attitude toward the creative person, a free society can actively insure its own constant invigoration.

This is the problem to which the following report is addressed. It is not too much to say that upon solution of this problem depends our survival and fulfillment—not just as a nation, but as a society of free individuals.

This report is a collaborative effort. Not every member of the panel subscribes to every detail, but it reflects our substantial agreement.

*JOHN W. GARDNER, president, Carnegie Corporation of New York; president, Carnegie Foundation for the Advancement of Teaching; chairman of Panel V.

J. DOUGLAS BROWN, dean of faculty, Princeton University; former member, Mobilization Program Advisory Committee, Office of Defense Mobilization.

LOWELL T. COGGESHALL, dean of the Division of Biological Sciences, University of Chicago; former special assistant for health and medical affairs, Department of Health, Education, and Welfare; president, Association of American Medical Colleges, and president, American Cancer Society.

PHILIP H. COOMBS, secretary and director of research, The Fund for the Advancement of Education, Ford Foundation; former executive director, President's Materials Policy Commission; faculty member, Amherst College and Williams College.

DANA L. FARNSWORTH, director, university health services, Harvard University and Radcliffe College; president, Group for the Advancement of Psychiatry; physician, Massachusetts General Hospital.

ELI GINZBERG, professor of economics, Columbia University; director, Conservation of Human Resources, and director of staff studies, National Manpower Council.

*CARYL P. HASKINS, president, Carnegie Institution of Washington.

*THEODORE M. HESBURGH, president, University of Notre Dame; commissioner, Civil Rights Commission; member, National Science Board.

*MARGARET HICKEY, public affairs editor, *Ladies' Home Journal.*

DAVID RIESMAN, professor, sociology department, University of Chicago.

J. E. WALLACE STERLING, president, Stanford University.

HOWARD E. WILSON, dean of School of Education, University of California, Los Angeles.

DAEL WOLFLE, executive officer, American Association for the Advancement of Science; former director of the Commission on Human Resources and Advanced Training; editor of *America's Resources of Specialized Talent.*

FRED M. HECHINGER, associate publisher, *Bridgeport Herald;* education editor, *Parents' Magazine;* secretary of Panel V.

JAMES R. KILLIAN, JR., president, Massachusetts Institute of Technology; served as chairman of Panel V until November 1957 when he was appointed Special Assistant to the President.

This report was written principally by the chairman with the assistance of his panel and the director of Special Studies. The panel appreciates the generous help of distinguished consultants from the field of education, labor, welfare, personnel, and population research.

* Also Overall Panel members.

# I. The Dignity of the Individual

The greatness of a nation may be manifested in many ways—in its purposes, its courage, its moral responsibility, its cultural and scientific eminence, the tenor of its daily life. But ultimately the source of its greatness is in the individuals who constitute the living substance of the nation.

A concern for the realization of individual potentialities is deeply rooted in our moral heritage, our political philosophy, and the texture of our daily customs. It is at the root of our efforts to eliminate poverty and slums at home and to combat disease and disaster throughout the world. The enthusiasm with which Americans plunge into projects for human betterment has been considered by some critics to be foolishly optimistic. But though we may have gone to extremes in a naïve belief that we could cure all of mankind's ills, we need not be ashamed of the impulse. It springs from our deepest values. We do not believe that men were meant to live in degradation, and we are foes of the poverty and ignorance that produce that result. We deplore the destruction of human potentialities through disease, and we are prepared to fight such destruction wherever we meet it. We believe that man—by virtue of his humanity—should live in the light of reason, exercise moral responsibility, and be free to develop to the full the talents that are in him.

Our devotion to a free society can only be understood in terms of these values. It is the only form of society that puts at the very top of its agenda the opportunity of the individual to develop his potentialities. It is the declared enemy of every condition that stunts the intellectual, moral, and spiritual growth of the individual. No society has ever fully succeeded to living up to the stern ideals that a free people sets itself. But only a free society can even address itself to that demanding task.

It is in this context that we consider the subject of individual excellence. To be sure, conditions in the world require that we think in terms of our performance as a nation. But in its deepest sense, our concern for human excellence is a reflection of our ideal of the overriding importance of human dignity. It is not a means but an end. It expresses our notion of what constitutes a good life and our ultimate values.

Our success or failure in this task is of crucial importance not for ourselves alone. All over the world peoples are striving for a new and fuller meaning of life. No challenge is more important than to give concrete meaning to the idea of human dignity. This task is all the more complex because the answer will be found less in what we say than in what we do. It will be found partly in the scale of our achievement, but even more importantly in the quality of our lives.

# II. The Nature of the Challenge

## THE SETTING OF THE PROBLEM: OUR POPULATION CHARACTERISTICS

The population of the United States is today over 170 million—and increasing rapidly. Since 1950, on an average day, there has been a net rise of about 7,600 in the population; over the year, a rise of some 2.8 million. This may give us a population of not quite 225 million by 1975.

We do not know with certainty what will be the trend of birth rates in the future. However, for the time span of our report, the problem of prediction is precarious only for the younger ages; everyone who will be twenty years old or older in 1975 has already been born. Therefore, we can predict with accuracy the age composition of the older portion of our population in 1975. Here are the estimates:

POPULATION OF THE U.S. BY AGE:
1955 AND PROJECTED FOR 1975

| | 1955 | 1975 | 1955–75 |
|---|---|---|---|
| | (*millions of persons*) | | (*per cent change*) |
| All ages | 166.0 | 222.3 | 34 |
| 0 - 4 years | 19.1 | 25.4 | 33 |
| 5 - 14 years | 30.4 | 41.9 | 37 |
| 15 - 19 years | 11.2 | 18.7 | 67 |
| 20 - 24 years | 10.8 | 19.3 | 79 |
| 25 - 44 years | 46.9 | 53.2 | 13 |
| 45 - 64 years | 33.4 | 43.2 | 29 |
| 65 years and over | 14.2 | 20.6 | 46 |

Source: U. S. Department of Commerce, Bureau of the Census, *Current Population Reports*, P-25, No. 123, "A" Projections.

As the table shows, the age composition of the population in 1975 will differ markedly from that of 1955. In recent years, as a

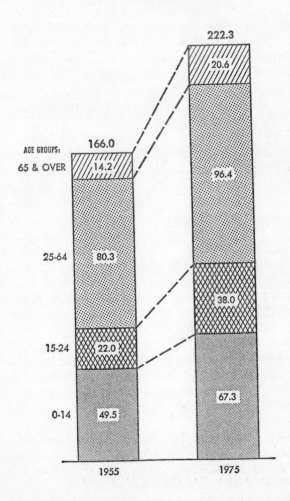

# POPULATION OF THE U. S,
## BY AGE

1955 AND PROJECTED FOR 1975
(in millions of persons)

222.3

20.6

166.0

AGE GROUPS:

65 & OVER    14.2

96.4

25-64    80.3

38.0

15-24    22.0

0-14    49.5    67.3

1955    1975

Source: U.S. Dept. of Commerce

consequence of the low birth rates of the thirties, we have been short on youths and young adults, while the high birth rates of the late forties and fifties have made children plentiful. In 1975, the situation will be radically changed. The recent baby boom will have resulted in an enormous increase in age groups fifteen to twenty-four; and as our present middle ages attain the later brackets, there will be a large increase in the age group sixty-five and over.

This pattern of future population will present two vital problems. The first concerns the flood of young people who will place an immense pressure on educational institutions in the next twenty years and on the labor market shortly thereafter. The second problem involves the social and individual problems posed by a rapidly expanding older group. Both of these problems will occupy our attention in later chapters.

In addition to these changes, there will be a continuance of long-term trends in the geographical distribution of the population. We are a people on the move—about 20 per cent or 34 million of us change our address each year, and there are great slow currents, northward and westward, that describe the drift of our people. Twenty years hence, California will in all probability be the most populous state and Nevada no longer the least populous. In certain aspects these migration trends make us a more homogeneous people. For example, they tend to diminish regional distinctions. Twenty years hence, the Negro will have shed to a greater extent than he has already his southern regional character, as a consequence of his steady migration to northern, midwestern, and western cities.

There are other signs of increasing homogeneity. Farmers, for example, are being transformed and reduced as a recognizable group. Not only are successful farms increasingly "businesslike" in their operation, but a million rural residents leave the farms each year. Among those who remain, many hold down a second job in a neighboring plant.

Thus, in some ways we appear to be becoming an ever more *national* community in which regional loyalties and sharp regional differences are diminishing year by year. And the fact that immigration is no longer a major factor has removed what was once an active force for heterogeneity in the population.

Another striking trend is the rise of the great metropolitan areas. In 1900, the average American lived in the countryside. By 1930, he lived in a small town of from 5000 to 10,000 population. Today, he lives in a big city or its surrounding area; by 1975, he will live in its suburban outgrowth. Four fifths of the nation's growth between 1950 and 1955 was concentrated in the urban fringe that rings each of the great cities and extends far into the countryside. Thus, in a sense, the typical American is on his way back to the country town. But he is no longer a rural person. The tempo of his life and work typically centers on the great metropolitan areas to which he commutes and toward which he is culturally oriented.

So we may expect for 1975 a nation both less regionally diverse and more uniform as to living environment.

What of the other characteristics of the individuals composing our society? The progress of science in combating diseases has been dramatic. It is an astonishing fact that our death rate from natural causes between age *one month* and age *forty years* is approaching—although it can of course never reach—zero. We may expect that within twenty years our life expectancy will be lifted from its present seventy years to seventy-five or eighty. It is reasonable to assume that the number of workdays that illness costs the nation should show a per capita decline and that our physical energies will be at least as robust as today. Whether our mental health will show a similar improvement is highly questionable. There is at least the possibility that an older and more urbanized society will be increasingly vulnerable to emotional disorders. The importance of counseling and guidance, for youths at the time of career decisions as well as for older people at the termination of their careers, will be correspondingly increased.

## THE CHANGING DEMANDS OF SOCIETY AND THE PRESSURE ON THE SUPPLY OF TALENT

Thus far we have sought to view our human resources in the light of certain characteristics they have as a population. Now we must view them in a different fashion. We must see them as a vast reservoir of human abilities and skills upon which our social and technical and economic institutions depend. What are these abilities and skills? What sorts of talent does our contemporary society demand of us, and what is the nature of the tasks it calls upon us to perform?

One of the striking features of contemporary life is the growing range and complexity of the tasks on which our social organization depends. This is dramatically apparent in science but is no less a reality in nearly every field of endeavor. It can be seen in the ever-increasing range of skills demanded of the doctor, the teacher, the government administrator, the labor leader, and the business executive.

The reasons are not far to seek. They lie in the explosive rate of technological change and the increasing complexity of our social organization. Not only are the tasks that must be performed to keep our society functioning ever more intricate and demanding, they are constantly changing in character. As a result, we are experiencing a great variety of shortages of human resources in fields requiring high competence and extended training. We are having to become more and more concerned with seeking and cultivating talent. We have become more conscious of the strategic importance of education in our society.

The demand for highly trained talent is not a sudden development. It has been coming for a long time. Certain critical manpower shortages of the past few years have forced it on our attention rather abruptly, but it is not a recent trend. If we compare the distribution of selected skills and occupations today with those of 1910, the long-term changes become vividly clear.

OCCUPATIONAL DISTRIBUTION OF LABOR FORCE
(*selected skills and occupations as per cent of labor force*)

|  | 1910 | 1957 |
|---|---|---|
| Professional and technical workers | 4.4% | 9.9% |
| Proprietors, managers, and officials, excluding farm | 6.5 | 10.3 |
| Clerical workers | 10.2 | 14.1 |
| Skilled workers and foremen | 11.7 | 13.3 |
| Total selected skills and occupations | 32.8% | 47.6% |

Sources: Statistics for 1910 from *America's Needs and Resources,* Twentieth Century Fund, N.Y., 1955, p. 730. Statistics for 1957 from *Current Population Surveys,* U. S. Department of Commerce, Bureau of the Census.

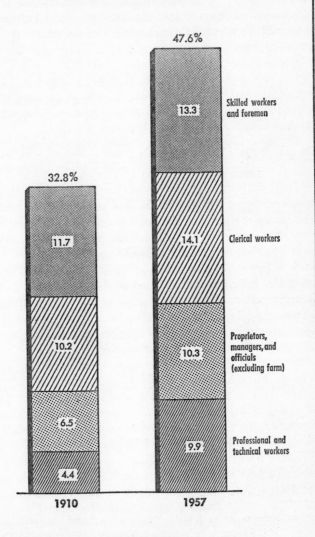

# OCCUPATIONAL DISTRIBUTION
## OF THE LABOR FORCE
### (PER CENT OF LABOR FORCE)

47.6%

13.3 — Skilled workers and foremen

32.8%

11.7

14.1 — Clerical workers

10.2

6.5

10.3 — Proprietors, managers, and officials (excluding farm)

4.4

9.9 — Professional and technical workers

1910          1957

Sources: Frederic Dewhurst, *America's Needs and Resources, 1955;* U.S. Dept. of Commerce

The table illustrates the increase in the degree of preparation demanded of our labor force. It is evident that whereas in 1910 highly developed skills and considerable educational background were demanded of less than a third of our work force, by 1957 they were necessary for almost half. The table further shows that the increase in employment has been greatest in precisely those categories that require the highest competence and the most extended training.

The increase in skill and training needed by our labor force can be expected to accelerate in the years ahead. One of its most interesting and widely publicized aspects is the impact on the labor force of the so-called automation revolution, whose substantial effects will be felt in the next decade.

The exact degree to which self-regulating machinery will replace human labor is a matter for debate. But there is no debate over the immediate impact of automation on the level of occupational skills. The consensus of engineers and economists who have considered the problem is that automation will reduce the number of routine jobs and will replace them by more demanding tasks of supervision, maintenance, and regulation in addition to the production of the machines themselves. Thus automation lends impetus to the trend away from unskilled and semi-skilled labor and toward skilled employments—a trend that had already gathered momentum with our gains in command of energy sources. And automation is adding this impetus in precisely those areas where the level of work is now least challenging—routine jobs in the factory and the large office.

Automation is not the only factor that will exercise an upward pressure on the level of skills in our work force. An equally powerful factor is the increasing specialization of our society. In all occupations, the level of competence required is constantly increasing. No scientist can hope to encompass more than a small sector of scientific knowledge. Military strategy is no longer only a matter for professional soldiers but rests importantly on the advice of scholars and technical experts. The conduct of government depends heavily on the talents of the economist, the agronomist, the public health officer, and similar experts.

Another factor creating a demand for talent is the recognized value of discovery. Discovery is no longer considered a matter of mere good fortune. It is consciously sought through large-scale, organized effort. This reliance on systematic research has long been growing. It is in one sense a culmination of our national habit of innovation. One of the factors in the dynamism of our economy has been our willingness to innovate. The development of systematic and organized research over the past fifty years is the institutionalization of a cardinal American faith in creative change and growth.

Another spur to systematic research is, of course, the imperative need to meet the Soviet military threat. For the first time in history, our survival is imperiled by the threat of technological inferiority, and the danger is all the more unsettling because we had taken our supremacy in the scientific field for granted. Our response has been to turn to organized intellectual effort as never before in our history.

In current discussions of shortages in high talent manpower, much attention is given to quantitative appraisal of the shortage in a given field at a given time. But of far greater significance than these appraisals of the moment is the long-term—and still continuing—upward trend in the demand for *all* trained manpower.

It must be recognized that the long-term trend toward greater demand for trained manpower is very different from the rise and fall of demand in a given professional field from one year to the next. This latter demand is at the mercy of a variety of circumstances in the manpower market. It is possible that in the near future we shall actually experience an oversupply in certain categories that now seem to be suffering shortages. This is not incompatible with the long-term upward trend in demand for talent. And it is important for the purposes of the present discussion to recognize that gross quantitative data on manpower conceal a deeper and more perplexing issue: the problem of quality. That is a problem that will preoccupy us throughout the remainder of this report.

In this day of technologies that become antiquated overnight, it is hazardous to predict a favorable future for any narrow occupational category. There will be economic advantage to the individual in acquiring the kind of fundamental training that will enable him to move back and forth over several occupational categories. Individuals so trained will find a market for their talents under most circumstances. Individuals more narrowly trained will be at the mercy of circumstances.

It is tempting to treat the problem of highly trained manpower in terms of the specific shortages that occur from time to time. But the true difficulty lies deeper. It is not a shortage, now of engineers, now of economists, that lies at the root of the problem. *It is the constant pressure of an ever more complex society against the total creative capacity of its people.* The problem breaks through to the surface in terms of specific lacks, but it exists as an underlying pressure at all times. A piecemeal approach defeats itself. In the first place, the "lead time" needed to train and develop talents is too long to allow crash programs to pay off. By the time we have brought up a generation of a particular kind of specialists, the need for the specialty may have been replaced by some other even more pressing need. We cannot now identify the skills needed ten years hence. Our most critical need a decade hence may be unknown today. Rather, we must prepare ourselves for a constant and growing demand for talents of all varieties and must attempt to meet the specific needs of the future by elevating the quality and quantity of talented individuals of all kinds.

This is a task of great difficulty. For some of the factors that produce the demand for talent also inhibit its development. Specialization, for example, is a vitally important force in the modern world; but it is unfortunately true that for many individuals specialization is a dead end rather than an avenue to deeper and broader understanding. This need not be so, and it is a challenge to our education to insure that it does not occur.

The trend toward specialization has created among other things an extraordinary demand for gifted generalists—men with enough intellectual and technical competence to deal with the specialists and enough breadth to play more versatile roles—whether as managers, teachers, interpreters, or critics. Such individuals will be drawn increasingly from the ranks of those whose education and experience have included *both* depth and breadth—who have specialized but have not allowed themselves to become imprisoned in their specialty.

We must never forget that the advances of science and technology have been paralleled by the increasing complexity of social organization. It is in the nature of a complex society that it depends simultaneously on the imaginative fulfillment of a multitude of tasks. A handful of scientists seem to bear a disproportionate share of the burden today, a handful of diplomats may be called upon tomorrow, and the next day an equally small number of doctors, teachers, political leaders. Our society is ever more interdependent, and with this fact has come a need for highly trained men and women in many fields.

Thus a society depends on achievement at many levels. Whether it is the general capabilities needed to man our industrial apparatus, or the more highly trained abilities required to staff the specialized functions of our society, or the supremely important achievements of creative thought, the need is for an unprecedented degree of individual effort and accomplishment. Not only must we have wise leadership in all areas of our national life, cultural as well as political, ethical as well as technological; not only must we have competent people in a wide range of key professions; but underlying it all we must also have an informed citizenry. Among the tasks that have increased most frighteningly in complexity is the task of the ordinary citizen who wishes to discharge his civic responsibilities intelligently.

In this context it becomes clear that the achievement of our objectives with respect to the cultivation of human resources is almost synonymous with our capacity to maintain the strength and vitality and growth potential of our society. At this level there is no conflict between our survival needs of the moment and our enduring needs as a society.

And it is not only in research fields that there is a premium on men and women with a talent for innovation, for individuals who can move beyond the limits of present practice. In a time of breath-taking technological and social changes, there is a need for people who understand the process and the nature of change and who are able to cope with it. One of our great strengths as a people has been our flexibility and adaptability under the successive waves of change that have marked our history. Never have we needed the trait more than today. It is for this reason that we should educate our young people to meet an unknown need rather than to prepare them for needs already identified.

In seeking to develop our human potential to meet the varied demands of the future, we shall find ourselves facing three obstacles. One of these is the inertia produced by doing familiar tasks well. Another is the ceilings on performance that exist in a highly institutionalized society. The final one is a deep philosophical rift within our own attitudes toward talent.

It is to these main obstacles that we now turn.

## THE PROBLEM OF CHANGE

One of the characteristics of a dynamic society is that its frontiers are constantly changing. The frontier of today becomes the familiar territory of tomorrow. The very effort of mobilizing energies for constructive tasks in one decade may inhibit creativity in another. The correctives of one age may become the roadblocks of another. Thus, the rewards and esteem that we attach to the fields in which we have been most successful may inhibit the development of talent in other highly important areas. We must recognize that one important factor in the unwillingness of youth to undertake certain critical tasks is due to a rather severe imbalance inherent in our current system of incentives. The skills that we need most critically today are not necessarily those that we reward most highly. Today we look especially to the scientist, the diplomat, the government administrator, the educator for critically important contributions to our society. Our scale of material and social rewards and incentives, however, still reflects an age when the attraction of talent into these fields was not accorded a very high priority. If teachers are not adequately paid today, it is at least in part because society has not yet come to esteem the teaching function sufficiently or to evaluate its social contribution adequately.

This existence of an older scale of material rewards is undoubtedly an important element in deflecting talent away from positions of presently critical social importance. But the problem cannot be met merely by increases of pay. If we are to develop adequately our talents in critical fields, we shall have to form a new estimation of certain kinds of work and to provide higher rewards of esteem and prestige in certain critical fields than now exist. The unfair caricature of the dowdy and fussy school teacher or the petty government bureaucrat may be as serious an impediment to the proper development and allocation of talent as the differentials in pay, which serve to reinforce and perpetuate the stereotypes themselves.

A dynamic society requires, above all, receptivity to change. To rest on achievement is a denial of creativity and an invitation to stagnation. The crucial questions then become: Are we fully manning the frontiers available to us? Are these current frontiers attracting our best people?

## THE SOCIAL CEILINGS ON
## INDIVIDUAL PERFORMANCE

Among the obstacles to the full development of individual talent is the nature of modern society itself. A consequence of the complexity and specialization of modern society has been the increasing prominence of organization in our lives. In every field—government, business, science, education, military affairs— activity is more formally structured, more bureaucratic, more "administered" than in the past. This is neither surprising nor in itself harmful. Delicately interdependent social activities cannot exist without synchronization and order. It is the purpose of organization to inject continuity, dependability, and orderliness into what would otherwise be chaos. The functioning of a modern city or factory is a miracle of voluntary co-operation that can only be accomplished by people who have developed deeply in- grained habits of playing by the rules, of self-discipline, and of internalized restraints. The same is true for most functions of a mass society.

But while complex organization is necessary, it is also costly. It is often a stifling atmosphere for the exercise of individual crea- tivity, and it may induce a conformity that becomes a threat to the society's vitality. In the atmosphere of regularity and order, the individual is under pressure to gear his performance to an acceptable common denominator. This may yield clear benefits in smooth organizational functioning but is hardly conducive to the kind of creative performance on which society now so im- portantly depends.

In short, the growing complexity of our social organization presents problems as well as opportunities for the cultivation of human capabilities. It tends to encourage effort—but often only up to a level of average acceptability. It opens avenues of advance, but these avenues converge on the citadels of routine where the individual pace must conform to fixed traffic patterns. It stimulates self-development but threatens to define the goal as mere competence. Meanwhile, the very contribution that a highly organized society most requires—original thought and effort—is precisely that which it unconsciously discourages.

Let us make no mistake about the alternatives. The notion that we might escape the complexities of modern life by returning to some simpler form of existence is sheer romancing. The interlocking complexities of modern society are an inescapable part of our future: if we are to nourish individual freedom, we shall have to nourish it under these circumstances. If we are to maintain individual creativity, we shall have to learn to preserve it in a context of organization. It is the predicament of Christian, in *Pilgrim's Progress*, facing the temptations of Vanity Fair: "The way to the Celestial City lies just through this town, where this lusty fair is kept; and he that will go to the City and yet not go through this town, must needs go out of the world."

The relevant questions then become: What organizational patterns and practices may be devised that are least destructive of individual initiative and autonomy? How is it that with all the intricacy of social mechanism, a good many astonishingly free, flexible, creative, and independent individuals exist—some of them in the very heart of the great bureaucracies? How may we best prepare our young people to keep their individuality, initiative, creativity in a highly organized, intricately meshed society? How may we rescue talented individuals from the lowered aspirations, the boredom, and the habits of mediocrity so often induced by life in a large and complex organization? How do we shatter the informal ceilings placed upon performance in an organizational setting in which order, harmony, and predictability seem to be given more emphasis than individual achievement?

When we arrive at questions of this import, we are no longer simply talking about the cultivation of talent. We are talking about some of the gravest issues in the future of our society. A continuing tension between the needs of the organization and the integrity of the person, between the effectiveness of the group and the creativity of the individual, may well be one of the most fateful struggles in our future.

## EXCELLENCE IN A DEMOCRACY

It is now widely recognized that our society has given too little attention to the individual of unusual talent or potentialities. To make such an assertion is not to deplore the unprecedented time and money we have devoted to raising the general level of achievement. It would serve no purpose to replace our neglect of the gifted by neglect of everyone else. We are all too prone to such wild swings of the pendulum in our national life. We must learn to view these matters in a perspective that will permit us to repair one omission without creating others.

It has not always been easy for Americans to think clearly about excellence. At the heart of the matter is a seeming paradox in democracy as we know it. On the one hand, ours is the form of society that says most convincingly, "Let the best man win," and rewards winners regardless of origin. On the other, it is the form of society that gives those who do not come out on top the widest latitude in rewriting the rules of the contest. It is crucial to understand this tug of war between equality and excellence in a democracy. When the rewriting of the rules is prompted by the standards of fair play, by elementary considerations of justice, by basic value judgments as to what sort of a "best man" the society wants, democracy can have no quarrel with it. Indeed, it is the core process of a democracy. But when the rewriting of the rules is designed to banish excellence, to rule out distinguished attainment, to inhibit spirited individuals, then all who have a stake in the continued vitality of democracy must protest.

Every democracy *must* encourage high individual performance. If it does not, it closes itself off from the mainsprings of its dynamism and talent and imagination, and the traditional democratic invitation to the individual to realize his full potentialities becomes meaningless. More, perhaps, than any other form of government, a democracy must maintain what Ralph Barton Perry has called "an express insistence upon quality and distinction."

The eighteenth-century philosophers who made equality a central term in our political vocabulary never meant to imply that men are equal in all respects. Nor do Americans today take such a view. It is possible to state in fairly simple terms the views concerning equality that would receive most widespread endorsement in our country today. The fundamental view is that in the final matters of human existence all men are equally worthy of our care and concern. Further, we believe that men should be equal in enjoyment of certain familiar legal, civil, and political rights. They should, as the phrase goes, be equal before the law.

But men are unequal in their native capacities and their motivations, and therefore in their attainments. In elaborating our national views of equality, the most widely accepted means of dealing with this problem has been to emphasize *equality of opportunity*. The great advantage of the conception of equality of opportunity is that it candidly recognizes differences in endowment and motivation and accepts the certainty of differences in achievement. By allowing free play to these differences, it preserves the freedom to excel, which counts for so much in terms of individual aspirations and has produced so much of mankind's greatness.

Having committed ourselves to equality of opportunity, we must strive incessantly to make it a reality in our society. This is a task that will concern us at many points in the present report.

With respect to the pursuit of excellence, there are several considerations that we must keep firmly in mind.

First, we must not make the mistake of adopting a narrow or constricting view of excellence. *Our conception of excellence must embrace many kinds of achievement at many levels.* There is no single scale or simple set of categories in terms of which to measure excellence. There is excellence in abstract intellectual activity, in art, in music, in managerial activities, in craftsmanship, in human relations, in technical work.

Second, we must not assume that native capacity is the sole ingredient in superior performance. Excellence, as we shall later have occasion to note, is a product of ability and motivation and character. And the more one observes high performance in the dust and heat of daily life, the more one is likely to be impressed with the contribution made by the latter two ingredients.

Finally, we must recognize that judgments of differences in talent are not judgments of differences in human worth.

To sum up, it is possible for us to cultivate the ideal of excellence while retaining the moral values of equality. Whether we shall succeed in doing so is perhaps the fundamental issue in the development of our human resources. A challenge must be recognized before it can be met. Our society will have passed an important milestone of maturity when those who are the most enthusiastic proponents of a democratic way of life are also the most vigorous proponents of excellence.

# III. The Educational System

## THE INFORMAL EDUCATIONAL SYSTEM

The formal educational system offers only part of the purposeful education that goes on in a society. Family, church, and school share the fundamental responsibility for education. But in a sense, every institution in a society is constantly teaching its members, molding their behavior, contributing to their development: in childhood it may be the scout leader, the playground director, the policeman on the corner; in later years the employer, the union, the mass media.

Family life is of basic importance in providing the emotional nurture and moral guidance the child needs if he is to develop fully as a person. Social circumstances that disrupt or degrade the quality of family life put in hazard this all-important emotional and moral nurture.

Clearly then, the social agencies, religious or secular, that concern themselves with the integrity of family life are insuring the soundness of the human material that will flow into our schools. In the same category belong the efforts of those who concern themselves with the physical and mental health of children. And here, too, one must list the contributions of those who have fought for the adequate education of our young women, since it is the young woman who largely creates the atmosphere of the home.

In short, the church, settlement house, day nursery, supervised playground, boys' club, Boy or Girl Scouts, and many other agencies contribute to the process by which a sound community delivers to the school a reasonably healthy and law-abiding child. As our great cities have learned to their sorrow, if the community delivers warped, criminal, or intractable boys and girls, there is little the school can do to save itself from havoc.

Seen in this light, even the city planners working on slum clearance and the governmental agencies engaged in public assistance programs are contributing to the conservation of those human resources that are the school's raw materials.

The contributions of these out-of-school influences to the emotional and moral life of the child are well known and understood. Less widely recognized is the fact that these influences have considerable effect upon the strictly intellectual motivations and academic fitness of the young person. Each year many thousands of young people with the ability to do well in college fail to go beyond high school. For many there are financial problems, but for a good many the primary reason is that their family and neighborhood environment have not provided them with the motivations and values that produce educational ambition.

The most effective educational system can be defeated by a social environment that blunts or destroys aspiration. There can be no striving for excellence without models to inspire emulation. There can be no greatness without the encouragement to ask much of oneself. It is essential for us to understand that the tone of our daily lives profoundly affects the quality of our society, and it is essential to recognize that of all factors involved in establishing that tone, the family is most important. It is not irrelevant to ask whether our families have too often relied on outside agencies, such as the schools, for the discovery of qualities that can best be developed at home; whether the pace of our lives permits the reflectiveness that is essential to creativity; whether we demand enough of ourselves or of our young.

## THE FORMAL EDUCATIONAL SYSTEM

Forty-three million Americans—one out of every four people in the nation—go to school. Almost two million Americans educate them in 150,000 institutions of learning. We have used our educational system as the basic instrument for realizing our ideal of equality of opportunity. It has been the great avenue along which any and all Americans might travel toward individual fulfillment and self-realization. The idea that any person regardless of back-

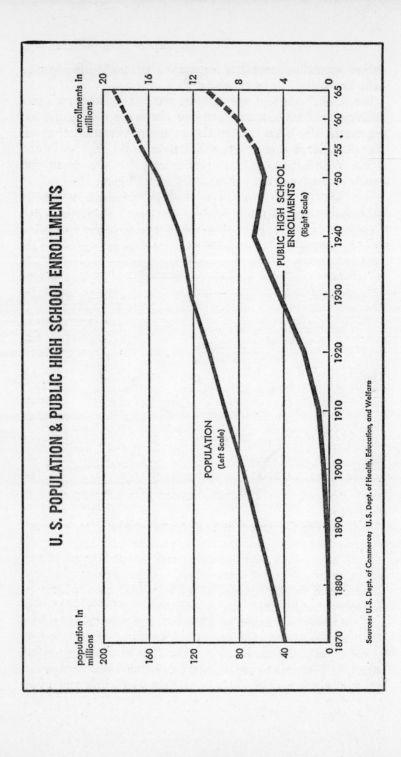

# U. S. POPULATION & PUBLIC HIGH SCHOOL ENROLLMENTS

population in
millions

enrollments in
millions

POPULATION
(Left Scale)

PUBLIC HIGH SCHOOL
ENROLLMENTS
(Right Scale)

Sources: U.S. Dept. of Commerce; U.S. Dept. of Health, Education, and Welfare

ground should be given the opportunity to develop his talents has been central to the system.

We have always told one another, sometimes with an all too shallow piety, that education is a vital element in the strength of our society. The times have grimly underscored the correctness of that view. But it is no longer sufficient to repeat it as an incantation. We must recognize that in many areas our educational facilities are poor and our educational effort slovenly.

Our schools are overcrowded, understaffed, and ill-equipped. In the fall of 1957, the shortage of public school classrooms stood at 142,000. There were 1,943,000 pupils in excess of "normal" classroom capacity. Some elementary and high schools and colleges had found it impossible to hire well-qualified teachers in such basic subjects as English, languages, and social sciences; some have even had to drop chemistry, physics, and mathematics from their curriculum since there were no teachers to teach them.

These pressures will become more severe in the years ahead. For the population bulge of the future will then press even more urgently on already overburdened facilities. Elementary school enrollments will rise from some 30 million today to about 34 million by 1960–61. By 1969, high schools will be deluged with 50 to 70 per cent more students than they can now accommodate; by 1975, our colleges and universities will face at least a doubling and in some cases a tripling of present enrollments.

If we are to meet these pressures, our schools will need greatly increased public support and attention, and much more money. But they also need something besides money: an unsparing re-examination of current practices, patterns of organization, and objectives.

In appraising the present state of American education, we must recognize that in the past seventy-five years we have heaped upon our educators one of the most heroic assignments a society could have invented. We have taken into the school system a greater proportion of our youngsters, and we have kept more of them in the system longer than any other nation. Between 1870 and 1955, while our population was increasing four times, our public high school population was increasing approximately eighty times. At the same time that we have forced this expansion upon the system, we have pressed our educators to include in the curriculum an incredible variety of subjects, to take over more and more of the functions of the home, and to accept a sense of responsibility for every psychic or civic crisis involving individuals below the age of consent.

That our educators did not founder completely under these chaotic pressures is impressive. That they may be credited with heroic achievements in creating a system of universal education is a simple fact.

And that their failures are in some measure failures of the American people is undeniable.

We do not wish to absolve our educators of the mistakes they have made. At the same time, we should not attempt to absolve ourselves. The fateful question is not whether we have done well, or whether we are doing better than we have done in the past, but whether we are meeting the stern demands and unparalleled opportunities of the times. And the answer is that we are *not*.

Not only must our educators handle a huge increase in the number of students, they must offer higher quality in education. From time to time one still hears arguments over *quantity* versus *quality* education. Behind such arguments is the assumption that a society can choose to educate a few people exceedingly well *or* to educate a great number of people somewhat less well but that it cannot do both. But a modern society such as ours cannot choose to do one *or* the other. It has no choice but to do both. Our kind of society calls for the maximum development of individual potentialities *at all levels*.

Fortunately, the demand to educate everyone up to the level of his ability and the demand for excellence in education are not incompatible. We must honor both goals. We must seek excellence in a context of concern for all.

If we are to do justice to these considerations, one of our most pressing needs is a revision of the false emphasis that the American people are coming to place on the purely formal evidence of education. Our dilemma with respect to higher education is illustrative. We have made of the receipt of a college degree an accolade of merit, not in terms of the intellectual achievement that it should symbolize, but in terms of the prestige that it attracts. To have received a college degree is becoming an essential qualification for entry into a great many careers, even though the careers may not utilize any of the particular kind of education that has been received. With these conditions prevailing, it is not surprising to find some people insisting that literally no one should be made "unequal" by a lack of higher education.

This dilemma is not limited to college education alone. It is manifest in the entire educational spectrum. By insisting that *equality* means an exactly similar exposure to education, regardless of the variations in interest and capacity of the student, we are, in fact, inflicting a subtle but serious form of inequality upon our young people. We are limiting the development of individual excellence in exchange for a uniformity of external treatment. Too many of our school systems have fallen into a chronological lock step under which all young people start off together at a given age and march forward one grade per year. Because many educators reject the idea of grouping by ability, the ablest students are often exposed to educational programs whose content is too thin and whose pace is too slow to challenge their abilities.

## THE TEACHING PROFESSION

No educational system can be better than its teachers. Yet we face severe problems both in the supply of teachers at all levels and in their quality. The number of new school teachers needed in the next decade is between one third and one half of all the four-year college graduates of every kind in the same period. Since only one out of every four or five college graduates enters school teaching, the magnitude of the problem is apparent, even allowing for the fact that recent college graduates are not the only source of supply. The danger of a decline in the quality of our corps of teachers is obvious. Even today it is in need of improvement: as of 1956, 33 per cent of the elementary teachers did not hold A.B. degrees, and more than 21 per cent of all public school teachers had less than four years of college.

At the college level, far from improving our corps of teachers, we may be slipping backward. The National Education Association reports that "since 1953–1954, holders of the doctor's degree among the newly employed full-time teachers have decreased 25.2 per cent." Although academic degrees and quality are not identical, it is clear that such a sharp decline in formal preparation may be symptomatic of decline in other respects. And the pressures immediately ahead are likely to make matters worse.

Under the present system of incentives, both financial and

social, it is likely that even those who have a formally adequate preparation contain a disproportionate number of individuals of low energy or over-all ability. This is particularly true at the college level. For many of the qualities that are most necessary for effective college teaching are in great demand in other fields as well. And since the financial rewards of nonacademic work are generally much higher, it is hard to attract the ablest people into academic life. There is a certain irony in this. The industrial and governmental organizations that are outbidding the universities for the young people who might have gone into college teaching are precisely the organizations that in the long run stand to lose most if the quality of our higher education deteriorates.

The problem of recruitment is inseparable from the preparation required to enter the teaching profession. If the programs for the preparation of teachers are rigid, formalistic, and shallow, they will drive away able minds as fast as they are recruited. Unhappily, preparation for pre-college teaching has come all too close to that condition. In some states the requirements for certification are so technical and trivial as to make it unlikely that individuals with a first-class liberal education would even apply —or be eligible if they did apply.

Perhaps no profession has suffered such a general neglect of specialized abilities as that of the teacher. Teachers at the pre-college level tend to be handled as interchangeable units in an educational assembly line. The best teacher and the poorest in a school may teach the same grade and subject, use the same textbook, handle the same number of students, get paid the same salaries, and rise in salary at the same speed to the same ceiling. Clearly, if the teaching profession is to be made more attractive, this will have to be changed.

Fortunately, there appears to be a lively movement to correct these difficulties. The Educational Policies Commission has recently* re-emphasized that "every teacher should have both a liberal education and a knowledge in depth of the field in which he teaches." Colleges of teacher education are re-examining their curricula with a new awareness of the problem. Groups concerned with teacher certification are reviewing state regulations in a similar spirit. The liberal arts colleges are once again accept-

* Written in June 1958.

ing some responsibility for teacher preparation. It is essential that all of these efforts to strengthen and enrich the process of teacher preparation be continued and given added impetus. It is necessary to clear away the deadwood of formalistic requirements and to provide a variety of stimulating paths to pre-college teaching.

As for the preparation of college teachers, the problem is one of reforming and expanding graduate education. There has been more emphasis on research and research training than on the preparation of teachers. The most farsighted leaders in the graduate schools have called attention to the conditions that make graduate education an interminable process for many students, that degrade the master's degree, and that belittle the importance of the teaching function. The graduate schools need courage and flexibility to correct these conditions. They also need money. It is essential that ample funds be made available for construction of new facilities, for remodeling of old facilities, and for the general operating budgets of the graduate schools.

But even with aggressive recruitment, there appears to be little or no likelihood that we can bring into teaching at any level anything approaching the number of qualified and gifted teachers we need. We can be certain that there will never be enough teachers with the extraordinary human gifts that make for inspired teaching. We must therefore utilize our superior teachers more effectively.

One way to make better use of the ablest teachers is to eliminate many of the petty tasks that occupy a teacher's time. Less highly trained classroom assistants may accomplish much in the lightening of this burden. Another measure is the employment of such devices as television to bring extraordinarily effective teachers into contact with larger numbers of students than they would otherwise face. Films may be similarly useful.

Such innovations as the teacher aide and television should not be thought of as stopgap measures to surmount the immediate teacher shortage but as the beginnings of a long overdue revolution in teaching techniques. The emergence of techniques that make it possible to reach large numbers of students economically (e.g., television and films) has led some observers to decry a mass approach to teaching. This is not a necessary consequence. All such techniques should only be used to extend the impact of exceptionally gifted teachers or to perform teaching tasks that may best be handled by such techniques, so that the teacher may be freed for creative attention to tasks that can *only* be accomplished through personal interaction.

In examining new patterns of teacher utilization, it is not important whether one agrees or disagrees with any specific measure. One may take any of several views of the usefulness of television or films in teaching. It *is* important to recognize that present patterns of utilization are simply not going to work except in a few institutions that are sufficiently prosperous to preserve them. It *is* important to accept the desirability of a rigorous reappraisal of present patterns and courageous experimentation with new patterns. This must include a candid weighing of essentials and nonessentials in the curriculum; more flexible and imaginative approaches to the problem of class size; and—at the level of higher education—the trying out of approaches that place more responsibility on the student for his own education.

But the root problem of the teaching profession remains financial. More perhaps than any other profession, teaching needs dedicated men and women to whom pay is not an overriding consideration; but until we pay teachers at least as well as the middle echelon of executives, we cannot expect the profession to attract its full share of the available range of talents. Salaries must be raised immediately and substantially. Almost as important as the level of pay is the fact that promotional policy for most school systems is routine and depends much more on seniority than on merit. And the top salary is not sufficiently far above the bottom salary to constitute a meaningful incentive. Those with more than modest financial needs and responsibilities can solve their problems only by becoming administrators or by leaving education altogether.

## THE CURRICULUM

Next in importance to teachers is what they teach. Reform of the curriculum is too large a subject to deal with here, but we can suggest some of its dimensions.

At the pre-college level, the gravest problem today is to reach some agreement on priorities in subject matter. There is little or no dispute about the content of the curriculum in the first seven or eight grades and relatively little about the "general education" provided for all pupils in grades nine to twelve. It is almost universal to require that all pupils study composition and literature for all four high school years. It is also widely accepted that all will study at least one year of high school mathematics, one year of science, and three to four years of social studies, including American history, in grades nine to twelve. We have been extraordinarily tolerant, however, in the matter of electives in the high school. In the great "democracy of subject matters," which we have allowed to develop, it is only a moderate exaggeration to say that beyond the prescribed subjects (which take about half the student's time) any subject has been considered to be as important as any other subject.

Deciding what is more important and what is less important among the electives is particularly vital in the case of the abler student, who must be challenged and held to high standards of performance. And establishing the relative importance of subjects for the abler student is not as controversial a matter as some seem to think. When educational leaders can be persuaded to list elective subjects in order of priority, a high degree of agreement emerges as to the top items on the list. Without presuming to lay down an inflexible set of recommendations, we may suggest what these high priority items in a solid high school curriculum might be for those of considerable academic ability. (These recommendations are based partly upon a recent study by Dr. James B. Conant and partly upon the findings of a conference sponsored by the National Education Association on "Education of the Academically Talented.")

In addition to the general education prescribed for all—four years of English, three to four years of social studies, one year of mathematics, and one year of science—the academically talented student should have two to three additional years of science, three additional years of mathematics, and at least three years of a foreign language. For certain students, the study of a second foreign language, for at least three years, might replace the fourth year of mathematics and the third year of science.

Particularly with respect to the highest priority subjects, we must modernize and improve the quality of the courses themselves. Virtually every subject in the curriculum would profit by a lively reform movement of the sort now going on in physics and mathematics teaching. Certainly every subject would profit by the attention of the best minds in that particular field. For too long the leading authorities in these fields, accustomed to the rarefied intellectual air of college and university teaching, could not be bothered to concern themselves with how their subject was taught in elementary and secondary schools, what kinds of courses were designed, or what sorts of textbooks were being written. In the past half dozen years, it has come as a shock to such people to realize that a poor harvest at the college level is often directly traceable to a failure of sound cultivation at earlier levels.

## SCIENCE EDUCATION

Though we cannot discuss in detail each of the fields of study, it is worthwhile to say a few words about education in science and mathematics. The public reactions to this subject have been so intense and so diverse that it has not been easy for the informed citizen to appraise the issues. The simplest way to avoid confusion is to keep a few basic ideas firmly in mind.

First, the crisis in our science education is not an invention of the newspapers, or scientists, or the Pentagon. It is a real crisis.

Second, the U.S.S.R. is not the "cause" of the crisis. The cause of the crisis is our breath-taking movement into a new technological era. The U.S.S.R. has served as a rude stimulus to awaken us to that reality.

The heart of the matter is that we are moving with headlong speed into a new phase in man's long struggle to control his environment, a phase beside which the industrial revolution may appear a modest alteration of human affairs. Nuclear energy, exploration of outer space, revolutionary studies of brain functioning, important new work on the living cell—all point to changes in our lives so startling as to test to the utmost our adaptive capacities, our stability, and our wisdom.

The immediate implications for education may be briefly stated. We need an ample supply of high caliber scientists, mathematicians, and engineers. Quantitative arguments over the shortages in these fields are beside the point. We need *quality*, and we need it in considerable quantity! Whatever the existing needs, it is in the nature of a revolution that its continuing impetus derives from the unknown needs, the new opportunities and vistas, which are the hallmark of creativity. We must develop guidance efforts designed to reach all able youngsters, and we must engage in a major expansion of the facilities for science teaching.

There is a danger of training scientists so narrowly in their specialties that they are unprepared to shoulder the moral and civic responsibilities that the modern world thrusts upon them. But just as we must insist that every scientist be broadly educated, so we must see to it that every educated person be literate in science. In the short run this may contribute to our survival. In the long run it is essential to our integrity as a society. We cannot afford to have our most highly educated people living in intellectual isolation from one another, without even an elementary understanding of each other's intellectual concerns. Such fragmentation must lead to a loss of social purpose.

This bears also upon the balance in education between the sciences, the social sciences, and the humanities. Each has a vital part to play and any policy that fails to nourish and strengthen all is shortsighted indeed.

## IDENTIFICATION OF TALENT
## AND THE USES OF DIVERSITY

Any educational system is, among other things, a great sorting-out process. One of its most important goals is to identify and guide able students and to challenge each student to develop his capacities to the utmost.

There is overwhelming evidence of a determination on the part of the American people that the sorting-out process be carried out mercifully and generously rather than ruthlessly, rigidly, or mechanically. But it has sometimes seemed that rather than admit differences in talent—or at least taking responsibility for assessing it—we prefer to accept mediocrity.

In recent months there has been much discussion of large-scale testing programs for the purpose of identifying talent. Used with a sound understanding of their strengths and limitations, present testing procedures can contribute significantly to a program of talent identification. When large numbers are involved, tests may uncover talent that would otherwise go unnoticed. And even when large numbers are not involved, a particular youngster's aptitude may be such as to defy easy diagnosis and may escape the attention of all but the keenest of teachers.

But testing procedures unwisely used can do harm. A few basic considerations with respect to them must be understood.

First, tests are most effective in measuring academic aptitude and achievement. There are certain other kinds of aptitude and achievement that they can measure, but with less assurance. And there are many kinds of talent that must go unmeasured because no adequate measuring instruments exist. In short, the tests are effective on a limited front. Decisions based on test scores must be made with the awareness of the imponderables in human behavior. We cannot measure the rare qualities of character that are a necessary ingredient of great performance. We cannot measure aspiration or purpose. We cannot measure courage, vitality, or determination.

Second, no single test should become a basis for important decisions. A series of scores obtained over the years enables teachers to achieve a reliable perspective on the young person's aptitudes and minimizes the possibility of false diagnosis.

Third, test scores are one kind of data to be placed alongside other kinds of data. The test score is not to be worshiped as a datum so decisive that it alone can be used to settle an individual's fate; it is a highly useful addition to other data but should not replace them. Unfortunately, the most powerful influence making for excessive dependence on test scores is the willingness of adults to evade their responsibility for complex and difficult decisions concerning the child. The test score should be regarded as an aid in making—not a device for evading—such decisions.

The identification of talent is no more than the first step. It should be only part of a strong guidance program. The word *guidance* has a variety of meanings; we use it here to mean advice concerning the young person's educational problems and the most appropriate course of study for him. It cannot be emphasized too strongly that such guidance is essential to the success of our system. As many teachers as possible should be trained to take part in it. As many high schools as possible should have special guidance officers to supplement the teachers where greater technical knowledge is required.

The objective of all educational guidance should be to stimulate the individual to make the most of his potentialities. The fact that a substantial fraction of the top quarter of high school graduates fail to go on to college is a startling indictment of our guidance system. It is not surprising that teachers, trained as they are to deal protectively and helpfully toward young people, should focus a major portion of their guidance efforts on those who seem most in need of help, such as the retarded and the delinquents. But there are students at the high end of the scale who present an equally great problem as far as their own self-fulfillment is concerned and an even greater problem as far as society is concerned. Within the framework of concern for all, guidance should give particular attention to able students.

The general academic capacity of students should be at least tentatively identified by the eighth grade as the result of repeated testings and classroom performance in the elementary grades. An adequate guidance system would insure that each student would then be exposed to the sort of program that will develop to the full the gifts that he possesses.

But the schools cannot do full justice to each young person in developing what gifts he may possess until they face frankly the need to provide different programs for different types and levels of ability. Our schools have made far more progress in *identifying* different levels of talent than in the *development of programs* for these different levels. Adequate attention to individual differences means rejecting a rigid policy of promotion by age; and it means sensible experimentation with various kinds of flexibility in the curriculum to meet the varying needs of young people. And especially, it means providing unusually able boys and girls with rigorous and challenging experiences.

In courses in which there is a wide spread of student ability—in English and other courses required of all students—there should be sections arranged according to aptitude *in that subject*. It is important to note that a student might be in a fast-learning group in mathematics, in a second group for history, and a third group for French. This is a very different thing from arbitrarily separating all students with intelligence scores above a certain figure and placing them in a separate curriculum as a block.

Some critics of our schools have advocated the European pattern of two entirely separate school systems after approximately the sixth grade—one system college preparatory and the other vocational in character. Such separation would be unpalatable to most Americans, and in any case separate school systems are unnecessary. There is no reason why youngsters at all levels of scholastic ability should not sit in the same homeroom, play on the same teams, act in the same plays, attend the same dances, and share in the same student government. And there are many reasons why such a common experience is important.

The argument against two entirely separate school systems need not rule out the possibility that in our larger cities we may develop special schools to meet special purposes, for example, the famed Bronx High School of Science. Our best guide in these matters is to vary the rule to fit the circumstances.

We have referred repeatedly to that portion of the high school population capable of high caliber college work—roughly 15 to 20 per cent of the students. A more special problem is presented by the top *two* per cent of the high school population. From this highly selected group will come many of the young men and women who will reach the pinnacles of intellectual achievement and creativity in the years ahead. No effort should be spared to provide them with the opportunities for challenging study.

For this group particularly, the Advanced Placement Program is important. Under this program, now sponsored by the College Entrance Examination Board, an expanding number of secondary schools, both public and private, is offering college-level courses to their best juniors and seniors. Many colleges are prepared to permit such students to "leapfrog" freshman college courses and get credit for them. Another approach is represented by the experimental Program for Early Admission to College, under which about 1,000 able students have entered twelve different colleges over the last five years *before* completing the last year or two of high school. An evaluation of the first two groups to graduate from college under this experiment shows that, on the whole, they have far outperformed their classmates academically; and despite their lower age, their social and emotional adjustment to college compares favorably with that of students generally.

The important thing is to rid ourselves of the notion that either a flexible promotion policy or flexible curricular arrangements are undemocratic in spirit. We cannot escape the fact of individual differences, and we cannot escape the necessity for coping with them. Whether we like it or not, they are a central fact in any educational system—and in any society. The good society is not one that ignores them but one that deals with them wisely and compassionately.

If we are really serious about equality of opportunity, we shall be serious about individual differences because what constitutes opportunity for one man is a stone wall for the next. If we are to do justice to the individual, we must seek for him the level and kind of education that will open *his* eyes, stimulate *his* mind, and unlock *his* potentialities. We should seek to develop many educational patterns—each geared to the particular capacities of the student for whom it is designed.

But though the educational patterns may differ, the goals remain much the same for all: enabling each young person to go as far as his aptitude will permit in fundamental knowledge and skills, and motivating him to continue his own self-development to the full along similar lines.

If we recognize the necessity of diverse educational paths, it may then be easier to accept the fact that education in a four year college is not the only road to a full and useful life. Americans who honestly believe in the full realization of every man's potentialities find themselves engaged in a two-front war. On the one hand, they must fight to make college education more widely available to those who are fitted for it. On the other, they must deny that college is the only key to success and happiness.

We will do well to stress the many kinds of achievement of which a human being is capable. The sort of capacity measured by the conventional scholastic aptitude test is very important; but we should be wary of putting too monolithic an emphasis upon this particular talent. Instead, we should encourage all kinds of individuals to run on all kinds of tracks. In this way we can distribute very widely the rewards of self-esteem and self-respect, which are the healthiest preventives of leveling reactions. We can encourage on the broadest scale the release of individual energy and positive motivation that have traditionally been among the greatest strengths of our society. We can then insist, as we must, that democracy is not to be conceived as an invitation to share a common mediocrity but as a system that allows each to express and live up to the special excellence that is in him. We can then demand the best of our most gifted, most talented, and most spirited youngsters. And we can dedicate ourselves to the cultivation of distinction and a sense of quality.

## FINANCING

All of the problems of the schools lead us back sooner or later to one basic problem—financing. It is a problem with which we cannot afford to cope half-heartedly. Education has always been essential to achievement of our political and moral objectives. It has emerged as a necessary ingredient in our technological advancement. And now events have underscored its value in terms of sheer survival.

It will not be enough to meet the problem grudgingly or with a little more money. The nation's need for good education is immediate; and good education is expensive. That is a fact which the American people have never been quite prepared to face. At stake is nothing less than our national greatness and our aspirations for the dignity of the individual. If the public is not prepared for this, then responsible educators, business leaders, political leaders, unions, and civic organizations must join in a national campaign to prepare them.

But first our national leaders will themselves have to grasp the true scope of the task. Perhaps the greatest problem facing American education is the widely held view that all we require are a few more teachers, a few more buildings, a little more money. Such an approach will be disastrous. We are moving into the most demanding era in our history. An educational system grudgingly and tardily patched to meet the needs of the moment will be perpetually out of date. We must build for the future in education as daringly and aggressively as we have built other aspects of our national life in the past.

Against a gross national product of $391 billion in 1955, total expenditures on formal education in the United States ran just under $14 billion, or 3.6 per cent of the GNP. This total breaks down as follows:

|  | Billions |
|---|---|
| Public Elementary and Secondary | $9.4 |
| Private Elementary and Secondary | 1.2 |
| Public Higher Education | 1.5 |
| Private Higher Education | 1.9 |
| Total | $14.0 |

Since 1930, this relationship of educational expenditures to GNP has remained relatively constant at about 3.5 per cent. This has meant, of course, a large increase in total dollars spent on education as the national product has risen, but the increase has not been sufficient to keep pace with the rise in enrollments, much less to outstrip it. The result is a proportionately smaller expenditure of the GNP *per pupil*.

Even allowing for considerably greater efficiency in the use of educational funds, it is likely that ten years hence our schools and colleges will require at least *double* their present level of financial support to handle our growing student population. In other words, by 1967, the entire educational effort is likely to call for expenditures on the order of $30 billion, measured in today's prices. Since the gross national product by 1967 has been estimated to be around $600 billion, educational expenditures would absorb about 5 per cent of gross national product in contrast with the current 3.6 per cent level.

A rise of this magnitude in the proportion of the gross national product devoted to education may require a sharp departure from past patterns of financing, particularly where public funds are involved. There has already appeared a tendency to shift the burden of school support from local to state government. The proportion of support coming from the state level shifted from just under 17 per cent in 1930 to over 37 per cent in 1954. The reasons are many—not the least compelling of which is the fact that sole reliance on local financial resources results in gross inequalities of educational opportunity from one district to another.

In the past, Americans have preferred to accomplish the financing of public education, like the financing of most nondefense public facilities and services, at the state and local level. But state and local tax systems are in some respects archaic, and it is very difficult to keep the revenues from this source growing in step with the economy or with the growing demand for governmental services that an expanding economy creates. This is due partly to the excessive dependence of state and local revenues—particularly the latter—upon the real property tax, which is notably laggard in its response to rising income. And it is due partly to the fact that state and local governments are reluctant to extend or expand their taxing systems for fear of placing their communities or states at a competitive disadvantage relative to other areas.

It is this weakness in the state and local taxing systems more than anything else that gives rise to current proposals for increased federal support of education. For those who wish to resist or postpone the resort to federal funds and at the same time not constrict educational services, there seems to be only one alternative: a thorough, painful, politically courageous overhaul of state and local tax systems.

The proposals for federal support of education have stimulated widespread public discussion, but there is an air of unreality about much of the debate. For a great deal of the debate centers around a doctrinal dispute over the dangers of such support. Over the years, while this full-dress discussion has been going on in the public eye, practical-minded legislators and executives on the one hand and hard-pressed educators on the other have been hammering out compromises almost unnoticed. And out of these compromises over the years has come a great variety of well-established federal programs in education. No discussion of federal support to education can proceed on a sensible basis without first recognizing this fact. Federal programs in education now exist on a large scale. They take a great many forms. It is certain that they will increase both in scale and in variety. It is a stark fact that there are educational problems gravely affecting the national interest that may be soluble only through federal action.

Under the circumstances, it is important for those who are apprehensive about the growth of federal support of education to examine the *direction* that it takes. There is no chance that we can turn back the clock and eliminate federal support of education. There is a chance that farsighted men may influence the *direction* of federal support or the *kinds* of federal support.

In seeking to exercise such influence, they would do well to bear in mind four principles in appraising proposals for federal support of education:

1. The federal government should address itself to those needs which educational leaders have identified as having a high priority. This may seem obvious, but governmental action is sometimes influenced more heavily by the political appeal of a program than by the need for such a program.

2. Federal funds should constitute one source of support among many. State, local, and private sources of funds should continue to be the major factor in the support of education. Federal funds

should be used only to balance the serious gaps in the total national educational system and should be given in such a manner as to encourage state and local governments to use their own resources, and where necessary to remove the barriers to use of their own resources.

\* 3. It should preserve local leadership and local control over education.

4. It should be based on a recognition that the government inevitably exercises a certain leadership function in whatever it does. The effect of a government scholarship program may go far beyond the immediate impact of the grants. The fact that the government chooses to recognize high talent could have far-reaching consequences in the attitudes of young people. Any federal support to education shall therefore be concentrated on certain strategic areas. The federal government should see its role as that of pacemaking rather than as confirming traditional and often outdated attitudes.

Perhaps the most popular form of federal support for education is the scholarship program. Scholarships appeal powerfully to our concern for providing opportunity to young people. And they involve a minimum hazard of federal interference. The money goes to the student, and he decides which university he wishes to attend. It may be public or private, religious or secular: the thorny problems involved in direct governmental dealing with certain kinds of institutions never present themselves.

The great political appeal of such programs makes it necessary to point out that however important in themselves scholarship programs may be, they are not a solution to the problem of financing higher education. There is no long-run gain in sending more and more youngsters to weaker and weaker institutions. As long as very few institutions charge tuition covering the full cost of education, a scholarship program that enables the student to pay his tuition should provide the college with a supplementary grant to make up the full cost of his education.

Another much discussed form of federal aid that involves a minimum of hazard to local initiative is funds for building construction. In the years immediately ahead, great expansion of the physical plant will be required at every level of the educational system. To the extent that the federal government can assist in this problem, either through loans or outright grants, it will be engaging in one of the most helpful and least hazardous forms of support to education.

One important question in the financing of higher education is the future of privately financed colleges and universities. Their share of total enrollments has already declined to well below 50 per cent; and within fifteen years their share of students could easily be closer to 25 per cent. If this decrease in percentage of students is accompanied by a waning of influence, it must be viewed with severe misgivings. Publicly financed and privately financed institutions have each made distinctive and essential contributions to the vitality of American higher education. We have come to recognize that the existence, side by side, of these alternative patterns of support and control is a healthy thing for all concerned. Here, as in so many other aspects of our national life, we find that diverse sources of control make for freedom and vitality in the system.

Some have urged that one solution of the problem lies in reform of the pricing system of the privately financed college. Today, tuition charges frequently represent 50 per cent or less of actual instructional costs, so that every student automatically receives a large *hidden scholarship* financed out of endowment income, current gifts, and low faculty salaries. Overt scholarships are then superimposed upon the hidden scholarships for those students who cannot even afford the cut rates. Some have suggested an alternate policy under which tuition would be set at the full cost of instruction, and each student would receive whatever amount of scholarship or other financial assistance he needed and would pay whatever proportion of the full tuition he could afford. This would eliminate hidden scholarships, put all student subsidies out in the open, and place all student charges on an ability-to-pay basis. No student would receive a subsidy if he did not need it, and not a dollar of alumni gifts or other income would be wasted on hidden subsidies to students whose families could well afford the real cost of a good college education. But many people disagree, basically and philosophically, with such a policy and find fundamental difficulties in it. One difficulty is that it might put the privately financed institutions at a severe disadvantage in attracting students as compared with the publicly financed institutions. Another is that such a plan would require that a large proportion of the student body be subjected to a *means test*, which would be very difficult in administrative terms.

Unquestionably the solution for the privately financed institutions lies not in any one device but in the simultaneous exploration of numerous paths—both for cutting costs and for raising money: for example, eliminating unnecessary frills in the curriculum; sharing facilities with neighboring institutions; dropping the extravagant notion that every institution must offer a carbon copy of the curriculum offered by every other institution; making radically better use of physical facilities; raising tuition; cultivating increased corporate and alumni giving; and obtaining certain kinds of federal support. Unless changes such as these are carried out, there is real danger that the influence of private higher education will progressively decline.

# IV. The Use and Misuse of Human Abilities

Unused talents lead to personal frustration, but they also deprive a society of the mainspring of its vitality. To realize our ideal of maximum personal development, it is not only essential that we inspire our people to the best that is in them, but it is also essential to give them an opportunity to exercise that best. A society must learn to regard every instance of a misuse of talent as an injustice to the individual and an injury to itself. And it must cultivate the ideal and the exercise of excellence by every means at its disposal.

These are the matters to which our report now turns.

## INADEQUATE USE OF TALENT

There exist at least four broad categories in which talent is wasted wholesale. The first one—and the one that must lie heaviest on our conscience—is our disadvantaged minorities. In addition, the better use of the talents of women and of older workers presents problems that are perplexing from the standpoint of social action. And the existence of economically depressed areas and segments of the population continues to be a challenge for all who are concerned with the development of individual potentialities.

### Fuller Use of Underprivileged Minorities

Primary among these groups is, of course, the Negro, who has been disadvantaged economically as well as politically and socially in the United States. Occasionally one hears it said that "the talented Negro will always make out all right." This misses the point. The smothering of talent under such circumstances is not an explicit, direct, observable act; it is a cumulative process. It is not so much that developed talent is rejected but that talent is not allowed to develop. It withers under the cumulative impact of poverty and ignorance at home, degraded neighborhoods, poor educational facilities, limited job opportunities, and the ever-present fear of rebuff.

What has until recently been thought of solely in terms of an abrogation of moral principle takes on even additional meaning in a society in need of talent. The denial of opportunity to the Negro results in the loss of potentially creative and skillful manpower.

The end of segregation, with all the difficult adjustments it imposes, is of course a step in the right direction. Legislation such as fair employment practices acts will add a necessary stimulus to private reorientation of attitudes. The migration trends that are distributing the Negro population throughout the nation will contribute to alleviation of the problem. Negro athletes, teachers, airline hostesses, diplomats, judges, government officials not only symbolize the fact that the problem is already on its way to being solved but serve to accelerate the trend. Yet all these are only first steps. Until the Negro has been offered equal opportunity with the non-Negro to develop and use his individual talents to the utmost, and until he can be encouraged to make the most of his opportunity, we shall have failed to achieve our moral goal.

## Better Use of the Talents of Women

As a recent report of the National Manpower Council made clear, women are playing an increasingly important role in the American economy: one out of every three workers in our regular labor force of nearly 70 million is a woman. To this already large contribution, we can expect a substantial increase over the next decades due to the age composition of our population. The average American woman today is married before she reaches voting age and frequently completes her family of two or three by her late twenties. Thus, some time in her thirties or early forties she may be in search of meaningful activity outside the home. Some women may find satisfaction in volunteer work, but many others will prefer or need a paid job on a part- or full-time basis.

Yet the availability will be wasted—despite the eagerness of many married women to work—if we do not take active steps to utilize this potential resource. In the educational, nursing, and welfare fields—all characterized by shortages—rigid training and licensing requirements make it difficult for able women to qualify for available openings. Outside of these professions, women are faced with other handicaps of a less formal but more prejudicial nature. There are still relatively few professional fields beyond nursing and teaching in which women participate extensively. Many firms still hesitate to use women in executive capacities or to include in executive training programs even those women who expect to remain in employment.

Finally, it is still true that women are typically less well prepared for careers than men. To a degree this reflects the continuance of nineteenth-century attitudes; to a degree it reflects a still ambivalent attitude toward work on the part of women themselves. Whatever the reason for the inadequate preparation, no improvement is likely to occur until there are substantially better opportunities for the gifted woman to find an occupation suitable to her capacities. And there is a growing need to provide educational opportunities for mature women on a part-time basis to help them qualify themselves for professional employment when their child-rearing responsibilities begin to ease. Nothing that we have said should be taken as belittling the meaningful and satisfying role of the wife and mother. Our earlier comments on the importance of family life stand as evidence of our conviction that no task could be more important to the nation than maintaining the integrity of the family.

## Rehabilitation of Economically Depressed Areas and Segments of the Population

When President Eisenhower asked Congress for legislation to assist the depressed areas of the country, he stressed the need for action on grounds of equity: why should a child born in the backwoods of the Appalachians be deprived of opportunities available to children whose parents are fortunate enough to be living in more prosperous regions?

The nation is paying a high price for its depressed areas in terms of the wastage of human abilities. Children who grow up under conditions that do not stimulate development not only suffer personal deprivation but are all too apt to be social liabilities. During the first year of the Korean conflict, the national failure rate on the Armed Forces Qualification Test was 19.2 per cent, but the failure rate for men from nine states where incomes and educational expenditures are relatively low ranged from 34 to 58 per cent. This illustrates the truth that poor education in any one area of the nation should be of serious concern to the whole nation. The constant movement of population from one part of the country to another makes the problem even more obviously one of national concern.

## Better Use of Older Workers

This problem has gained prominence because of the changing age composition of our population, but it is hardly a new problem. In our society the role of the older person is difficult, perhaps more for psychological than for material reasons. The grandparent is not a figure of authority as in some cultures but is relegated to the periphery of family life. Part of the problem is that health and longevity standards have improved markedly, so that an individual at sixty-five has higher potentialities than was the case a generation ago. Neither our houses nor our values are such as to accommodate the old. They must largely fend for themselves.

These facts have had significant consequences. The specter of dependent old age has been a powerful factor in the emphasis on pensioned retirement as a goal of American life. Retirement security in all its various forms has made enormous gains in recent decades. But as these gains were achieved, the problem has unexpectedly shifted in focus. It was not foreseen in the thirties, when many of our retirement ideas became widely accepted, that the man facing economically secure retirement at sixty-five would fear boredom as intensely as an earlier generation had feared want. Nor was it foreseen that the enterprise, public or private, that had lost his services might find itself not rid of a burden but deprived of a still active personality.

The truth is that only for a portion of older people has retirement with economic security become a treasured period of leisure when one can do "what one always wanted to." For others, it is a dreaded break in the texture and tempo of life, leading to personal dissatisfaction on the one hand and to wasted ability on the other.

To a certain extent this is unavoidable: in a highly organized society there must be compulsory retirement, not only to provide security for the individual but to assure a steady turnover of opportunity at the top. Yet the waste of human talent in the premature retirement of still vigorous people clearly calls for remedial action. In some instances this action might take the form of a latter retirement age. Or it might involve the development of special job opportunities for people over sixty-five. Such opportunities have already been provided in college teaching: the professor retiring from one campus may be hired on special status by some other college.

## USE OF TALENT IN LARGE ORGANIZATIONS

An imaginative policy to nurture talent would include not only an effort to identify talent at all age levels but a continuous development operation to rescue able people—at whatever age level —from situations that stifle individual potentialities. Such talent development should become a settled policy of every organization. Every corporation, union, government agency, military service, and professional group should—in its own best interest as well as that of its personnel—conduct a never-ending search for talent within its own staff.

This sort of operation is likely to test severely our ingenuity and wisdom. For part of the problem of rescuing talent is to *recognize* talent. Any organization or society is all too likely to get trapped in its own stereotyped notions of what constitutes talent. As a result, an apparent shortage of talent may often represent only a shortness of vision.

Sometimes a change of jobs is extremely useful in lifting the individual out of his rut and exposing him to new challenges. In this connection, it must be noted that nontransferable pension and benefit plans weaken the incentives of men and women to move to positions where better use could be made of their capacities and experience. There seems to be a need for more vesting of pension rights so that the employee who moves to another job need not leave behind years of accumulated benefits.

Another problem is the large organization itself. The traits commonly associated with a high level of creativity (e.g., in the best scientists) are not always such as to make for success or even happiness in a large organization. Since many large organizations today cannot function without men of these gifts, a good deal of effort has been expended to resolve this dilemma. Some industrial concerns, particularly those that depend on a high level of technological innovation, have learned much about how to attract and hold persons of high creativity and intelligence. The military, bound by many rigidities in the treatment of its personnel, has done less. And labor unions still have far to go if they are to develop a forward-looking policy for the nurture of talent within their ranks.

Improved opportunities for advanced education within employing organizations and under community auspices can help mature people to test their own unexplored interests and abilities and to develop their potentialities more fully. Education is never finished. One must be continually exposed to it if one does not wish to stagnate. A degree is not an education, and the confusion on this point is perhaps the gravest weakness in American thinking about education.

One consequence of the scarcity of professional skills is the hoarding of talent—a practice visible in a good many areas of government, business, and academic life. In its most blatant form hoarding involves the stockpiling of personnel in scarce categories. Thus a number of industrial firms have hired large numbers of engineers for whom they had no immediate need. The damage done to other organizations which might use such talent more constructively is appreciable but less disturbing than the damage to the able individuals who are thus deprived of constructive assignments.

There are many less obvious, less deliberate forms of talent hoarding. Scientific personnel is jealously sought by different branches of the Armed Forces, and the results of scientific research are not properly shared. Every government department now has its own staff of economists. Corporations bid indiscriminately for high talent on the campus without careful consideration as to the long-term prospects that they can offer to those talents. Universities, often within the same community, vie with one another for personnel to build up replicas of one another's offerings.

One obvious need is to broaden the mechanisms for sharing

of personnel. Certainly there is little excuse for the absence of such sharing among government agencies. Competitive corporations may be understandably reluctant to share their scientific or technical personnel, but an increased movement of able people back and forth between government and business might be a helpful step. Tours of duty of several years' duration in the government might well be recognized by some corporations as a regular stage in the development of a man's career, and experience in private business might enhance the value of a career civil servant. In academic life, the sharing of intellectual talents, along lines already begun by a number of smaller colleges, and an attempt to dovetail rather than duplicate one another's offerings might yield important benefits. And a healthy traffic between the academic world and government and business is highly desirable.

But great as they are, the opportunities for the better utilization of our talents and human abilities is only a partial answer to the larger problem before us. The fundamental challenge has to do with the motivation of the individuals comprising the society. It turns on their notion of what in the ultimate sense life is *for*; what, in short, gives it its value.

# V. Motivation and Values

Excellent performance is a blend of talent and motive, of ability fused with zeal. Aptitude without aspiration is lifeless and inert.

And that is only part of the story. When ability is brought to life by aspiration, there is the further question of the ends to which these gifts are applied. We do not wish to nurture the man of great talent and evil purpose. Not only does high performance take place in a context of values and purpose but if it is to be worth fostering, the values and purpose must be worthy of our allegiance.

Some of our more discerning critics are uneasy about the current aspirations and values of Americans. They sense a lack of purpose in Americans; they see evidence that security, conformity, and comfort are idols of the day; and they fear that our young people have lost youth's immemorial fondness for adventure, far horizons, and the challenge of the unpredictable.

The critics point to the extraordinary difficulty we are having in persuading young people to enter some fields of work that are vital to our future as a nation. We cannot fill innumerable important assignments in the overseas activities of our government. There are not enough able people in basic research. There are not enough able people in teaching. The difficulty—the critics argue—is that these jobs require a measure of sacrifice or dedication and some deviation from the standard formulas of American life.

One may wish to apply a slight discount to these alarms and anxieties. Such self-criticism of our society is something of a national tradition. But one would be foolish to discount altogether the penetrating observations made by so many qualified observers. Fortunately, we do not need to decide whether the situation is seriously deplorable or only mildly so. It is possible to identify a posture more constructive than hand wringing in connection with the problem. The truth is that never in our history have we been in a better position to commit ourselves wholeheartedly to the pursuit of excellence in every phase of our national life.

Those who place little value on our material progress and fear the growing complexity of our society must reflect on the fact that precisely these circumstances have increased the possibility of a striving for excellence for its own sake. For thanks to technological advances on the one hand and the complexity of social organization on the other, hard dull toil and the routine chore are slowly giving way to a new, more exacting, and more imaginative level of work. And those who must still engage in tasks too cramping for the exercise of self-expression have much increased leisure and resources to pursue avocations of a more self-fulfilling variety. The demands of society and the desire of the individual for self-realization are in this particular dimension more compatible than ever before.

The cultivation of excellence—the pursuit of achievement for its own sake—is a latent force in any society. Every society has had its fine craftsmen. Now, with the changing nature of work needs and the social demand for skill and talent, the opportunity exists to bring that latent force to fuller expression.

And it bears saying that among the many kinds of excellence of which the human is capable, intellectual and moral excellence has come to play a uniquely important role. Intellectual excellence has not always ranked high in the scale of values of Americans generally; but with our rising educational level and increasing prominence of intellectual pursuits, there are signs that this evaluation is changing. The desirability of such a change cannot be too strongly stressed. As we shall have occasion to note again, a nation only achieves the kind of greatness it seeks and understands. Only if we value intellectual excellence shall we have it.

It is clear, then, that a substantial part of our task is to insure that the individual may be exposed to a context of values in which high performance is encouraged. It is essential, for example, that we enable young people to see themselves as participants in one of the most exciting eras in history and to have a sense of purpose in relation to it. It is essential that we enable them to see that they are living out in their own lives—in their own convictions and fears and tensions—one of the gravest crises that has ever occurred in man's relationship to man. And they must see, too, that it is a time of great opportunity for man—if he has the wisdom and the courage to profit by it.

Another task is to insure that young people are exposed to sufficient variety and challenge in their lives—to insure that they not be placed too early on an inflexible schedule of education, career preparation, and job. Certainly for the most talented segment of our population, we must leave ample room for the sort of lesson one learns when one goes down a blind alley of one's own choice, for the sense of adventure involved in doing something unpredictable, for the zest generated by pursuing one's own inner urge rather than always doing what is "sensible."

Still another challenge is that of providing "models" for young people. The life goals of young people are in considerable measure determined by the fact that they identify themselves with admired figures in the adult world. A society is fortunate if the adults who enjoy the most prominent positions in the public eye, who are most applauded and admired and respected, are also the most suitable models for young people to follow if the society is to meet the challenge of its own future. It is fair to ask whether our young people can find in our gallery of national heroes enough models of, let us say, the gifted scientist, the dedicated Foreign Service officer, or the inspired teacher.

With rare exceptions, it is probably true that a society produces great men only in those fields in which it understands greatness. Spain in the sixteenth century produced Cortez and Pizarro and a dozen more who rank with the most extraordinary explorer-conquerors who ever strode the pages of history. It is unthinkable that the same society at the same time would have produced a Jefferson. The society that produced Jefferson produced Franklin, Monroe, Benjamin Rush, John Adams, and other philosopher-statesmen of breadth and brilliance. It is less easy to believe that it could have produced a Mozart.

The kinds of greatness that our society produces over the years ahead will be the kinds of greatness we inspire and will have to be securely rooted in our values.

If we ask what our society inspires in the way of high performance, we are led to the conclusion that we may have, to a startling degree, lost the gift for demanding high performance of ourselves. It is a point worth exploring.

There is no good reason to believe that the American people are any less capable of devotion or courage or response to challenge than they ever were. Everyone knows a parent, a teacher, a doctor, a friend who has acted with spirit and dedication in the service of our society's highest values. But there is some reason to believe that American life today is not such as to call forth these qualities on a wide scale and in their highest form. There is reason to believe that we have lost some of our talent for evoking these qualities.

The characteristic picture of the citizen-as-consumer has taken a firm grip on the national imagination; and the consumer is, almost by definition, a creature devoted to self-gratification. He must be constantly and ingeniously served milder cigarettes, softer mattresses, and easier-driving cars. If his dollars are to continue flowing, he must be endlessly catered to, soothed, anointed, protected, healed, cajoled, and generally babied. Add to this the fact that we get on with our national life through the mediation of representatives, agents, or delegates of various sorts; and that whether these are congressmen serving their constituents, corporation executives representing their stockholders, labor leaders serving union members, or lobbyists representing their various employers, they are all committed to protecting and nourishing the interests of those by whose sufferance they hold their posts. It is their professional role to be selfish for their constituents, to defend them from incursions on their comfort and convenience.

We would certainly not wish to have businessmen who cared nothing for the wishes of the consumer, nor representatives who cared nothing for the interest of their constituents. The only point to be made is that the images of citizen-as-consumer and citizen-as-constituent may have led us to think of the man in the street as guided only by his self-gratifying impulses. We may have fallen into the habit of thinking that the citizen's resources of devotion are slight indeed, and that to seek to tap these resources would be, if not indecent, then politically dangerous, or at the very least futile. The result may be a national habit—shared by political leaders, teachers, social and cultural leaders—of underrating the capacity of the American people for devotion to anything but the more and more luxurious furnishing of their private worlds.

This cult of easiness is a wholly inadequate guide to understanding the springs of human action. What most people, young or old, want is not merely security or comfort or luxury—although they are glad enough to have these. They want meaning in their lives. If their era and their culture and their leaders do not or cannot offer them great meanings, great objectives, great convictions, then they will settle for shallow and trivial meanings. "Our chief want in life," said Emerson, "is someone who will make us do what we can." People who live aimlessly, who allow the search for meaning in their lives to be satisfied by shoddy and meretricious experiences have simply not been stirred by any alternative meanings—religious meanings, ethical values, ideals of social and civic responsibility, high standards of self-realization.

This is a deficiency for which we all bear a responsibility. It is a failure of home, church, school, government—a failure of all of us.

In the context of the present discussion, there should be a general recognition that development of the individual's potentialities occurs in a context of values. Education is not just a mechanical process for communication to the young of certain skills and information. It springs from our most deeply rooted convictions. And if it is to have vitality both teachers and students must be infused with the values that have shaped the system.

No inspired and inspiring education can go forward without powerful undergirding by the deepest values of our society. The students are there in the first place because generations of Americans have been profoundly committed to a republican form of government and to equality of opportunity. They benefit by a tradition of intellectual freedom because generations of ardent and stubborn men and women nourished that tradition in Western civilization. Their education is based upon the notion of the dignity and worth of the individual because those values are rooted in our religious and philosophical heritage. They are preparing themselves for a world in which, as Thornton Wilder said, "Every good and excellent thing . . . stands moment by moment on the razoredge of danger and must be fought for." They are preparing themselves for a world which has always been shaped and always will be shaped by societies that have placed at the service of their most cherished values a firmness of purpose, discipline, energy, and devotion.

We would not wish to impose upon students a rigidly defined set of values. Each student is free to vary the nature of his commitment. But this freedom must be understood in its true light. We believe that the individual should be free and morally responsible: the two are inseparable. The fact that we tolerate differing values must not be confused with moral neutrality. Such tolerance must be built upon a base of moral commitment; otherwise it degenerates into a flaccid indifference, purged of all belief and devotion.

In short, we will wish to allow wide latitude in the choice of values, but we must assume that education is a process that should be infused with meaning and purpose; that everyone will have deeply held beliefs; that every young American will wish to serve the values that have nurtured him and made possible his education and his freedom as an individual.

# Report VI

# THE POWER OF
# THE DEMOCRATIC
# IDEA

(First published September 8, 1960)

# A Word by the Overall Panel

Democracy is a powerful idea. It is powerful because it respects the desire of every man to share in his own rule. It is powerful because it is based on the belief that every man has the capacity to learn the art of self-government. And it must be clear to everyone everywhere that a belief in this capacity and a recognition of this desire speak to the deepest and most pervasive aspirations of modern man.

Democracy is a powerful idea because it draws much of its strength from religions that posit the sanctity of the individual and the brotherhood of man. In a democracy, as in a moral order, none can be excluded, none left out. In a democracy, responsibility for everyone rests in some measure upon all.

Democracy is a powerful idea because it both assumes and is built upon the moral commitment of its supporters. It will require all the power this commitment can generate in the decades ahead to deal affirmatively and courageously with the vast and pressing problems faced by all countries of today's world. But to do so without sacrificing the real source of democracy's permanent strength—the independence and integrity of its citizens—will require the very best that is in each of us, all the time, for as long as we can see.

And so we present this report—a realistic yet hopeful statement of the idea of democracy as it has found expression in the American scene. It recognizes the central problems of our democratic society but does not despair about the prospects for their resolution. Not all of us will agree in all particulars. But we believe it is an honest picture of our democratic system and its prospects.

We are sobered as we reflect on the tasks to be performed, yet confident in the power of the democratic idea to help us perform these tasks and maintain our liberties.

The Overall Panel members are grateful to a writing committee chaired by James A. Perkins. Charles Frankel was the principal author involved in the preparation of this report and should, therefore, receive our special thanks.

JAMES A. PERKINS, vice-president, Carnegie Corporation of New York; chairman of the writing committee.

CHARLES FRANKEL, professor of philosophy, Columbia University.

LEWIS GALANTIERE, counselor, Free Europe Committee, Inc.

AUGUST HECKSCHER, director, The Twentieth Century Fund.

PENDLETON HERRING, president, Social Science Research Council.

# Introduction

The history of the last three centuries is in large part the history of the democratic impulse. Democratic aspirations have moved with mounting force in the world, and any people that has felt their contagion has never been the same afterward. Masquerades of democracy have sometimes been taken for the real thing. The power of democratic ideals is now so great that even the most militant opponents of democracy must speak the language of democracy to justify themselves to those they rule. A fundamental reason why our era is so unsettled and turbulent is simply that the attraction of democratic ideals has come to be felt everywhere in the world. It is the democratic dream that is keeping the world on edge.

The story of modern democracy is more than the story of an aspiration. It is also a story of practical accomplishment. Democratic social institutions have steadily expanded, giving ordinary men and women opportunities they never had before to educate themselves, to enjoy the good things of life, and to take part, as free citizens, in the great enterprises of human civilization. And although free democracies are rare occurrences in the history of mankind, the governments that have endured unchanged in form for the longest time in the modern world are almost without exception democratic. Modern democracy has known defeats as well as victories, and there are dark spots in its history as well as signal achievements. But modern democracies have repeatedly shown that they have an inner gristle and that they can outlast other social systems when their citizens have the education, habits, and courage that make democracy work.

Yet this record of accomplishment offers no guarantee for the future. For the problems that democracy faces today are in many respects unprecedented. Science, technology, and economic expansion have produced a world that is shrunken in size, immeasurably larger in the number of its inhabitants, and almost unimaginably quicker in its tempo of change. Mass production, mass communication, and large organizations have changed the normal context in which most citizens of industrial societies lead their lives. In the more prosperous countries, there is an era of high consumption and growing leisure that requires democratic citizens to develop a new sensibility and a new personal ethic. There is an explosive demand for education at all levels, an urgent need for technical skills and social imagination, and a redoubled effort by those who have been victims of racial prejudice to be admitted to free and equal partnership in the democratic enterprise. And in the less prosperous countries, people who have never known democracy have also been touched by its spirit. They are pressing for full citizenship in their societies, for a decent share of the world's goods, and for a chance to educate their children. Whether they can move toward these goals within a framework of freedom, and whether the peace of the world can be preserved while they do, remains to be seen. And as democracies wrestle with these problems, they must face the steady dangers of the totalitarian challenge.

The preceding reports of the Special Studies Project have dealt with questions of national defense, foreign economic policy, the national economy of the United States, education and the nurturing of talent, and foreign policy. These are questions with which the United States must deal if it is to maintain and strengthen its own democratic system and if it is to play its necessary role on the world scene. An even deeper question is whether American democracy can act with the force, resolution, and imagination necessary to meet the problems it faces in the second half of the twentieth century.

A report such as this can provide only the beginning of an answer to this question. In the final analysis, it can be answered only by what Americans do in their governments, their private organizations, and their daily lives. But a study such as this can do two things. It can state reasons why democracy is worth working at, and it can examine the American democratic process in an effort to see what resources Americans have at their disposal for meeting the problems they confront.

Certain self-imposed restrictions have been accepted in writing this report. We deal with ideals that Americans share with many other people, but our focus is on the special means and methods by which Americans have come to pursue these ideals. This study does not pretend to describe democracy as it is or must be elsewhere in the world; it is an attempt to help Americans appraise what they are doing in their own democracy. While it is not easy for men to maintain an objective attitude when they are examining a way of life to which they are passionately committed, we have made the effort to describe the processes of American democracy as realistically as possible and to distinguish between what is essential to democracy and what is not. Where American actions, in our judgment, are not in accord with American democratic principles, we have said so; and where conceptions of democracy that are current in America seem to us to be mistaken, we have pointed this out. We have tried, in short, to follow the ancient maxim "know thyself" in the belief that this is the way in which American democratic principles and practices can be clarified and strengthened. Such a belief, we cannot help but think, lies at the very heart of the democratic faith.

We have also tried to do something more. For nearly two centuries the American democracy provided the rest of the world with a testing place for democratic principles. It is still a testing place for these principles. And the test these principles must meet is the same test they have had to meet in the past: they must demonstrate their power to generate visions, to set programs in motion, to lift Americans above mere getting and spending, and to kindle the hopes of people elsewhere. At the greatest moments in the American past, Americans had an image before them of what free men, working together, could make of human life. The great question that the present generation of Americans will answer is whether the American democratic adventure can be continued and renewed and whether American life can be lit by a sense of opportunities to be seized and great things to be done. This report is an effort to indicate that the problems America faces today, although they are heavy, are not burdens but invitations to achievement.

# I. The Ideals of Democracy

Every society gives spontaneous signs of the moral weather in which it normally lives. The attitudes of the men and women who compose it will be revealed in their manners, in their behavior toward their parents, their children, and one another, in the atmosphere of their schools, churches, and public squares, in their games and jokes. What the members of a society expect in life and what they think is right and decent will show itself not only in what they explicitly say but in what they do not bother to say.

This is as true of a democratic society as it is of any other. Because democracy gives so much freedom to the individual and leaves so much to his powers of judgment and self-discipline, it depends more than most other forms of government on an unspoken atmosphere and on the willing allegiance of most of its citizens to certain moral principles. A democratic form of government may exist in a society where this atmosphere and moral outlook are weak or still in the process of development. But in any society where democratic government can be said to be reasonably safe, certain attitudes will be deeply ingrained and certain ideals will be widely shared.

What are the fundamental ideals that distinguish a democratic moral outlook?

## DEMOCRACY'S COMMITMENT
## TO AN OPEN SOCIETY

A distinctive conviction marks a democratic society. One part of this conviction is that all human arrangements are fallible. A second part is that men can improve the societies they inhabit if they are given the facts and are free to compare things as they are with their vision of things as they ought to be. It is a defining characteristic of a democratic society, accordingly, that nothing in its political or social life is immune to criticism and that it establishes and protects institutions whose purpose it is to subject the existing order of things to steady examination.

This process of self-examination has certain special features. It is conducted in the open. All members of the community are presumed to be free to engage in it, and all are held to be entitled to true information about the state of their society. Moreover, in a democratic society such public criticism has immediate and practical objectives. Men who are imbued with the democratic attitude are not likely to be content with the promise that the realization of their ideals must be put off to an indefinite future. They will want to see these ideals make a difference here and now.

A commitment to democracy, in short, is a commitment to an "open society." Democracy accepts its own fallibility. But it provides a method by which its mistakes can be corrected. It recognizes that men can be power-hungry and prone to self-delusion, that they can prefer old errors to new truths, that they can act without caring about what they are doing to others. And it believes that these human tendencies can only be held in check if they are exposed to the open air and subjected to other men's continuing judgment. This is the way, in the democratic view, that the goodness and rationality of men can have a chance to grow.

## EQUAL MEMBERSHIP
## IN THE MORAL COMMUNITY

This belief in a process of criticism that is open to all brings us to another fundamental principle of a democratic outlook. The man with democratic feelings and convictions looks upon all men as members of the same moral community and as initially endowed with the same fundamental rights and obligations. He does not determine his obligations to others by considering their status in society or their racial or religious backgrounds. The respect and concern that a democratically-minded person shows for other men are shown for them as individuals; this respect and concern do not depend on their membership in any group.

Ideas that have kindled the struggle for democracy in the modern world—the rights of man, the dignity of the individual—have expressed this attitude. In this sense, the history of democracy records the growth in scope of man's sense of moral concern. Moreover, this democratic moral sense generally implies something not only about the goals that men should seek but the spirit in which they should seek them. A man of democratic temper will pursue human welfare, but he will not do so in a context of rigid ranks and hierarchies. For he seeks more than the improvement of men's material condition, he seeks their development as independent individuals and their entrance as full participants into the enterprises of their community. To believe in democracy is to wish to help individuals by giving them the tools to help themselves.

## RESPECT FOR INDIVIDUAL DIVERSITY AND PRIVACY

This sense that all men have an initially equal right to membership in the same moral community suggests another element in the democratic image of the good society. This is the acceptance of the simple fact that human beings are different. It is one thing to believe that all men have a right to be treated in accordance with the same fundamental rules. It is quite another thing to believe that there is any single style of life that is good for everybody. The democratic view is that the burden of proof rests on those who argue that the individual is not the best judge of the way to run his own life. To care about democracy is to care about human beings, not en masse, but one by one. It is to adopt the working hypothesis that the individual, if given the right conditions, does not need a master or a tutor to take care of him. The devoted believer in democracy will act on this hypothesis until he is proved wrong. And he will act on it again when the next individual comes along. For he believes that the exercise of individual judgment is itself an ultimate good of life.

A considered democratic outlook, therefore, will place a special premium on the value of privacy. It will hold that there are aspects of the individual's life that no government may touch and that no public pressure may be allowed to invade. In the absence of very strong considerations to the contrary, these include the individual's right to bring up his children as he desires, to go where he wishes, to associate with those he chooses, and to live by his own religion and philosophy, staking his destiny on the rightness of his choice.

There is, therefore, an extraordinary degree of human discipline involved in allegiance to a democratic ethic. It asks men to exercise their own judgments and to choose their own ultimate beliefs. But it asks them to care just as much about the liberties of others and the right of others to think differently. That such a discipline has actually been developed, and that it thrives at all, is a remarkable achievement. It is testimony to democracy's faith in the power of human intelligence and good will. But the very difficulty of this discipline indicates that the citizens of a democracy can never take the continued success of their social system for granted. There is always the temptation to relax such a discipline or to resent it. The survival of this discipline calls for constant vigilance.

## GOVERNMENT BY CONSENT

Obviously, a society that accepts the moral ideals that have been described can never say that its work is done. Nor can such a society have a neat and symmetrical design. It will be a mobile society without fixed class barriers, offering opportunities to individual talents and providing an arena within which diverse individuals can struggle for the achievement of their own purposes. Inevitably, furthermore, it will be a society in which groups clash and contend with one another and in which the determination and implementation of public policy must depend on something other than unanimous agreement.

We come at this point to a distinguishing feature of democracy as a political system. Democratic political arrangements rest on the recognition that shared purposes and co-operative endeavor are only one side of any complex society and that disagreement and conflict of interests are also persisting characteristics of any such social order. The working principle of a democracy is to deal with such conflicts by bringing them out in the open and providing a legal and social framework for them. It is this principle that gives a distinctive meaning to the classic political ideal of democracy—the ideal of government by the consent of the governed—as it is understood in the United States and other democracies, and that sets off the theory and practice of these democracies from totalitarian forms of government that use and abuse democratic language.

In the American tradition, "the consent of the governed" has meant a number of things. It has meant, to begin with, that public policies should be subject to broad public discussion, that political leaders must be chosen in free elections where there is honest competition for votes, and that no one is punished or restrained, legally or extralegally, when he works for the political cause of his choice and remains short of violence and insurrection. But government by consent has also meant some things that are perhaps less obvious. For public discussion, free and honest elections, and the rights to freedom of speech and association are essential to achieving government by consent; but the history of democracy in the last century is marked by the growing recognition that they are not sufficient.

In addition to the legal guarantees that are implied by the ideal of government by consent, certain broad social conditions are also implied. Individuals with grievances, men and women with ideas and visions, are the sources of any society's power to improve itself. Modern democracy is an effort to provide such individuals not only with the freedom to struggle for what they think right but with some of the practical tools of struggle. Government by consent means that such individuals must eventually be able to find groups that will work with them and must be able to make their voices heard in these groups. It means that all important groups in the community should have a chance to try to influence the decisions that are made. And it means that social and economic power should be widely diffused in the community at large, so that no group is insulated from competition and criticism. The maintenance of such conditions is the steady business of a democratic society.

What such a society seeks is responsible government. Moreover, it seeks this ideal in a special way. Judged from its working procedures, a democracy does not define "responsible government" as government by men who are benevolent, intelligent, and unselfishly interested in the general welfare. Naturally, a democracy seeks such men, and it will prosper if it finds them. But in aiming at responsible government, a democracy has its eye mainly on institutions, not persons. No matter how able its leaders, or how morally responsible they are as individuals, it reposes only a careful and limited confidence in them.

From the democratic point of view, a government is a responsible government only when those who make the decisions on which other men's destinies depend can be held effectively accountable for the results of their decisions. This means that they can be asked questions, that they have to give answers which satisfy those who ask them, and that they can be deprived of their power if they fail to do so. It means, moreover, that the decision makers in a society are visible and that it is possible to fix responsibility for a policy on definite individuals or groups. Finally, it means that those who ask the questions must know how to ask the right ones and must have sufficient information and good sense to judge the answers they receive intelligently. To list these criteria of responsible government is to remind ourselves not only of what democracy has achieved but also of how much still remains to be accomplished and of new and urgent problems that have emerged in the present generation.

Thus, the ideal of government by consent involves more than free elections and constitutional government. It calls for the existence of instruments of communication that men can use to get in touch with one another when they wish to join together in a common cause. It demands that these instruments of communication be generally available to the community rather than monopolistically controlled. It requires the existence of independent groups that can give expression to the diverse interests that are bound to prevail in any sophisticated modern society and that can do so openly, legally, and without fear of persecution. It requires that these groups be democratically controlled. Most of all, if government by consent is to work over the long pull, it needs the support of a population in which the average level of education is high. A people that dedicates itself to free government cares about its schools as it will care about little else. Government by consent does not exist once and for all, and a people cannot passively enjoy it. They must steadily create it.

Free government thus depends on men and women who possess a subtle blend of skills and attitudes. The ideal citizen of a de-

mocracy has enough spirit to question the decisions of his leaders
and enough sense of responsibility to let decisions be made. He
has enough pride to refuse to be awed by authority and enough
humility to recognize that he, too, is limited in knowledge and
in the power to be perfectly disinterested. And while he is good-
humored when others win fairly, he is implacable toward those
who play unfairly. Such qualities of mind and character are not
easily come by, but they are the secret, the inner mystery, of a
flourishing democracy.

## THE DEMOCRATIC WAGER

Democratic ideals, like any other ideals, do not exist in a void.
They rest on assumptions and express a faith. There is an ultimate
conviction and a supreme act of faith behind the ideals of democracy. The conviction is that the value of all human arrangements
must be measured by what they do to enhance the life of the
individual—to help him to grow in knowledge, sensitivity, and
the mastery of himself and his destiny. The faith is that the individual has the capacity to meet this challenge.

The faith must be stated carefully, for it is complex and subtle.
Restraints that democracies place on the men who govern them
are based on a tough and realistic conception of the actual character of human beings. Constitutional government is a conscious
effort to place checks on the power of all individuals; it foresees
no time when men can afford to assume that any among them
are free from imperfection. "Sometimes it is said that man cannot
be trusted with the government of himself," Jefferson once observed. "Can he, then, be trusted with the government of others?
Or have we found angels in the forms of kings to govern him?"

Jefferson's remark catches both sides of the democratic faith.
Democracy does not expect men to be angels; but it does not
propose to treat them, therefore, as sheep. The great wager on
which it stakes its destiny is that the imperfectible individual is
improvable. And it believes that the best way to improve him
is to let him improve himself, to give him as much responsibility
as possible for his own destiny and for the destiny of the community to which he belongs. Democratic governments have been
prepared to take positive steps to free the individual from avoid-
able handicaps so that he can run the race on fair terms with

others. They are committed today to providing all individuals with the basic forms of economic security that are essential to a decent life. But their objective is not to produce tame, well-tended men and women who are easy to harness to a master plan. Their objective is to release the powers of individuals and to turn loose the flow of human initiative.

There is, therefore, a kind of inner tension that is perennially present in the democratic way of life. A democracy must balance its faith in the potentialities of the individual against its realistic appraisal of his capacities for judgment and responsible behavior. It cannot simply give him room to live his own life; it must also place restrictions upon him. Each generation must make new decisions on this issue, and there is no easy formula by which the questions it raises can be settled. In large measure, men must deal with them by deciding what they wish human life to be and placing their faith and effort on that side of the scales. Democracy, if it must err, chooses to err by trusting the ordinary individual. If it must choose between what he is and what he can be, it leans in the latter direction and places its long-range bet on what he can be.

This faith and purpose give dynamism to the democratic principles that have been described. A democracy's commitment to the continuing criticism of itself is not due to an inner malaise or lack of confidence. It expresses the belief that nothing deserves a higher loyalty from men than the truth and that the only way in which fallible men can find the truth is to keep the process of inquiry open. Democracy bets that men can bear the rigors of this process and learn to love it. And it bets that it will be a stronger social system as a result. For it is the one form of society that has institutionalized the process of reform.

A democracy, therefore, will measure its success in a distinctive way. In the last analysis it will judge itself by the character of the men and women who make it up and the quality of the lives they lead. A democratic society cannot be indifferent to the condition of its economy, the development of its technology, or the material possessions in the hands of its people. It is dangerous sentimentality to think that such issues are unimportant either practically or morally. But a democratic society that has kept its balance and sense of direction will recognize that they are means, not ends.

The end is the individual—his self-awareness, his personal powers, the richness of his life. Democracy aims at the individual who can live responsibly with his fellows while he follows standards he has set for himself.

## A DEMOCRACY'S NEED TO BE ON THE MOVE

There are many reasons for believing that this democratic wager has been worth making. In the United States, a continental nation has been governed. Successive waves of immigrants have been absorbed into a common way of life, and their children have found the opportunities for which their parents came. American democracy has gone far in delivering men from poverty, in releasing them from the stifling boxes of caste and class, in opening careers to talent, and in making performance rather than inheritance the key to men's positions in life. And having accomplished its great absorbing work of settling a continent, American democracy has gone on to other tasks and carried them off with equal *élan*.

Within the last generation, it has modernized its economic system and fought, together with its allies, a victorious war against an extraordinary threat to the values of all civilized men. It has turned almost overnight from a long policy of isolation to one of active participation in keeping the peace of the world. It has shown itself capable of original social inventions like the Marshall Plan abroad and the Tennessee Valley Authority at home. It has accomplished all this, furthermore, while preserving individual freedom and extending it at many points. American democracy has shown that it has resilience, flexibility, and the power to meet emergencies. The achievement justifies the democratic faith that free citizens can successfully work out their problems together if they are given the chance to try.

While a democracy can take confidence from its past accomplishments, it cannot live on them. Democracy is a system which aims at the minimum of coercion and the maximum of voluntary co-operation. If it is to excite men's devotion it needs to be on the move, and it needs citizens who are alert to the business they have left unfinished and the new business they must undertake. The citizens of America have an educational system that needs strengthening. The problem of mass media of communication as a source of public information and not only as a form of entertainment, intensified by the coming into existence of television, has only begun to receive the attention it requires. The elimination of racial barriers is another piece of unfinished business, and time is growing short. The American people have only begun to realize the extraordinary perils for them and for all humanity in the contrast between their own wealth and the poverty of most of mankind.

Not least, few have as yet asked themselves, earnestly and steadily, what their prosperity is for and where their real wealth lies. A transition to an economy of comfort has been made, but the development of discriminating standards and the projection of goals that will excite the imagination of the concerned citizens of America has still to come. In the past, Americans have responded well when confronted by immediate emergencies and obvious injustices. The great question is whether a comfortable people can respond to an emergency that is chronic and to problems that require a long effort and a sustained exercise of will and imagination.

## QUESTIONS DEMOCRACY MUST FACE

The marshaling of democratic energies will have to take account of emerging conditions that obscure the democratic idea at many points and challenge its viability at others. The questions American democracy now faces range from the rebuilding of American cities to the proper organization and encouragement of scientific research, from the co-ordination of our foreign activities to the co-ordination of the activities of our state and federal governments, and from the allocation of our national wealth between public and private purposes to the development of new skills in the use of leisure. But underneath these and the myriad other problems that confront the United States, there are certain long-range conditions with which our country, as a country in the modern world, must deal.

First and foremost, it faces the problem of keeping the peace and the related problem of maintaining the climate of freedom, at home and in the world, through a prolonged period of international tension. American democracy confronts a massive challenge—the rise to power of enormous nations charged with a sense of mission and governed by men who have set out to prove that our social order cannot keep up the pace if it is put to the test of serious and sustained competition. America today must obey an ultimate imperative—the imperative to survive and to survive in freedom. It must do so while the world confronts the unprecedented danger of nuclear weapons. It will be a complex and subtle effort for Americans to keep their defenses in order and to steer a sane course between impulsiveness and irresolution while they seek to avoid nuclear war and to find ways of assuring the peace of the world.

The success of America's efforts on the international scene will depend in large part on what Americans do at home. Both at home and abroad, American democracy must wrestle with other fundamental issues. One is the unprecedented speed and the radical impact of technological change. A second is the preservation and nourishing of individual freedom, originality, and responsibility in the world of large organizations that has come into being. A third is the impact at home of what has come to be known as "the revolution of rising expectations." This revolution is stirring millions of people abroad and creating for their governments tremendous tasks in economic growth, education, and communication. It has begun to make a visible difference within the Soviet Union and its satellites. And it is taking place in the United States as well, where there is an extraordinary pressure not only for material goods but for the qualitative enrichment of individual life through education, music, books, and the significant use of leisure.

These are interests that have traditionally been the special prerogative of the few. The expectation that they can be shared by the many is fundamentally democratic. If it is to be satisfied and if the standards and the sense of excellence of a discriminating civilization are to be preserved, a major effort in education and communication is required, and a thoroughly reconsidered one. Democracy thrives on the virtues of patience, good humor, and moderation. It will need all these. But it needs excitement, too. There is more than enough excitement in the problems it faces to keep American democracy occupied for some time.

Is American democracy capable of dealing with these issues? Is democracy too loose, too slow, too inefficient, to move with the speed, concentration, and daring these problems demand? Can it set definite goals, follow long-range plans, and pull its citizens together for a concerted effort to achieve clearly formulated objectives? Is democracy a dangerous luxury or an historical anachronism for which there is no longer any room? To begin to answer these questions we must stand back and see what we have. So it is to an account and appraisal of the fundamental characteristics of the American democratic process that we now turn.

# II. Consensus in a Democratic Society

American democracy faces the test of an era in which the pace and scope of change are unprecedented. Everywhere, and not least in the United States, habits of thought and patterns of behavior that represent the inheritance of centuries are rapidly losing or have already lost their force. And in many parts of the world, aggressive ideologies have arisen that exercise a wide appeal. Leaning on democratic ideals at some points and subtly distorting them at others, they also challenge the democratic outlook in fundamental ways. If a democratic society is to sail through such storms and arrive successfully at destinations of its own choosing, it must possess inner forces of stability and cohesion on which it can call.

The first question we must therefore consider is the way in which the many groups and interests that compose a democratic society are held together. When a society concerts its efforts for the sake of common goals and when it does so without recourse to violence or terror, it counts on the existence of certain generally held beliefs, attitudes, and feelings. Let us begin by asking what kind of agreement a democracy may and must enforce.

## ALLEGIANCE TO THE RULES OF THE GAME

The answer must begin with the recognition that democratic ideals have their origins in a variety of religious and secular traditions and that there is no single embracing philosophy which all citizens of a democracy can be expected to share. Experience shows that men can be equally loyal to democratic ideals even though they give different ultimate reasons for their loyalty. In the United States, Protestants, Catholics, Jews, and freethinkers have all found it possible to agree about the validity of democratic ideals. The practice of toleration that characterizes free societies is the hard-won product of bitter experience. As the religious wars of the sixteenth and seventeenth centuries and the ideological purges in contemporary totalitarian societies indicate, the effort to impose unity of belief in matters of religion and ultimate philosophy, far from unifying a society, can lead to extraordinary bloodshed and brutality and can breed hostilities which it can take centuries to erase.

Accordingly, there is no official creed—religious, philosophical, or scientific—that a democratic state can impose on its citizens. Each individual is free to try to win his fellows to his own views by every fair means. Truth in matters of religion, philosophy, or science cannot be determined by vote, popular pressure, or governmental fiat. The issues with which these fundamental human enterprises are concerned are too important to be regulated by political expediencies, real or alleged. In a democracy the state is neutral with regard to religion, philosophy, or science, and citizens are free to decide for themselves where they stand in relation to the ultimate questions concerning the nature of the universe and man's place within it. This is one reason why those who are deeply concerned about these matters are likely to prize democracy. Democracy does not ask them to conceal, compromise, or apologize for their views on issues so important that concealment, compromise, and apology are incompatible with honor and conscience. In short, cohesion is achieved in a democratic society, in the first instance, by carefully removing certain questions from the sphere of politics, by separating the things that are Caesar's from the things that are God's.

But if a democracy does not demand that all its citizens accept a common religion or view of the cosmos, what is the nature of the agreement at which it must aim and which successful democracies have largely achieved? It consists in a shared allegiance to the rules by which social decisions are reached.

In a democratic society it is expected that men will hold different aims and ideas and that these aims and ideas will sometimes clash. If common policies are achieved and enforced in such a society and if citizens accept peaceably the defeat of their hopes in the public arena, the reason is that they believe it better in the long run to yield and fight another day rather than sacrifice the rules by which victory in such a struggle is determined. In a democracy the preservation of those rules normally takes priority over the achievement of any other social purpose. This is the heart of the democratic political ethic, and the allegiance of an individual to this ethic is the acid test of his allegiance to democracy.

Allegiance to the rules of the democratic competition is not pure ritualism. Written into the rules governing the democratic process are principles that provide for orderly change in the rules themselves. Moreover, the rules that define fair democratic competition are of at least two kinds. Some, like the electoral process or the right of freedom of assembly, are set forth in explicit laws. If governmental decisions are made in contravention of rules of this sort, they lack authority and do not carry a mandate that must be obeyed. Other rules of the democratic process, however, are matters not of legal procedure but of ethical principle. They cover matters too subtle and intricate to be spelled out in detail, but they are exemplified by such principles as honesty in stating the facts, a separation of a public official's public duties from his private interests, and refusal to impugn the loyalty of one's opponents in legitimate democratic competition. The success of the democratic process depends to a considerable extent on the degree to which citizens adhere to such unwritten rules. For unwritten moral assumptions affect the way that written rules are applied and the respect that men hold for these rules. If men think the rules of the game are mere rituals without an ethical substance behind them, they will look upon the rules as deceptions or as meaningless frivolities. When a democratic consensus is vigorous, therefore, loyalty to the rules of the game is loyalty to the inner spirit as well as the external forms of democracy.

## FORMATION OF A
## DEMOCRACY'S WORKING CONSENSUS

A minimal agreement to abide by the rules of the democratic process is not enough, however, to produce effective and resolute government in a democracy. Free discussion will yield no practical results unless men talk directly to each other, unless they address themselves to common problems and share some common assumptions; disagreement and conflicts of interest cannot terminate in agreements that men accept voluntarily unless they find a common ground on which to negotiate. In addition to generally shared allegiance to the rules of the game, democracy also requires a practical working consensus about definite issues.

What is this "working consensus"? In any stable democracy that has the power to get ahead with its business, a body of opinion and principle tends to grow up and to be widely shared. Men are not forced or legislated into such a consensus, and no one in a democracy can be required to accept it. But habit, sentiment, common experience, and the appropriate social conditions all contrive to produce it. And if it does not exist, even common allegiance to the rules of the game is jeopardized.

The working consensus serves to define the issues that must be solved and the effective limits of the political dialogue at any given time. Disagreements, often fundamental ones, arise within it; and citizens who stand outside the prevailing consensus often make precious contributions to democracy precisely because they do so. Nevertheless, when such an informal working agreement exists, it serves to define what is and what is not a significant matter for public debate; and in a successful democracy such a consensus usually does exit. Thus, there may be controversy today about the priority that should be given to slum clearance in comparison with other projects, but there is now no debate about whether the elimination of slums falls within the area of the public interest. In short, the decisions that are made in a democracy, the compromises that are reached, and the actions that are taken are made in an environing moral and intellectual atmosphere.

## Role of Compromise

How is this working consensus achieved? To a large extent it is achieved by compromise, which is the workaday instrument of practical democracy. In the best of worlds, men have different interests, and since resources are scarce, no individual, no matter how admirable his purposes, can do everything he pleases. The effort of a democracy is to arrive at arrangements that will convince most men that their interests have been taken at least partly into account. Democracy thus depends on the ability of its citizens to negotiate peacefully with each other, to give as well as receive, and to arrive at understandings to which they will mutually adhere. Such understandings form the point of departure for the next round of the democratic debate.

Far from representing a lapse from principle, compromise thus represents one of democracy's most signal achievements. Compromise is incompatible with an unbending commitment to an abstract ideology; but it does not imply weak wills or fuzzy minds. Groups within a democracy may and do struggle hard for the achievement of their purposes; and if they do not achieve their full program at any given moment, they can continue to struggle until they do. The ethic of compromise does not call for them to abandon the struggle for their ultimate purposes. It calls for them only to carry on their fight at all times within the rules of the democratic process. They will use the courts, the press, peaceful public demonstrations, strikes, and elections; they will not use violence, slander, personal threats, or bribes. A notable example from the past of this sort of resolute struggle was the campaign for legislation against child labor. A current example, remarkable for its courage, restraint, and respect for democratic procedures, is the campaign American Negroes are waging for full citizenship.

## Focusing the Public Interest

The striking of bargains between different interest groups is only part of what is involved, however, in the formation of an enlightened democratic consensus. Contemporary American society is a complex social order composed of many different groups with conflicting interests. But it is also an intricately co-ordinated society in which the actions of any group can ramify outward, affecting the welfare of great numbers of people and perhaps the security of the democratic process as a whole. When strong-minded groups take decisions, or when they struggle with other groups, the pressure on them to behave responsibly cannot come only from within the groups themselves. It must also come from the outside. Something we know as the public interest must be focused, expressed, and brought to bear on the contending parties.

To give the conception of the public interest specific content and to make it come alive in the day-to-day affairs of a democracy is the task of many agencies. The press, the churches, the universities, civic groups, eminent individuals, political parties, all play a part. They will often have different views about the true nature of the public interest, and none of them, in a democracy, will occupy a position as a privileged interpreter and spokesman for the common good. But there is one agency that has an unequivocal responsibility to protect the public interest and a special opportunity to make it come alive in a democracy's day-to-day existence. This is government—at all levels. Government cannot claim greater intellectual authority for its judgments than other institutions in democratic society. Within a constitutional framework, however, it has ultimate legal authority, and it has the greatest power to voice the public interest forcefully and to see that it is protected. A democratic government's task includes much more than appeasing and conciliating different groups. It includes the duty to remind citizens of the larger frame of reference within which they act and to embody and enforce the common purposes to which they must contribute.

In any society there are certain common interests which men must seek together because they cannot seek them separately. The concept of the public interest stands first and foremost for such common interests. At the most elementary level, these include certain common necessities such as a sound currency, protected natural resources, roads, schools, police, sanitation facilities, and instruments of communication. But at a higher level they include values and purposes to which a society, by tradition or by its deliberate decision, is committed. In a democratic society the preservation of the fundamental rights of the individual and of the democratic decision-making process is itself a supreme part of the public interest.

Among the more important matters that today fall within the range of the American public interest so defined is an economy that combines stability of the general price level and a low rate of unemployment with a high rate of growth of production; an adequate system of national defense; a well-conceived and supported foreign policy aimed at preserving the freedom of the American people and at using the power of the United States to work for a peaceful and productive international order; a vigorous program of research in the physical, biological, medical, and social sciences; the orderly renovation of our metropolitan areas; an educational system that draws out the potential excellences of each individual, while at the same time cultivating in the young the habits of democracy and producing the trained intelligence, general and specialized, on which a twentieth-century democracy must depend.

As this imposing but incomplete list suggests, the agenda of activities that must be matters of organized and official public concern at any particular moment is not inscribed for all eternity. Nor is it an agenda which is self-evident. The determination of what lies within the public interest is probably the fundamental task that each successive democratic government must undertake. Its achievement in conciliating and adjusting the opposing interests within a democracy is not complete unless government itself affirmatively represents the overriding public good that must also be taken into account. For a democratic government does not exist simply to please as many groups as possible. It is the trustee of fundamental and common concerns which can otherwise be smothered in the conflict between special interests.

Moreover, there is a second meaning of "the public interest" with which a democratic government must also be concerned. The classic image of "John Q. Public" waiting outside the door while the men inside the smoke-filled room are plotting or quarreling catches this meaning exactly, although a little melodramatically. At times the idea of the public interest stands for interests that are likely to be forgotten, interests that are indirectly affected by an issue although not directly involved in it. To speak of a "public interest" in such contexts is to call attention to values that may be overlooked, to people who may be neglected, to damage that may be done because men are acting within too narrow a conception of their responsibilities.

While a democratic government is not the only agency that exists to bring such neglected interests to the fore, it is one of the principal instruments for doing so. It exists not only to represent interests that have already found themselves but to give a voice and shape to interests that without it would be silent and unformed. Government in a democracy, if it is good government, is more than a broker for those who have the power to bring their interests and opinions to its attention. It is a watchman against injustice and irresponsibility and a representative of those who need the helping power of government if their interests are to see the light of day.

## CONTINUING RECONSTRUCTION
## OF THE DEMOCRATIC CONSENSUS

The political leader cannot, by himself, create a conception of the public interest. He helps form, but he also leans on, the working democratic consensus. And the formation—or destruction—of this consensus is not an organized process. It goes on whether anyone wills it or not. Events take place and men respond to them, changing their beliefs about the kind of world in which they live and altering the judgments they pass on that world.

A little more than a century ago, for example, reports by parliamentary commissions revealing conditions in British mines and factories provoked a revulsion of conscience in Great Britain that affected people in all classes and that fundamentally changed the context of political discussion and action. Thirty years ago, similarly, Americans clashed in their interpretation of unemployment. Some took it to be a sign of individual failure, others of an iron economic law. An overwhelming majority now believes that unemployment is a social ill that can and should be substantially moderated by government action.

In the long run, few things are more important in the politics of a nation than such changes in the terms of debate and in the subjects around which discussion turns. This is why the mere presence of a consensus is not enough. Agreement about the wrong things can be immensely damaging. Nor does it suffice for a democracy merely to give answers to the questions it asks itself. It is important that it asks the right questions in the right terms and avoid wrestling with the ghosts of problems of a preceding era. While the preservation of the conditions that make for consensus must be the constant object of a democracy, it is not the preservation of the existing consensus in all its parts but rather the steady criticism of that consensus that should concern such a society.

In the end, a task that is indispensable to the politics of democracy is carried on outside the political arena. Scholars who conduct deliberate and detached inquiry into the facts, critics who attack encrusted habits of thought, moralists who glimpse new values of which their contemporaries ought to be aware, these and others contribute decisively to the course of democratic politics.

Much that such men do may be misguided and wasted, and such success as their ideas achieve is usually achieved slowly. But the health of a democracy depends on its ability to sustain and respect those who disengage themselves from the currents of prevailing opinion. A democracy cannot stand a consensus from which there is no dissent.

Nor should the consensus that prevails be one that invites only apathetic assent. It is possible for a society to deal with its problems efficiently, to satisfy the private and practical interests of most of its members, and still to leave them unmoved and uneasy. Most men also desire something more from the societies they inhabit. They want a sense that large projects are under way and that they are part of some significant and enduring human enterprise. If their society does not give them such a sense, it is possible for them to be physically contented and yet morally indifferent or alienated. Totalitarian ideologies have exploited this demand, but they are not the best means by which this demand can be satisfied. A society that is moved by an image of what it can be and that translates this image into definite programs of action can also satisfy the human impulse to idealism.

# III. Social Conditions of a Democratic Consensus

In the democracies that are functioning most successfully, there is both a remarkable degree of allegiance to the rules of the democratic game and a large measure of consensus about the important issues to which the political dialogue should be addressed. This is what makes these democracies successful. Yet this is not a state of affairs that comes merely for the asking. It is the product of appropriate social conditions, sometimes happily inherited and sometimes deliberately created. To regard the conditions that make for consensus as inherently precarious and to tend them with the greatest deliberate care should be the working principle of any democracy.

## HABIT AND TRAINING

The primary conditions that affect an individual's allegiance to rules of conduct of any kind are obviously his habituation and training. The greatest part of human behavior is determined not by conscious decisions or articulate ideas but by habits and attitudes that usually lie below the level of awareness. The home and the school, accordingly, are among the primary agencies by which democratic patterns of behavior can be fostered and consolidated or, conversely, discouraged and weakened. The neighborhood, the church, the civic group, and the general tone of informal community relationships are hardly less important. And it is what the child actually finds in such contexts, it should be added, as well as the explicit moral teaching he receives, that is likely to exercise an influence upon him. For habits and values, generally speaking, are caught, not taught. They develop by imitation, emulation, and the force of example.

They also need regular exercise. If faithfulness to the rules of the democratic process is in large part a matter of habit and training, the individual must have reasonably frequent opportunities to practice such rules actively and to practice them successfully. When the rules of democratic procedure are remote from the everyday experience of the ordinary citizen, when he does not respond to a breach of those rules with an instinctive aversion, a democratic consensus has lost some of its spontaneity and vigor.

In addition to the immediate, practical work that they do, therefore, the myriad voluntary organizations that exist at the local level in the United States perform a more general function. They are training grounds for democratic habits. The consequences for a democracy are considerable if such organizations lose their power, if their democratic procedures break down, or if such procedures regularly yield disappointing results. It is a matter for concern, therefore, when voluntary organizations become impersonal, when membership in them is passive, or when, as studies indicate, large numbers of citizens, either through lack of interest or of opportunity, are not members of any formally organized voluntary associations. For the habits and attitudes on which the democratic process depends are plainly affected by the circumstances that the citizens of a democracy meet in their everyday lives.

## FORCE OF EXAMPLE

The citizen's allegiance to the rules of his society also depends on general conditions in the society at large. A society's public ceremonies symbolize the principles on which it professes to stand; its games dramatize the social as well as physical traits it admires; its religions evoke its ideals. Stories about ancestors, heroic and venerated figures, great experiences that men share together, all give them the sense that they are part of an ongoing enterprise and that they owe it their allegiance. And the past by itself has a momentum that propels men's actions into molds which, for better or worse, they often find it uncomfortable or agonizing to break.

Not least among these influences on the individual's feeling of allegiance to the basic rules of his society is the behavior of certain key individuals and institutions. In any society, some persons and certain institutions acquire symbolic functions. They come to be examples of a society's dominant aspirations. The actual character of such persons and institutions is bound to affect the regard that ordinary men hold for the rules of their society. The respect that the major institutions in our society show for democratic principles of behavior is thus a matter of great importance.

A refusal to include a particular racial group within the activities of such organizations, for instance, does more than penalize this group unjustly. Those who are not directly affected are invited to be skeptical about the workability of democratic principles and the genuineness of our society's commitment to these principles. Similarly, the use of symbols of democracy and patriotism to sell a product or to win a momentary political advantage helps to cheapen the currency of these symbols. Not least, when elected leaders, political parties, or the media of communication hesitate to give difficult and controversial issues the extended and frank discussion they deserve, the democratic dialogue is robbed of its seriousness and the respect in which it is generally held is likely to be weakened. For the kind of respect for the rules which is essential in a democracy depends peculiarly on the kind of respect that is shown toward those rules by its most representative institutions. Any sharp contrast between rhetoric and reality, between the ideals such institutions profess and their actual behavior, endangers the credit rating that democratic principles enjoy in the public mind.

Force of habit and force of example are both ingredients, then, of the process that produces general allegiance to the rules of the democratic competition. There are other conditions, however, that must also be satisfied. And one of the most important is that men and women feel that the rules to which they are asked to conform are good rules. Among other things, this means that they must feel that these rules generally protect and advance their vital interests and the values, selfish or unselfish, to which they devote their lives. Of course, a democratic society cannot undertake to advance the values, say, of criminals. But in order to maintain general respect for the rules by which it lives, a democratic society must achieve a reasonable measure of success in satisfying the individual interests of its law-abiding citizens. What are the conditions on which this depends?

## CIVIL LIBERTIES

A democratic society has an enormous source of strength in its commitment to civil liberty. For there are two fundamental conditions that must be met if individuals are to retain their respect for democratic principles of behavior. The first is that they shall not be required to sacrifice what they cannot sacrifice and keep their self-respect. The second is that they shall believe that there are avenues of legitimate action available to them through which they can register their complaints and struggle to improve their condition. Without the presence of civil liberties, no social order can claim to be a democracy in the sense of the term that is habitual in the Western world.

The first function of these liberties is to allow the individual citizen to remain true to the values he cherishes most. A democracy must of course set limits to the individual's right to carry his beliefs and values into action. But if it adheres to its commitment to civil liberty, in spirit as well as in form, it does not require the citizen to conceal or deny his beliefs and values. Moreover, a democracy also permits him to do something about them. Within very broad limits, the citizen is free to speak, to publish, to raise his children according to his own lights, to worship or not to worship, to travel, and to associate with those he chooses. And so he is able not simply to enjoy his privacy without interference but to give his inner beliefs and feelings at least some external form.

The role of civil liberties in protecting the individual, however, is generally recognized. What is not so fully understood is their role in making the achievement of a democratic consensus easier. A defining characteristic of democratic government is that it maintains a "loyal opposition" and takes elaborate steps to protect and preserve organized disagreement with its program. Far from encouraging social instability, this encourages social cohesion. For it makes dissent a legitimate part of the system. To those who have reason to be dissatisfied with their lot in life, civil liberties can be at once symbols and instruments of hope. They permit and encourage the growth of visible agencies—newspapers and journals, unions and political parties, civic associations and private enterprises—by which those who have grievances and discontents can push for the correction of what disturbs them. Thus, by offering its citizens instruments for changing a social system that are themselves parts of that system, a democracy can convert even dissatisfaction into a reason for allegiance to democracy as a whole.

## DISTRIBUTION OF POWER
## AND OPPORTUNITY IN THE COMMUNITY

Yet the existence of civil liberties is generally not enough to ensure an individual's allegiance to democratic principles. Without the proper social structure, civil liberties can seem empty abstractions, inviting the comment, like Anatole France's, that they forbid the rich and the poor alike to beg in the streets and sleep under bridges. A full-fledged desire to give meaning to civil liberties calls for continuing concern, not only with legal safeguards but with the economic and social conditions that can make those liberties instruments that ordinary citizens actually prize and use.

Ideas first arise in the minds of individuals, and the record of democracy is replete with examples of individuals who have started out alone, who have fought courageously for an idea, and who have ultimately won through to victory. But this has meant that such individuals have eventually been able to find others who shared their purposes and have had ways of communicating with them. To achieve social purposes, groups must normally be formed. They may consist of obscure or eminent people, rich ones or poor, or of all manner and variety of men and women. But if they are to wage an effective struggle they must find effective leadership and have or develop economic or social leverage. Their power to do so does not depend simply on legal guarantees of civil liberty, but on the means to make these rights effective through access to the necessary resources of talent, wealth, and influence in the community, and a democratic society has the obligation to see to it that all citizens have access to these practical tools of struggle.

This is why, for over a century, a recurrent issue has preoccupied democracy in all countries. It is the tension between those who already enjoy the full rights and powers of democratic citizenship and those to whom these rights and powers have not yet been extended. Where this issue has been solved, and solved without leaving a heritage of distrust and resentment behind it, democracy has been highly stable. Where it has not been solved, or solved slowly and bitterly, democracy has been unstable. The speed and good grace with which a democratic society admits groups that have hitherto been excluded from full membership is a major determinant of its subsequent health and cohesiveness.

Such an issue, of course, is not one that can be settled once and for all. In every generation new groups are likely to arise that knock at the door of democratic society and demand admission. The Jacksonian era is one such episode in American history. The struggle of industrial workers for recognition of the legitimacy of their major instrument of social power, the labor union, is another episode, and one that has marked the history of all modern democracies. The contemporary struggle of American Negroes for equal civil rights and educational opportunity is the present chapter of this story in the United States. New economic or political conditions may at some future date lead other groups to believe they are excluded from the rights and powers that go with full membership in the democratic community, that they are in democratic society but not of it. Whatever groups these may be, the success of democratic government will depend in the future, as it has in the past, on its responsiveness to them and its willingness to make a place for them in the democratic process.

As these examples suggest, there are potent dangers to the democratic process in the existence of sharp and rigid divisions between social classes or between religious, ethnic, or racial groups. The compromises on which a democratic society rests are possible when it contains citizens whose interests overlap at many points and who do not believe that their entire destiny in life depends on the solution of some one all-embracing issue. Rigid distinctions of class and caste, in contrast, create resentments around which all other issues cluster and divide a society into large and mutually exclusive groups whose experience is different and whose outlooks may be wholly opposed.

## ECONOMIC CONDITIONS OF EFFECTIVE DEMOCRACY

Equally important is the maintenance of an economy that leaves most of its members with the conviction that they or their children have a chance to move upward and that status in their society is something achieved, not inherited. "Equality of opportunity" is, therefore, one of the most important things that democracy means when translated into economic and social terms. Political democracy gives citizens a say about public affairs. It is buttressed by an economic system which gives citizens a share in the well-being of their society. The success of American democracy in building a voluntary consensus based on competition and compromise is to a large extent the result of the fact that we have been a prosperous society that has given its members economic elbowroom.

A democratic society must therefore be committed, for practical as well as moral reasons, to a struggle against poverty. The ethic of compromise and the mutual understanding on which democratic political processes rest require citizens who do not feel that their backs are against the wall, and who do possess a broad spectrum of interests and associations. Poverty is incompatible with this state of affairs. Moreover, the economy of a democracy must be relatively free from major shocks like widespread unemployment or uncontrolled inflation, which upset established expectations concerning the justice of social arrangements. Such events touch individuals along the whole range of their interests, leave profound and lasting psychological shocks, and destroy the conditions of compromise by creating pervasive divisions and hostilities. The preservation of a democratic society requires positive and deliberate action to protect the economy against such catastrophes.

The history of the last thirty years, however, has focused the attention of most citizens on such dangers. With regard to economic issues, a practical working consensus has been reached in the United States. Government, it is agreed, has an obligation to prevent violent changes in over-all price levels and to pursue policies aiming to maintain the economy at or near the level of full employment. Important disagreements exist with regard to these matters; but they have to do with ways, means, and priorities, and not with fundamental objectives.

## A PLURALISTIC SOCIETY

The consideration of these issues leads us to a concluding topic —the general shape of the social order that makes democratic political processes vigorous and successful. A society with a thoroughly democratic social order will be a "pluralistic society." Such a society is the opposite of a totalitarian or monolithic society. It contains and protects many religions, many philosophies, many ethnic groups, many different people trying different ideas in different ways. It is marked by the wide dispersion of power throughout its various sections and by the existence of autonomous centers of decision-making authority. It offers individuals a chance to vote for more than one party, to choose among municipal or state governments that have different patterns, to change their jobs freely, and to join—or to refuse to join—many different groups.

In a pluralistic society, such groups have distinctive characteristics. They are independent of one another, autonomous and self-supporting, and are strong enough to resist pressure from the outside and to maintain their integrity when the struggle is severe. Moreover, on the contemporary scene, these groups are usually specialized groups—a farmers' co-operative, a professional association, a chamber of commerce—which do not represent all the manifold interests of the individuals who belong to them. They represent only a limited and selected set of these interests. The great boon conferred on its members by a society organized in this way is that it releases them from total dependence on any single human organization. They do not have to accept the unlimited authority of any group of men; they can turn from one organization to another for protection; they can spread their interests so that few defeats need to be final disasters.

But a pluralistic society provides more than freedom. It provides conditions in which the habit of compromise has a chance to develop and opportunities for reasonable and rewarding compromises are likely to flourish. In such a society the citizen has many different interests and associations; no center of power and interest embraces all the others; no single issue becomes so dominant that all other issues pile up around it. When an individual has many interests and belongs to many groups, he is unlikely to risk everything on a single issue, and he is likely to bring an external perspective to the struggles in which he engages. Some of his interests may overlap those of men and women who are among the innocent bystanders. Some even may be identical with those of members of the group directly opposed to his own. Wittingly or unwittingly, in consequence, he is likely to see things a little from the outside and to rehearse the larger social issue in an inner debate in his own mind.

Thus, conflicts in a pluralistic society are likely to be milder than those that arise in societies in which the individual is wholly encased within the group to which he belongs. Specific clashes of interest are limited, and they occur within a network of intersecting loyalties. One of the most important reasons why compromise has been an effective instrument of American democracy is that American society has been pluralistic.

On the rapidly changing contemporary scene, attention must be steadily focused on the conditions on which a pluralistic society depends. Relatively few individuals in any modern society can accomplish their purposes without the protection and support of powerful social groups. Accordingly, a democratic society must meet two imperatives. It must see to it that all its citizens have the opportunity to join groups that can protect and represent them; at the same time, however, it must see to it that none of these groups exercises monopolistic power over the individual.

In the contemporary world, the totalitarian state and monolithic political parties have been the most vivid examples of this danger. But the danger is present even in the absence of overt totalitarian commitments. As the social democratic parties of Western Europe seem now to agree, the state cannot be the only employer in the community; its power over the individual must be checked by the existence of other possible employers. Similarly, the individual must be protected against private employers by his union and by the state, and his rights must also be protected within his union by the action of the state or by other appropriate means.

The objective of a pluralistic society is to give the individual a wide variety of real and interesting alternatives among which he can choose. When men speak of a free society, this is primarily what they mean.

# IV. The Consent of the Governed

A democratic society has stability and ballast when its citizens adhere to its fundamental rules. It has a place to begin its political dialogue when most of its citizens are in agreement about the character of the issues that must be met. But rules to follow and a place to start are not enough to produce programs and set goals. Decisions must be made and translated into action. The process by which this is done is the process of government.

We must turn, therefore, to an examination of a fundamental idea. That governments derive "their just powers from the consent of the governed," that here on this continent the effort has been made to establish "government of the people, by the people, for the people"—these classic phrases express the heart of the American political creed. Since this creed was formulated, the United States has become a large, complex, and specialized industrial society, but the idea of government by consent of the governed continues to be valid. Yet there are few ideas that require more careful and candid scrutiny by the citizens of democracy.

Equipped with ill-considered notions of what is meant by "the consent of the governed," many American citizens have an improper conception of their rights and responsibilities and their powers and privileges under a democratic government. Armed with equally inaccurate notions, many critics of democracy have argued that it proposes a system of government that cannot be achieved or that would fail disastrously if it were achieved.

There have been two classic and influential interpretations of this idea of consent of the governed. The first is that a society is democratic when its members participate directly in making its decisions. The second is that a society is democratic when it elects its representatives by majority vote and when the majority of the elected representatives exercises the authority for determining a course of public policy. The first of these interpretations may be called the "town meeting" ideal of democracy, and the second, the "representative government" ideal.

## GOVERNMENT BY TOWN MEETING

From the time of the Greeks, the idea of government by citizens who meet face to face to discuss their problems has been a fundamental impulse behind many of the most influential theories of democracy. The town meetings of the New England colonists exemplified this idea in the New World. One great theme in the history of contemporary democracy, it may be said, has been the attempt to adapt an ideal of government developed in an atmosphere of intimate community life to an era of great nation-states, large and centralized organization, and highly specialized knowledge.

Such an ideal is by no means entirely inapplicable to a modern industrial society. In thousands of American communities, effective power in determining zoning ordinances, school budgets, and other local issues still lies in the institution of the town meeting. When the group concerned is relatively small, face-to-face consultation continues to be an important part of the democratic process of self-government. But it is plain that no city, state, or national government can conduct its business by direct consultation with all citizens or by submitting all major issues to popular referendum. It must make decisions on its own, and frequently they are difficult technical decisions whose details the great proportion of citizens cannot be expected to grasp.

These facts, of course, are generally understood and accepted in the United States and in other large nations. Yet underneath the apparent acceptance of these facts, the ideal of the town meeting still persists. Men unconsciously use it in evaluating the institutions of contemporary democratic government. Thus, there is still widespread suspicion of the "expert" and the "bureaucrat" in government, not because they are thought to know less than they claim or to be more officious than they should be, but because it is felt they do not belong in a truly democratic government. Such government, it is erroneously supposed, should be direct government by the people. For the same reason the professional politician is sometimes regarded as an undesirable appendage of democracy rather than an essential feature. Such views rest upon a definition of democracy that is not only irrelevant to contemporary conditions but describes democracy as it has hardly ever existed.

The lingering and unobserved influence of the town-meeting ideal of democracy is responsible for other kinds of misdirected thought and behavior as well. For example, it stands behind claims that democracy does not "really" exist because military or diplomatic decisions are regularly made without substantial popular participation beforehand—even though these decisions are made by those who have the constitutional responsibility to do so. It also stands behind practices that are parodies of democratic processes. The mass meetings that were standard weapons of fascism are one example. Another is the direct appeal which demagogues in many democratic countries have regularly made to "the people" when they have wished to justify a violation of normal democratic procedures. There are other examples, although relatively harmless ones, in practices that are frequently praised in free societies as instances of "democracy in action." The annual meetings of stockholders in large corporations are a case in point. Such meetings have both symbolic and practical uses, but the decision-making power normally remains in the hands of management.

There are aspirations behind the town-meeting conception of democracy, however, that must be recognized as indelible parts of the democratic creed. The town-meeting conception of democracy is an idealized way of expressing the democratic hope that those who are governed will be able to reach those who govern them, that they will be able to make their voices heard where it counts and will be recognized as persons and not as faceless cogs in an efficient machine. It speaks for the belief that a society is safer and freer when the bulk of its citizens understand the programs and goals that their government has chosen and when they have achieved this understanding because these programs and goals have been honestly debated in public.

Not least, the town-meeting ideal catches an important meaning of freedom and expresses a classic conviction of believers in democracy. The ordinary man may or may not be the best judge of his own interests, but if he does not exercise effective authority over matters that are in his immediate range of interest and competence, he may be a well-tended animal, but he will not be a free man. Freedom in the concrete, freedom as it is experienced in daily life, is the experience of having a hand in the determining of issues that touch the individual closely and intimately.

There is a dignity in democracy based on individuals working together seeking solutions for their joint problems. Since the time of the Greeks, it has been part of the democratic outlook that this kind of dignity is the reward of a free way of life and that the chance to participate as an equal in communal ventures is one of the ways in which men educate themselves best and one of the major joys of being alive. It is because democracy has been thought to make such an opportunity more generally available that it has been prized by most of its adherents.

Despite its limitations, the town-meeting conception of democracy is useful, therefore, as a warning against making wholesale judgments about the much mooted issue of "centralization" or "decentralization." The movement toward highly centralized government at the national level has been a natural and a necessary response of American democracy to the problems faced by the American people at home and abroad. Military defense, foreign policy, or the control of the business cycle are all matters that cut across inherited state and local lines and that require decisive action at the center of things. It should be noted that this tendency has been given added impetus because states and communities have frequently shirked their own direct responsibilities.

But such big questions, although they are questions of national significance, are not necessarily the questions that make the most important difference in the quality of the ordinary citizen's daily life. He spends this life at work, in a neighborhood, and inside his home. If he is not directly consulted face to face each time that national decisions are made, he will not necessarily feel that his democratic rights have been violated. But if he believes that he has no voice in the control of the immediate forces that affect his home, the character of his neighborhood, or the conditions under which he works, he is likely to have just this feeling. In the day of the automatic calculator, therefore, a degree of local variety and autonomy may well be a price worth paying—even if, as is by no means certain, it means a sacrifice in organizational efficiency. Paternalism is the uninvited guest at most banquets in honor of efficiency.

## REPRESENTATIVE GOVERNMENT

There is another classic view of political democracy, however, which is even more influential than the view that democracy is government by town meeting. This is the belief that democracy means government by representatives who are chosen by vote. In the traditional interpretation of this doctrine, it is held that these representatives will do the people's work for them, expressing and implementing the desires of the majority. Probably no idea of the nature and rationale of political democracy is more widespread. It is one element in the conception of the United States as a constitutional republic, and it conforms to the formal mechanisms of existing democratic governments.

An unquestionable hallmark of genuine democracy is the individual citizen's right to vote in free elections for his representatives in government, to choose them from among competing groups, and to do so without fear of penalty. The concept of free elections thus implies a good deal more about the meaning of democracy than the existence of elections alone. It implies that legal means of criticizing a government's policies must exist, that there must be freedom of thought, speech, and association, that the opposition to a government must have a chance to be organized, and that the electoral majority must respect the rights of the minority. The classic definition of "representative government" as government by men chosen in free elections is thus an accurate and suggestive definition of democracy.

Nevertheless, this conception of democracy can also be misleading unless it is analyzed. The idea of majority rule through a representative assembly rests on two concepts. The first is the concept of "majority rule." The second is the concept of "representation."

### The Concept of "Majority Rule"

The most usual interpretation of the idea of "majority rule" is that it refers to the election of governments by majority vote. It has happened that presidents have been elected in the United States by pluralities rather than majorities, and even that individuals have been elected who have won a smaller popular vote than the defeated candidate. Despite these exceptions, the election of governments by majority vote is obviously the norm in the United States and a significant determinant of government policy. Through elections, citizens have the opportunity to pass judgment on the performance of their government and to determine some of the major lines of policy of the next government. The existence of elections is a major reason why democratic governments are under steady pressure to be responsive to the opinions of ordinary citizens.

But while elections influence the policies of government, they are not the only determinants of these policies. These policies are forged in the teeth of events, amidst the day-to-day pressures of different groups, and with the advice of administrative officers who have not themselves been elected. They are explained and propelled by political parties, and tested and changed in the competition that goes on within and between these parties. When the actual processes by which democratic governments make decisions are examined, "majority rule" stands for something much more complicated than the choosing of a government by free election. It stands for the formation of policies in a context of continuing public discussion and debate. Above all, it stands for a decision-making process that is not dominated by a single minority group or oligarchy.

Indeed, the phrase "majority rule" has a certain inexactness about it when the most important feature of the democratic decision-making process is taken into account. At the heart of this process is the competition among the organized interest groups in the community. All these groups speak for minorities. When we speak of "majority rule," we largely mean that most of the important organized groups in the community are able to make themselves heard at some point in the elaborate process by which government decisions in America are made. The ideal of majority rule expresses the democratic antipathy to the domination of society by any single center of power. It speaks for the democratic effort to achieve government that will serve the interests of a steadily larger portion of a nation and that will do so because all its citizens possess instruments for affecting its decisions.

The politics of democracy, therefore, is primarily the politics of what are known as pressure groups. The existence of such groups is frequently taken, even by the strongest partisans of democracy, as a sign of democratic weakness. It is an error to do so; the statement does not imply that democratic politics are inherently dishonest or that behind the façade of "majority rule" and "government by consent" sinister interests dominate the American system of government. On the contrary, such conclusions are drawn only when a simplistic conception of democratic processes of government is accepted. Pressure groups, for example, have fought against minimum-wage laws; but other pressure groups have fought for them. The groups that make their weight felt in the democratic process are sometimes self-seeking, sometimes public-spirited. Some democratic political figures think only of the next election; others try to determine their position on the basis of a conscientious and independent examination of the issues. But the politics of pressure groups is not in itself incompatible with democracy. The only alternative to this kind of politics is a government that rules over isolated and rootless individuals who have no groups other than the government to protect them and no stable and independent social power of their own. This is the pattern at which totalitarian government aims.

## The Idea of "Representation"

The idea of majority rule is intimately tied to another central idea in the theory of democratic government—the idea that such government is "representative." This has sometimes been interpreted to mean that those who are elected to political office are merely the agents of the electorate and exist simply to translate into action such views as the electorate holds. As a result of this notion, grave doubts are sometimes expressed about the viability of democracy. It is argued that not many citizens vote unselfishly, that most of them vote impulsively or irrationally, and that few or no citizens have the knowledge that is a necessary prerequisite to warranted judgments about public issues. Democracy, it is therefore suggested, is based on a false view of human capacities and on oversimplified notions about the nature of the problems with which a modern government must grapple.

These skeptical doubts are better directed at faulty assumptions —conceptions of representative government to which no contemporary representative government in fact conforms—rather than at the actual way in which democratic government operates.

There is a fundamental error in the notion that a democratic government can be, or should be, merely the passive spokesman of the popular will. The error lies in assuming that a definite popular will actually exists in the absence of government, political parties, media of communication, and all the other agencies in society that register what is known as "public opinion." For these agencies do not simply reflect such opinion. They form and inform it and give it its direction and mode of expression.

No one forms his opinions in a void. The citizen must get his information somewhere. He will attach more weight to the views of some people than to the views of others; certain groups in his environment, as a result of their proximity or their power, will inevitably have a better chance than others to get his ear. Indeed, such political preferences as the individual may express will be preferences with regard to issues that have been formulated expressly for him. Not only do the political parties propose the candidates among whom he must choose, but they define the questions about which the individual citizen is asked to make up his mind. Together with the media of communication and voluntary associations, they bear the crucial responsibility for determining whether the political dialogue will be serious or merely superficial, informed or studiously ignorant.

This is why such groups, and particularly their leaders, may be justly accused of attempting to shift their responsibility when they claim that they are merely giving the American citizen what he wants. What the citizen wants can only be determined by observing how he chooses among the alternatives that are presented to him; if other alternatives were presented, his choices might possibly be different. This principle applies, indeed, to much more than politics. The television, radio, newspaper, housing, or automobile industries do not simply react passively to public demand. They shape and limit that demand and, for better or worse, are therefore among the makers of the so-called "popular will."

This is not an abuse of the democratic process. It is an inevitable concomitant of the process by which opinions and tastes are formed in any society. Undoubtedly, there is justified concern today about the manipulation of opinion and the engineering of consent. Despite the fact that a modern educated population develops some powers of resistance to calculated attempts to deceive it, such attempts remain assaults on the spirit and ethic of democracy. The individual citizens of a free society should have a chance to understand what they are choosing and a chance to impose their own standards after genuinely critical reflection upon them. But this does not eliminate the role of leadership or the responsibility of leaders for the decisions which they and not others make. Unless the political parties, the media of communication, and the leaders of voluntary organizations perform the function of directing the democratic debate, this debate will be aimless and unformed. It is their responsibility to put before the citizen a rationally considered and imaginative set of alternatives among which he can make his choice. For the importance of the right to vote is directly proportional to the importance of the issues that are determined by the vote.

The view that a definite popular will can exist without the help of leadership ignores the fact that there is a difference between having an opinion on matters that are immediate and close at hand and having an opinion on matters of government policy. A housewife, for example, in the course of her daily experience and as the keeper of the household budget, is likely to develop her own views about the honesty of the corner grocer. They probably will be rather sensible views, and they will not depend entirely on the testimony of others. But when she moves to the question whether the United States has adequate deterrent strength in intercontinental missiles, she will merely be arrogant if she believes that she can come to a responsible judgment without time and study that may not be hers to give. Moreover, government secrecy about such matters—which may or may not be necessary —may prevent her from obtaining the essential facts she must have if her opinion is to be an informed one.

Many issues, of course, lie in between the areas in which the ordinary citizen has a practical competence and those in which he is almost wholly ignorant. Responsible and intelligent citizenship in a modern democracy nevertheless entails a willingness on the part of citizens to recognize that there will be areas in which they inevitably will be ignorant. The statement "I do not know" is too frequently taken to be a confession that an individual has failed in the performance of his democratic duty. It is an unreasonably undervalued remark. For in many circumstances it reflects intellectual probity and civic good sense.

A more balanced position would acknowledge that there are

matters on which an individual citizen is quite competent to make informed judgments, matters on which even modest study and reflection will greatly improve his understanding, and other matters on which it will be impossible for him to have really informed judgments of his own.

In short, the concept of representative government makes sense only if the relationship between those who govern and those who are governed is properly understood. Democracy is not a system in which the citizenry governs through representatives who are its passive agents. It is a system in which the authority to govern is acquired through competition for the citizens' votes. Those who hold elective positions in a democracy are the representatives of the people in the sense that it is the people who choose them and remove them. They are the representatives of a popular will in the sense that it is their obligation to make the decisions they do only after extended consultation with individuals and groups outside government. But it is the function of the electorate to choose and remove a government; it is the function of the government to govern. It makes decisions and does not merely enact decisions already made by the population. Few things can harm the cause of effective democratic government more than a faulty view of the role and responsibility of leadership.

Effective democratic government depends on social and educational conditions that produce good leadership and that give this leadership a chance to function. The political life of a democracy must be such that it does not suffer in comparison with other areas of activity and attracts its fair quota of gifted and responsible people. Such people must not only respect the political life but feel a duty to take an active part in it. The electorate, although it cannot be informed on every issue that confronts government, must be sufficiently informed to understand the main drift of the issues and sufficiently shrewd to detect ability and to tell the charlatan from the genuine article among the candidates that are proposed to it. And although the driving purpose of those who engage in democratic politics, inevitably, is to beat the opposing party, a sufficient number of those who are active in politics, and especially the most powerful among them, must recognize that government has other business as well. Of course, no administration in power in a democracy will be indifferent to the outcome of the next election. But the capacity of democratic government in the United States to meet its responsibilities in the era that is taking shape depends on its capacity to think beyond elections as well.

## INSTRUMENTS OF DEMOCRATIC SELF-CONTROL

No democracy can sustain itself if either its government or its citizens lack the capacity for self-restraint or the habit of looking upon the "majority opinion" of the moment as something that may well be wrong. Happily, democratic institutions give both government and citizens a number of instruments that reinforce and implement these attitudes. At many points the idea of government by majority rule is hedged and qualified by other institutions and practices.

### Political Parties

One of the most notable of these instruments is the party system. Political parties are normally regarded as the major instruments of democratic rivalry, and it is obvious that this is a major purpose for their existence. In the United States and in many other democracies, however, they also serve a complementary function. Each party is an instrument by which differences are ironed out, tensions reduced, and interests of extraordinary complexity and diversity are brought together. It is within, and not only between, the two great political parties in the United States that a major part of the struggle between competing interests has taken place, and has been softened and negotiated. In this way, the parties, by means of the political processes that go on within them, contribute to the construction of a democratic consensus as well as to the maintenance of democratic competition.

It is as vehicles of competition that political parties perform their distinctive democratic function. Not all systems of party competition function like the American system, and whatever the special advantages of a two-party system may be, such a system cannot be said to be a necessary characteristic of political democracy. What is a defining characteristic of political democracy, however, is the existence, legally and openly, of an organized party or parties that are in opposition to the party in power. This is a major instrument of democratic self-control. The subtle notion of a loyal opposition takes us to the center of the democratic process of government. In the large perspective, the opposition party is really part of the government. Its presence means that a democratic government is forced to seek as broad and tolerable a synthesis of interests as possible, and that the minority will be represented to some degree in the policies such a government eventually adopts.

## Judicial Review

The competition between political parties, however, is not the only instrument of democratic self-control in the United States. The prescriptions of the Constitution and the entire legal framework in which the Constitution is embedded not only set limits to the powers of elected officials but also establish a system of checks and balances. Within this system, which distributes power between the legislative, executive, and judicial branches of government, appeal to the courts, and particularly to the Supreme Court, has been a traditionally effective instrument for preventing the "majority will" from having its way. Moreover, the courts have not only acted as negative and restraining influences. Many of the most fundamental arrangements that govern the relations of American citizens to one another have been created not by explicit legislation but by judicial action.

Politics, in a democracy and in any society, is constantly in danger of passing under the rule of the urgent moment and the immediately expedient. Judicial review is one of American democratic society's instruments for checking this tendency. For judicial reasoning ideally demands that a judgment be guided not simply by an immediate end in view but by principles and standards whose validity transcends the case at hand. The judicial reasoner seeks more than a convenient result. He seeks results that meet the test of principles that are neutral and general and can be applied to cases other than the one under adjudication.

The application of the principle of judicial review to legislative as well as executive action is one of the most distinctive contributions made by America to the theory and practice of democratic government. It provides one instrument for giving effect to the recognition that a nation is a community with interests and principles that transcend the life of a single generation and that must be protected against the momentary views of shifting majorities. These interests and principles can be changed and reinterpreted: the courts themselves are not immune to changes in the working democratic consensus, and the process of constitutional amendment is always open. But the institution of judicial review helps to ensure that such changes will not take place without extensive and deliberate examination by more than one agency of government. Despite differing reactions to recent decisions of the Supreme Court in different parts of the United States, the existence of the Court is one of the fundamental circumstances responsible for the maintenance over the years of the American consensus.

## The Federal System

The limitations imposed by American democracy upon simple rule by legislative majorities or an elected executive go beyond provisions for checks and balances and judicial review. The American federal system, with political power dispersed among the fifty states and the national government, provides a highly significant built-in limitation. Since federal authority is specified in the Constitution and residual powers remain in the states, the power of national majorities to regulate local conditions is obviously limited. Whether the present geographical boundaries between the states are anachronistic, whether the federal government needs more centralized power than it now has, or whether its powers already go beyond those proper to a federal form of government—all these are questions that are currently debated. But there is little dissent from the principle that, in a continental nation like the United States, a federal form of government is an important condition of continuing consensus.

## Regulatory Commissions and Administrative Services

Political democracy, we have observed, is a system for choosing governments by electoral competition. But it is also a system in which, by the action of elected representatives, increasingly large areas of government action have been placed in the hands of independent regulatory commissions. The Federal Communications Commission, for example, or the Securities and Exchange Commission exercises great power but is only indirectly governed by an electoral mandate. Similarly, independent public corporations like the Tennessee Valley Authority, although established by a majority decision of elected representatives, are not themselves engaged in the competition for votes. As a number of events over the years have revealed, the technical independence of regulatory commissions unfortunately fails to guarantee that their members will be immune to political or other forms of influence. Probably such corruption can only be fought by the relentless use of the democratic methods of investigation and exposure. In principle, nevertheless, these commissions represent the recognition that democratic government is a complex affair requiring professional as well as political advice and decisions.

Another important branch of government that is relatively insulated from the political arena is the permanent administrative service, both civil and military. Here the principle is established that service should be nonpolitical and that loyalty must be given to whatever government holds office. It is this branch of government, more than any other, that brings technical expertise to the government process and continuity in the implementation of government policy. Even more, it is this branch that makes it possible for democratic government to take account of issues that transcend the next election and that are more important than the victory of a particular party. For the separate departments and bureaus that constitute the administrative branch of democratic government are themselves among the pressure groups whose power must be reckoned with in the determination of governmental policy. The judgments expressed by these groups are not inevitably more immune to bias and self-seeking motives than are those of other pressure groups. The administrative services are nevertheless peculiarly capable of organizing and representing public interests that would otherwise be neglected in the push and pull of democratic competition.

The construction and preservation of a strong administrative service, free from political threat, is a necessary condition of democratic success in handling contemporary problems. One of the most important long-range tasks of American democracy is that of advancing the respect in which this branch of government is held and of recruiting and training talented people for careers within it.

# V. The Private Sector

Elections, the rugged competition of political parties, the processes of compromise within a pluralistic social order, the working of judicial review, the principle of federalism, and the maintenance of a nonpolitical administrative service are among the mechanisms American society employs to preserve government by consent. No one of them, however, and not all of them together are enough to guarantee free government. An essential condition for securing these ideals is the vigorous and independent activity of private citizens possessing sources of power and wealth that lie outside the government sector.

## THE LINE BETWEEN THE STATE AND SOCIETY

A competitive political process is not self-sustaining. It requires a society organized on the principle that the state is only one form of human association and that it exists side by side with a host of other associations that are to some extent autonomous. A democratic state is limited by its constitution in what it can do, and it is also limited in fact by the existence of significant centers of decision-making authority outside itself. The American pattern of private enterprise and voluntary associations is not the only mold for a free society. But such a society must contain groups that can make decisions and take action without asking repeated permission of the state or depending on its largesse. The existence of such autonomous and powerful groups in a society gives substance to classic democratic slogans such as "government that rests on will, not force" and "government by consent." To act with one's friends, one's co-believers, or one's associates and to know that the state will not interfere so long as one remains within the law—this is the heart of what men have fought for under the name of freedom.

It is wrong to imagine, of course, that there is a violent antithesis between "freedom" and the restraints imposed by laws of the state. The restraining of individual behavior in certain respects is the necessary condition for individual freedom in other respects. The thief is not free to take property that does not belong to him; his lack of freedom in this respect is what gives the right to property its meaning. In states where anti-discrimination laws in housing have been enacted, a landlord is not free to pick and choose his tenants only from the racial and religious groups he finds congenial; his lack of freedom in this respect spells freedom for members of minority groups to live where they desire. It is a society's business to choose which freedoms it particularly values. The one thing it cannot do is to choose freedom in the abstract. Few social controversies are more stultifying than those that revolve around the issue of freedom but do not specify which freedoms are desired and which are endangered.

But if restraints are conditions of freedom, they are not the same thing as freedom. As the old ex-slave is reported to have said, he liked freedom because "there's a kind of looseness about it." In a democratic society the area of legal coercion and state control cannot be all-encompassing. There must also be room, and considerable room, for individuals to do as they please and to face the consequences of their actions. The restraints that a democratic society imposes on its members, therefore, are presumed to have as one of their principal purposes the preservation or the extension of areas of free, personal choice.

In practice, this means that the law must permit citizens freedom of association. It also means that they must enjoy social and economic circumstances that actually provide them with more than one avenue to the realization of their desires and more than one channel for making their careers. If they are frustrated in one area, they must have the chance to turn around and try somewhere else. For if they find themselves confronted by the same monolithic structure of power wherever they turn, they do not have freedom in a substantial sense, no matter what the official rhetoric of their society may proclaim.

In a speech before the Indian Parliament, Mr. Khrushchev referred to "the monolithic pattern" of Soviet society—a society which, according to him, does not have "any intermediate social groups or strata with some special class interests of their own." He went on to say, "The Soviet society is a society of workingmen, peasants and intellectuals with their roots in the people, united by a community of interests and a singleness of purpose. The interests of the Soviet people are expressed and upheld by one party—the Communist Party." And he concluded, "This is what accounts for the absence of any other parties in our country."* It is to be doubted that the Soviet Union has quite the monolithic structure that Mr. Khrushchev describes: the record of purges in the Soviet Union, to mention only one bit of evidence, suggests something less than "a community of interests and a singleness of purpose" in that country. But in any case, there is no adherent of democracy, as it is understood in the noncommunist world, who would regard such a statement as anything but the description of profound unfreedom. It describes a society in which all groups but one have lost their autonomy.

The monolithic structure at which the Soviet system aims highlights the quite different characteristics of American society on which American freedoms hinge. At the same time, however, this monolithic ideal calls attention to a constant danger that exists in any society and against which it is the business of a democratic society to be alert. Particularly in times of emergency, but even at other times, there is a besetting temptation in political life. It is the temptation to push reasons of state into the private areas of society and to turn nonpolitical voluntary associations into instrumentalities of an encircling political power. The extralegal persecution of conscientious objectors, the refusal of private enterprises to give employment to individuals only because these individuals subscribe to radical doctrines—these are examples of practices that erase the line between the state and the rest of society.

Such practices have not been the rule in the United States, and they sink into insignificance when compared with the scope, severity, and centrally organized character of similar practices in Communist countries. Their rarity, nevertheless, does not make them more compatible with democratic ideals. They represent lapses from the principle that the state shall not be a ubiquitous

* From Mr. Khrushchev's speech of February 11, 1960, as reported in *The New York Times*, February 12, 1960.

and constant presence in all the affairs of men; and to a thorough believer in democracy, even minor defections from this principle will be noted and fought. The issue, indeed, is not simply a matter of personal liberties. It is a matter of intellectual atmosphere. The politicizing of all important issues—the insistence on appraising literature, scientific ideas, art, philosophy, or international athletic competition always in terms of their political implications, real or alleged—does more than make cultural life a bore, which is bad enough. It implicitly converts activities that free men have always regarded as ends in themselves into instruments of the state.

## EVER-CHANGING RELATION OF THE PRIVATE AND PUBLIC SECTORS

These questions bring us to a fundamental issue. It is a mark of a free society, we have said, that it draws a line between the areas that are subject to state control or legal coercion and those in which the private judgment of individuals or voluntary groups will prevail. At any given moment, however, there is usually an entire zone where the public and private sectors fade into one another. The recognition that certain private associations serve crucial social interests that must receive public support is reflected, for example, in provisions of the income tax laws which make contributions to private educational and charitable institutions in part tax deductible. Again, associations within the professions—for example, bar associations—have long enjoyed a delegated authority from the state and are recognized as the quasi-official representatives and protectors of particularly important sectors of the public interest. To take still another example, in recent years a new form of partnership between government and private enterprise has been worked out in the field of atomic energy. On all sides, during the last generation, new hybrids have emerged—independent public corporations, private corporations that are created to do only government work, research centers staffed by private groups and financed by public funds. Few of these activities fit into simple and conventional categories separating the "private" and the "public."

The lines that mark off the private from the public steadily shift and move, and so does the shadow zone between them. Must employers protect their employees against the hazards of their jobs? This was once a matter of individual discretion; it is now a legal obligation. Is the owner of a restaurant that is not a private club free to pick and choose his customers? The laws of some states now answer this question in the negative; in other states the issue is still being fought. As the social and physical environment changes, the reasons that once existed for drawing the line between the private and the public at a certain place are subject to reassessment. Thirty years ago, a basketball coach looking for tall players would have accepted a six-foot candidate. Today, he would classify him as short. The relation between the private and the public is similar.

The fact that a sharp line is hard to draw does not mean, of course, that there is no difference between the "private" and the "public." We can usually tell the difference between a merely portly man and a fat man even if we have difficulty drawing an exact line. Similarly, in the politics of a free society, there are relatively few questions about what is private and what is public until we come to the border areas where the battles are being fought. In contrast, there are no recognized border areas in a totalitarian society: the distinction between the private and the public has in principle been erased.

A democratic society, accordingly, is recurrently confronted by the problem of where to draw the line between the private and the public, and it cannot be definitely settled for all time. Nor should we be beguiled in dealing with it by either of two unexamined assumptions. The first is that all social control must be governmental control. There are other alternatives, such as community opinion or voluntary agreements among private citizens and groups. Indeed, even in countries in which governmental control has proceeded very far, it is probably less influential in the hour-to-hour behavior of men than the controls of tradition, moral beliefs, personal relations, habit, informal understandings, and the established code of manners and etiquette. In determining whether social controls are necessary, therefore, it is also necessary to determine what sort of control—governmental or nongovernmental—is desirable.

The second assumption to be avoided is that each instance of governmental or other restraint reduces the total area of freedom. The compatibility of freedom with varying amounts of governmental regulation is not an issue that can be settled by dogmatic pronouncements on either side. It is plain, of course, that any instance of restraint, if considered in and by itself, is a limitation of freedom. To take a hypothetical example, if the drivers of private passenger automobiles were prohibited from bringing their cars into the central part of New York City, they would lose their freedom in precisely this respect. But such a law might create conditions that gave the former drivers of automobiles more freedom to go where they wish quickly, comfortably, and cheaply. And it might also enhance the freedom of pedestrians and advance the cause of a great many other interests that are now smothered by an adherence to the principle that the private automobile has supreme rights.

Whether this would turn out to be the case is not, of course, to the point. The example merely illustrates the principle that governmental restraint is not automatically to be equated with a net loss of freedom. Much useless debate would be avoided if this principle were recognized. Only by examining the specific consequences of a particular action can it be determined whether freedom will or will not be diminished. This is not to deny, however, that liberty is seriously threatened if any single agency in the community monopolizes all economic resources. One of the clear imperatives of democratic policy is the preservation of an economic system that diffuses power and contains autonomous centers of authority within it.

There is a consequence that follows from this principle that cannot be too greatly emphasized. It is a principle of democracy that the government will not be the only rule-making body in the community, and that associations that are independent of it will have the right and the power to make socially significant decisions. This implies, however, that these associations are themselves governments in the most meaningful sense of the term. They make rules and exercise genuine and effective authority over those who work for them or belong to them, and they establish arrangements that affect the general character of the community at large. The phenomenon of widespread private government, nourished and supported, indeed, by the deliberate action of the state, is an intrinsic feature of a free society.

Accordingly, the same sort of question that can be asked of other governments can also be asked of these private governments. The democratic ideals by which the state is properly judged may also be applied to the ways in which the lives of men are governed in the private sector. If the individual is smothered, if power is excessive, democratic principles are violated as surely as they are violated by similar conditions in the public sector. The proper balance between private government and public government is always a precarious one. It is a matter of reciprocal checks and restraints and of balancing forces that are equally necessary to democratic freedom.

A democratic way of life includes more than the relation of the individual citizen to his city, state, or national government. It includes the kind of experience he has in his everyday activities and the expectations on which he and his fellows act in their private dealings with one another. The great goal of democracy is a change in the intimate quality of human experience. Democracy seeks a world in which men meet in the mutual respect that equals give to one another. It seeks a kind of life for the individual in which he will know that all men are limited and checked in the powers they can exercise but that every man is counted as important for the potential excellence that is in him. Such an ideal of life refers to much more than politics. It is for the sake of this ideal that the democratic process should be cherished and its performance constantly re-examined.

# VI. The Power of the Democratic Idea

The desire for freedom is very old; the experience of freedom is very rare. American democracy is young, as age is measured by the nations of the world. Its work is far from finished. It is only one among the many forms that a democratic society can take. But nowhere has the democratic idea been tested by so large a society over so long a period as in the United States.

It is not surprising that throughout its existence the American democratic system has been a puzzle, a portent, and a symbol of hope. To skeptics, to lovers of order and hierarchy in human affairs, to those who distrust ordinary human beings when they are not held on tight checkreins, democracy in America has been a paradox. They have wondered how a system that puts its leaders under so many restrictions and gives common citizens so large a voice in the making of policy can possibly meet the trials of life in a dangerous world. To those who exercise despotic authority, democracy in America has been—and continues to be—a source of constant danger, a great center from which the belief that freedom is possible and desirable has radiated. To masses of men and women everywhere, American democracy has stood for a change from the hereditary condition of mankind. It has given them the courage to hope that they need not be locked in the boxes into which birth and inherited position have put them, that they can carve out their own careers, enjoy what other men enjoy, reach their leaders and influence them, and live without deferring to a ruling group.

Can the democratic idea continue to exert this power? Can the desires and hopes it has set loose be satisfied under contemporary conditions and within the framework of freedom? America is not the only country where the democratic idea has found a home or where it is being tested as it has not been tested before. But what America does will determine a large part of the answer to these questions. And what America does will be governed by two principal considerations: the inherent resources of its democratic system and its ability to adjust its policies to the imperatives of the radically changed environment in which the democratic system must make its way.

## DEMOCRACY'S CHANGING ENVIRONMENT

Men everywhere are living through a change in the human scene that challenges most ideas and institutions inherited from other days. Man's relation to his physical environment has changed; his relation to other men, his distance from them, and his impact upon them have changed; his sense of himself and of the possibilities of human life have changed. And behind these changes there are momentous and irreversible movements that have brought a tidal shift in the course of human affairs.

### Technology and Large Organizations

A major source of these changes is technological innovation. Changes in technology have always been a major cause of change in government, economic relations, and social institutions. But technological innovation is no longer the work of isolated, ingenious inventors; it is the product of organized scientific enterprise and is constant, insistent, and accelerating. One of its most notable effects is upon the tempo of social change itself, which is enormously quicker than it has been and which subjects every inhabitant of a technological society to its pressures.

Technological innovation thus poses a series of issues with which our democracy will have to deal. It will need to strengthen its techniques for applying enlightened social forethought. It may have to enlarge its existing programs for cushioning the shock of technological unemployment. It will have to explore the question whether it is possible for a democracy to arrange for the orderly and considered introduction of technological innovations without limiting freedom of inquiry or stifling the spirit of invention. These are large issues that will test our democracy's capacity to manage this new and complex technological environment.

Moreover, the growth of a technological society has changed the traditional environment in which men have enjoyed freedom. Large and complex organizations have become the order of the day. In the United States they touch the lives of almost all citizens at some point. Programs for the preservation and strengthening of individual freedom in the modern world must assume the existence and the inevitability of such organizations.

Large organizations are often considered to be inimical to individual freedom because they lead to a phenomenon known as "bureaucracy"—in essence, the effort to co-ordinate the work of many people by requiring common standards and fixing precisely their specialized responsibilities. The bureaucratic administration of large organizations, private as well as public, has been a steadily more prominent feature of all industrial societies for over a century. There can be no question that it raises issues of the sharpest sort for a democracy. The central issue is whether bigness and bureaucracy are inherently incompatible with freedom and democracy.

The issue has many sides. Large-scale organization and the growth of bureaucracy have contributed to the progress of democracy in a number of ways. In making possible the development and enforcement of general rules covering diverse techniques, multiple systems, and geographically dispersed operations, they have contributed to the productivity of modern industry and have helped create the conditions of economic plenty in which democracy normally thrives. By developing clear standards that stress performance, they have accelerated the decline in influence of class and family prerogatives and have opened new channels of achievement for able individuals. Most important of all, the administrative techniques employed by bureaucracy have generally brought a decline in the influence of personal and arbitrary authority. Bureaucracy limits the power of officials by definite rules, thereby making slavish conformity to their wills less necessary. Nor does it automatically close off competition among individuals. In America today, the large-scale organization has become a major arena for individual competition.

Nevertheless, the fears aroused by bigness and bureaucracy do point to dangers that test our society's alertness and ingenuity. The rights of individuals within large organizations require protection, and internal democratic procedures need to be strengthened. The largest challenge of all is to find ways of arranging the work of large organizations that will give individuals more discretion, a maximum opportunity to show their personal capacities, and a greater chance to feel personally responsible for the contribution they make to a larger effort. It may well be in industry that the ultimate value of automation will reside not in the increase in individual productivity or leisure time but in the elimination of routine work and the creation of more positions in which decision and discretion are essential.

Vigilance against the hardening of the arteries in modern organizations must be matched, furthermore, by encouraging their sense of responsibility to the larger community. Too many large organizations, especially in business and labor, still betray a tendency to bring up their officers in a tradition of narrow loyalty to the corporation or the union, which dulls their awareness of the effects of their decisions upon the community as a whole. Such organizations can themselves do a great deal to correct this tendency. Steps in the same direction could usefully be taken by non-economic associations.

Significant safeguards, however, are at the disposal of a democratic society. These include bringing the instruments of public criticism to bear on those who mismanage administrative machinery; assigning elected or politically appointed officials to positions of authority over public agencies; maintaining competition among private organizations; and introducing public regulation as well where that is necessary. Probably the most important means for controlling the dangers implicit in large-scale organization, however, is the vigorous activity of private citizens in their political parties and private associations.

We come here to an issue that lies at the heart of much current debate about democracy. An increasing number of large voluntary associations in the United States are composed of active organized minorities and large, inactive majorities. To a great extent, this is a consequence of the problems with which these associations must deal. The complexity and technical character of most important issues have greatly increased, and they have become national and international in scope. As never before, events and decisions in distant places touch the lives of individual citizens intimately. These changes in the character of the problems with which democratic society must grapple have inevitably encouraged the feeling that democratic citizens, despite the personal liberties and voting rights they enjoy, are remote from the centers of power and cannot bring their personal weight to bear on the events that affect their lives.

The growing complexity and scope of public issues cannot be reversed. Yet, the fact remains that more, not fewer, individuals have some chance to exert influence in a modern democratic society than in any other society that has existed. The practical problem is to find ways and means to protect and reinforce the power that individuals can bring to bear on their environments. The purposeful reorganization of our cities to provide neighborhoods that will encourage people to meet and work together is one example of what can be done. The granting of larger power to local units in voluntary organizations and the expansion of the responsibilities of employee organizations are other examples. Neither bigness nor bureaucracy need be the inherent enemy of individual freedom so long as the deliberate and active object of our democracy is to spread the experience of self-government as widely as possible.

## "Revolution of Rising Expectations"

These problems have a special urgency because they have emerged in a radically altered moral setting. American democracy has moved into a world in which the overwhelming majority of its own citizens, and an increasing number of people everywhere, have come to entertain new expectations about the things they should have a chance to do and enjoy and the place they should rightfully occupy in their societies. This change in human moral horizons has led to turbulence and dissatisfaction, has prepared the way for authoritarianism in some countries, and has thrown every society that has been touched by it on a path that is strewn with perils. But every one of a democracy's fundamental principles commits it to welcoming this remarkable alteration in the feelings of ordinary human beings about the lives to which they may aspire.

Our own democracy has been the scene of this revolution for a long time and is continuing to feel the impact of this revolution in many ways. It is basically because so many of our Negro citizens take the American democratic creed seriously that they are struggling for the removal of the barriers to their full participation in our society. More broadly, there is emerging in the United States a society with a shape hitherto unknown in history. An unprecedented proportion of the population will be in schools; a steadily growing proportion will live to what was once known as old age; young, middle-aged, and old will have more leisure than all but a privileged few have enjoyed in the past, and they will have more to buy and consume.

The vista is exciting, but it will also bring issues that have never troubled any nation on so vast a scale. In such a world, more than ever before, a society should be able to offer its members something better than a life of mere accumulation and of sensation without commitment. A still further expansion of our educational effort will be required, and the demand for improvement in its quality will have to be satisfied. New public and private facilities will be needed to make leisure an opportunity for steady and cumulative personal fulfillment. Work at its best has always been a chance for personal accomplishment and social service. Particularly when leisure comes to occupy a progressively more important place in the life of the individual and of society as a whole, it must be measured by the same standard. Finally, individual citizens in the new society that is emerging will have a greater need than ever for an active, informed taste, for a sense of responsibility, and for personal standards that will allow them to discriminate among the welter of goods, some meretricious, some genuine, that are put before them. It is a demand that has never been made on so large a portion of a society.

Nor is this the only demand American citizens will have to satisfy. The discrimination and sense of purpose that America shows in using its wealth—the way in which it allocates its resources, the shape it gives to its civilization—will affect our democracy's influence abroad as much as anything else we do. There will also be required a public understanding, at once subtle, compassionate, and widespread, of the relationship of the United States to other nations. No country today, and the United States least of all, can move toward its future with its eyes turned within. It is understood, though not yet sufficiently, that the peoples of the less developed nations need many forms of help from the United States, of which economic assistance is only one, if they are to realize their aspirations within the framework of freedom. It is less well understood that such co-operation as the United

States undertakes is unlikely to achieve the purposes for which it is intended unless Americans develop to a greater extent the capacity to project themselves across cultural lines. Different peoples construe their welfare in different ways, and there is no single pattern to which all societies that desire freedom must adhere. The imaginative understanding of the situation of people elsewhere has always been in short supply in all nations. It was never more needed than it is today.

## A World Between War and Peace

We come at this point to the overhanging challenge that faces our society. The United States and its allies are confronted by disciplined nations, rapidly growing in size and power, whose leaders have so far shown themselves incapable of understanding the reasons why free men cherish their liberties. A twilight world that is neither at peace nor wholly at war has existed since the end of World War II. It has led to tensions and deep anxieties and to a variety of problems that are new to the democratic scene.

One of the most perplexing problems of the cold war is how to deal with the efforts of the international Communist apparatus. The perplexity arises from the skillful use by this apparatus of democratic symbols and machinery to subvert democratic processes. The American Communist Party is too insignificant to be a present danger, but the total international apparatus of communism is powerful and is always ready to use underhanded methods. Toughness and realism are required to deal with this conspiracy. If fundamental democratic values are to be preserved, however, restraint is also necessary. The excesses of various loyalty programs illustrate this aspect of the problem. When government clearances require the individual to prove his loyalty, a basic democratic postulate is ignored.

A closely connected problem is raised by the need to restrict public access to information pertaining to military or foreign affairs. Some restriction, particularly in the military area, is probably necessary, although even this proposition has been questioned by well-informed men. But it is important to recognize that the policy of restriction at best delays, but does not ultimately prevent, the acquisition of scientific and technical knowledge by other governments. There appear to be no basic scientific secrets anywhere in the world.

A policy of restricting information has serious consequences for the health of a democratic system. It undermines the trust that ordinary citizens repose in public discussion, leaving them with the feeling that they cannot perform their roles as democratic citizens and should not bother to try because they cannot obtain the reliable information essential to responsible judgment and action. Restriction gives the citizen a feeling of distance between himself and public problems and encourages him to leave the disposition of these problems entirely to those who allegedly know all the facts. The practice of restricting information is fundamentally disturbing, in short, to democratic attitudes and expectations. Unless its necessity is clear and immediate, it is not worth the risks it entails.

These problems bring us to the underlying issue that the present crisis raises for American society. Democracies are not warlike. Large military budgets, recurrent alarms and excursions, a state of prolonged international tension are all foreign to the normal climate of freedom. Many of the practices this state of affairs requires, such as centralized controls at many points, long-range planning, and the maintenance of a constant state of military readiness, have not been habitual in the United States. It is natural that they should be employed reluctantly and that the belief should persist that a democracy cannot do more than respond to the initiatives taken by its enemies.

But this belief is incompatible with our wealth, our past, and the inherent resources of our democracy. Our material resources, though not unlimited, are abundant. Democratic citizens, here and in other countries, have repeatedly shown that they can pull together and pull hard when the purpose is clear. But for the long pull that must now be made, this purpose must be defined by leadership. And the support for this definition of our national purpose will have to be won in the way that enduring support for any policy must be achieved in a democracy—by honest and fearless exploration of the issues, conducted on the premise that a democracy's citizens want to listen to reason and deserve to be told the facts. Hesitation in setting this process in motion reveals only a failure to understand the inherent resources of the democratic system.

## RESOURCES OF DEMOCRACY

What, in summary, are the resources of democracy? What are its inner strengths that give it the power to meet its problems? The democratic system, we believe, is built to manage the complex problems of our era. It is one that aims at the most important form of efficiency. And it puts its trust in the one place where trust must be placed—in the spirit, the talent, and the intelligence of its citizens.

### Democracy Is Built to Manage Complexity

There is no alchemy that will make the problems of the contemporary world simpler than they are. Their solution depends, in every social system, on four essential conditions—on the quality of the men who occupy positions of leadership, on the information and resources available to them, on the circumstances in which they work, and on the support they receive from their fellow citizens. Examination of democracy from any one of these viewpoints suggests that in its essentials it is built to manage complexity as well as any human arrangement can be.

The quality of the individuals who occupy the positions of leadership in any system of government depends, in general, on the methods by which they are selected. In practice this means that they are selected by a competitive process that is governed by certain rules. Competition for leadership is not a distinguishing characteristic of democracy. It is an inevitable characteristic of any system of government. Rivalry, the struggle for power and authority, "politicking," go on in every society—openly or surreptitiously, peacefully or violently, but rarely gently. Democracy is an effort to tame this competition and to turn it to constructive use.

It is not competition, then, but the rules democracy employs to regulate this competition that differentiate it from other systems of government. Just as the rules of football make it likely that those with weight and speed will be outstanding and the rules of chess favor more strictly intellectual qualities, so the rules of the democratic process favor men of one kind and the rules of other systems of government favor men with different qualities.

The democratic method of competition does not guarantee that men of humane intelligence and integrity will come to the fore. But it is more likely to produce this result than methods of competition that depend on conspiracy, violence, and authoritarian claims to infallibility.

The democratic process, furthermore, gives those who acquire the authority to govern an extraordinary opportunity for a continuing liberal education. The decisions that men make are determined in large part by the information that is available to them. When the problems with which a public official has to deal are complex, he needs information from many different quarters and he needs the chance to hear many different points of view. In the modern world, the funneling of information to those in key positions is an extraordinarily complex task. Where totalitarianism tends to clog the channels through which information flows, democracy tends to open them up.

The evidence we have about the workings of the Nazi regime indicates that the difficulties of communication are doubled when subordinates in a hierarchy are fearful of extreme punishment for their mistakes or when they feed their superiors only the information their superiors want to hear. Democracy minimizes such dangers. In contrast, it provides the general conditions for the growth of informed intelligence. It provides liberty of thought and conscience and the chance for open debate. It makes it possible for men to exchange information freely and to criticize and amplify one another's beliefs. And it does something more. In a world in which problems are difficult, it diffuses power and decentralizes the decision-making process, thus permitting men to try different ideas simultaneously. It permits leadership to arise in many parts of society. It gives energetic men multiple chances to take responsibility and does not discourage them by insisting that all their efforts be controlled from one great center.

In other words, democracy refuses to make the most tempting and the most misleading assumption that can be made when problems are complex. This is the assumption that all knowledge and good sense reside in a single, tightly-knit ruling group. A democratic system, in contrast, keeps its leaders under steady pressure. Needless to say, no social policy can please everybody, whether in a democracy or a dictatorship, and no government that has character and integrity of purpose will try to please everybody.

But a democratic government is constantly hearing from those who are displeased. And if it makes its decisions on narrow grounds, if it ignores any considerable set of interests held by its citizens, the penalty is likely to be reasonably swift.

Democracy is thus a method for keeping the leaders of a society steadily reminded that their problems are more complex than they may like to think. This does not make the life of those who govern easier, but it helps the lives of those who are governed. Moreover, it gives to their lives a special quality. When a government has earnestly listened to the opposition and when it has made an honest effort to reach a consensus before determining its policies, the citizens who must execute these policies are less likely to feel that they are doing so under coercion. Their views have been asked and their dignity respected, and they can feel that the support they give their government is given freely.

The issue is more than a question of practical efficiency. It is a question of attitude. Men who are attached to democracy speak of the complexity of present-day problems partly because they are aware that the impact of any social policy will vary from person to person. They recognize as well that in every society there are bound to be individuals who suffer from the irresponsibility, the cruelty, the indifference, or the ignorance of their fellows. They therefore propose to maintain a social order that gives these individuals the chance to speak up and fight back. For they cherish the variousness of human beings and the differences between them and count this variousness—this complexity—the mark of a high civilization. And they prefer this vision of human life to the lure of simple solutions and the seductions of a master plan that solves all problems by ignoring the existence of most of them.

In the end, the totalitarian method is not a method for dealing with complexity. It is a method by which the desperate, the impatient, or the ruthless can come to convince themselves that life is simpler than it really is; it is a method by which the weary can escape the need to think at all. When frustration accumulates in a society, it is intelligible that its members may be tempted to turn to such a method. But totalitarianism is not an answer to the question of complexity, it is a refusal to ask the question. The democratic method, in contrast, is for the confident and the tough-minded. It does not promise that all problems can be solved;

it relieves no one from the pain of thought or from the responsibility of facing as many facts and respecting as many human values as possible. But it accepts the difficulties of government for what they are, and it aims at a level of human achievement that is only possible when men face their difficulties squarely and overcome them honestly.

## Democracy Judges Efficiency in Democratic Terms

Such a commitment, like any commitment, has its risks. Democracies, with their habits of prolonged public discussion, have often been thought, even by their friends, to be inefficient. This fear is bound to be more insistent when a democracy is faced by ruthlessly organized totalitarian regimes, which seem to determine their policies with speed and to execute them with rigor. But speed, rigor, organization, and discipline are virtues only when the goals they serve are intelligent. The arbitrary fixing and refixing of goals are surely less adequate devices for insuring intelligent policies than the more protracted and self-critical deliberative processes that democracy employs. Moreover, the human cost of forcing individuals to work toward the execution of purposes they do not share or cannot accept is notoriously high. Wherever such a policy has been attempted in the modern world, a large proportion of a society's resources has been spent on secret police, political prisons, propaganda, and party functionaries. Even in the narrowest terms, such methods are more wasteful than methods that place their faith in humane education, free communication, and the open competition of opposing groups.

Moreover, if "efficiency" is construed to mean simply the capacity to attain a narrow set of purposes, then efficiency is not the only value that a democracy seeks. But if "efficiency" stands for an effort to produce the largest result for a given application of resources, then democracy does not suffer by comparison with any other system. For the democratic idea asks that a society measure the results it achieves by the extent to which it nourishes human rationality and human capacity for willing service to one's fellows. A society guided by this idea believes that the intelligence and integrity of its citizens are its richest resources. It aims to find that intelligence wherever it is and to create a fluid society that will allow this intelligence to flow where it can be used. It tries to build its power, in short, on the power of its individual citizens, and it judges the efficiency of its various enterprises in these ultimate terms.

## STRENGTH AND
## WEAKNESS OF DEMOCRACY

The virtues possessed by the democratic form of government, however, do not guarantee that it can deal with its problems successfully or that its triumph is assured when it finds itself in competition with an authoritarian social order. History affords too many somber examples to the contrary. Democratic governments can meet and master great dangers. They have done so on innumerable occasions in the past. But they have only been able to do so when the social conditions that support democracy have been strong, and when democratic citizens have had the habits and attitudes that make democracy work and a firm commitment to democratic ideals.

Ultimately, therefore, the capacity of a democratic government for great achievement depends on the qualities that the citizens of a democracy are willing to call forth in themselves. Democratic debate is a source of strength; it is wasteful only when the debaters put forward irresponsible or foolish views. Public discussion of the policies of government can make the formulation of these policies more intelligent and their execution more resolute; it fails to do so only when citizens fail to distinguish between dissent and obstruction and when they lack the self-control and the love of the democratic process that keep criticism within the bounds of reason and decency.

When there is weakness in democracy, it does not lie in the inefficiency of the process by which democracy reaches its decisions. It lies in the values held by the individuals who take part in these decisions—in what they hold dear and in what they regard as right and wrong. The inefficiencies in the American debate over civil rights, to take a current example, are not a consequence of procedural safeguards that allow a minority voice to be expressed. They are a consequence of the actual values that are espoused. The democratic system, in short, provides its citizens with the basic instruments they need for government that is both efficient and just. But it will not give them efficient and just government; they must create that for themselves.

## DEMOCRACY'S CHALLENGE

An analysis of democracy ends, then, where it begins. The adherents of democracy stake their destinies on the inherent capacity of the individual to play his part in the system and to carry his share of the public responsibility. The viability of democracy does not depend on any fixed structure, public or private. It turns, finally, on the soundness of a fundamental commitment.

Democracy aims to provide a mobile society and a free political process that will give the individual the opportunity to participate in the affairs of his community and to bring to bear on those affairs the best that is in his mind and spirit. Are there enough individuals whose sense of responsibility to themselves and their fellow men will lead them to take this opportunity? Are there enough who will use this opportunity with intelligence, integrity, and care? This is the challenge that democracy puts to its citizens. The democratic faith is that they will respond.

For democracy is built on the belief that the purpose of a society is to emancipate the intelligence and protect the integrity of the individual men and women who compose it. Democracy relies on rationality as against irrationality. It is the application of mind and spirit to the serving of public ends and to the routing of ignorance, fear, and superstition. The whole conception of liberty for the individual and freedom of thought and conscience rests on the conviction that such freedom nurtures intelligence and that this in turn will carry men toward truth and away from error. It is this faith that our institutions fortify. No guarantee can ever be given that truth will triumph or that fallible human beings will win out over all obstacles. But our system provides a means for putting intelligence and good will to work.

This is what gives diversity of interests within a society and mobility for the individual their significance. It is the justification for the classic democratic conception that careers must be open to all talents. It is the inner meaning for tolerance of argument, debate, and the rough-and-tumble of political controversy. It brings urgency today to the pursuit of excellence in education, to the nurturing of human gifts at all levels, to a wider understanding of the nature of research and scholarship and science.

The citizen who casts his lot with the democratic idea will find that it asks difficult things of him. It asks him to act with conviction while recognizing his fallibility; to enjoy, and not merely to accept, the inconvenient fact that others disagree with him; to fight hard and then to compromise; to distinguish between helping others and dictating their lives. But it offers him rewards, and the most important of these rewards are not external. They are these traits of character themselves, the chance for choice, the sense of dignity that comes to a man when he knows that he should and will be consulted about his society's affairs. The citizen of a democracy has an immediate stake in his society because that society itself stakes its strength and continuity on his resourcefulness, energy, and good will. And he will find that he can play his part in that society in many ways that go far beyond casting his ballot. He can initiate action and not only follow or applaud it; he can work for others from an inner drive and not external necessity; he can respect the rights of all his fellow men without bending his knee to any of them. The appearance of such citizens not in a special class or protected group but throughout a society is what democracy seeks and is its ultimate reason for being. The power of that idea has already transformed the quality and feeling of life for millions of human beings.

It is an idea that can put the issues of the present era in perspective and can sustain the citizens of this democracy in the purposes they set themselves. Mankind is going through one of its most fateful moments. Throughout the world there are people who have never counted in the affairs of their society, whose powers have never been tested or used, and whose feelings have never been trusted or given a full measure of respect. They are emerging from their ancient condition. Never before has mankind lived with the fear that it might totally destroy itself; but, on the other hand, never before have so many men and women had the chance to live in hope, and never before has there been the chance to release so much human intelligence, talent, and vitality. The democratic vision is the reason why this chance exists. To seize this chance and to act on it with faith and confidence is the great privilege of Americans of this generation.

# Consultants and Authors

William Attwood
Stephen K. Bailey
Frederick C. Barghoorn
Lincoln Barnett
Willard Bascom
John R. H. Blum
C. H. Bonesteel, III,
   Maj. Gen., USA
Howard L. Boorman
Maxwell Brandwen
Kershaw Burbank
John F. Cady
Robert L. Calhoun
Ansley J. Coale
Joseph I. Coffey*
Wilbur J. Cohen
Gerhard Colm
Dwight Cooke
L. Gray Cowan
H. H. Critz, Brig. Gen., USA
James E. Cross
Robert A. Dahl
Martha Dalrymple
Kingsley Davis
Cornelis W. de Kiewiet
H. A. DeWeerd
Byron Dexter
Eugene P. Dvorin
Robert B. Ekvall,
   Lt. Col., USA (ret.)

William Y. Elliott
Grover W. Ensley
Merle Fainsod
Clarence H. Faust
William J. Fellner
Louis Finkelstein
Joseph L. Fisher
Lloyd A. Free
David F. Freeman
Andrew J. Goodpaster,
   Brig. Gen., USA
Lincoln Gordon
Morton Grodzins
N. E. Halaby
Elizabeth Ann Hawley
Robert L. Heilbroner
William Henderson
Roger Hilsman
Edgar M. Hoover
J. C. Hurewitz
F. Ernest Johnson
Amos A. Jordan, Jr.,
   Lt. Col., USA
Hugh B. Killough
William R. Kintner,
   Col., USA
Dudley Kirk
Charles Kline
Howard N. Knowles
Fritz G. A. Kraemer

* Served as Assistant to the Director from August 27, 1956 to June 30, 1957.

Wladyslaw W. Kulski
John LaFarge, S.J.
S. M. Levitas
Walter J. Levy
Paul M. A. Linebarger
David Loth
R. M. MacIver
Arnold Miles*
Arthur T. Mosher
John Courtney Murray, S.J.
Richard A. Musgrave
Robinson Newcomb
Waldemar A. Nielsen
Fairfield Osborn
George S. Pettee
William T. Phillips
Rt. Rev. James A. Pike,
   J.S.D., S.T.D.
Don K. Price
Lucian W. Pye
Froelich Rainey
Carl G. Rosberg, Jr.
Walt W. Rostow
Wallace S. Sayre

Robert A. Scalapino
Richard M. Scammon
Thomas C. Schelling
Theodore W. Schultz
Robert G. Snider
Herman M. and Anne R. Somers
Nicolas Spulber
Herbert Stein
Donald B. Straus
Robert Strausz-Hupé
Irene B. Taeuber
Charles A. H. Thomson
A. A. J. Van Bilsen
Richard L. Walker
Avra Warren*
Howard Whidden
Arthur P. Whitaker
John C. Whitehorn, M.D.
Ernest W. Williams, Jr.
Bryce Wood
Coleman Woodbury
Edwin M. Wright
Paul Ylvisaker

* Deceased

# Index